Contents

For Andrea

The Sea! The Sea!

The Shout of the Ten Thousand in the Modern Imagination

Tim Rood

Duckworth Overlook

London • Woodstock • New York

Paperback edition 2006
First published in the UK in 2004
and in the USA in 2005 by
Duckworth Overlook

LONDON
90-93 Cowcross Street
London EC1M 6BF
inquiries@duckworth-publishers.co.uk
www.ducknet.co.uk

WOODSTOCK
The Overlook Press
One Overlook Drive
Woodstock, NY 12498
www.overlookpress.com
[for individual orders and bulk sales in the United States,
please contact our Woodstock office]

NEW YORK
The Overlook Press
141 Wooster Street
New York, NY 10012

A catalogue record for this book is available
from the British Library and the Library of Congress

ISBN 0 7156 3571 9 (UK)
EAN 9780715635711
ISBN 1 58567 824 4 (US)

Typeset by e-type, Liverpool
Printed and bound in Great Britain by
Biddles Ltd, King's Lynn, Norfolk

The Sea! The Sea!

Acknowledgements

I have been helped by many people in the course of writing this book. Franco Basso, Kristina Boden, Patrick Bradley, Nicholas Horsfall, Robin Lane Fox, John Ma, Greg Rowe, John Taylor, and Stephanie West all drew my attention to poems or passages or films I would probably have otherwise missed. John Ma also discussed Xenophon with me rather more than I discussed Hellenistic history with him; and he and Claire Bergmann both looked at some books not available in libraries in the UK. Gijsbert Loos, Slawomir Sprawski, and Stephanie West translated Dutch and Polish poems; Ben Earle, John de Falbe, Andrew Marsham, Christopher Tuplin, and Steve Crook helped on points of detail; and Gregory Hutchinson, Oliver Lyne, and Luke Pitcher were among those who made useful comments on a paper I gave in Oxford in a seminar series on 'The Sea' organized by Matthew Leigh. Lavinia Wellicome, Curator at Woburn Abbey, Timothy Huw Davies at the Courtauld Institute of Art, and Victoria Lane at Sotheby's helped me to track down Haydon's painting of Xenophon; Julia Brotherton kindly let me see the painting itself and also allowed it to be photographed. I also gained some interesting thoughts about Haydon's painting from some of the Oxford Classics applicants whom I interviewed in 2001 and 2003. The BBC Written Archives Centre sent me a copy of the script of Louis MacNeice's radio play on Xenophon, while the librarians in the Upper Reading Room of the Bodleian Librarian cheerfully served up a bizarre range of books. Tom Harrison offered valuable comments on the whole script; Jonathan and Kristina Boden, Christopher Krebs, Lynette Mitchell, Christopher Pelling, and my parents Pearce and Beaujolais Rood kindly read some of it; Binkie Biggs, Angus Bowie, Armand D'Angour, Stephen Harrison, Simon Hornblower, Katerina Ierodiakonou, Christina Kraus, Robert Parker, and Simon Price read an earlier piece from which this book developed; and Andrea Capovilla provided stimulating criticism as that piece and as the book itself took shape. I must also thank Deborah Blake at Duckworth and the two Oxford colleges at which I was based while I researched and wrote the book: Queen's (as Junior Research Fellow) and St Hugh's (first as Lecturer, then as Fellow, in Classics).

The President and Fellows of Corpus Christi College, Oxford, kindly gave me permission to reproduce extracts from the unpublished travel journals of Major Thomas Crowder, held in the College's Archives. Other copyright material is reproduced by permission of the following: extracts from *Thalassa Thalassa* by Javant Biarujia by permission of the author; 'Anabasis', from *Report from the Besieged City and Other Poems* by Zbigniew Herbert, trans. J. and B. Carpenter, © 1995 Zbigniew Herbert, by permission of Oxford University Press and HarperCollins Publishers (New York: published by Ecco Press); extracts from *Collected Poems* by John Betjeman by permission of John Murray (Publishers); extract from *Flight among the Tombs* by Anthony Hecht by permission of Carcanet Press Ltd; extracts from *The Complete Poems of Heinrich Heine: A Modern English Version* by Hal Draper, © Suhrkamp/Insel, by permission of Suhrkamp Verlag; extract from 'The Deconstructed Man' by James Laughlin, from *Poems New and Selected*, © 1996 James Laughlin, by permission of New Directions Publishing Corporation; extracts from *Collected Poems* by Louis MacNeice and from *The March of the Ten Thousand*, © 1941, 2004 Louis MacNeice, by permission of David Higham Associates, on behalf of the Estate of Louis MacNeice; extract from *Selected Writings* by Christopher Middleton by permission of Carcanet Press Ltd; extract from *Through the Forest* by Jaan Kaplinski, trans. H. Hawkins, published by The Harvill Press, by permission of The Random House Group Ltd; extract from the song 'Thalatta, Thalatta' by Libitina by permission of Jamie; extract from *The Nine Days Wonder* by John Masefield by permission of the Society of Authors as the Literary Representative of the Estate of John Masefield; extracts from *Downriver* by Sean O'Brien by permission of Pan Macmillan Ltd; extracts from *Flying Blues* by Rodney Pybus by permission of Carcanet Press Ltd; extracts from 'Birds of Passage' by Esaias Tegnér, from Judith Moffett (ed. and trans.), *The North! To the North!: Five Swedish Poets of the Nineteenth Century*, © 2001 Judith Moffett, by permission of Southern Illinois University Press; extracts from 'Descent to the Sea' by V. Uroševik, in Ewald Osers (ed. and trans.), *Contemporary Macedonian Poetry*, by permission of the translator; extract from *Omeros* by Derek Walcott by permission of Faber and Faber Ltd and Farrar, Strauss and Giroux Inc.; extracts from *Paterson* by William Carlos Williams, © 1946, 1948, 1949, 1951, 1958 William Carlos Williams, by permission of New Directions Publishing Corporation. Particular thanks are due to the Jowett Copyright Trustees, who helped to pay for the reproduction of copyright material, and to those copyright holders who not only gave permission for material to be reproduced free of charge, but also showed a generous interest in the book: Ewald Osers, Jamie from Libitina, and above all Javant Biarujia. Every effort has been made to trace other copyright holders: all omissions drawn to the attention of the publishers will be remedied in any future edition. Finally, I must thank Christopher Tuplin for his help in supplying Plates 14 and 15.

T.C.B.R.
February 2004

Plates

Xenophon, *c.* 428 – *c.* 354 BC
Greek historian

θάλαττα θάλαττα
The sea! the sea!

Anabasis bk. 4, ch. 7, sect. 24

The Oxford Dictionary of Quotations

1

The Black Sea

'God,' he said quietly. 'Isn't the sea what Algy calls it: a great sweet mother? The snotgreen sea. The scrotumtightening sea. *Epi oinopa ponton*. Ah, Dedalus, the Greeks. I must teach you. You must read them in the original. *Thalatta! Thalatta!* She is our great sweet mother. Come and look.'

James Joyce, Ulysses

As he looks out on Dublin Bay, stately, plump Buck Mulligan echoes many others who have echoed a shout first heard on a mountain in Eastern Turkey two thousand four hundred years ago: 'Thalatta! Thalatta!', 'The Sea! The Sea!'. That shout was first uttered by an army of Greek soldiers (the famous Ten Thousand) who had been stranded in Mesopotamia, in the heart of the Persian empire, a thousand miles from home, and had marched through the formidable tribes and across the snowy mountains and plains of Kurdistan and Armenia until they came at last to a mountain named Mount Theches. It was on that mountain that they first caught sight of the Black Sea – a scene described by one of the participants, the Athenian historian and philosopher Xenophon, in a passage that was 'once one of the most celebrated … in all of Greek literature':

> When the men in front reached the summit, there was much shouting. Xenophon and the rearguard heard it and thought that there were some more enemy attacking in front. … But as the shouting kept on becoming louder and closer, and the successive groups going forward kept on running towards the men in front who kept on shouting, and the more there were of them the more shouting there was, it seemed then to Xenophon as though this was something of great importance, and he mounted his horse and taking Lycius and the cavalry with him rode forward to give support; and soon they heard the soldiers shouting 'Thalatta! Thalatta!' and passing the word down the column. Then they began to run, the rearguard and all, and the baggage animals and horses were driven on. When they had all got to the top, they embraced each other, and the generals and captains, crying. And suddenly someone gave the word, and the soldiers brought stones and made a great cairn.[1]

Xenophon himself may have given a memorable description of the scene on Mount Theches, but the story of 'The Sea! The Sea!' itself has never been told before – not even by Iris Murdoch. Xenophon's shout has had an extraordinary afterlife. It has captured the imagination of nearly everyone who has read Xenophon's account or simply heard the story of the Ten Thousand's long march to the sea. It has been invoked in literary masterpieces by writers as diverse as Heine and Joyce and in stirring adventure stories set in the Middle East and elsewhere. It has appeared in settings ranging from sober Victorian periodicals to popular romantic novels. It has even been depicted in one of the large historical paintings by the megalomaniac Benjamin Robert Haydon. 'Thalatta! Thalatta!' and its variant form, 'Thalassa! Thalassa!', have also been on the lips or in the thoughts of many travellers who have followed in Xenophon's footsteps and looked down on the Black Sea from the spot where Xenophon first saw it; and on the lips or in the thoughts of travellers in many other parts of the world (Alexander Kinglake struggling through the Egyptian desert, the young T.E. Lawrence cycling through Southern France, Louis MacNeice on a holiday trip with his father to Connemara) when they have suddenly caught a glimpse of the sea. Xenophon's shout has also been echoed by countless others who have yielded once more to the sight of the sea without ever setting down their feelings in writing. And it is still occasionally heard in modern Greece as an expression of sudden joy – a less self-promoting version of Archimedes' 'Eureka!'.

This book tells the story of 'Thalatta! Thalatta!', the shout uttered by some Greek soldiers in 400 BC and echoed by numerous others since. It may seem excessive to devote a whole book to two words – especially when they are both the same. But it is precisely the simplicity of those two Greeks words that makes the story of 'Thalatta! Thalatta!' so fascinating as a case study of the workings of the literary imagination. Because the writers and adventurers who have responded to those words have all been responding to the same memorable description, we can trace the political and cultural concerns that mould reactions to *all* literary works far more forcefully than if we were looking at the reception of a whole text. Exploring later responses to Xenophon's account of the scene on Mount Theches also allows us to see with particular clarity the way in which historical events come to be transformed into 'myths'. The Greeks' shout has gripped the imagination of readers of the *Anabasis* because it is the climax to a long narrative of toil and suffering. Its appeal is a reflection of our desire for the satisfactions of closure. This does not simply tell us something about the attractions of Xenophon's story. It tells us something about the attractions of narrative itself.

Telling the story of 'Thalatta! Thalatta!' will itself involve telling some stirring and poignant stories. We will relive the experiences of school-children reading the *Anabasis* (*The March Up Country*), Xenophon's account of his adventures. We will explore the emotions of travellers and adventurers who have followed, literally or figuratively, in Xenophon's footsteps, and the emotions fostered by the sea itself – the sea of youth, the romantic sea, the sea that stands for eternity, the sea to which we all long to return.

We will see how modern writers starting with James Joyce have twisted and played with the bewildering range of associations that 'Thalatta! Thalatta!' had come to acquire by the beginning of the twentieth century. Following the stories of some of the writers who have responded to that shout will also shed light on how modern ideas of democracy and freedom have shaped our views of Xenophon's story. It will shed light, too, on how an event in the distant past and in a distant land can help individuals and nations fashion an identity for themselves.

No less intriguing are the attempts by later writers to tell the remarkable adventures of the Ten Thousand. Even though Xenophon's own story is celebrated for its brilliant novelistic instinct, it has often been retold – in books for children with titles like *Ten Thousand Heroes* or *The Long March Home*, or in plays for radio by Louis MacNeice and Wolfgang Weyrauch. The opening years of the twenty-first century have already seen a paraphrase-cum-travelogue, John Prevas' *Xenophon's March: Into the Lair of the Persian Lion*, and a fictional retelling, Michael Curtis Ford's *The Ten Thousand*. Xenophon's story has also been transferred to very different settings. It has been the model for stories about a gang fighting through the streets of New York and about an American division trapped in Central Europe under a resurgent Germany – and it has even been the inspiration for a recent sci-fi trilogy set on the planet Marduk.[2]

Despite all these retellings and adaptations, and despite the excellence of Xenophon's own account, the adventures of the Ten Thousand are now relatively little known. We will be concentrating here on just one moment in their long retreat from Mesopotamia – the moment when they finally caught sight of the Black Sea. But how had they come to be stranded so far away from Greece in the first place?

*

The story of the *Anabasis* was like that of the Grand Old Duke of York – with a twist. The Ten Thousand were Greek mercenaries hired by Cyrus, a young Persian prince, soon after his brother Artaxerxes' accession to the Persian throne. Cyrus marched them up country, and Xenophon marched them down again. Only it was not quite as simple as that. It is often claimed that the march down to the coast was led by Xenophon, but Xenophon himself makes it clear that he was just one of the generals, with joint command of the rearguard. And Cyrus in fact had more than ten thousand men. His Greek force numbered almost thirteen thousand: they are known as 'the Ten Thousand' because that is a nice round figure (and also, perhaps, because that is roughly how many of them arrived back at the sea). They were at first not a united force, but separated into contingents led by various Greek generals who had raised them on Cyrus' behalf. It was a good time for raising

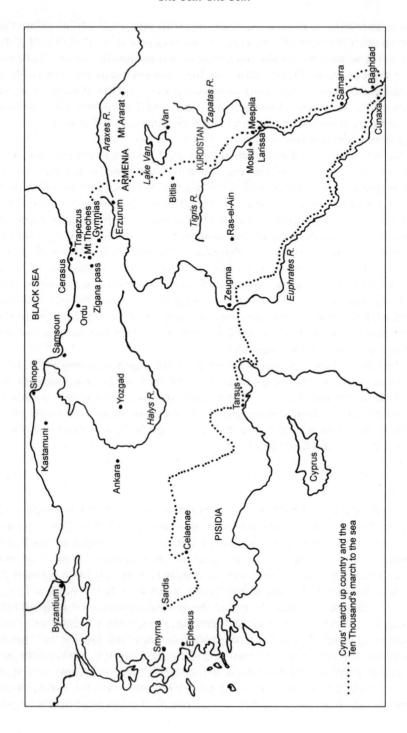

Cyrus' march up country and the
Ten Thousand's march to the sea

mercenaries: the long war between the Athenians and the Peloponnesians, the so-called Peloponnesian War, which had lasted on and off for almost thirty years, had just come to an end. Cyrus was able to raise troops from all over the Greek world, but above all from the poor regions of Arcadia and Achaea, the central and north-western regions of the Peloponnese. This Greek force was only a small part of Cyrus' army: he also had one hundred thousand non-Greek troops, if Xenophon's figure can be trusted.

Cyrus' claim was that he was going to use his army against the Pisidians, an obstinate mountain tribe in Southern Turkey. He led the army away from the Lydian capital Sardis. He marched through Lydia and Phrygia, past the river Meander, past one of his own hunting parks (or 'paradises'), and on to the place where Apollo was said to have flayed the satyr Marsyas who had challenged him to a contest with the lyre. It was here, at Celaenae, that Cyrus was joined by troops under the blunt Spartan general Clearchus. His Greek force – the elite of his army – was now complete. About eleven thousand of them were hoplites – heavy-armed troops who could stand and charge in line together, a fearsome sight on level ground for opponents who were only lightly armed.

From Celaenae Cyrus marched across the plain of Lycaonia, and then down through the narrow Cilician gates to the south coast of Turkey. By the time the army got to Tarsus, the Greeks had come to realize that they were not being led against the Pisidians. They refused to go further. Clearchus – the only man in the Greek army who did in fact know what Cyrus was planning – put on an act and persuaded them to carry on. Cyrus now told them that they were to fight against a rebel on the Euphrates. And so he marched into Syria and across the desert to the Euphrates. And it was there that the Greeks learnt what they had long been suspecting. They were being led against the Persian king himself: Cyrus wanted to take his brother's place on the throne. They crossed the river, and Cyrus again marched forth, and his troops followed (they could scarcely turn back now), on and on towards Babylon, with the river to their right, waiting to meet the army that did not appear, the army that had to appear before they reached Babylon, or else the prize Cyrus yearned for would be his. On they went, past a great ditch supposedly dug to stop Cyrus' advance. And then finally, late one afternoon, 'there appeared dust, like a white cloud, and some time later a sort of blackness in the plain stretching a long way. And when they were closer, there was suddenly a flashing of bronze, and spears and the enemy ranks began to come into sight …'.

The battle was fought at a place with no name, at least in Xenophon's account. Later authorities called it Cunaxa. The Greeks were stationed to the right of Cyrus' line, near the Euphrates. They did their bit. They avoided, as best they could, the scythe-bearing chariots that were driven against them, and advanced together through the enemy lines. But Cyrus had in fact wanted them to march directly against his brother, and Clearchus had refused to budge from the river, fearing that the vastly superior enemy forces would outflank them on the right. So Cyrus took his personal brigade of cavalry, six hundred strong, and charged against the Persian centre, where his brother was posted. Rode the six hundred through the troops defending the king, but Cyrus became isolated, with only a few of his followers left around him. All the same, he made straight for his brother ('I see the man'), and as he raised his weapon for the kill he was struck himself under the eye with a javelin. When the Greeks came back from what they thought was a victory, they found their camp sacked and their employer dead.

What were the Greeks to do? They could suggest to Cyrus' subordinate Ariaeus that they could try to put him on the Persian throne, but he would have none of that. They could yield to the king's demand that they surrender their weapons, but they would have none of that ('we have nothing of value left to us other than our weapons and our courage: if we keep our weapons we think we would be able to use our courage'). At first they joined Ariaeus, and negotiated a truce with the king and Tissaphernes, one of his satraps (governors). They agreed terms for buying provisions and for guidance home, and set off northwards, for they could not return by the way they had come, across the desert. They marched in step with the Persian army, a few miles apart, each side wary of the other. Soon Cyrus' other troops joined the Persians, and the Greeks marched on by themselves. They came to the Tigris, and crossed to its right bank, and kept going north, fording all the irrigation ditches, still watched over by Tissaphernes. And so they came to the Zapatas, the Greater Zab, and here the Spartan general Clearchus started discussions with Tissaphernes to try to remove the suspicions that threatened to lead to war. He went to Tissaphernes' tent once. He went there again, this time with four other Greek generals. They were all seized and killed.

What were the Greeks to do now? Perhaps at this point we should let Xenophon tell the story:

> The Greeks were in great difficulty as they considered their position: they were at the gates of the king; in a circle on every side were many peoples and cities who were their enemies; no one was any longer going to provide them with a chance of buying food; they were no fewer than ten thousand stades away from Greece; there was no guide to show them the way; uncrossable rivers in the middle of their homeward journey shut them in; the barbarians who had marched up country with Cyrus had betrayed them; they had been left alone, without a single horseman to help them, so that it was clear that if they were victorious they would kill no one, but if they were themselves defeated no one would be left alive. Reflecting on these things, despondent, few of them tasted food that evening, few lit fires, many did not come to the camp that night, but rested wherever they happened to be, unable to sleep through grief and longing for fatherlands, parents, wives, children, whom they thought they would never see again. Such was their mood as they were all taking their rest. But there was in the army a certain Xenophon, an Athenian ...

1. The Black Sea

This description, with its vivid accumulation of short clauses, is the darkness to the light of 'Thalatta! Thalatta!' – or even to the light of the following morning. This Athenian man named Xenophon was distressed like the others, and unable to sleep. But he did get a little sleep, and it was then that he saw a dream – a dream of his father's house being struck by a bolt of lightning and lit up all around. A good omen? Or a bad one? Time would tell. As soon as he woke up, a thought struck him: 'Why am I lying down?' And now Xenophon became a hero, rousing the captains around him, insisting that they choose new leaders, and, at dawn, addressing the army as a whole, lifting their spirits, and finding himself elected general. 'The sun must have risen in burning splendor over the parched and yellow plains of Shomamok, for it was early in the autumn. The world has rarely seen a more glorious sight than was witnessed on the banks of the Zab on that memorable morning.' Those are not the words of the boastful Xenophon, but of the archaeologist Henry Layard, looking back on his own journey to the spot where that fateful night was passed.[3]

The Greeks set off on their retreat, with Xenophon in the rear providing (or so his account implies) both moral and strategic guidance. As they made their way, they were pressed by the Persians with both cavalry and archers, and they could only respond themselves with slingers. Harassed from the sides and from behind, they marched past the ruins of two deserted cities, Larissa and Mespila, as Xenophon calls them – Nimrud and Nineveh, romantic names to his nineteenth-century readers, enthralled by their biblical resonance and by Layard's exciting discoveries. For the Greeks, continually pressed by the enemy cavalry, it was a relief to get past those cities to the hills. But even here the Persians could fire on them from the hilltops while the Greeks suffered below – until they sent their own light-armed troops to dislodge the Persians. And so they marched on again, with the Persians sometimes close at hand, at other times out of sight, until they would suddenly appear again, holding a hill above a pass, and then the Greeks would have to race up and try to seize a hill that could itself command the hill from which the Persians were blocking them. The Persians in turn began to burn the villages the Greeks were using for supplies, and now the Greeks found themselves caught with the great Tigris, unfordable, to their left and mountains all around. They quizzed some captives about the lands around them, and found that the path north would take them into the mountains of the people Xenophon calls the Carduchi, the mountains of Kurdistan. Into those mountains, the captives said, the Persian king had once sent an army of one hundred and twenty thousand men, and not one of them had returned.

Into those mountains the Ten Thousand went, and the Carduchi fled from their villages as they approached. But then they harassed the Greeks from above, rolling rocks down slopes as they struggled along narrow, winding mountain paths, paths that were at times too narrow for the baggage animals, so that the Greeks would have to seek other ways round for them. And they also began to gather their forces, and to start blocking the passes ahead, so the Greeks were again and again forced to find ways round, or to take to the mountain heights themselves. Finally they came out of the mountains to a plain, but still there was a fierce river to ford, with enemy behind them and enemy on the other bank. Even when Xenophon had another dream, and they fought their way across that river, and came out into the highlands of Armenia, they still had to march through deep snow, against a wind blowing from the north that cut into one's face like a knife, and there were men who were blinded by the snow, and others who lost toes through frostbite. But they managed to make their way through to villages with strange under-ground houses, but well stocked, and not least with a drink made from barley, and stored in great bowls, with grains of barley floating on top, and reeds one would drink it through – 'a very strong wine, unless one mixed it with water, and then, when one had got used to it, very pleasant'.

The Greeks had to move on from the brew-town they had stumbled across, and still there were more mountain passes to overcome, passes protected by the natives, the Chalybes, the Taochi, the Phasiani, Xenophon calls them, people who carried large knives on their belts, handy for cutting throats, and then cut off their enemy's heads and carried them as they went, singing and dancing. And finally they came to a large and prosperous town which Xenophon calls Gymnias, and the governor of the town sent the Ten Thousand a guide who would lead them in five days to a place from where they could see the sea. As they went the guide urged them to burn the land, for, it was clear, they were now in territory hostile to the people of Gymnias. And it was on the fifth day that this guide led them to a mountain, and the name of the mountain was Theches, the Holy Mountain, and here the rear-guard heard shouting ahead, and Xenophon rushed up and realized that they were shouting because they had seen the sea, and the sight was good.

But the sea was still some days' march away, and first there were more hostile tribes to pass through, the Colchians, 'the only people in the way of our being where we have long been eager to be'. Xenophon told his men: 'we should eat them raw if we can.' And so at last they came to the sea, and to a Greek city called Trapezus (later Byzantine Trebizond, now Turkish Trabzon), where the astonished inhabitants gave them presents of oxen and barley and wine, and the Greeks offered sacrifices to Zeus the Saviour and to Heracles, and they told a Spartan named Dracontius, a man who had been exiled in his youth for killing another boy, to organize athletic games for them, and he said that they should run and wrestle on the rough hillside where they were all standing, and 'all the worse for the man who gets thrown'.

*

1. The Black Sea

The Ten Thousand's March to the Sea has often been regarded as one of the greatest achievements of military history – 'more than could have been expected from human means', as the distinguished geographer James Rennell wrote. What of Xenophon himself – the star of 'The Sea! The Sea!', the man without whom that shout would not be known at all? Since our story depends so much on this one man, it would be helpful to say something of how he came to take part in this great eastern adventure and of what happened to him afterwards.[4]

Xenophon was born around 430 BC to a rich Athenian family. In the aftermath of Athens' defeat in the Peloponnesian War in 404 BC, he seems to have served in the cavalry under the 'Thirty Tyrants', a junta imposed by Sparta. It was after democracy had been restored at Athens that he received a letter from a friend, Proxenus, who promised that he could make him a friend of Cyrus – a man, he said, who was more important to him than his own fatherland. Xenophon consulted his teacher Socrates, who was cautious, because Cyrus had helped the Spartans in the war against Athens, and advised him to consult Apollo's oracle at Delphi. But Xenophon did not ask the oracle whether or not he should go, as Socrates had recommended, but which gods he should propitiate to help him get back successfully. And off he went.

Some time after the expedition, Xenophon was exiled from Athens, either because he had served with Cyrus, as Socrates had feared, or because he subsequently served with the Spartans. He was then settled by the Spartans in the Peloponnese, on an estate near the small town of Scillus, close to Olympia. He provides in the *Anabasis* a brief but vivid glimpse of his life there. He set up a temple to Artemis of Ephesus and a festival in her honour,

> and the men and women of the neighbourhood would take part in the festival. The goddess would provide for them barley meal, loaves, wine, and dried fruit, and a share of the sacrificial victims from the sacred herd and of the animals caught by Xenophon's sons and the sons of the other citizens when they went out hunting for the feast; and anyone else who wanted would join in the hunt, and boars, roe deer, and stags would be caught ...

The good life did not last. Some time after 371 BC, as the Spartans' control of the Peloponnese weakened, Xenophon was forced to leave his estate at Scillus. He is thought to have settled in Corinth. Whether he ever returned to Athens is not known. He died perhaps in the later 350s. A few centuries later, at least, the inhabitants of Scillus could point to a local grave as Xenophon's. But this perhaps tells us more about the later fame of Xenophon than about where he was really buried.

*

Xenophon's account of his life at Scillus has encouraged many to think of him as a retired general fondly writing up his memoirs, a pious country gentleman with keen sporting tastes. Such a view of Xenophon scarcely does justice to this extraordinarily versatile writer. The *Anabasis* itself is a bold enough work: the first military memoir, published perhaps under the pseudonym Themistogenes of Syracuse, and with Xenophon himself called by the third person throughout. Xenophon also wrote a regular work of history, the *Hellenica*, or *Greek Affairs*, which finishes Thucydides' incomplete history of the Peloponnesian War, and continues down to 362 BC. To Xenophon also belongs the distinction, if it is a distinction, of having written the first historical novel, the *Cyropaedia*, or *Education of Cyrus* (the elder Cyrus, that is, founder of the Achaemenid empire in Persia in the sixth century BC). This is no *Waverley*, however, but a heavily didactic work illustrating the art of ruling. Xenophon also wrote philosophical dialogues such as the *Hiero*, a dialogue in which the Syracusan tyrant Hiero outlines the unhappiness of the tyrant and the poet Simonides gives advice on how a ruler can be happy and make his subjects happy too. Like Plato, he wrote several Socratic works: a *Symposium*, telling of a dinner party attended by Socrates, which ends with an erotic dance that sends the guests rushing home to their wives; and an *Apology*, a version of Socrates' speech at his trial. In his *Oeconomicus*, Xenophon showed Socrates discussing household management. His major Socratic work, though, was the *Memorabilia*, where Socrates discusses a wide range of topics, among them justice, temperance, and divine providence. As if this were not enough, Xenophon also wrote an encomiastic biography of the Spartan king Agesilaus; technical treatises on hunting, horsemanship, and cavalry leadership; and even a pamphlet advising the Athenians how to reform their financial system. Not bad for a crusty old bore.

It is the *Anabasis*, though, that is regarded as Xenophon's masterpiece. Indeed, it has often been seen as one of the classic works of literature. 'No more graphic and stirring narrative ... was ever written', claimed Sir Alexander Grant, Principal of Edinburgh University, in 1871. A century earlier, the historian John Gillies found that the expedition was 'related ... with such descriptive beauty, with such profound knowledge of war and of human nature, and with such inimitable eloquence, as never were re-united in the work of any one man'. And Gillies' contemporary William Mitford thought that Xenophon's 'beautiful narrative ... remains, like the Iliad, the oldest and the model of its kind'.[5]

Yet to talk of Xenophon's account as a classic runs the danger of making its reputation seem too cosy, too static. It may now be the case that the *Anabasis* is judged his masterpiece, but this has not always been so. In the sixteenth and seventeenth centuries, his overtly didactic works were preferred – and especially the *Cyropaedia*, which could appeal to some for its apparent defence of monarchy, and to others for the tragic love story interwoven with the political

10

lessons – the story of Abradatas and Panthea, the archetype of all romantic suicides. Popular too were the *Hiero* – another text that could seem to promote monarchy – and the *Oeconomicus*, itself the forerunner of many treatises on marriage. In the eighteenth century, the *Anabasis* was greatly admired, as Gillies' praise shows, but Xenophon was best known for the *Memorabilia*, with its agreeably practical and down-to-earth Socrates, and above all with its famous allegory, the 'Choice of Hercules' (or 'Hercules at the Crossroads'), which recounts how the young Hercules was wooed by two women, stern Virtue and bawdy Pleasure, and won over to the cause of virtuous toil.

It was only in the nineteenth century that the *Anabasis* came to be universally regarded as Xenophon's masterpiece. The excessive didacticism of some of Xenophon's other works was no longer so agreeable. As a philosopher and a historian, Xenophon could now be berated for failing to be a Plato or a Thucydides. His Socrates succumbed to the more ironic and more sublime Socrates of Plato, and, as new conceptions of historical method took hold, his historical writing now became notorious for some awkward omissions. The *Anabasis* alone was immune to such criticisms. It took the schoolroom by storm. But it was not a victory by default. It was strongly admired for reasons of its own – and above all for the descriptive beauty praised by Gillies. Indeed, the greatest of eighteenth-century historians, Edward Gibbon, had already contrasted the 'vague and languid' *Cyropaedia* with the 'circumstantial and animated' *Anabasis*: 'Such is the eternal difference between fiction and truth.' Many later readers might well disagree with Gibbon's generalization – but still prefer the animated *Anabasis*. And nowhere was the *Anabasis* more animated than when the Greeks shouted as they caught sight of the sea.[6]

*

The fortunes of the Greeks' shout of 'Thalatta! Thalatta!' have been no more fixed than the fortunes of the *Anabasis* itself. Hardly any writers before the nineteenth century echoed that shout or exploited it as a symbol. And even though it has often been thought to encapsulate the Greeks' attachment to the sea, it was neglected by ancient writers – to judge from what remains of their works (which is only a fraction of what was written). One echo from antiquity can be detected – in an unexpected place, the *Acta Philippi*, a life of the disciple Philip written several centuries after Christ. Philip, caught out at sea during a great storm, stood at the prow of his boat, and 'shouted out so as to be heard by everyone: "Thalassa, Thalassa – Sea, Sea, Jesus Christ, who walked on your waters, orders you, through me his servant, to check your fury." ' But this command to the sea does not have much to do with Xenophon's exclamation of joy. The scene on Mount Theches could still be evoked by ancient writers even if that exclamation was not echoed: in a geographical treatise on the Black Sea, the second-century historian Arrian wrote that he had seen the sea from the same spot as Xenophon; and in a funeral oration for the Emperor Julian the fourth-century rhetorician Libanius conveyed the feelings of some prisoners seeing their friends and family again by evoking the shouts, tears, and embraces of the Ten Thousand when they saw the sea. Yet this is still a slender haul given the enormous popularity that Xenophon enjoyed in later centuries – and the enormous popularity that 'Thalatta! Thalatta!' has enjoyed since the start of the nineteenth century.[7]

The sudden rush to 'The Sea! The Sea!' in the last two hundred years comes in part at least from the growing popularity of the *Anabasis*. But many other reasons will emerge for the fascination with Xenophon's shout in modern times. After all, not everyone who shouts 'Thalatta! Thalatta!' has been engaging closely with the world of Xenophon and his Ten Thousand. Its popularity may simply be due to the intriguing sound of the Greek words.

The sound of the Greek words is suggestively exploited by George MacDonald Fraser in *Flashman at the Charge*, one of his amusing novels about the improbably successful afterlife of Harry Flashman, anti-hero of the most famous of the Victorian public school novels, Thomas Hughes' *Tom Brown's Schooldays*, and last seen slinking off from Rugby School, expelled for drunkenness. The cowardly Harry Flashman, with his uncanny knack for being present at almost all the great military events of the Victorian era, has found himself riding with the Light Brigade on its charge through the valley of death – and somehow emerging once again an undeserved hero. But he has been taken prisoner and now, as he is being hauled in a cage across the Ust Yurt desert, he suddenly catches sight of the Aral Sea: 'we came through more salty flats to a long coastline of rollers sweeping in from a sea so blue that I found myself muttering through my beard "Thalassa or thalatta, the former or the latter?", it seemed so much like the ocean that old Arnold's Greeks had seen after their great march' (the 'Arnold' here is Thomas, the renowned headmaster).

Flashman's neat pun could be a fragment of a longer verse illustrating the difference between two Greek dialects – the Ionic 'thalassa' and the Attic 'thalatta': the sort of rhyming *aide-mémoire* that Victorian schoolteachers were fond of inflicting on their pupils. (Xenophon himself wrote in the Attic dialect that was spoken in Athens, his home city.) But in fact the rhyme just came to Flashman (or rather, to George MacDonald Fraser) on the spur of the moment.

If it is a rhyme, that is. It only works if one pronounces 'thalatta' in the British way – with a soft first syllable and the stress falling on the second syllable. The stress in the Greek in fact falls on the first syllable, and the Greek theta is more like the 'th' in 'Thomas' than in 'thanks'. Xenophon's shout sounded more like 'tallata' than 'the latter' – but why let pedantry spoil a pun?[8]

Particularly a pun that could also occur on the spur of the moment to a six-year-old – albeit an unusually precocious one: Ronald Knox, later famed for his detective stories and satires as well as his religious writings. Evelyn

Waugh, who wrote a respectful biography of Knox, tells the story that 'when the two little boys, aged seven and six, were taken to the sea, Wilfred asked: "Ronnie, do you consider that Xenophon's men cried "θάλαττα" or "θάλασσα"?" and Ronald answered: "The latter".' But even Waugh added that this nice paradox was of 'rather doubtful authenticity'.[9]

'The latter! The latter!' is also one of the many distorted echoes of Xenophon's shout included by James Joyce in *Finnegans Wake*. Also to be found in that riddling work are 'The letter! The litter!'; 'ye seal that lubs you lassers, Thallassee'; 'kolassa! kolassa!'; 'Galata! Galata!'; and even 'tha lassy! tha lassy!'. Or perhaps the Greeks' cry of triumph sounds a bit like a sneeze? That, at least, is what the modern Dutch poet Ben Zwaal suggests with his variant 'hatsjie thalassa' – 'hachoo thalassa'.[10]

Many who have echoed Xenophon's shout have, it seems, simply been fond of the sound of 'Thalatta! Thalatta!'. And this delight in the sound of the phrase is of course part of our story. Indeed, these echoes highlight an important – but often neglected – point about the way in which texts like the *Anabasis* are received by later readers. A common justification for studying the reception of literary works is that the changing horizons of different generations of readers mould the way we ourselves view the original works. But reception does not work through a slow and steady accretion of data: writers at different times may respond in similar ways without knowing that they are echoing earlier instances of reception – just as George Macdonald Fraser did not know that Flashman's pun had already been made by Ronald Knox. The very independence of different responses does not detract from their significance: on the contrary, it sheds even more light on the cultural assumptions that have shaped modern responses to the *Anabasis*. The assumption that later echoes of Xenophon's shout affect the way we read the original text should also be questioned. Many later responses to 'Thalatta! Thalatta!' may seem tenuous – yet their very tenuousness is proof of that shout's hold on the modern imagination. Nor need we judge these reactions by their relation to the source text. Literary works are there for later writers to use in whatever way they like, and responses that break free from the original text may be artistically rich and suggestive in their own right.

There have also been many people who have staked a claim for themselves by echoing Xenophon's shout, a claim that their own experiences merit some sort of comparison with Xenophon's. This temptation, we shall see, was particularly strong for British officers engaged upon eastern adventures of their own: for was there not, as Sir John Fortescue, the historian of the British army, wrote in 1895, 'somewhat of a Britannic character' about Xenophon's adventure itself?[11]

13

2

Eastern Adventure

Eight British officers are hiding in thick scrub outside a deserted village in the lower reaches of the Taurus mountains. It is late August 1918, and more than three weeks have elapsed since the men escaped from an internment camp at Yozgad ('pronounced Useguard') in the great central plateau of Turkey. At the time of their escape, they decided not to head north to the Black Sea, or east towards the Russian front, or west towards the Aegean coast, but south – even though it meant travelling some one hundred and fifty miles across salt desert. They have since been moving mainly by night across bare plains and rocky hills, across the Kizil Irmak river (the Halys of antiquity), and up into the ridges of the Taurus range. By day they have slept as best they can in the heat. They have had some adventures along the way, posing as a German surveying party and narrowly escaping discovery. Now they know they are getting near the coast. Yet each ridge has opened out onto another ridge hiding the sea from view. One of the men has even climbed an oak-tree in the hope of a glimpse of the sea. But now a couple of them have gone off in the early morning to fetch food, and returned with the news that they have seen the sea. Two of the officers, Captains Johnston and Yearsley, describe what happens when the group sets forth, incredulous, from its hiding place:

> Five minutes later the party as a whole had its first view of the sea. The morning sun was on it, making sky and sea one undivided sheen. ... As we scanned the water through the field-glasses, it looked as dead as the adjacent country. Not a sail was in sight anywhere, not a single ripple disturbed the shining sheet of glass in front of us. With heads uncovered, and with thankful hearts, we stood gazing, but without being in any way excited. Thus it was that no shout like the 'Thalassa! Thalassa!' of Xenophon's Ten Thousand broke from the lips of our little band that still August morning, although here was the end of our land journey at last in sight after a march of some 330 miles.

As it turned out, they could have expressed some joy. When they got to the coast, they hid in a ravine, and soon found a boat, stole it, and crossed to Cyprus, a British colony, and the endpoint of their *Four-Fifty Miles to Freedom*.[1] Why do the writers of this modern adventure tale evoke the most famous ancient tale of 'real life' adventure – Xenophon's *Anabasis*? If the men had

14

shouted 'Thalassa! Thalassa!', the implication would be clear: like the Ten Thousand, they had survived many dangers in a foreign and hostile land. But why point out a failure to echo that shout? Perhaps they are implying that they would normally have been expected to shout 'Thalassa! Thalassa!' – that they would have shouted those words, if only there had been some boats about. Their very remark that they failed to shout 'Thalassa! Thalassa!' proves to be an even more telling sign of Xenophon's hold on the imagination of escape than if they had actually shouted it.

Johnston and Yearsley were not the only British officers in Turkey whose thoughts turned to Xenophon. Xenophon's shout of the sea had also been in the minds of some prisoners who had escaped one year earlier from a camp in the town of Kastamuni, in a fertile valley close to the mountains that skirt the northern coast of Turkey. These men had not had to ponder which way to turn when they escaped. They had immediately headed north, towards the Black Sea. One of their number, E.H. Keeling, wrote for *Blackwood's Magazine* in May 1918 an account of what happened next: 'We were now on the north side of the watershed, and suddenly we beheld the Black Sea stretched out before us in the sunshine – only forty-one hours after we had decided to strike for it. Xenophon's Ten Thousand can scarcely have been more elated when they sighted the same sea two or three hundred miles further east.' When Keeling re-published this account in 1924, in his book *Adventures in Turkey and Russia*, he added a touch of melodrama ('It was a thrilling moment') and a touch of scholarship (after 'Xenophon's Ten Thousand', he added: 'or what was left of them'). He also gave the chapter in which he told of that first sight of the sea the heading 'Θάλαττα, θάλαττα' – and this despite the fact that his account alludes merely to the elation felt by the Ten Thousand, not to their actual shout.[2]

So Johnston and Yearsley were following the pattern set by a fellow British officer when they alluded to Xenophon's account of the Ten Thousand catching sight of the Black Sea. And that pattern was also followed by another member of Keeling's escape party, H.C.W. Bishop, when he recorded their first sight of the sea in more or less the same terms as Keeling (though without the Greek font) in a book published in 1920: 'It looked about fifteen miles off, but the mere sight seemed to raise our spirits marvellously, and we were, perhaps, almost as elated as Xenophon's men when the same sea greeted their gaze at Trebizond.' Bishop even seems to have had Keeling's words before him as he wrote: Keeling had made the very slightly bolder claim that the Ten Thousand 'can scarcely have been more elated'.

Johnston and Yearsley were perhaps contrasting their own position with Keeling's when they remarked on their failure to echo Xenophon's shout. They had themselves been interned at Kastamuni with Keeling and the rest of his escape party: it was after the escape of Keeling's group that the other prisoners were moved further away from the coast, first to squalid stables at Changri, and from there to the aptly named camp at 'Useguard'. Johnston and Yearsley also start their own story with news of Keeling's escape – and with a tribute to the men who had helped his group (they allude to Keeling's piece in *Blackwood's Magazine* and explain that Keeling himself, writing while the war was still going on, could not tell the full story).[3]

Or perhaps Xenophon's shout was simply so famous that anyone mildly cultivated enough to become a British officer would be more or less bound to think of it if he found himself on the run in Turkey and making for the sea. Johnston and Yearsley were not, after all, catering for devotees of fancy intertextuality. They were writing for the firm which had published popular wartime morale-raisers such as Ian Hay's *The First Hundred Thousand*, and for readers seeking excitement and adventure, and groping for proof that there was still a place in the world for the values of chivalric romance. By looking back to a Greek army that had extricated itself from danger after a succession of exciting adventures nearly two and a half thousand years earlier, these British officers were implying that there was still a place for heroism and endurance in the modern world.

*

It is telling that Xenophon's escape to the sea should have been recalled by these four British officers towards the end or in the immediate aftermath of the First World War. This era was a boom time for escape stories. To be captured had previously been viewed as shameful, but it had lost some of its stigma as developments in air and tank warfare made it more common for large bodies of soldiers to be encircled through no fault of their own. Still, it was better for soldiers to try to escape when they had been captured. And for those prisoners who did get away an allusion to a great classic like the *Anabasis* was a good way of elevating their achievements and restoring lost honour. Even though the Ten Thousand had evaded captivity rather than escaped, prisoners who had escaped would still find themselves in much the same position as the Ten Thousand, forced to survive a succession of pressing dangers as they tried to avoid capture.

As a story of evasion, Xenophon's account resembles not just the new breed of escape stories that became popular after the First World War, but also many of the established classics of fictional adventure. Just as Xenophon shows how the Greeks adapt to unusual surroundings, so too many adventure stories explore what happens to people left to their own devices in a new and strange location. The *Anabasis* is a grown-up version of island adventures like *Coral Island* or its negative counterpart, *Lord of the Flies*. It has even borne comparison with the archetype of all island adventures: 'Robinson Crusoe's reflections on his own plight barricaded on his island by the ocean' have been likened to Xenophon's 'superb description of Greek despondency' in the evening after the murder of the generals. Xenophon's gripping tale is also set in a suitably remote region, with an exotic landscape of mountain and desert (shades of Ouida's *Under Two Flags* and other novels of the Foreign Legion?). And this region is, perhaps, ripe for imperial exploitation (like the Africa of *King Solomon's Mines*), or even for colonization by the adventurers, a new (old) world, an ancient El Dorado. The adventurers' capacity to exploit that region is affirmed by the qualities that the story celebrates: masculine prowess, quick-wittedness, pluck – qualities well conveyed by the 'straightforward manliness' of Xenophon's style (as the 1911 edition of the *Encyclopaedia Britannica* characterized it). Perhaps Xenophon wrote the world's first eastern.[4]

Gibbon thought that the superiority of the animated *Anabasis* to the languid *Cyropaedia* marked 'the eternal difference between fiction and truth'. But perhaps the *Anabasis* became so popular because it almost read like fiction – like 'a chronicle of the most chivalrous knight-errantry', as one reader wrote in 1842, or 'a boy's own adventure story', according to a more recent assessment. Many others have invited comparison with the modern genre by calling the Ten Thousand 'adventurers', or by speaking of their 'magnificent adventure'. *Xenophon's Adventure* was the title of a re-telling of Xenophon for children by Geoffrey Household – or the title, at any rate, of the British edition. The American title, *The Exploits of Xenophon*, had stressed Xenophon's individual prowess, aligning him with muscular heroes like Hercules. But the taste for adventure was not restricted to the British. When Stephen Marlowe's 1963 historical novel, *The Shining: A Novel about Alcibiades*, was reprinted as a mass market paperback for the American public (it has never been published in Britain), the original subtitle was dropped, and the novel was promoted as the story of the March of the Ten Thousand, 'one of the greatest adventures of all time' – even though that great adventure accounts for less than a fifth of the book. And thirty years earlier an American college teacher could write, in opposition to those who 'disparage the *Anabasis* as a war book which will arouse war feeling among the young', that it was rather 'a great book of adventure and exploration, picturing many young Greeks on a holiday expedition'. This teacher was yielding (if a few years' anachronism may be allowed) to a bizarre Blyton-esque fantasy, an image of the *Anabasis* as *The Famous Five* two thousand times over.[5]

Xenophon himself could easily be seen as a rather English figure – 'the supreme model of the gentleman adventurer', who 'stands out, as he does from his own account, as a rather superior person, an amateur among gentlemen'. So wrote a journalist in *The Times* in 1930, reviewing an American book with the ungentlemanly title *Xenophon, Soldier of Fortune*. Many others have portrayed Xenophon's character in similar terms. For the

German scholar Werner Jaeger, it was 'his own burning passion for adventure and for war' that 'drew him to the young prince Cyrus, that romantic rebel' – as if Cyrus were a Bonny Prince Charlie in Achaemenid clothing. Indeed, Sir Alexander Grant could write that 'at first sight there is a halo of romance over the whole episode, not unlike that which surrounds the ill-fated Rebellion of 1745' – before admitting the qualification that the Greeks were without a cause, and Cyrus himself a traitor. Still, the notion of Xenophon's passion for adventure could survive all such qualms. Many, indeed, have imagined that Xenophon joined Cyrus' army because he had a taste for action and because he wanted to escape from the city – that is, from the oppression of the restored Athenian democracy – to the freedom of a frontier region.[6]

Xenophon emerges from such accounts as a Frederick Burnaby, the legendarily strong British army officer who would dash off on arduous rides through the desert to Khiva or across Asia Minor in the middle of winter as soon as he got a few weeks of leave. Or as a Fitzroy Maclean, applying for a transfer from Paris to Moscow because he had gained the impression that it offered 'a better chance of adventure' than most places, because he had seen something of the west, and now wanted to see the east and tread the golden road to Samarkand. Or perhaps (and the point is that there are many such figures) as a Peter Fleming, off up the Amazon on a Brazilian adventure in response to a newspaper advertisement, or crossing the wastes of China to bring back news from Tartary – but above all ('of course') because he thought he would enjoy it.[7]

But perhaps it is more apt to compare Xenophon not with these solo adventurers, but with the generals of the imperial armies that found themselves operating in unfamiliar terrain – or even with the journalists who followed those armies. As an eye-witness report on an ambitious expedition, the *Anabasis* could perhaps bring to mind the tales of G.A. Henty (*With Cyrus to Cunaxa?*). The historian J.B. Bury even thought that 'if he had lived in modern days', Xenophon 'would have made his fortune as a war-correspondent' – Henty's original occupation.[8]

Scarcely any terrain was more terrifying to the British than the bleak mountain passes of Central Asia – scene of the disastrous British retreat from Kabul in January 1842, when one man out of more than ten thousand reached Jalalabad. Small wonder that W.F. Ainsworth noted in a book published two years after the disaster that the military exploits recorded in the *Anabasis* offered 'a remarkable contrast to the recent campaign in Affghanistan'; or that Thomas De Quincey, in an essay written in the same year, called the original British advance into Afghanistan an 'anabasis'. Forty years later, General Roberts would march his own Ten Thousand from Kabul to Kandahar. That sort of British army could all too easily resemble Xenophon's Greeks as they battled against barbarian hordes – the few against the many, the disciplined against the wild. At the same time, the British were busy creating myths of their own: the famous imperial sieges – Cawnpore and Lucknow from the Indian Mutiny, Mafeking and Ladysmith from the Boer War – that became legends of endurance, or Gordon martyred at Khartoum, or Rorke's Drift, a hundred odd men defending an isolated post against an army of Zulus storming at them, few against many, those few with rifles against the many with spears, but, like Dr Brydon's solo arrival at Jalalabad, fitting material all the same for the brush of Lady Butler.[9]

We can perhaps understand, then, why Sir John Fortescue commented (in the year of the Jameson Raid) on the 'Britannic character' of Xenophon's adventure. At the same time, Fortescue's complacent assertion helps us to see even more clearly the political implications of adventure stories that pit plucky European heroes against the native inhabitants of lands ripe for exploitation. In the ancient world, the story told by Xenophon was often interpreted as proof of the weakness of the Persian empire – and even used to support expeditions against Persia. Fortescue's claim that the Ten Thousand showed a British spirit in their march justifies the British involvement in distant lands by appealing to that ancient precedent – while also using the British character as the norm by which other adventures can be judged. Yet Fortescue was evidently flattening out the experience of adventure. We would nowadays want to be a bit more wary of making such vast historical leaps: Xenophon's soldiers are not quite the same as British officers. Fortescue was also ignoring shifts within the British experience of adventure – shifts that themselves mirror the British experience of empire. We can trace these shifts by following how Xenophon's shout of 'The Sea! The Sea!' has been evoked by writers of real and fictional adventures from the first great English master of adventure tales, Daniel Defoe, to that emblem of modernity, T.E. Lawrence.[10]

*

In 1720, the year after *Robinson Crusoe* first appeared, Daniel Defoe published *The Life, Adventures, and Pyracies of the famous Captain Singleton* – a work presented, like *Robinson Crusoe*, as a true story, the memoirs of Singleton himself. Captain Singleton starts by telling how he took to the sea and joined a party of sailors who then mutinied and were abandoned on Madagascar. They managed to make their way across the sea to the east coast of Africa, and then they started on the long journey across Africa. It is in this section of the narrative that there appears what has been called a 'spontaneous allusion to Xenophon's Ten Thousand'. Singleton is describing their ascent of a band of hills: 'we were surprized when, being not quite come to the Top, one of our Company, who, with two Negroes, was got up before us, cry'd out, the *Sea*! the *Sea*! and fell a-dancing and jumping as Signs of Joy.' Singleton evokes Xenophon not merely by that cry of 'the *Sea*! the *Sea*!', but also by describing how he hears that shout from the rear, as Xenophon had done.[11]

But can we be sure that Defoe (or Singleton) is indeed echoing Xenophon? The cry of 'the *Sea*! the *Sea*!' rather than 'Thalatta! Thalatta!' leaves the matter in some doubt. The use of the English phrase is doubtless eloquent of the more robust manner of the eighteenth-century novelist. And these are not educated people that Defoe's narrator, Singleton, is describing – nor is Singleton especially educated himself. So it could be that Defoe is echoing Xenophon, but dulling the echo to suit the persona of his narrator. Yet it is not in fact certain that Defoe himself knew Greek or that he had read the *Anabasis* even in translation. A modern scholar has argued that there are more detailed correspondences between the *Anabasis* and *Captain Singleton*, but not all of these are convincing. Perhaps all we have is a coincidence of narrative strategy between two good storytellers.

A more definite glimpse of the attraction of Xenophon's sight of the sea to adventurers is offered by the scientist hero of Mary Shelley's *Frankenstein*, first published in 1818. It is easier for us nowadays to think of *Frankenstein* as a classic of gothic horror or as a parable on the dangers of scientific discovery than as an adventure story. But we should not forget the narrative setting of Shelley's story. Frankenstein is on a ship in the icy north, telling his story to a polar explorer, Robert Walton, who tells it in turn in a letter to his sister at home. Before we encounter Frankenstein, we hear Walton tell of his own dreams of reaching the North Pole and of the childhood reading that fostered them. And it is while he is pursuing those dreams, on a ship making its way slowly through vast fields of ice, that he first sees in the distance Frankenstein's monster, and then meets Frankenstein himself. So Frankenstein has himself entered the world of Arctic adventure when he tells his strange tale of creation and loss and loneliness.

It is towards the end of Frankenstein's narrative that he alludes to Xenophon's Greeks. After the monster he created has killed his brother, sister, and bride, Frankenstein has pursued it down the Rhone, across the Mediterranean to the Black Sea, and then across the wastes of Russia to the frozen north. But the monster always remains out of his grasp, taunting him with messages: 'My power is complete. Follow me; I seek the everlasting ices of the north, where you will feel the misery of cold and frost, to which I am impassive.' The creator is at the mercy of the being he created. Frankenstein goes on:

> calling on Heaven to support me, I continued with unabated fervour to traverse immense deserts, until the ocean appeared at a distance, and formed the utmost boundary of the horizon. Oh! how unlike it was to the blue seas of the south! Covered with ice, it was only to be distinguished from land by its

superior wildness and ruggedness. The Greeks wept for joy when they beheld the Mediterranean from the hills of Asia, and hailed with rapture the boundary of their toils. I did not weep; but I knelt down, and, with a full heart, thanked my guiding spirit for conducting me in safety to the place where I hoped ... to meet and grapple with him.

Here the joy felt by Xenophon's Greeks is likened to the joy felt by a wanderer over the empty northern wastes that fascinated the nineteenth-century English imagination. Frankenstein himself is like Xenophon's Greeks in another way too: he is seeking a return of sorts – a return to a past before he created the monster. But while the Greeks hail 'the boundary of their toils', Frankenstein remains thwarted, his heavenly aspirations 'blasted', as if he were a titan blasted by the thunderbolt of the gods.[12]

Shelley here is offering a comment on the spirit of adventure. The same heavenly aspirations that made Frankenstein create life are driving Walton towards the north – far from the home of the sister he addresses in his letters. But Walton too is thwarted, painfully conscious that he has no friend to share his adventures, and finally broken down by a mutiny when his sailors refuse to go further (no Cyrus, he). The monster alone achieves an end he has set for himself, the death of Frankenstein. But it brings him no satisfaction. Those toils finished, his own sublime aspirations for comradeship damned by his creator, he is last seen heading further north, to burn himself in an icy wasteland, alone. Frankenstein may recall the Greeks weeping with rapture, but none of Shelley's romantic trio is granted any such triumphant return.

*

Fictions of adventure like *Captain Singleton* and *Frankenstein* fed off the 'real life' narratives that told of the great British imperial adventure. At the time Defoe was writing, this was still predominantly a naval adventure. The crossing of Africa was itself only part of the adventurous life of Captain Singleton. His was predominantly a story of the sea: Singleton gains a vast wealth in Africa, but loses it at home, and the second half of the novel describes how he takes to the waves once more, as a pirate in the West Indies and in the east. A century later, sea voyages could still provide the best standard for measuring the endurance of the Ten Thousand: the geographer James Rennell compared the Greeks with Captain Cook in the *Endeavour*, 'engaged in the intricate, and imminently dangerous navigation, amongst the reefs and shallows of New Holland', and with Captain Bligh and his crew, 'driven by mutineers from his command of the *Bounty* and committed to an open boat with scanty provisions, on which they sailed 3,618 miles in 41 days'.[13]

At the time Rennell was writing the terrain of the African interior that appears in *Captain Singleton* was becoming more familiar to explorers endowed with a new spirit. This new spirit was the will to overcome obstacles of desert and mountain and ice, the passion to fill in the blank spaces on the map, to make light where there was darkness, the cult of the explorer, of Parry and Franklin in the Arctic, of Burton and Livingstone in Africa. This spirit could even endow Xenophon himself with a new sort of glory: Xenophon was 'in the position of a geographical explorer, or at least of a traveller through almost unknown regions', one historian of ancient geography could claim, or the leader of 'a magnificent feat of exploration', as Sir Percy Sykes, himself a notable explorer of Persia, wrote.[14]

More counterparts to Xenophon's tale would be provided by the deeds of great nineteenth-century explorers like John McDouall Stuart, leader of the first expedition to cross Australia from sea to sea. When the expedition was approaching the Indian Ocean in July 1862, Stuart alone had worked out how near to the sea they were. As he recorded in his journal, he told two of his colleagues, and one of them rode out in advance and 'called out "The Sea!" ', at which the others 'were so astonished, that he had to repeat the call before they fully understood what was meant. Then they immediately gave three long and hearty cheers.' So a shout of 'The Sea! The Sea!' was heard – even if there was a bit of a pause between the two parts. But giving three cheers was a more common way of celebrating the sight of water. When Richard Burton was approaching the east coast of Africa on his return from his search for the source of the Nile, his servants from Zanzibar 'screamed with delight at the sight of the mango-tree' while three days later 'we greeted, with doffed caps and with three times three and one more, as Britons will do on such occasions, the kindly smiling face of our father Neptune'. The masculine sea of father Neptune is to the British what soft fruits (mango, pineapples, limes) are to the natives – except that the British greet their native element in a more restrained way than those screaming natives: hip-hip-hurrah three times, and once more for luck. Another African explorer, Samuel White Baker, drawing near to the 'great inland sea' that he named Albert N'yanza – the second source of the Nile – was also aware of the English way to behave. He saw the lake suddenly 'like a sea of quicksilver', a 'reward for all our labour ... England had won the sources of the Nile! Long before I reached this spot I had arranged to give three cheers with all our men in English style in honour of the discovery ...'. More enterprising Englishmen could come up with other ways of expressing their pleasure at arriving at the sea – 'God save the King' and 'Rule Britannia', for instance. Those, at least, were the words that G.F. Lyon, who ventured to the African interior early in the nineteenth century, chanted when he saw the Mediterranean again, and he chanted them 'as loud as I could roar', and 'to the great astonishment of my fellow travellers, who no doubt thought me mad'.[15]

2. Eastern Adventure

Other great journeys of exploration could be given the Xenophontic treatment after the event. An American journalist in 1906 could claim that the survivors of De Soto's 1539 expedition into North America had uttered at the sight of the Gulf of Mexico a cry of 'The Sea! The Sea!' as joyful as Xenophon's – even though earlier accounts of De Soto's march did not mention any such cry. What, if anything, Meriwether Lewis and William Clark, leaders of the first expedition to cross the breadth of North America, shouted when they first saw the Pacific in November 1805 is not recorded. Clark did write in the table of courses and distances: '*Ocian in view! O! the joy.*' But it took a later writer to make the proper comparison: 'The Corps of Discovery felt like Xenophon's Greeks on the day when ... a cry of "Thalassa! Thalassa!" ran down that heroic column.'[16]

A firm allusion to Xenophon could elevate a much lesser venture into the interior than these expeditions across continents. In one of the most famous travel books of the nineteenth century, *Eothen*, first published in 1844, Alexander Kinglake recounted a trip made nine years earlier through the Ottoman dominions: from Constantinople through Asia Minor, across to Cyprus, and from there to Palestine and Cairo. The classical world was with him as he went, and nowhere more so than in the Troad, where he reflected on the childhood delights of the *Iliad*. (It was from Homer that he took his precious title – the epic word for 'from the east', as is hinted in the subtitle, *Traces of Travel Brought Home from the East*.) The classical world even helped him survive an adventure en route – a rough crossing to Cyprus, when the Greek crew suddenly took on 'the spirit of the old Demos'. As he journeyed down through Palestine, the biblical world started to take over his thoughts – or at least it should have done, but he was constantly drawn to contemplate the 'mysterious' desert stretching forth into the distance. The desert alone, he thought, would satisfy his 'moody longing for Eastern travel' and provide him with relief from his 'weariness of that ... pedantic and painstaking governess, Europe'. But when he did travel through the desert to Egypt he was disappointed: 'Childe Harold would have found it a dreadful bore to make "the desert his dwelling-place", for, at all events, if he adopted the life of the Arabs, he would have tasted no solitude.' Kinglake would walk away as his attendants pitched the tent to 'feel the loneliness of the desert' and be filled 'with a sort of childish exultation in the self-sufficiency which enabled me to stand thus alone in the wideness of Asia'. But it was not until he was travelling through the desert from Cairo to Suez that he enjoyed real solitude – and the defining adventure of his journey. He went ahead of his party, and after a couple of hours found himself all alone:

It was not without a sensation of awe that I swept with my sight the vacant round of the horizon, and remembered that I was all alone and unprovisioned in the midst of the arid waste; but this very awe gave tone and zest to the exultation with which I felt myself launched. ... now, at least, I was here in this African desert, and I *myself, and no other, had charge of my life.*

Thirsty, he encountered some Bedouins, and drank, without asking, from their water-flask:

> before me now, and on either side, there were vast hills of sand and calcined rocks that interrupted my progress and baffled my doubtful road, but I did my best. With rapid steps I swept round the base of the hills, threaded the winding hollows, and at last, as I rose in my swift course to the crest of a lofty ridge, Thalatta! Thalatta! the sea – the sea was before me!

And so to Suez, and the home of the British agent, and the delight of fresh sheets.[17]

Xenophon's shout seems to come into its own as it enters the thoughts of Alexander Kinglake, educated at Eton and Cambridge, a bored barrister set free suddenly in the wastes of the Near East. Here we have the Greek words themselves, not Defoe's English. And here we have the will to identify oneself with the Ten Thousand and their great shout. Alone, unprovisioned, in the midst of hostile terrain: Kinglake is in an archetypally imperial setting, and his exclamation is an archetypally imperial gesture.

*

At the same time as he elevates his struggle through the Egyptian desert by echoing Xenophon's cry of joy, Kinglake presents us with a rich sense of the landscape that elicits from him that shout. Before he is saved by the sight of the sea, he is lost in a romantic desert – a boundless desert that he compares several times with the sea, a place of danger where it is all too easy to disappear without trace, but a place that can also promise a freedom of sorts. He is alone in a vast and empty expanse – rather as the Ten Thousand themselves could be pictured as isolated in the great landscapes of the Kurdish mountains and the Armenian plateau. That at least is how their adventures were recreated in a poem written in 1906 by a popular novelist, Mrs Baillie Reynolds:

> When those ten thousand Greeks – a downcast host –
> Tramped starving on, in hostile deserts lost;
> When with each mile the land more sterile proved,
> More faint their hope of finding what they loved: -
> One day, one moment found them unawares -
> Flashed on their sight the answer to their prayers!
> Their own true element, the boundless main,
> Gleamed in the sun across the barren plain,
> Their goal! – Where no man deemed such goal could be ...
> '*Thalassa*!' was their cry – 'The Sea! The Sea!'

24

The same romantic aura was conveyed by a Polish poet K.M. Górski in a poem 'Thalatta' written a few years earlier:

> On the boundless wilderness, the Greeks were marching slowly
> Freezing under the stars, falling down under the killing sun.
> And they even began to doubt whether they would ever come back
> Where their women were left in sorrow for them.

Xenophon orders some men to go ahead to look out for a town or a river –

> And a shout: Sea! – growing up among the Greeks.
> There were ten thousand of them in that sweltering day
> There were ten thousand of them in that remote land
> And in front of their eyes they can see in the frame of the hills
> A long stripe on the horizon …

The Greeks, suddenly stumbling across the sea when they were lost in the desert, are here in the position of Frankenstein or Kinglake, traversing immense deserts when they suddenly see the promise of safety and an end to their toils. Like Mrs Baillie Reynolds, Górski pares down Xenophon's geography to a symbolic opposition of desert and sea.[18]

It was not just the ambivalent charms of the desert that made it attractive to imagine Xenophon's Greeks lost in a flat desert until they were unexpectedly saved by the sight of the sea. Such depictions were also moulded by an even more romantic concern: they made the Ten Thousand themselves seem like shipwrecked sailors cast off in a boat or raft and waiting for salvation from a passing ship or from the sight of land.

The nautical parallel for the Ten Thousand's escape from the interior had already been observed in antiquity. In his life of Mark Antony, Plutarch recounted Antony's disastrous retreat from Parthia to Armenia – in the course of which Antony 'often cried "O the Ten Thousand!", in admiration of Xenophon and his men, who made an even longer march back down to the sea from Babylon, and fought with many times as many enemies, and yet came through in safety'. Antony's army came at last to the river Araxes, which divided Media and Armenia, and 'word went round that the enemy were lying in ambush there and would attack them as they crossed. But when they had safely got across and set foot in Armenia, as if they had just seen that land from the sea, they saluted it and in their joy turned to weeping and embracing one another.' The false expectation of another attack, the salute, the joyful tears and hugs recall Xenophon – while the phrase 'as if they had just seen that land from the sea' points to what was unusual about his achievement. The joy of sailors seeing land was a natural comparison for the less common pleasure of adventurers emerging safely from the dark interior. Indeed, the only ancient parallel one eighteenth-century commentator could find for Xenophon's 'Thalatta' scene was the joy felt by Virgil's Aeneas as he sails from Troy to a new home in the west and sees Italy for the first time: 'We see Italy. Italy Achates shouts first, Italy his companions greet with a cheerful shout.'[19]

The analogy between the Ten Thousand and sailors finding safety from the dangers of the sea would appeal especially to the romantic generation – to imaginations obsessed by shipwrecks and alive to the romance of the desert. The Ten Thousand's theatrical display of emotion when they saw the sea found naval counterparts in the narratives collected in anthologies like the three-volume *Shipwrecks and Disasters At Sea* edited by Sir John Dalyell in 1812. The narratives gathered by Dalyell include descriptions of sailors crying and shouting for joy as they catch sight of the ships that will save them; or else caught between joy and apprehension when they catch sight of land – joy at the prospect of escape from the sea, but apprehension at the dangers in steering to shore and at the savages waiting for them. Many more such incidents would occur in the years after Dalyell's anthology was published. Most notorious were the sufferings of the passengers abandoned on the raft of the *Medusa* – sufferings that turned to joy when the survivors sighted a ship in the distance, and, as two of them later recalled in a famous memoir, shouted 'Saved!', and 'all embraced each other with transports that looked like delirium, and tears of joy rolled down our cheeks, shrunk by the most cruel privations'. Closer still to Xenophon's 'Thalatta! Thalatta!' was a shout of 'A sail! A sail!' – the shout made by Defoe's mutinous sailors in *Captain Singleton* when they are marooned on Madagascar, and by Byron's corsair when he sees a ship to attack, but also by shipwrecked sailors like Coleridge's ancient mariner or Tennyson's Enoch Arden – who shouts 'A sail! A sail! / I am saved!' and dies. 'A sail! A sail!' was also shouted in a fiction inspired by the wreck of the *Medusa*, Eugène Sue's *La Salamandre* (1832). Sue had his shipwrecked men and women go through all the moves required by the grammar of disaster narratives: they embrace each other; they fall to their knees as a sense of religious gratitude floods through them; some start to sing a hymn; and some are even happy enough to be able to weep ('pour pouvoir pleurer') – as if they weep because that is what is expected of them, because that is what happens in the classic accounts. Closest of all to the Greeks' shout of 'Thalatta! Thalatta!' was Columbus' shout of 'Tierra! Tierra!', 'Land! Land!', at his first sight of the New World: many readers would be reminded of that eloquently simple shout as they came to Xenophon's climactic scene.[20]

*

When Alexander Kinglake identifies himself with the Ten Thousand as he catches sight of the sea, we may suspect that 'Thalatta! Thalatta!' is the more alluring for its seductive similarity to the shouts uttered by sailors struggling across the desert-like expanse of the sea. But while the romantic fascination with shipwrecks may have given Xenophon's exclamation a paradoxical resonance for nineteenth-century explorers emerging from the darkness of the interior, 'Thalatta! Thalatta!' could also appeal directly to actual sailors. And not just to sailors simply admiring the open sea around them, but to sailors engaged in adventures of their own – to the followers of Mary Shelley's Robert Walton, men who felt the pull of the north and were driven to confront the icy wastes of the Arctic, that blank expanse whose appeal was as strong as the deserts of the south.

In 1893, the great Norwegian explorer Fridtjof Nansen set sail on his most ambitious expedition to the north. His ship, the *Fram*, had been strengthened so that it could be locked into the ice and allowed to drift along with the current. A year and a half after his ship had become bound in the ice, Nansen set off with one colleague on a long march across the ice, and succeeded in penetrating further north than any explorer previously. His ship meanwhile continued to drift with the ice, and another long year passed before the ice began to break up (Plate 2). In July 1896 the *Fram* did at least start to make its way through broken floes towards the open sea, but even now its progress was slow and the ice threatened to close in again. At last in August the ice opened further, and a wide channel lay ahead, and there loomed the prospect of liberation from the ice and the sight of the open sea. It was now that one of these adventurers turned his thoughts to Xenophon: 'Perhaps we can soon celebrate with the classic greeting Tallata Tallata. Don't know if it's written correctly, but what the hell.' So Scott Hansen, a Norwegian naval lieutenant, wrote in his journal as he came off watch one morning. After three years in a ship stuck in the ice, his carefree tone can easily be forgiven – and 'tallata' (the Finnish word for 'trample') is not far off the sound of Xenophon's shout (the polar writer Roland Huntford adds, perhaps unfairly, that Hansen 'meant "Thalassa! Thalassa!" '). Xenophon's classic greeting has here become a shout of joy at the thought of the freedom of the open sea after long years of confinement within the ice. That greeting could, it seems, appeal as readily to explorers in the Arctic north as to travellers in the Egyptian desert.[21]

A few years after Hansen's Arctic jottings on board the *Fram*, Xenophon's versatile greeting was shouted further south even than Egypt. The shout was heard towards the end of a military adventure described in an extremely vivid Boer War memoir, *Commando*. The author, Denys Reitz, was son of the President of the Orange Free State (then still an independent Republic). He followed his father into exile at the end of the war, unwilling to accept British rule, and wrote his account in Madagascar in 1903 – though it was only published in 1929, when he was a Cabinet Minister, long reconciled to the united South Africa (he was later High Commissioner in London).

Reitz's memoir tells the story of a small commando group led into the

Cape Colony by Jan Christiaan Smuts. At first they were very hard pressed, as Basuto tribesmen attacked them in the rear and the British used the railways to throw cordon after cordon in their way. They found themselves 'beset on all sides', but they constantly managed to evade the British with the help of local guides. They heard that Kitchener had demanded the surrender of all Boer arms. They lived off what they could get from farms, at one time falling sick from a poisonous fruit, at another coming across an inn well-stocked with beer and spirits (with terrible results for the man who was left behind asleep and caught by the British).

Reitz could have suggested parallels from Xenophon for many of these episodes. As it is, he only alludes to Xenophon once – when Smuts, quartered on the banks of the Olifants River twenty-five miles from the sea, sent word to the nearby units that all those who had never seen the sea were to be sent to him:

> Some sixty or seventy men arrived within the next forty-eight hours, and with these we set off for a small inlet on the coast called Fishwater. We rode via the Ebenezer Mission Station, and towards afternoon caught a glint of the sea through a gap in the dunes. It was amusing to watch the expression on the men's faces as the great expanse of ocean burst on their view, for few of them had seen anything bigger than the dam on their parents' farms, and, as we topped the last sand-hills, they looked in amazement on water that stretched beyond the horizon.
>
> With one accord they reined in their horses in silence, and then, like the Greek soldiers, rushed forward in a body, crying, 'The sea! The sea!' each wanting to be first on the beach.

Boers too, it seems, could feel the freedom of the sea after a long trek across mountains and forests and veld.[22]

Reitz's evocation of Xenophon gains a particular resonance from an event in the march that he does not himself record. In the early stages of the expedition, Smuts pilfered from a farmhouse a copy of the *Anabasis*, along with a Latin edition of Erasmus' *Praise of Folly*. Three weeks later, Smuts had to extricate himself from a tight corner at Moordenaarspoort. He had gone to scout a pass with three others, when, as he wrote in his journal, 'suddenly and unexpectedly we were surrounded by a strong force of the enemy'. His comrades and all the horses were killed, and Smuts 'alone escaped without a scratch by creeping through the enemy's lines'. Smuts' narrow escape cost him his copy of the *Anabasis* – but he lived on to become Prime Minister of the Union of South Africa (and later Chancellor of the University of Cambridge).[23]

While Nansen's shipmate brought us back to the world of *Frankenstein*, Smuts' commando evokes again the landscape of Defoe's African adventure – except that the Boers were battling for national freedom, not for private gain. Other adventurers and travellers in the nineteenth and early twentieth centuries would transport Xenophon's shout to yet more varied settings – and even away from the sea itself. When an English aristocrat looked back in 1905 to a journey across North America that he had made more than fifty years earlier, Xenophon provided the right register as he recalled the great moment when, after an increasingly difficult trek from Fort Laramie across the Rockies to Oregon, he caught sight of the military post at the Dalles: 'our cry of "The tents! the tents!" echoed the joyous "Thalassa! Thalassa!" of the weary Greeks.' (Yet in the account the Hon. Henry J. Coke had published as a twenty-five-year-old the only exclamation came from an Indian squaw who was guiding him – and what she cried out was 'Soljar house!'.) Other sights, too, could inspire such passion. The Greeks' joyous shout was irresistibly brought to the mind of an American soldier in the Confederate army during the Civil War when his mountain-bred comrades cheered as they came in sight again of the high country with which they were familiar. Similarly a German soldier retreating through Macedonia at the end of the First World War thought of 'The Sea! The Sea!' when he finally caught sight of a railway line.[24]

Xenophon's shout was heard in an even more exotic setting in the world of fiction – at the end of a *Journey to the Centre of the Earth*. In Jules Verne's famous story of 1864, a young German, Axel, accompanies his uncle, a frenzied geologist, and their placid Icelandic companion, Hans, down a series of tunnels leading deeper and deeper into the earth. It is a voyage into the past, as they come across earlier and earlier geological formations, until finally they discover a vast sea deep within the earth where the conditions of early life are preserved. 'La mer!' is how Axel greets this surprising sea. But one early translator made Axel an English boy, Harry, and had him cry 'The sea – the sea'. Another, Frederick Amadeus Malleson, of The Vicarage, Broughton-in-Furness, went even further. He acknowledged in his preface that he had corrected some of Verne's scientific errors. But he did not restrict himself to 'trifling deviations' intended to increase the usefulness of the work. In his version, when Axel first sees 'a vast sheet of water, the commencement of a lake or an ocean' spreading far away beyond the range of the eye, it reminds him 'forcibly of that open sea which drew from Xenophon's ten thousand Greeks, after their long retreat, the simultaneous cry, "Thalatta! thalatta!" the sea! the sea!'. Malleson even made 'Thalatta! Thalatta!' the heading of the previous chapter, at the end of which Axel, separated from his companions and then fortuitously saved, hears a strange lapping sound: the cry of Xenophon's Greeks both signals Axel's joy at finding his companions again and anticipates his sight of the immense sea at the centre of the earth. We may well feel that this translator has overseasoned his Xenophontic broth – but his very extravagance is telling. For both adventurers in the flesh and adventurers in the imagination, 'Thalatta!

Thalatta!' was not just a cry of relief and joy at the prospect of a safe return home but also an assertion of heroic endeavour and achievement.[25]

*

It has been slightly less easy for more recent adventurers to bridge the historical gulf separating them from antiquity and to identify directly with the heroic Ten Thousand. An Etonian traveller like Kinglake, saluting the Red Sea with 'Thalatta! Thalatta!', did not have quite same the same feelings as another Etonian, Peter Fleming, when he evoked Xenophon's shout in a chapter heading a century later. Fleming belonged to the generation of travellers like Evelyn Waugh and Graham Greene who, as Greene himself later reflected, had been 'brought up on adventure stories', but had 'missed the enormous disillusionment of the First War' and so 'went looking for adventure'. The sort of adventure that Fleming (as a Special Correspondent of *The Times*) undertook in 1935 and described in *News from Tartary*: a journey of seven months and three thousand five hundred miles from Peking to Kashmir at a time when parts of China were split by civil war. Fleming's aim (apart from his own enjoyment) was to find out what was happening in the province of Sinkiang (Chinese Turkistan), then ruled by a government that, though nominally loyal to Nanking, was more or less under Soviet control. Getting to Sinkiang was far from easy: since the normal routes were closed, Fleming and his companion (a Swiss woman) spent several weeks crossing a corner of the Tibetan plateau, a desolate upland region of mountain, marshland, and desert without a house or tree, before descending to Cherchen, one of the oasis towns on the southern rim of the Takla Makan desert.[26]

It is the chapter where he describes his first sight of Cherchen that Fleming designates 'Thalassa, Thalassa'. It may seem odd that Fleming uses Xenophon's shout of the sea to celebrate his arrival at an oasis town. Other writers, admittedly, had already used that shout to bring out the joy of seeing tents or mountains or even a railway line, but they had made the point of the comparison clear. Fleming, moreover, seems to be inverting the more usual image of the desert as a sea – an image he uses earlier in his journey across the bleak Tibetan plateau when he approaches a rare settlement 'as castaways in a rowing boat draw nearer to an island' and when he greets the arrival of camels with the delight of castaways hailing a ship. It is as if Fleming has intuitively picked up how Xenophon's Greeks could be imagined toiling through the desert when they saw the sea and the promise of an end to their ordeal. The unexpected chapter heading is not, however, totally isolated. In the next chapter, when he arrives at Cherchen, Fleming explains that 'the earth offers no greater contrast – except that between land and sea – than the contrast between desert and oasis. ... we slipped into coolness and delight as smoothly and abruptly as a diver does.' 'Thalassa,

Thalassa' indeed. Fleming may even be recalling the feelings of his fellow Etonian Kinglake – but not so much his excited 'Thalatta! Thalatta!' at the sight of the Red Sea as his feelings when he passed from the desert into lands watered by the Nile and 'floated along (for the delight was as the delight of bathing) through green wavy fields of rice ... and dived into the cold verdure of groves and gardens'.[27]

By citing Xenophon, Fleming seems to be striving for the heroism of the generation that had fought in the Great War – the heroism of his own father, 'V. F., Killed in Action, May 20th, 1917', as the dedication of *News from Tartary* reveals. That is not the only reminder of the war that Fleming himself missed: the first section of his march across the Tibetan plateau is entitled 'No Man's Land'. In his preface, Fleming also invites comparison with the heroic adventure stories on which he had been raised: 'the situation in the Province was as dark as Darkest Africa in the days when that Victorian superlative was current.' One might suppose that Fleming saw himself as reviving the spirit of Victorian adventure. But that would be to mistake his intention. Fleming had, in Anthony Powell's words, 'a preoccupation, almost an obsession, with not appearing to "show off" ', and the great popu-larity of his travel books stemmed precisely from the comic, self-deprecating tone that he cultivated. In *News from Tartary*, Fleming is careful to separate his own journey from the worthwhile travels of specialists who bring back Knowledge ('We measured no skulls'). He is himself 'eternally the amateur', engaged on a 'comic expedition' that was 'undeservedly successful'. He plays with the tradition of the desert island adventure (as they cooked a goose Fleming had just shot, 'we felt very Swiss Family Robinson') while also suggesting that the status of adventure has been cheapened in the modern world: he speaks of his 'abhorrence of the false values placed ... on what can most conveniently be referred to by its trade-name of Adventure'. Perhaps, then, the chapter heading 'Thalassa, Thalassa' is not after all a gesture towards identification with the heroic Ten Thousand. Its inflated tone fits the persona Fleming creates for himself perfectly – since it is a prelude to another confession of bumbling amateurism. As Fleming and his companion approached Cherchen they had been speculating lazily about it with a 'chronic lack of advance information ... unexampled in the annals of modern travel': 'Cherchen, for all we knew or could find out, might be a walled city, or a cluster of tents, or almost any other variation on the urban theme.' And their joy at their arrival is short-lived: they are soon hauled before the police, and it looks as if they may not be allowed to go any further (they have been travelling without the proper permit). But they are surpris-ingly released, and so they proceed to the home of the local British agent, and the sight of a Union Jack, and another designedly bombastic chapter heading – 'Rule Britannia'. Like that heading, 'Thalassa, Thalassa' stands in counterpoint with the understated title of the whole section – 'No Picnic'.[28]

Peter Fleming does not seem to be using Xenophon's exclamation in quite the same way as Alexander Kinglake. They both offer only an isolated citation of Xenophon's shout, without any reference to Xenophon himself. But while Kinglake seems to be directly engaged with that shout, Fleming is ironic, the child of an age more detached and questioning in its use of the classical past, and more sceptical, too, of the place of adventure in the modern world.

*

It was while Peter Fleming was at the oasis town of Yarkand that he rifled a postbag, borrowed a copy of *The Times*, and read of the death of T.E. Lawrence – perhaps the most famous of all twentieth-century adventurers. Fleming describes how, as he read of Lawrence's death, he reflected on the strange rumours he had heard that Lawrence himself was present in Sinkiang, helping the rebels who were fighting the provincial government – 'not the least fantastic part of the Lawrence legend', and also, perhaps, the sort of adventure for which Fleming feels a certain nostalgia (he later mentions that a communist paper in Britain made him out to be an 'agent of Imperialist intrigue, a kind of shady Lawrence; and I could not help feeling pleased that anyone should take me so seriously'). Fleming seems to be distancing himself from the legendary Lawrence, and this sense of distance is suggestively mapped out in their different responses to Xenophon. The ironic and insouciant allusion to Xenophon's shout made by Fleming, a Special Correspondent resigned to his own belatedness, is telling enough. But the pre-war and wartime adventures of T.E. Lawrence, a member of the generation that had experienced at first hand the enormous disillusionment of the First War, reveal even more sharply the changing value of 'Thalatta! Thalatta!' in the modern world.[29]

As an undergraduate, Lawrence had an engaging Xenophontic experience during the summer vacation of 1908. Escaping from Oxford for a long cycling trip across France, he reached Aigues-Mortes on the southern coast – the town from which St Louis set out for his crusade. From there, on 2 August, a fortnight or so before his twentieth birthday, he wrote a letter to his mother, describing his recent adventures in the hills of the Auvergne. He started by saying that he consoled himself 'with the idea that my sufferings were beyond the conception of antiquity, since they were a combination (in a similar climate) of those of Sisyphus who pushed a great weight uphill, of Tantalus who couldn't get anything to drink, or any fruit, or of Theseus who was doomed ever to remain sitting'; then, as he reached a peak,

> I had a most delightful surprise. ... suddenly the sun leaped from behind a cloud, & a sort of shiver passed over the grey: then I understood, & instinctively burst out with a cry of θάλασσα, θάλασσα that echoed down the valley,

& startled an eagle from the opposite hill: it also startled two French tourists who came rushing up hoping to find another of the disgusting murders their papers make such a fuss about I suppose. They were disappointed when they heard it was 'only the Mediterranean'!

Lawrence's heightened mood stayed with him as he reached the coast and had a swim: 'I felt that at last I had reached the way to the South, and all the glorious East. ... I fancy I know now better than Keats what Cortes felt like, "silent upon a peak in Darien". ... Really this getting to the sea has almost overturned my mental balance: I would accept a passage for Greece tomorrow.'[30]

Lawrence does not name Xenophon or the Ten Thousand when he tells of his own instinctive echoing of their shout. The mere shout, and the Greek letters, are enough to keep up the spirit of the account. The shout celebrates his release from Sisyphean toil. Unlike the Ten Thousand, however, the release Lawrence sees in the shivering sea is not the promise of home. His shout is an expression of a Mediterranean passion, a gesture of arrival at a new world, the world of the south, the south. But it is also a return to somewhere that feels like home to someone like Lawrence, educated in the classics at Oxford High School and eager for all things medieval.

Lawrence's instinctive shout on top of a steep hill in Southern France takes on a new interest when considered alongside the achievements of the older Lawrence, the Lawrence who fomented the Arab revolt. Lawrence's wartime adventures could easily bear comparison with Xenophon's. Like Xenophon, Lawrence was the successful leader of a difficult march over tough terrain. Like Xenophon, he was young when he carried out his great exploits. And like Xenophon, he later wrote a famous account of those exploits. Italo Calvino has even claimed that Lawrence is the contemporary writer who is Xenophon's nearest equivalent. *Seven Pillars of Wisdom*, Lawrence's account of his role in Britain's 'war-time Eastern adventure', is – as Calvino acknowledges – a very different sort of work from the *Anabasis*. There is some overlap in the bare account of desert marches (descriptions of gazelle hunts, for instance), but Lawrence pays far more attention to geological vagaries – to what it felt like to tramp (or ride on a camel) across different sorts of terrain. His work is also much more psychologically complex. For all these differences, Lawrence himself was aware of the comparison with Xenophon. When he took up Greek again in 1927, he started with the *Anabasis*, and told George Bernard Shaw that he found it 'charming: so cunningly full of writing tricks, by an amateur soldier who had (like a recent fellow of my experience) obviously studied better men's books and copied them carefully.' No need to say who that 'fellow' was. And in *Seven Pillars of Wisdom* itself Lawrence used Xenophon to bring out his conception of his exploits in Arabia.[31]

Lawrence first hinted at Xenophon by writing of the 'moral greatness of the march up-country' to Wejh ('march up-country' is a traditional translation of 'anabasis'). He then described how he gained a new insight into military strategy while he lay for ten days sick in a tent in the desert (a conventional place for enlightenment). He pondered the 'algebraical' and 'biological' factors of warfare in Arabia, and saw the need to fight 'a war of detachment', containing the enemy 'by the silent threat of a vast unknown desert'. There remained 'the psychological element': 'I went to Xenophon and stole, to name it, his word *diathetics*, which had been the art of Cyrus before he struck.' Lawrence here presupposes a quite detailed knowledge of Xenophon: he forms a new noun ('diathetics' is not in the *Oxford English Dictionary*) from a verb used once in the *Anabasis*. This new coinage describes the psychological element which will be the key to his thinking: the Arab revolt will be the stirring of an idea. He put his new thinking to the test with a bold plan to win the strategic coastal town of Akaba. Since Akaba was well protected against attacks from the sea, Lawrence set off from Wejh on a long march inland through the desert before looping back towards the coast and capturing Akaba – the supreme Xenophontic moment of his Arabian campaign. He described his arrival at the sea at the end of Book IV of *Seven Pillars of Wisdom* (just as Xenophon reaches the sea at the close of Book IV of the *Anabasis*): 'we raced through a driving sandstorm down to Akaba, four miles further, and splashed into the sea on July the sixth, just two months after our setting out from Wejh.' We find here a sense of liberation, certainly, and a nicely sibilant 'splashed into the sea'. But there is no shout of 'Thalassa! Thalassa!' – no echo of the sound of the sea itself (Plate 3).[32]

Lowell Thomas, the American journalist who first created the myth of Lawrence, did succeed in giving Lawrence's arrival at Akaba a slight Xenophontic aura. Lawrence, he wrote in *Strand Magazine* in 1920, had led an army 'of about ten thousand Bedouins' down into Akaba. That number was a vast exaggeration – one of countless mistakes in Thomas' account. Yet for all the cult of heroism that he built around Lawrence, Thomas did not follow up the parallel that could easily have been suggested by that mistaken number. And when he came to write his book *With Lawrence in Arabia*, he changed the wording and wrote of Lawrence 'leading his scraggly, undisciplined horde of Bedouins'. No chance there of a parallel with Xenophon leading the Ten Thousand.[33]

One of Lawrence's later biographers, B.H. Liddell Hart, himself one of the foremost military historians of the twentieth century, had no doubt about the appropriate parallel for Lawrence's arrival at Akaba. 'While the post was being looted,' he wrote, 'Lawrence raced on to Aqaba, only four miles further, and splashed into the cooling sea. If "Thalassa, Thalassa" was not on his lips, it was in his thoughts.' Liddell Hart was here playing the great classical historian, freely attributing thoughts to his hero. But that hero was someone he knew. So he sent Lawrence his first two drafts to comment on. And that 'Thalassa, Thalassa' passage did not survive intact: 'T. E. had made no comment on this in the first draft, but now he put brackets round the sentence ... and said that, in fact, his thoughts were entirely "on his feet" – his one idea was to plunge into the water and cool his burning feet.' Hence Liddell Hart's final version: 'Historical aptness should have called to his lips the cry of the Ten Thousand – "Thalassa, Thalassa". But, in fact, his thoughts were entirely "on his feet" at this moment of triumph.'[34]

Why did Lawrence object to the way Liddell Hart had read his thoughts? Perhaps his thoughts had in fact been on his feet rather than on Xenophon. But this answer will scarcely do in the case of someone as dedicated to creating, and concealing, a mythology of himself as T.E. Lawrence, Shaw, Ross etc. (Liddell Hart himself anticipated a favourite postmodern gesture, inverted commas, by calling his biography '*T. E. Lawrence*' – for the British market, at least; the Americans got the gruffer *Colonel Lawrence*.) What does seem clear is that Lawrence was becoming increasingly wary of the romantic way that Liddell Hart was portraying him. He told Robert Graves that Liddell Hart 'seems to have no critical sense in my regard' – a comment glossed by Graves as follows: 'L. H., he knew, had come to see him as a historical character, the most recent of a long line of Great Captains, with Alexander and Belisarius as his predecessors.'[35]

But perhaps we should ourselves suspect Lawrence's suspicion of Liddell Hart. We may recall that Lawrence did not object to Liddell Hart's sentence when he read his first draft (though we do not know how carefully he read); and also that Lawrence sprinkled his own account of his exploits with allusions to Xenophon. It was not just that 'march up country' and that erudite 'diathetics'. He also wrote, while describing his operations in the desert later in the war, that 'the Zaagi had shot a bustard, and Xenophon did rightly call its white meat good'. Suspicious, too, is the fact that he was as careful to rewrite his own work as Liddell Hart's (when he was not forced to rewrite it by his penchant for losing manuscripts). And one sentence that was dropped between the 1922 'Oxford' version (first published in 1997) and the version of *Seven Pillars* published in 1935 was the reference to the 'march up-country'. Doubtless it came to seem too obvious.[36]

Lawrence's ambivalent response to Xenophon in his own and in Liddell Hart's writings seems to support a recent characterization of *Seven Pillars* as a work 'penetrated by a passion for adventure, but also by a sense of the fraudulence of adventure for the modern Englishman, condemned to a life of inner complexity'. Equally suggestive is the ambivalence in Lawrence's admiration for Xenophon the writer. What is at issue in this ambivalence is precisely the degree of self-revelation appropriate for the writer of military memoirs. Lawrence could praise Caesar's *Gallic War* as 'a miracle of self-suppression: one of the most impressive things in print': 'Hats off to Caesar

... for really pulling off the impersonal thing, and yet leaving his stuff palpitant with excitement'; compared with this, 'my Seven Pillars is nearer Xenophon, a much less ambitious ancient'. Yet Lawrence could also contrast his work with Xenophon's. In response to H.G. Wells calling *Seven Pillars* 'a great human document but not a work of art', Lawrence remarked to Liddell Hart: 'the opposite – not a human document like Xenophon's Anabasis but an artificial straining after art'. Then again, he could imply to George Bernard Shaw, as we have seen, that both the *Anabasis* and *Seven Pillars* were 'cunningly full of writing tricks'. Even more strikingly, he writes in the same letter that the *Anabasis* is 'pretentiously simple'.[37]

Lawrence's ambiguous regard for Xenophon as the paradigm of both the great general and the great writer tells us something about Lawrence himself. And that something about Lawrence also tells us something bigger, something about why one might no longer find it so simple to shout with the Ten Thousand 'Thalassa! Thalassa!' again. For the inspiration behind the Arab Revolt to be caught with that shout on his lips – well, it was all a bit embarrassing, a bit too much like that youngster cycling in the Auvergne, a bit too much like those escaped officers writing their popular adventures. It would not do after the bitterness of the war – and especially not after the disingenuous British treatment of the Arabs whose cause Lawrence had championed.

*

We are faced with a paradox. We have seen how Defoe's Captain Singleton, giving an account of some mutineers crossing the African interior, uses Xenophon's shout in a rather simpler way than more romantically engaged travellers like Mary Shelley's Frankenstein, A.W. Kinglake, and the young T.E. Lawrence; and also how the charged mood of those travellers contrasts with the more reserved and ironic attitude of Peter Fleming and the older Lawrence. We have traced, it seems, a change in the spirit of adventure. Yet not all of Lawrence's contemporaries shared his increasing ambivalence towards the great heroes of antiquity. The British prisoners of war in Turkey who escaped to the sea *were* keen to recall Xenophon and the Ten Thousand. And yet few participants in the war had suffered more than those prisoners. Lawrence may have playfully written in 1908 that his sufferings on a cycling holiday in the South of France were 'beyond the conception of antiquity'. Those prisoners had to come to terms with sufferings that could more seriously be thought beyond the conception of antiquity. They had been taken prisoner at the surrender of Kut-el-Amara in April 1916 – the low point of the British campaigning in Mesopotamia in the First World War, and one of the British Army's greatest defeats. They had then been subjected to a terrible march across the desert to Turkey – a march that led T.W. White, an

Australian airman taken prisoner in the attempt to relieve the siege at Kut (and later High Commissioner in London), to write that 'the hardships of the Ten Thousand of Xenophon ... would pale before the record of suffering of the prisoners from Mesopotamia on their seven-hundred mile march over much of the same territory, more than two thousand years later'. It is hard to disagree with this claim. Twelve thousand or so British troops surrendered at Kut (the majority of them Indian); twelve thousand or so Greek mercenaries were cut off in Mesopotamia after Cyrus' death at Cunaxa. Yet the fatality rate among those prisoners of the Turks was greater than that among those Greeks, cut off in the heart of the Persian empire.[38]

Unlike T.E. Lawrence, the British prisoners in Turkey, survivors of the Kut debacle, could all too easily remove their experiences from the context of Britain's great eastern adventure, and render them timeless, as real and as mythical as the experiences of the famous Greek army they could remember from their schooldays, the Greek army whose great shout they could still evoke, and with Greek font if need be. The identification they felt with Xenophon was not just a matter of a bit of mountaineering somewhere near the Black Sea, but born of a long engagement with the Ten Thousand as a paradigm of endurance.

How had these men come to be trapped, like the Ten Thousand, so far from home? At the start of the war with Turkey, the British had taken measures to protect the oilfields near the Persian Gulf. They had seized Basra, and then turned north, towards Baghdad, to try to make the position even more secure. A small flotilla led by Major-General C.V.F. Townshend had pushed up the Tigris, for there was no other way north, over the flooded plains. They forced the Turks back and pressed on, capturing first one town, Amara, then another, Kut-el-Amara. Kut would have been a good place to stop, for it was where one of the main canals to the Euphrates started. But the order came to press ahead, and they pushed further into the desert, up to Ctesiphon, where a single vast arch proclaimed the site of a great Sassanian palace. Here, a mere twenty or so miles from Baghdad, they encountered fresher, tougher, more experienced troops. The small force had done a lot, but now it was isolated, far apart from any supporting force. Townshend cut his losses and retreated quickly back to Kut, where the weary troops settled in for a siege and waited for the relief promised from the south. But it proved no easy thing to help the men at Kut. Relief efforts were thwarted by the Turks and by the flooding of the Tigris, and many men were lost in attempts to extricate the troops besieged amidst the mudbrick buildings of Kut and slowly falling prey to disease and hunger. Finally, after enduring a siege for five months with provisions meant for two, they surrendered.

Now began their historic trek. The officers were taken by boat up the Tigris to Baghdad, and by train to Samarra; from there they walked, or rode on donkeys, north to Mosul, across the river from Nineveh; they then left the Tigris and travelled across two hundred miles of desert (partly in carts, partly on foot) to the railhead at Ras-el-Ain; and so by train to Ankara, with breaks for the journey through the Cilician gates and across the Taurus mountains, where the line was not finished; and on to internment in central Anatolia. A journey estimated by one of them at one thousand seven hundred miles – 'probably the longest distance across country any prisoners of war have had to travel to their place of confinement'.[39]

In retrospect, there could seem something Xenophontic about the early days of the Mesopotamian campaign and the thrill of that initial push up river. The parallel is suggested in a novel, *Blow, Bugles, Blow: An English Odyssey*, written by a man who had endured the siege of Kut, E.O. Mousley. Mousley has his hero join the force sent to relieve Kut, and become troubled by how things had got into such a mess: ' "Were there no other troops in the country when Ctesiphon was fought? That's five hundred miles up river, isn't it?" "None whatever! Like Xenophon's ten thousand, a single division started walking over a continent without communications." Laughing the same bitter laugh, he turned with a grimace.' The parallel seems strained. The Ten Thousand were left to their own resources because they had no other choice, and when they were retreating, not when they were on the offensive. But perhaps that makes the anger at military incompetence the more cutting. To court the authentic Xenophontic experience was foolhardy.[40]

Mousley himself could write an account of his own experiences as a Kuttite and his adventures in captivity without mentioning Xenophon. But it still seems unlikely that he would have thought to compare Townshend's division with the Ten Thousand but for the long trek that the British soldiers endured after the surrender of Kut. The British prisoners were conscious as they marched that they were moving over ground covered by the great names of antiquity – Xenophon, Alexander, Julian, Belisarius .... But it was Xenophon who aroused most interest. E.H. Keeling, one of the officers who escaped to the Black Sea, described how as far as Mosul, a distance of one hundred and eighty miles, they 'kept close to the Tigris, like Xenophon's Ten Thousand'. 'But Xenophon', he added, 'went up the left bank while we followed the right. His was much the better choice ...'. Not that the British prisoners had any choice at all.

One of the problems faced by the British prisoners was that transport was hard to find, and here too Keeling and his colleagues could look back to the Ten Thousand – thanks to a young Oxford classicist:

> the commandant ordered that each officer's baggage should not exceed 20 kilograms. As blankets, cooking-pots and a certain quantity of food were included in this allowance, there was little room for spare clothing, and the small supply we had brought with us from Baghdad had to be cut down still further. One of

our party, fresh from Pass Mods., drew attention to a remarkably similar incident in the experience of Xenophon's men a little further up the river ...

Like the Ten Thousand, these British officers were confronted by an unfamiliar world as they moved up the Tigris. 'At Sharqat', Keeling reports, 'milk and eggs were brought across the river to us by Kurds, who supported themselves on inflated goatskins. ... Again Xenophon supplied a precedent, for he mentions that at Coenae, not far from Sharqat, "barbarians" brought food across to the Ten Thousand in exactly the same manner, though in the opposite direction.' 'Again Xenophon supplied a precedent ...': Keeling even seems to imply that these similarities were pointed out at the time. Had that Oxford classicist remembered that name 'Coenae'? Had he remembered where that place was? Had he even remembered Xenophon's phrasing? 'Fresh from Pass Mods.' indeed. When Keeling – himself well-educated, the son of a distinguished headmaster of Bradford Grammar School, with an Oxford degree, albeit in Law – goes on to provide, in a footnote, the precise reference to the *Anabasis* (book, chapter, and section), we suspect that he has gone back to his Xenophon after the event (understandably enough: the classical allusion justified including a good photograph of a Kurd swimming on a goatskin – see Plate 4). At any rate, his later comrade-in-escape, Bishop, is rather more vague – and also unsure of his dates: 'Arabs could be seen swimming across the river supported on inflated skins, in exactly the same way as Xenophon has described their forefathers doing 2,000 years ago.'[41]

For the prisoners from Kut, to remember that the Ten Thousand had followed more or less the same route over two thousand years earlier was to give some sort of meaning and dignity to their humiliation. Or rather, it was the officers from Kut, schooled in the classics, who were happy to look back to the Ten Thousand in this way. The eastern adventures that we have encountered so far were adventures for the officers. They had it comparatively easy. They had a tough trek, but it led to a not too uncomfortable internment – to games of cricket, in-house versions of *Punch*, spiritualist hoaxes, and dreams of escape. They could even enlist divine help. As they headed to the south coast of Turkey, Johnston and Yearsley were aware that St Paul had described adventures like their own in almost the same region; and it struck them that 'the escape of our party was due to a higher Power'. The 'other ranks' at Kut did not have things so easy. Sick and undernourished as they were at the surrender of Kut, they were forced to march all the way, without help from donkeys or carts, constantly mocked and humiliated, and assaulted, if they slackened, by bull-pizzle whips, or worse. The strong men who survived the march were forced to work on the railways. At the end of the war, they did not rush into print with accounts of their life in captivity. And when, years later, some of them did tell of their sufferings, they could mention inflated goatskins without bringing in Xenophon. If they were reminded of the past at all, it was in a more earthy way: 'The sanitary arrangements in those barracks beggar description, so foul were they. I have never seen anything quite like them in the East, before or since, and we came to the conclusion that they had not been cleaned out since the days of Nineveh!'.[42]

The greater sufferings inflicted on the other ranks of Kut tempt one to read rather differently the escape narratives of those lucky officers, with their proper supply of classical allusion. Those escape narratives remain moving tales of suffering, and many of them are sensitive to the treatment of the lower ranks. Keeling (later Conservative MP for Twickenham) would write letters to *The Times* and ask questions in Parliament about the treatment of prisoners of war. But perhaps it could come to seem rather insensitive, rather elitist, to keep on harking back to the great classical examples. It is still hard to avoid the feeling that what these officers offer is in places a rather tired re-playing of the familiar trope of an unchanging east where things are much as they were when Xenophon passed through. A trope so familiar that it could even occur to Proust – or rather (and significantly) to one of his characters who dabbles in journalism. As Proust's narrator talks to Gilberte de Saint-Loup about the ideas that her dead husband Robert had about the art of war, they marvel how often he has been proved right. He had predicted Hindenburg's tactics, and foreseen the role of aeroplanes,

> 'And then,' she went on, for now that she 'lived only for the mind' she had become a little pedantic, 'he maintained that we return always to the methods of the ancients. Well, do you realise that the Mesopotamian campaigns of this war' (she must have read this comparison at the time in Brichot's articles) 'constantly recall, almost without alteration, Xenophon's *Anabasis*?'

Gilberte goes on to mention the British use of the same long narrow boats as the Chaldeans, and the narrator has 'a sense of the stagnation of the past through which in certain parts of the world, by virtue of a sort of specific gravity, it is indefinitely immobilized'. Yet, for all the narrator's reflections on temporality, there is also a sense that Gilberte is unduly reverent to her late husband's platitudes – that she is just trotting out tired material from newspapers, just as the officers from Kut rework a small range of predictable allusions.[43]

At any rate, the contrast between the accounts of the officers and those of the other ranks at Kut is another reminder of the ideological undercurrent in responses to Xenophon. When the officers alluded to 'Thalatta! Thalatta!', they were not just proclaiming their triumph over a series of dangers in a foreign land: they were also laying claim to a position within their own society, to a membership of an elite bound together by a shared cultural heritage – by a familiarity with a repertoire of classical exempla instilled in the schoolroom. So it is no surprise, perhaps, that a recent historian has picked on 'Thalatta! Thalatta!' as a symbol in an impressionistic account of the siege of Kut and its aftermath, an angry denunciation of the leadership of Townshend:

> The officers' parties … were Xenophon's Greeks retreating, rather than slaves driven into the wilderness: and one day, just as Xenophon's troops had cried 'Thalassa, thalassa … the sea, the sea,' because they had triumphed over the desert, so they would cry, 'It's over,' because their friends now concentrating at Amarah would have triumphed over the Turks. … meantime, treat the Turk like a sepoy.
>
> Meantime, said the Turks, treat British soldiers like slaves: and their slaves, to whom all thoughts of sea and peace had become as grotesquely unreal as the trees and streams they constantly saw, but knew to be illusions, marched in a trance of exhaustion, hunger and thirst …[44]

3

Our Friend of Youth

In the latter years of the Napoleonic Wars, a young English aristocrat, the Hon. Frederick Sylvester North Douglas, set off on a grand tour. Travelling by the route used by many others at this time (not least Byron's Childe Harold), he sailed from Britain to the Iberian peninsula, and then across the Mediterranean to the Ionian islands and on to the Greek mainland. He described his impressions of the modern Greeks in a book he wrote in 1813, *An Essay on Certain Points of Resemblance between the Ancient and Modern Greeks*. As he looked back, he was still struck by his first arrival at the Ionian island of Zante two years earlier: 'The remembrance of the first Greek sentence I heard upon landing in that beautiful island will never be effaced. I doubt whether the θάλασσα of Xenophon's soldiers was productive of more lively sensations than those I experienced at the first sight of the Morea' (the Morea was the medieval term for the Peloponnese). Such was the appeal of Xenophon's description of his arrival at the sea that Douglas could evoke it even though he had himself arrived at land. By alluding to Xenophon, Douglas was able to transform his first sight of Greece into a return to somewhere familiar.[1]

The tenor of the rest of Douglas' book makes his first response to Greece seem slightly odd. Douglas resisted the growing tide of philhellenic sentiment. He did see some traces of the ancients among the modern Greeks, but on the whole he thought they were a degenerate race. Many of the philhellenes shared that distaste for the modern Greeks. The difference was that the philhellenes hoped that the Greeks would recover their ancestral spirit when they regained their freedom. Douglas, by contrast, wanted the Turks to keep control of Constantinople: the Greeks would harm British interests by appreciating the city's naval potential – in that at least they would resemble their ancestors.

For all his hostility to Greek independence, Douglas still elevates his first arrival in Greece into a return home by comparing his feelings with Xenophon's. The point is that he has arrived at a world made home by a schooling in the classics – in his case, Westminster School and Christ Church, where he received a first class degree in 1809 (one of the first Oxford firsts, for classification of degrees had been introduced only two years earlier). He even mentions the Greek words he heard when he landed before he describes his emotions at the first sight of land: in retrospect, his memory of that first sight has been enriched by his memory of that first Greek sentence.

*

The easy familiarity with the *Anabasis* implied by Douglas' response to the Morea was shared by many boys and by the increasing number of girls who studied Greek at school. The Ten Thousand have been described as 'the romantic heroes of every Victorian schoolboy' in a recent anthology of travel-writing on Turkey. That claim is doubtless slightly exaggerated, but it is true that the *Anabasis* was often the first Greek text to which school-children were exposed. Indeed, Xenophon's use as a school text was so common that one notable Victorian scholar, J.P. Mahaffy, could write that 'there is no figure in Greek history now so prominent in the classical world'.[2]

It was thanks to Xenophon's use in schools that the shout of those romantic heroes secured a place in the minds of excitable young men like Douglas – just as it later became fixed in the minds of Alexander Kinglake, T.E. Lawrence, and the British prisoners taken at the surrender of Kut-el-Amara. But when and why did the *Anabasis* establish itself as the archetypal school text? And how did classroom encounters with Xenophon affect perceptions of that shout of the sea? Three more encounters with Xenophon in the latter years of the Napoleonic War will help to set the scene.[3]

The *Anabasis* was the second Greek book that John Stuart Mill (born 1806) read, after Aesop's *Fables*. Mill started to learn Greek at home when he was three – even younger than Ronald Knox. That was exceptional.[4]

The theologian E.B. Pusey (born 1800) was also exceptional, for an Etonian at least. At Eton, he read the whole of the *Anabasis* for enjoyment in less than a week, when a bad foot had confined him to bed. Or that was what he said to encourage his brother. But it is not hard to believe. Pusey had been sent aged seven to a preparatory school for Eton in Mitcham, where the boys would translate from Latin and Greek without cribs, tearing out the Latin translations that accompanied some Greek texts, and write Greek verses of their own. Pusey would later say in Council at Oxford that half the boys at that school could have passed Moderations at Oxford at the age of eleven – but for the logic paper.[5]

In Oxford itself, one undergraduate, Thomas Jefferson Hogg, friend and biographer of Shelley, was reading the *Anabasis* for the first time in January 1811, a few months before he was sent down for refusing to condemn Shelley's discourse on atheism. The *Anabasis* was, he records, 'a book deservedly in high repute at Oxford': 'I perused it very carefully, with the lexicon and atlas by my side, for the first time, with unspeakable gratification, and endless, abiding pleasure.' Hogg's account is perhaps a bit exaggerated. He had, he says, just returned from a weary walk from Oxford to Salisbury and Winchester and back: 'The first-fruits of my sitting-still, and of this strong disinclination ever to go out of the college gates again, were to read the Going-up of Cyrus.' He is evidently concerned to build up a contrast between reading about a long walk while sitting in front of a fire, and going on a long walk oneself. Why had Hogg not read Xenophon earlier, like Mill or Pusey, when he was at Durham Grammar School?[6]

These three examples suggest that, early in the nineteenth century, the *Anabasis* had not yet become *the* school text. Mill read it before he went to school, Pusey only read it at school because he had hurt his foot, and Hogg did not read it at school at all. Doubtless this is not a representative sample. But the picture suggested by these three cases is confirmed by a survey made by Nicholas Carlisle in 1818, published as *A Concise Description of the Endowed Grammar Schools*. Carlisle wrote to all the grammar schools in England and Wales seeking information about the education they offered, including the Latin and Greek texts studied (teaching of the classics was often laid down in their statutes). From the information he gives, we can see that Xenophon was often read, but only alongside a number of other writers. And often it was not the *Anabasis* that was specified. At the Grammar School at Witton, near Chester, for instance, the *Cyropaedia* and *Memorabilia* were read, along with the Greek Testament and the *Iliad*. At Louth in Lincolnshire, boys would start Greek at eleven, or even earlier, when they had mastered Latin grammar, and they would read the *Anabasis*. But they would also read Xenophon's *Cyropaedia* and *Agesilaus*, and, so Carlisle was informed, an impressive range of other authors, including the difficult Pindar. How much of these authors was read is not revealed. At Harrow, teachers used the Eton grammars for Latin and Greek, but saved face by printing some texts for their exclusive use. One of Xenophon's works was among these – the short *Agesilaus*. Many other schools noted that they used the Eton grammars – perhaps including *Scriptores Graeci*, a selection of excerpts from Greek prose writers published by Eton. The only Xenophon to be found in that 'wretched compilation' was taken from the *Cyropaedia* and *Memorabilia* – as we have seen, the most popular works of Xenophon before the nineteenth century.[7]

The general picture is clear. English schoolboys who read Xenophon in the eighteenth or early nineteenth century were more likely to be subjected to excerpts from the *Cyropaedia* or *Memorabilia*. And this was true in other countries too. To give just one example: John Adams recorded that his son, John Quincy Adams, had read the 'Choice of Hercules' from the *Memorabilia* before he went to Harvard in 1785. The father must have been pleased: nine years earlier, he had himself proposed that an engraving of the painting of the 'Choice of Hercules' commissioned by Shaftesbury should be used as the seal of the United States of America.[8]

The situation had changed by the middle of the nineteenth century. By the 1848 edition of the Eton textbook *Scriptores Graeci*, the *Anabasis* had made its appearance – and it was not just a scrap or two, but the first book in full (the earlier selection had been heavily criticized, not least because boys would leave Eton without having read a full book of Herodotus, Thucydides, or Xenophon). In a lecture a few years later, John Henry Newman imagined a university interview in which a tutor tests a dim pupil on a single word – 'anabasis'. The position of the *Anabasis* became even more entrenched with the introduction of common examinations. In the Oxford and Cambridge Local Examinations, first set in 1858, part of the Junior examinations, for children under sixteen, was a Greek paper with one prose and one verse text. For the first fifteen years, both the Oxford and Cambridge boards set Xenophon as the prose text, and more often than not a book of the *Anabasis* (at Cambridge, every year but one; at Oxford, ten out of the fifteen years).[9]

More and more school editions of the *Anabasis* began to appear to meet the demands of the new market. Whereas the school editions in the first half of the century had often included the whole text, now they would tend to cover just a single book. The *Anabasis* may now have been read much more at schools, but very few boys would read all of it, as Pusey had done in his bed at Eton. Often they would not get as far as the fourth book, where the Greeks reach the sea. But they could still be exposed to Xenophon's shout. The Rev. J.D. Collis produced a book called *Pontes Graeci*, sub-titled *A Stepping-Stone from the Beginning of Greek Grammar to Xenophon* (one of a number of grammatical works geared particularly to Xenophon). For the third edition, in 1879, he added some extracts from the *Anabasis* – culminating in the passage where the Greeks shout 'Thalatta! Thalatta!'. That passage was included in many other textbooks for beginners: a more recent popular example is Wilding's *Greek for Beginners* of 1957, where it is one of the first extracts (with suitable changes – like the substitution of 'thalassa' for 'thalatta').[10]

The entrenched position of the *Anabasis* is shown, paradoxically, by one of the criticisms made of the new standardization of exams. One teacher imagined 'a class that had not read Greek very long, only long enough to be called well drilled during a year or rather more in a book of Xenophon (naturally *Anabasis*, book i) and a book of Homer', and complained that the examination board might choose books that the boys had already read – not that one or two of them would mind that, he acknowledged. What stands out here is not just that he imagines the class reading Xenophon, but that he takes it for granted that they would be reading the start of the *Anabasis*.[11]

By the start of the twentieth century, the place of Greek at schools, and the position of the *Anabasis* with it, were coming more and more under attack. The typical path for learning Greek was set out by the Rev. C. Eccles Williams in a Board of Education Special Report on Preparatory Schools published in 1900. Boys would start to learn Latin at nine or ten, and Greek two years later. They would start with excerpts from Morice's *Attic Stories* or from Xenophon himself, and then in their second year they would move on to the *Anabasis*, with perhaps an easy Greek play by the end of the year. And so they would be equipped for entrance to public school. Williams was keen to defend this system. Others were less happy with this early and time-consuming exposure to Greek. The opponents won through: the Headmasters' Conference agreed in 1908 to abandon the requirement of Greek for the public schools.[12]

The key battle was over the requirement of Greek for entrance to Oxford and Cambridge. At Oxford there were no formal entrance requirements, but to study for a degree one had to pass Responsions (or 'Little-go'), and to pass them one had to know some Greek and Latin – enough to be able to read, or at least translate from, three books of the *Anabasis* and four books of Caesar's *Gallic War*, say. That is what T.E. Lawrence studied for his Responsions, which he took when he was still at school. (After 1874, a good enough performance in the Oxford and Cambridge Local Examination could give one exemption from Responsions, but Lawrence, no great grammarian, had done indifferently at Latin and Greek.) The *Anabasis* was now a hurdle to get through, and not the rage among undergraduates, as in Hogg's time. It had no place in the rest of the syllabus – not even in Pass Mods., the exam which E.H. Keeling's comrade in Mesopotamia had recently sat. And it was no longer a hurdle for all undergraduates after 1920, when the debate was finally lost by the defenders of compulsory Greek – elderly dons who, as one of the greatest classical scholars of the twentieth century, E.R. Dodds, then fairly fresh from Oxford himself, satirically portrayed them, would 'die in the last ditch like scholars and gentlemen that budding botanists may still acquaint themselves under penalty with a certain number of highly irregular plurals and commit to memory the crib of a small portion of Xenophon's *Anabasis*'.[13]

*

The *Anabasis* gained its classic status in the classroom alongside the *Gallic War*, the text through which schoolchildren learnt to grapple with the gerund and other eccentricities of Latin syntax. Xenophon and Caesar were the Hobbs and Sutcliffe of the schoolroom – opening partners in the teaching of Greek and Latin. A writer in the *Boy's Own Paper* in the 1890s could ask how many boys now 'puzzling over their Caesar and Xenophon' had ever considered for themselves the advantages of a classical education. And if one wanted to argue that compulsory Latin should be ditched sooner than compulsory Greek, it was easy enough to point out that Xenophon was better than Caesar.[14]

Xenophon and Caesar were picked for much the same reason: they were not too difficult to translate. Xenophon's *Cyropaedia* was also a fairly easy work, but already in an edition of 1785 it was argued that the *Anabasis* was more appropriate for school use because it was more varied and interesting. Children would actually want to know what happened next. Or at least boys would: for, as Sir John Fortescue wrote in 1895, Xenophon had 'not a little that appeals to the boyish mind' – like hunting, presumably, to judge from the title of his essay, 'A Day with Xenophon's Harriers'. And also war: 'boys like generals, like fighting, like accounts of battle', Woodrow Wilson wrote in 1888, when asked, as Professor of History at Bryn Mawr (a women's college), to explain the attraction of Caesar.[15]

The *Anabasis* was all the better for not being as overtly moralistic as the Socratic works or the *Cyropaedia*, which was boring for those who had not engaged in politics themselves. The *Anabasis* had a subtler moralism. It could promote the virtues of courage, nobility, and self-control, while boys could also, as Simon Goldhill has noted, 'read the easy Greek as an adventure story (without any sex, philosophy, or tragedy)'. Not that the *Anabasis* is in fact sexless: Xenophon does mention a pederast or two, but they could always be taken out of school editions.[16]

Girls were much less likely to learn Latin or Greek at all. Anthony Trollope could recommend that 'all young ladies' read the volumes on the *Iliad* and the *Odyssey* in a series of 'Ancient Classics for English Readers' published by his friend John Blackwood. He wrote a volume for the series himself, and 'a well-educated girl' who had read that 'would perhaps know as much about Caesar and his writings as she need know'. Trollope was assuming a well-educated boy would have read Caesar in the original.[17]

If girls did learn Latin or Greek, they could still be subjected to the same diet that was forced on boys. Virginia Woolf could describe a congregation reading out a passage from the Old Testament 'very much as schoolboys translate an easy passage from the *Anabasis*' (the novel, aptly enough, is *The Voyage Out*). When she herself was learning Greek aged sixteen, she struggled through Homer ('I have made out three lines unhelped this afternoon and I feel very wise'), but found Xenophon 'too dull to read much of'. Some teachers would insist on a dose of Xenophon all the same. Judith Hallett, a modern Classics professor in the United States, attended an all-female college, but went to a co-educational summer school where one of the teachers 'pronounced "these women's colleges" disgracefully negligent for failing to provide me with the requisite year of Xenophon. He insisted that I meet him twice weekly to march through the *Anabasis*.' That Classics teacher would presumably have been more happy with the requirements at one of the most prestigious woman's colleges, Bryn Mawr, in the 1880s (when Woodrow Wilson was teaching there). These requirements were identical with those at Harvard – translations of Virgil's *Aeneid* and the two military classics, Caesar's *Gallic War* and Xenophon's *Anabasis*. In their early days, at least, the likes of Bryn Mawr evidently felt that inflicting Caesar and

Xenophon on the girls would show that they were as rigorous as the traditional men's colleges.[18]

For all their fondness for fighting, boys too could find a diet of Caesar and Xenophon hard to digest. Woodrow Wilson thought that teaching Caesar could be made more interesting by telling boys that Caesar was in his youth 'a fop and a lady-killer' who yet became an incomparable commander, and that he wrote with the deeds 'fresh in the mind – perhaps also heavy on the muscles'; and by getting boys 'to *play* at the campaigns' – '*any*thing to dispel the idea that Caesar wrote grammatical exercises in hard words!'. But that idea was hard to dispel. More familiar were the Latin classes described in Anthony Hecht's poem 'The Mysteries of Caesar': 'Through a long / Winter campaign of floundering, grief, and wrong, / That little army force-marched without resting.' That 'little army' of schoolboys struggling through Caesar's sentences is like Caesar's not so little army struggling through Gaul.[19]

Hecht's poem could as easily have been called 'The Mysteries of Xenophon'. Like Caesar, Xenophon suffered from his use in schools. W.W. Tarn aptly applied to Xenophon Juvenal's most famous lines: 'he performed a march without precedent across savage mountains, his reward has been to become a text for schoolboys.' Except that while Hannibal, the object of Juvenal's satire, thrilled schoolboys by providing a theme for declamations, Xenophon bored them by providing material for language teaching. 'We loathed Xenophon and his ten thousand': that was how those romantic heroes were viewed by Sir William Osler, Regius Professor of Medicine at Oxford, and also a President of the Classical Association, when he recalled his schooldays in Canada in the 1860s. Schoolboys could even be encouraged to dislike Xenophon. Alfred Pretor, who edited the whole of the *Anabasis* in the Pitt Press series for schools (and whose own schooldays at Harrow had featured an affair with the Headmaster), confessed in the final volume that 'I have but little admiration either for Xenophon or his writings, and am glad to find myself approaching the termination of an ungrateful task'. And a modern professor has lamented that few American students of Greek 'get through the mountains of Xenophon even to the waters of the *Apology*' – as if they would feel like shouting 'Thalatta! Thalatta!' when they finally got to read some Plato (and he must mean Plato's *Apology*: he seems to forget that Xenophon also wrote a work with that title).[20]

The hostility to Xenophon came from the way the language was taught. The Cambridge scholar W.G. Clark (himself a former pupil of the famous Dr Kennedy of Shrewsbury) insisted that 'a young boy can be allowed to take but a feeble interest in … the up-country marches of Cyrus', since 'his whole attention is centred in the language, the difficulties of which, requiring to be mastered step by step, compel him to proceed so slowly as to lose all interest in the story'. Not everyone was so complacent. 'The book itself', George Cawkwell has written, 'was also an expedition, not without hardships', and

3. Our Friend of Youth

Andrew Lang offered a gloomy view of the results of this way of teaching Xenophon:

> Ten lines of Xenophon, narrating how he marched so many parasangs and took breakfast, do not amount to more than a very unrefreshing sip of Greek. Nobody even tells the boys who Xenophon was, what he did there, and what it was all about. Nobody gives a brief and interesting sketch of the great march, of its history and objects. The boys straggle along with Xenophon, knowing not whence or whither:
> 'They stray through a desolate region,
> And often are faint on the march.'
> One by one they fall out of the ranks; they mutiny against Xenophon.

Lang himself had been a victim: 'Xenophon routed me with horrible carnage. I could have run away to sea' – but then Homer came and saved him. (Lang was writing as one of the most notable literary figures in Victorian Britain: poet, essayist, novelist, translator, folklorist, anthropologist.) 'Ranks' of schoolboys 'faint on the march' and mutinying against a writer/general who turns against the troops under his command and routs them: Lang's schoolboys are even worse off than Hecht's little army force-marched through Caesar or Judith Hallett marching through the *Anabasis*. The military metaphor was an especially apt response to the likes of Clark, defending the traditional method of proceeding through the text 'step-by-step'.[21]

The horror of reading Xenophon at school was particularly associated with a single word – parasang (the Persian unit of distance). In his popular work *The Glory that was Greece*, J.B. Stobart pictured schoolboys 'struggling in a wilderness of parasangs and paradigms', and H.W. Allen assumed in a lecture in 1920 to the Classical Association of Victoria that his audience 'thought ... that Xenophon's *Anabasis* was the dullest book in all the world': 'it connotes to you only "parasangs." ' What had the parasang done wrong? Xenophon used it in a notorious formula in his account of the march up country (and many schoolboys would get no further than that section of the work): Cyrus marched forth so many stages, so many parasangs, and then again Cyrus marched forth another few stages, another few parasangs. Cyrus would march forth so often that the verb 'march forth', *exelauno*, has even had an affectionate tribute paid it: Exelauno Day is celebrated every year at Roxbury Latin School in Massachusetts – on March the fourth.[22]

The hostility that Xenophon has aroused in schools presents us with something of a paradox. If Xenophon's familiarity as a school text helps to explain the popularity of 'Thalatta! Thalatta!', why did that shout appeal to people who had been bored by Xenophon at school?

Adults could always change their minds about the book they had loathed as children. When H.W. Allen imagined his audience thinking the *Anabasis* 'the dullest book in all the world', he added 'and so did I once' – before he had served in the Great War. Now he could draw comparisons between the Ten Thousand and the Anzac troops, with their blunt speech and earthy humour (hence his lecture title: 'Xenophon's Greek Diggers'). When Italo Calvino recalled the *Anabasis*, he thought not of the parasangs but of Xenophon's long speeches: 'My classroom memory of these rhetorical excerpts was one of great boredom.' 'But,' he went on, 'I think I was wrong.' Not everyone loathed the *Anabasis* in the first place: think of Pusey at Eton, and Hogg at Oxford. And 'Thalatta! Thalatta!' could keep its allure even for the little armies of schoolboys force-marched through Xenophon's text parasang by parasang. Like Andrew Lang, they could always think of the sea as a world away from school – or of 'The Sea! The Sea!' as a great moment isolated from the tedium of the *Anabasis* itself.[23]

This brief survey of Xenophon's role in the classroom has suggested that it was only in the nineteenth century that the *Anabasis* gained the priority that it held for a hundred years and (in some countries at least) still holds. Xenophon's text assumed this position at a time when more attention was being paid to Greek in schools (the requirement of Greek for entrance to Oxford and Cambridge, abandoned in 1920, was itself only a nineteenth-century invention). And it is Xenophon's primacy in the classroom that explains the pervasiveness of 'Thalatta! Thalatta!' in the modern imagination. An easy familiarity with that shout could be assumed in a wide range of literary works – and assumed even in people who had not opened Xenophon themselves but had simply heard at second hand of the dramatic moment when some Greek heroes reached the safety of the sea. Even though the shout of those Greek heroes has become known to thousands who have never studied Greek or even read the *Anabasis* in translation, it is still apt that their shout has left a strong imprint on imaginative re-creations of the long years of childhood, when an exotic adventure like the march of the Ten Thousand offered a glimpse of broad eastern horizons. This imprint is especially marked in Philip Glazebrook's 1987 novel *Captain Vinegar's Commission*, set in the nineteenth century and inspired by the world of the classic British adventurers.

*

Glazebrook introduces his hero, Tresham Pitcher, as a schoolboy wearily sitting over his Xenophon in an attic room in a villa in Clapham in south London:

> He defeated the Greek words one by one and forced them to contribute their mite of sense to the narrative. By these laborious means he had followed Xenophon and his mercenaries across the Mesopotamian deserts to Persia; and he felt he had crawled after them on all fours every inch of the way. He was

bored by the book's contents till he hated every inkstain and blemish upon the book itself.

He looks through his window to try to catch a glimpse of the sails of ships on the river:

> It was possible in a clear light to glimpse the coloured sails of barges on the river. This hint of voyages – firing memory of his own travels by sea that summer – could scarcely be resisted whenever it crossed his mind that the sails might be there to be seen if he looked up. So he looked up. Smoke lay in windless drifts too close upon the dark mass of the city for the river's course to be traced through it, and he saw no coloured sails. The grey gravel plains of Mesopotamia cannot have looked more dreary to Xenophon's Ten Thousand, or more unlike the sea-girt isles they pined for, than the scene from his window looked to Tresham.

Even though he is slowly defeating the language, not being routed by it like Andrew Lang, Tresham is still looking for release from his slow crawl through Xenophon, and even the sight of a sail will be enough to take him away from the world he hates to the sea, to that world of adventure which he has tasted briefly and which he longs to recapture.

Thoughts of that battle with Xenophon return to Tresham later. Forced to leave school, and miserably working as a clerk, he rows in a skiff to stay with a schoolfriend in a castle near the sea in Wales. He finds himself slightly overwhelmed by the opulence of the castle, with its medieval aura: blazing fires, sconces, trophies, tapestries – 'it was journey's end'. His friend's father had even brought a Turkish servant back from his travels. Tresham is also anxious because he has promised to describe his adventurous canal trip. He is regretting that promise as he sets off for a walk to the sea. He climbs up the dunes, feeling 'the pain of longing, for he knew not what'. Now he reaches the top:

> There lay the sea, the limitless flux of water surrounding the island. Journey's end. And how was the journey to be described? … the reality … must be transformed. Courage, pace, adventure – that was the nature of the journey, more true than mere reality … Below him the cold dull waves broke on the stones, broke and receded, broke again with their monotonous chant. And this was supposed to be the sea! The Θαλασσα of Xenophon's poor soldiers! How much it needed changing before it could figure as the element of adventures and romances. There it lay, the restless unhappy sea. He looked at it without satisfaction, as if he had not known that this boundary to his travels existed.

The sea for which he had longed disappoints him. It must be transformed – just as a journey must be altered, made more heroic and dangerous, by the travel writer to fit his sense of inner reality. Glazebrook here points ahead to the main conceit of his novel: when Tresham Pitcher himself and his school-friend travel to Xenophon's Near East, they invent for themselves the persona of the intrepid Captain Vinegar (after Henry Fielding's pseu-donym?) – and Tresham ends up the author of O.Q. Vinegar (Capt.), *Journal of a Land-March towards India*.[24]

It would have been easy for Glazebrook to handle Xenophon's sea rather differently. We might have expected Pitcher to find the release he was seeking. Dreams of adventure, the deeds of Xenophon's heroic soldiers, could have transformed the sea for him as he looked down on it. Instead, he reflects that it needs changing *before* it can 'figure as the element of adven-tures and romances'. This seems to be rather demanding. The mere thought of Xenophon's sea had been enough for George Macdonald Fraser's Flashman when he suddenly caught sight of the Aral Sea as he was being dragged across the desert, and the words of the Ten Thousand – 'old Arnold's Greeks' – came to his mouth ('thalassa or thalatta ...'). 'Old Arnold' in turn takes Flashman back to his schooldays: 'suddenly I could close my eyes and hear his voice droning away on a summer afternoon at Rugby, and smell the cut grass coming in through the open windows, and hear the fags at cricket outside, ... and it was such a sweet, torturing longing that I groaned aloud.' Tresham Pitcher, by contrast, had felt the pain of a longing that could not be articulated before he saw the sea.[25]

Why do Fraser's and Glazebrook's heroes respond to the sea in such different ways? Fraser, writing to please, is happy to offer a pleasant pastiche of a common vision of England, that elegiac land of flannelled fools and warm beer. Glazebrook, by contrast, is exploring the spirit of adventure, the need for a sense of the heroic as a safeguard against the dullness of reality.

But it is not just that Glazebrook and Fraser are writing different sorts of novel. Fraser's hero, looking back on childhood with some experience of the world of adventure, naturally has a different perspective from Glazebrook's, an adolescent trying to shape an identity for himself. And while Glazebrook's novel may seem the more intellectually demanding, Fraser has in fact caught very well the nostalgic appeal of schooldays. We need only compare a remark in George Gissing's partly autobiographical novel *The Private Papers of Henry Ryecroft*: 'By some trick of memory I always associate school-boy work on the classics with a sense of warm and sunny days.' Gissing's character, absorbed in his books and the countryside, relishing solitude, is a far cry from Flashman. But in both cases it is Xenophon who calls those sunny schooldays to mind. While Flashman thinks of Xenophon when he sees the sea, Ryecroft describes how he turns back one summer to 'books such as mature men rarely read at all – books which it is one's habit to "take as read" ': 'Thus, one day my hand fell upon the *Anabasis*, the little Oxford edition which I used at school.' He opens it and begins to read, 'a ghost of boyhood stirring in my heart', and 'glad this happened in the summer-time': 'I like to link childhood with these latter days, and no better way could I have found than this return to a school-book, which, even as a school-book, was my great delight.' 'Were this the sole book existing in Greek,' he adds, 'it would be abundantly worth while to learn the language in order to read it', so fresh is it 'with the air of mountain and of sea'.[26]

While Tresham Pitcher's ambivalence towards Xenophon's sea stems from his own awkward self-consciousness, with Flashman and even more with Henry Ryecroft thoughts of Xenophon are enriched by association with youth. For these two fictitious characters, it is pleasant to look back at schooldays, and schooldays are summer. For Sir Max Mallowan, by contrast, the Assyrian archaeologist, and husband of Agatha Christie, it is less pleasant to look back at schooldays, and schooldays are winter. But for Mallowan, too, thoughts of Xenophon help to weigh the experiences of childhood against those of later life.

In his memoirs, published in 1977, Mallowan recalled his schooldays at Lancing College:

> I shall not forget the harsh impression of my first arrival at school on a cold midwinter afternoon, in January of 1917. This was my first sight of the grey granite prison walls, framed by the dark cloisters and the gaunt length of the tall Victorian chapel thrusting itself like a long spear against the bleak base of the Sussex Downs, and looking out on its other side towards the rushing waters of the river Adur.

That first arrival in the middle of winter contrasts with his impressions when he returns to the school for the first time since he had left:

> This desolate scene remained in my mind for more than fifty years until I returned to behold in the summer a landscape unspoiled, which unfolded itself to me in its incomparable setting, untarnished by any modern building, pristine in its beauty and bounded by the sea, against the river Adur which was now transformed into a sweetly flowing silver ribbon. ... I felt like the soldiers in Xenophon's mercenary army when they caught their first sight of the Black Sea, after their long march from Mesopotamia, and set up the cry, *Thalassa, Thalassa*.

Once more Xenophon's sea is transfigured by an imaginative leap to the world of youth. Unlike Flashman, however, Mallowan is not looking back to days of summer, but finding in the unspoilt beauty of the school's setting the summer that should have been his all those years ago. And he is able to find this summer because he is belatedly redefining his origins. Through Xenophon, he makes Lancing a home that it had not been for him in those dreary schooldays he shared with Evelyn Waugh.

But why give Xenophon this symbolic weight? The elderly Mallowan was writing as a man who had excavated at Nimrud and Nineveh (Plate 5) – sites passed by the Ten Thousand in their retreat, not long after the slaughter of Clearchus and his fellow generals (an early Murder in Mesopotamia). Later, he will evoke Xenophon as he describes his excavations at Nimrud: 'the last man before our time to record this tremendous quay was Xenophon, who ... jotted down for posterity notes, substantially correct, to which we were able to add 2350 years later.' Mallowan here makes Xenophon a sort of amateur archaeologist, whose brief jottings yield to the greater rigour of the modern professional. So as we come to Mallowan's later story, we re-interpret that story of his return to school, much as Mallowan seems to re-interpret his own schooldays. Like Xenophon, he has returned home from the plains of Mesopotamia.[27]

*

The power of Xenophon's shout as a symbol of youth was fully grasped in 'Thalassa!', a novel by Mrs Baillie Reynolds published in 1906. Mrs Baillie Reynolds (whose early novels were published under her maiden name of Gertrude M. Robins) wrote more than fifty books between 1886 and her death in 1939, and not without success: a profile in *The Bookman* in 1907 noted that 'her novels are running into their fifth and sixth editions'. Her success was not just financial. That same profile asserted that many of 'the best novels in our days are being written by women', and 'Mrs. Baillie Reynolds has written more than one of them'. And along with the likes of Baroness Orczy and Rose Macaulay, she was included, or patronized, in a 1927 book as one of the 'goddesses of the pen' – goddesses not because their works would last, but because Art with condescension had invested them with a Divine spark. The writer of novels such as *Phoebe in Fetters* and *The Judgement of Charis* perhaps deserves more attention. But here we will just look at 'Thalassa!'.[28]

Reynolds alluded to Xenophon in her title, in the epigraph (a poem she composed on the retreat of the Ten Thousand), and in key scenes towards the start and end of the novel where 'Thalassa!' is part of a dialogue between the voices of youth and maturity. The heroine, Aldyth Staveley, has been living in Italy with her father, an aristocrat who has quarrelled with his family. She knows nothing of her mother. Her father suddenly dies, and she moves, at the age of twenty, from the mellow Mediterranean to the North of England, to the home of her father's childhood friend, Geoffrey Orme, who lives alone with a slightly wild daughter. At first, Aldyth finds him rude and aloof. She stands up for herself, and starts to teach her one friend, the girl. One evening, as they are being driven home in a carriage, Orme suggests that they ride a bit further to see the moonlight on the water. They reach the summit of a pass through cliffs: 'Behold, there below her, at a distance of two or three miles only, lay the sea, a sheet of placid silver, rhythmically heaving like the slow, evenly-drawn breath of the world. "The sea!" she cried, under her breath, but with a kind of excitement in her voice.' Orme comes to stand beside her, and he recalls an experience not too dissimilar from T.E. Lawrence's on his cycling trip to the South of France, two years after Reynolds' novel was published. But where Lawrence describes a Xenophontic experience in his youth, here Xenophon helps to bring out what it means to look back on youth:

> 'When Reg [Aldyth's father] and I were kids,' he said, in an absent voice, more as though thinking aloud than speaking to her, 'we used to push our bicycles up this hill, pretending we were the ten thousand Greeks in retreat. We starved, and fought natives, and had all kinds of adventures until we gained the summit, and cried, "*Thalassa*! We are saved!"'

But his is the voice of adult disenchantment:

> 'I used to think,' he added ... – 'I used to think, later, when I was growing up, and things were going hard with me, that if I got my heart's desire, I would come up here, and cry "Thalassa!"' He broke off and laughed grimly.
> 'And did you?' suggested the girl timidly.
> He made a derisive sound, climbing into his seat once more.
> 'That's only a story, you know,' said he. 'The Greeks never really found the sea; they died in the desert. There is no Thalassa, only Mirage in real life.'

Not long after this, when Orme is recovering from being shot by one of his more radical labourers, Aldyth finally learns from his doctor the secret of her own and Orme's pasts. Her mother had lived locally, in the home of a crooked spiritualist. When she married Aldyth's father, the spiritualist used his powers over her to make her steal some family jewels. The theft was discovered, and she collapsed and never recovered. It was after this that Aldyth's father had fled to the continent. Orme had been no more fortunate. He had married another woman in the spiritualist's entourage, only to discover that she was married already.

Aldyth hears at the same time that her father's brother has just died. She is now a peeress – if she wants to make a claim to the title. Provoked by Orme's temper, she flees to London. There, friendless and still unsure of herself, she resolves to support herself as a governess. And now it even becomes doubtful whether she could inherit the title if she wanted to. Her parents, it seems, had only married after her birth.

Aldyth decides to return to Orme's house when she hears that his daughter is ill and that Orme himself is abroad. A few days later, however, Orme returns. And soon they find themselves driving again through the Gap, the place they had once before visited under the midsummer moon. This time it is very dark. But they can at least hear the ocean. Aldyth reflects:

When last she topped that hill, she was an alien – tossed like a ball into a far country, her past all cut away … And now? The man whose head and shoulders she could just descry in the lamplight, standing very still, and with his back to her – this man had cleared away her difficulties – had taught her who she was, had watched over her interests, fought her battles … Could she now call herself homeless? She knew that to her, Wildmarsh was home in a true sense.

She is home because she has found out that this is where she was born, and she is home in another sense too. In her early days at Orme's home, she was 'Alone in the Wilderness' (one of the chapter headings) thanks to what she took as his hostility. Yet Orme, she has now learnt, has been investigating the mysteries of her parents' marriage for her sake. He has found out that they had had an earlier Quakers' marriage, and that Aldyth herself had been born and raised secretly near to Wildmarsh. He has fought her battles, this hero, a bit like that Xenophon, perhaps, who had cleared away the difficulties for the Greeks when they were alone in the wilderness, that Xenophon who had led them home.

The previously timid girl soon reveals her love to Orme. As they drive out a third time to the same vantage point, Orme promises her that he will try to recapture his lost youth. Once again it is night. But now the moon does appear from behind clouds (rather as the sun appeared suddenly for T.E. Lawrence):

They were on the summit of the Gap, and far below them, the sea caught the shimmer and dazzle for a brief, unutterable instant.

The girl turned to the man, struggling with sobs, shaken through and through.

'*Thalassa!*' she cried brokenly.

'Thalassa!' he echoed, his voice full of triumph and attainment. 'In sight of it, beloved – all that remains is to reach it, and launch away.'

The retort Aldyth had made at their first visit to the Gap is justified: 'There is no Mirage in real life; Mirage is what we make ourselves.' And this adult joy outdoes the dreaming of youth. As the hero had earlier explained, when as a boy he looked out towards the sea from that vantage-point, 'the point of the thing was … that very often, if it was a bit thick, we couldn't see it at all'.[29]

It would be easy enough to dismiss 'Thalassa!' as a pleasant period-piece, written under the spell of the Brontës. Characters in the novel allude to *Wuthering Heights* and *Shirley*, and it did not need much perspicacity for a contemporary reviewer to conclude that Reynolds 'consciously took for her model *Jane Eyre*'. The bleak northern setting, with a house named Wildmarsh and a village Grimwold; the brusque man who lives in isolation, his life blighted by a mysterious marriage; the wilful child; the gentle young woman who wins the child's trust, and softens and wins the heart of the older man, but leaves his house, friendless, before returning and taking the initiative ... All that is missing is an attic and a fire. There is also more than a sniff of Wilkie Collins (jewels stolen under a psychological disorder, a legal mystery over the heroine's legitimacy, a page torn out of a marriage registry ...). Despite the slightly second-hand feel to the story, Reynolds pulls it off quite well. She establishes a spiritual geography of Thalassa and Mirage matching the physical geography of her poem on the Ten Thousand – where they are described as 'in hostile deserts lost' until 'one day, one moment found them unawares'. And the very conventionality of her plot merely points up the emotional appeal of 'Thalatta! Thalatta!'. This is no experimental writer toying with an unexpected symbol. This is a popular novelist giving the slightest of twists to a familiar motif, and reinforcing its appeal as a shout of youth and hope.[30]

*

Another weary middle-aged man is rescued by Xenophon in 'O You Xenophon', a short story written for *Atlantic Monthly* in 1920 by S.H. Kemper, a fairly frequent contributor of stories and poems to such journals. The story is rather less charming than Mrs Baillie Reynolds' novel, but it endows Xenophon's shout with much the same symbolic force. A businessman is being driven to his weekend retreat, a house on the coast, and then

> on this particular afternoon somehow the first faint glimpse of the sea caught his attention. It stirred an indistinct memory of a brave dramatic climax to some long effort coming with the sight of the sea. He seemed to remember – Oh, yes: it was that fellow Xenophon, with the ten thousand Greeks. Goodness! How many years had passed since he thought of Xenophon; and once that frank Attic spirit had been his constant companion. ... Back in Goodall's bookish boyhood the sea had meant a great deal to him. ... And he still liked it. ... only he had been so busy all these years, that he had had no time to think about it.

Now the sight brings some words to his mind: 'When you would shout with the Ten Thousand, *"Thalassa! Thalassa!"* again!'. And those words become the refrain to the first lines of verse he has ever written:

> The restless and mighty sea-longing, the love of the unquiet main:
> And always the ancient deep shall call to the deeps of your spirit,
> 'When you would shout with the Ten Thousand –'

And then, 'with an astonishing facility', he has his opening:

57

How did you see it again, after long times that detained you
Inland and far from the sight, from the sound and scent of the sea?
How was it with you, shaking off all the poor and landward cares that
    had chained you
With the thrill of a primal emotion, the leap of the spirit made free?

'The ancient deep' calling to 'the deeps of your spirit', 'the thrill of a primal emotion, the leap of the spirit made free': small wonder our businessman discovers that writing poetry is more relaxing than golf. The poem is even accepted for publication – but the poet shies away from showing it to his wife. For all the refound sense of freedom that is caught by the refrain, he is too scared of the thought of being called to address his wife's club. But he does at least advise his 'racially and ineradicably amicable and acquiescent' chauffeur to write a little poetry – if he likes a good deal of excitement in his life, that is. Kemper himself, it seems, was not too embarrassed to have his own story published.[31]

Xenophon may have saved Kemper's poet, but he cannot save everyone – not even all characters in magazine stories. The popular novelist Blanche Willis Howard wrote a story in *Scribner's Magazine* in 1897 about a sixty-eight year old shopkeeper from a small town in Germany who has for the first time in her life some money spare, thanks to a secret speculation. She wants to spend the money on a visit to the sea, for seeing the sea has been her greatest desire since childhood. Indeed, she often dreams of the sea, seeing it sometimes amidst ships and crowds, sometimes in a quaint foreign scene, 'like pictures on tea-cups', but most often picturing

> a vast expanse of rocky coasts, *It* surging gloriously, and a group of strong men hailing *It* with cries of joy … She had waked, indeed, with that triumphant cry almost upon her lips, but never in all the years could she carry it quite over the mystic boundary of dreamland, though a subtle sense of gladness and exhilaration would linger, and pervade her homely and monotonous duties.

An odd dream, perhaps. What is this 'group of strong men', what are their 'cries of joy' that can be reduced to a 'triumphant cry'? The title of the story – 'Thalatta' – must offer a hint. That group of strong men must be Xenophon's Ten Thousand (even though they were nowhere near the sea's glorious surge when they hailed it), that triumphant cry must be 'Thalatta! Thalatta!'. But she never gets to make that cry for herself. She finds out that her nephew has defrauded her of her money, and probably headed to Hamburg to catch a ship: 'Suddenly into that narrow room, between her and the solicitous face upon which her physical eyes were gazing, broke space – strength – freedom – the slow plunge of breakers – the poise of wide-winged birds. "He will behold it," cried her heart with a mighty pang.'[32]

3. Our Friend of Youth

The sorry experience of this elderly shopkeeper may be contrasted with the nostalgic farewell to the West of Ireland made by Mary McHugh in her 1931 memoir, *Thalassa: A Story of Childhood by the Western Wave*. McHugh lamented 'all that world, the beautiful, simple world of my childhood' that 'has vanished into the past', and closed by picturing herself 'sitting in the train, a dull ache in my thoughts, catching my last glimpse of the distant ocean. Farewell, my childhood!'. McHugh's evocative title suggests that we should read that last glimpse of the sea as an inversion of a famous first sight.[33]

*

Blanche Willis Howard's heroine dreaming of the sea since childhood, Mary McHugh looking back to the sea of her childhood: the experiences of both women suggest that Xenophon's sea was linked with youth not just because of his use in the classroom but also because the sea itself came to be seen as a 'friend of youth' – as in Byron's fine lines in *Childe Harold's Pilgrimage*, the book that was in the mind, if not the hand, of nearly all nineteenth-century travellers:

> Yet once more let us look upon the sea;
> The midland ocean breaks on him and me,
> And from the Alban Mount we now behold
> Our friend of youth, that ocean, which when we
> Beheld it last by Calpe's rock unfold
> Those waves, we followed on till the dark Euxine roll'd.[34]

When did the association of the sea with youth begin? The Mediterranean only became a friend for Byron's Childe Harold late in his youth, when he roamed overseas, tired of his dissipated life. But as the nineteenth century went on, the sea would be a friend to the increasing number of children who would spend part of their summer at the seaside. The trend towards seaside holidays was analysed by the Rev. M.G. Watkins in an article published anonymously in *Cornhill Magazine* in 1875. He argued that 'our longing for seaside pleasures is a direct growth of the peaceful times which followed the Great War' – that is, the war against Napoleon. Seaside residence had been too expensive and dangerous during the war itself. But he did admit that people had enjoyed the seaside even before Waterloo, in the eighteenth century, when 'George III showed the fashionable world that life was endurable at Weymouth'. It was perhaps for his periodical readership that he underplayed what Alain Corbin has called 'the initial primacy of the aristocracy'. A code of social behaviour for aristocrats had been established in the eighteenth century not just at Weymouth, but at other seaside towns too, most notably Brighton. The rituals of the spa towns like Bath could easily be transferred to the seaside when doctors started to hail the medical benefits of sea water and sea air: Scarborough, which combined the advantages of both a spa and the sea, led the way in the 1730s. It was in the aftermath of Waterloo that the rush to the sea accelerated, as the increasingly prosperous middle classes began to copy the aristocratic habit. Better transport helped as well. Soon one no longer had to go by steamer to Ramsgate or Margate. One could go by train to Great Yarmouth or Brighton. Trains were cheaper, and good for conveying children. Seaside resorts would now offer the middle classes escape in summer from the heat of the industrial cities. And increasingly towards the end of the nineteenth century they would likewise offer escape for the workers, who could take a day trip on the new Bank Holidays.[35]

The new trends can be illustrated from fictional and artistic portrayals of childhood. Virginia Woolf drew on her own childhood holidays in Cornwall in several of her novels – in the opening of *Jacob's Room*, for instance, and above all in *To the Lighthouse*. Hers was a privileged late Victorian upbringing. More people would have recognized the scene of children at play on the beach offered in Frith's panoramic *Life at the Seaside (Ramsgate Sands)*, painted in the 1850s and bought by Victoria. Equally revealing are some of the light stories found in nineteenth-century periodicals. The story of 'A Trip to the Sea' in the *New Monthly Magazine* in 1830 tells of a husband and wife keen to escape London during the languid heat of July, remembering a seaside holiday early in their marriage, but especially concerned for their children's health. So off they go, with the youngest child urging his father in the carriage to sing 'Rule Britannia', and they come at last to the road to the shore, 'my boys shouting from wonder, surprise, and delight, and myself almost wishing that some such ebullition were permitted to my own strong and excited feelings'. Anxiety about children's health also leads to 'A Family Trip to the Sea-side' in a story in *Bentley's Magazine* in 1852. The father is also excited – but dismayed to find that you can only get the previous day's paper there. One did not need to have children oneself to think of the seaside as a place for children. Even the languid visitor slumbering over a book, an optimistic contributor to *Cornhill Magazine* wrote in 1861, could gain pleasure from watching children enjoying themselves at the seaside – 'digging holes in the sand with wooden spades', for instance, like the children in the beach scene depicted by Dickens in 'The Tuggses at Ramsgate'.[36]

The sense of adventure was another reason why the sea was thought to appeal to the spirit of youth. The English schoolboy's feelings for the sea were bred by reading *Robinson Crusoe* and Cook's *Voyages*, a writer in the *Dublin University Magazine* argued in 1855. The same view was expressed by the Rev. Watkins in his article in *Cornhill Magazine*, where he recreated the child's view of the sea: 'far away one white sail which was carrying modern Robinson Crusoes to islands of the blest, decked with all the wealth of tropic vegetation which a child's imagination could conceive.' The sight of ships, he went on to argue, 'feeds that passion for adventure, inherent in all English hearts, which led his forefathers to range the deep and claim the supremacy of the sea', while coastal parts without ships are less interesting, 'at least with masculine minds'. We may recall Tresham Pitcher looking out of his study window, and seeking relief from dull Xenophon as he tries to glimpse the sails on his Thames, sails that would transport him to the world of travel and adventure.[37]

An aetiology for this youthful fascination with the sea as a realm of adventure was supplied by Millais' famous painting of 1870, *The Boyhood of Raleigh* (Plate 7). By depicting the young Raleigh at the seaside, Millais implies that Raleigh's later attachment to the sea (and Raleigh stands for all the maritime adventurers that the Elizabethan and later ages produced) was fostered in childhood. But what is Raleigh doing at the seaside? He is not playing in the sand or even looking out over the sea that stretches to the horizon. He is listening intent to a rough old man telling stories. As Tresham Pitcher first understood when he himself looked down on what 'was supposed to be the sea', 'the Θαλασσα of Xenophon's poor soldiers', the sea 'needed changing before it could figure as the element of adventures and romances'. Or rather, it was precisely the element of adventure, the potential for narrative, that changed the sea.

*

As children became increasingly familiar with the seaside, 'The Sea! The Sea!', the shout of ardent adventurers, could also come to convey the more mundane world of the family trip to the coast. That world – still familiar to many of us today – was nicely caught by John Betjeman in his 1958 poem 'Beside the Seaside', where summer arrives, and

> Very soon the town
> Will echo to the groan of empty trams
> And sweetshops advertise Ice Cream in vain.
> Solihull, Headingley and Golders Green,
> Preston and Swindon, Manchester and Leeds,
> Braintree and Bocking, hear the sea! the sea!

The poem follows a family as they return to the same lodging house as every year, with its petty rules and notices ('Still unprepared to make a picnic lunch / Except by notice on the previous day'), its Do's and Don't's, the smell of the overcrowded lounge when it's wet,

61

> Ah, still the same, the same
> As it was last year and the year before –
> But rather more expensive, now, of course.
> 'Anne, Jennifer and Michael – run along
> Down to the sands and find yourselves some friends
> While Dad and I unpack.' The sea! the sea!

'The sea! the sea!'. Who speaks or thinks those words? The narrator, the children, the parents as they unpack (or whatever they do in the children's absence)? It does not matter who speaks the words: the sea, Xenophon's sea, speaks through us. And there at the sea is Mr Pedder, 'schoolmaster and friend / Of boys and girls – particularly girls', still organizing games of rounders. But not everything is still the same, the same: poor Jennifer is dismayed to find that she is no longer his favourite.[38]

For all his light-hearted and slightly sardonic tone, Betjeman still hints through that repetition of 'the sea! the sea!' at something deep within us – at the voice of our subconscious. Yet a voice that can be heard by Headingley and Golders Green, Manchester and Leeds, the cities and towns and suburbs that expanded in the industrial nineteenth century, is not a voice that can be heard by all cities and towns at all times. Betjeman knowingly plays off the seemingly timeless and mythical cry of Xenophon's soldiers against the cadences of town life in contemporary Britain.

For other writers, Xenophon's shout could itself be a simple emblem of nostalgia for the seaside of one's childhood, much as, for Flashman and others, it expresses nostalgia for schooldays. A traveller in the 1950s who found himself travelling by Xenophon's road down to the Black Sea thought that 'the joy of Xenophon's soldiers had perhaps something in common with my own experiences as a very small boy, anxiously peering out of railway-carriage windows on the way to an annual seaside holiday'. The same idea is far more memorably conveyed by the Welsh poet Duncan Bush in an account of childhood trips to the sea, by a railway line now long since closed. The article, published in 1985 in the journal *Poetry Wales*, is entitled 'The Sea, the Sea':

> The sea has always been important to the imaginative life of South Walians: not only because of a maritime past, and the stories which came out of that, but because of ordinary but ineradicable private memories … which not all littoral people share. Perhaps this sense is best expressed by the exultant massed shout of 'Thalassa! Thalassa!' in Xenophon when, after weeks of travelling, the sea is finally descried; and any kid who has been to Lavernock or Barry or Porthcawl on a summer daytrip will have experienced that moment too. Here, of course, it is no wine-dark Aegean that we confront, but, often enough, that cement-grey gleam of the Bristol Channel under a wash of low cloud. But that instant of simultaneous expectedness and surprise, that slight lift to the heart, remains the

same; and I experience it undiminished now – and almost every day, I suppose – at St Donat's when, at certain points of the road or turns in the driveway, suddenly the sea, and on a clear day Devon, are glimpsed across the last fields.

As in Betjeman's poem, the names speak powerfully for themselves. But here the names are the names of the seaside towns, not the towns of the interior. Lavernock, Barry, Porthcawl .... Reading Bush's words is itself enough to give that slight lift to the heart, even if those names mean nothing – for one can replace them with names of one's own, Muizenberg or East London or Umtata Mouth, any names will do.[39]

Something of that nostalgic yearning, something even of that instantaneous excitement, can be heard in a poem written by Louis MacNeice in 1961, 'Round the Corner'. He ponders the meaning that the sea has had for him at different times in his life:

> Round the corner was always the sea. Our childhood
> Tipping the sand from its shoes on return from holiday
> Knew there was more where it came from, as there was more
> Seaweed to pop and horizon to blink at. Later
> Our calf loves yearned for union in solitude somewhere
> Round that corner where Xenophon crusted with parasangs
> Knew he was home, where Columbus feared he was not,
> And the Bible said there would be no more of it. ...

MacNeice captures the simple contentment of children playing at the seaside – just as in his poem 'Autobiography' he pictures the paradisiacal garden of his youth: 'In my childhood trees were green / And there was plenty to be seen.' This world of plenitude soon vanishes, and the simplicity of the sea disappears with it. 'Round that corner where Xenophon crusted with parasangs / Knew he was home ...': it is still the sea round that corner, but no longer the same sea. The circumlocution itself expresses the poet's initiation into culture, into a world where thoughts of Xenophon, of the world of adventure, of the apocalyptic vision of *Revelation*, intrude upon the child's plainer perceptions of the sea. Xenophon is 'crusted with parasangs': the image marks the imprint of a classical education on the poet's developing imagination. And with knowledge of Xenophon there appears a sense that something is lacking, as those youthful passions yearn for a 'union in solitude' that they will never find. Xenophon's return to the sea stands for the accomplishment of all that eludes those 'calf loves' – as if 'Thalatta! Thalatta!' were a cry of sexual climax. The poem has traced a path from the fullness and fulfilment of childhood, with the wonderfully evocative image of the sea always round the corner, to the lack felt by adolescents, cut off from that sea to which Xenophon returned, a sea that is still round the corner, but now harder to find.[40]

63

*

While Xenophon's shout of the sea acquired new resonances during the nineteenth century as children were more and more exposed both to the sea and to Xenophon himself, there could also be a danger in those childhood days at the seaside – a danger to 'Thalatta! Thalatta!' at least. 'Any kid who has been to Lavernock or Barry or Porthcawl on a summer daytrip' may well have experienced 'that instant of simultaneous expectedness and surprise, that slight lift to the heart'. But would their thoughts turn to Xenophon when they first saw the sea? 'Round the corner was always the sea' – but it is only later, in adolescence, that the sea arouses a picture of Xenophon crusted with parasangs. Young children would be much less likely to think of Xenophon when they first caught sight of the blue expanse of the sea.

Children's first sight of the sea fascinated the Victorian imagination. What that first sight meant was discussed by 'H' (Vere Henry, Lord Hobart, later Governor of Madras) in 'A Chapter on the Sea', first published in *Fraser's Magazine* in 1857. Hobart argued that 'the strongest, if not the most delightful sensation which one has about the sea' is in childhood: 'What a field for wandering interest in the dawning intelligence of six or seven years, when it is first told "you will soon see the sea." ' He then turned to describe his own memories of his first sight of the sea:

> along hot, dusty, chalky roads, winding, as it seemed for ever, over breezy, turf-clad downs, the lumbering old carriage had dragged its way; and there was in the air that strange sense of freshness and freedom, and that delicious odour caused by the proximity of the sea; but these sensations could scarcely be noticed or understood at seven years old; and the feeling, when they said we should soon 'see the sea', was one of far more pain than pleasure – that pain I suppose which the human race incurred when it ate of the 'tree of knowl-edge', – the dawning, half-conscious apprehension of the great mystery of life. And when between the horizon and the turfy hill the sea itself appeared, I remember no pleasure in the sight of it – I remember nothing but an all-pervading sense of novelty and wonder.

No joyful shout of 'Thalatta! Thalatta!': he was evidently too young for that (or at least, he was no Ronald Knox). Indeed, no joy at all. 'The first impression received from contemplating the sea is fear', as another periodical writer proclaimed. The fear felt by the son of the painter Benjamin Robert Haydon, who recorded in his diary that 'Frank, the first time he saw the Sea, ran away screaming, "It's coming, it's coming." '[41]

Children were now seeing the sea before their imaginations had been moulded by the spirit of romanticism. Summers spent amidst the sand and waves may have given them the benefit of 'that sense of vastness and power which the sea confers', but an important pleasure was denied them – or so

3. Our Friend of Youth

the Rev. Watkins argued in his *Cornhill* piece: 'How many have wished to recollect their thoughts on first seeing the ocean! Memory cannot recall them. This is a penalty for travelling at so much earlier an age than did their fathers. Other generations saw the sea for the first time when their mind was formed. Then they could register their feelings as they called Thalatta! Thalatta!'.

Watkins had a point. Just think of Hobart trying to recall his first sight of the sea: he describes sensations that 'could scarcely be noticed or understood at seven years old', and philosophizes that first sight into a fall from prelapsarian grace and innocence. And while Watkins was of course exaggerating when he implied that everyone who first saw the sea when their mind was formed would shout 'Thalatta! Thalatta!', his remark does suggest that the romantic sensitivity to nature is an important part of the story of Xenophon's sea. It is time to turn away from schoolboys at the seaside, to see how 'Thalatta! Thalatta!' has been a way for sentimental poets to register their feelings as they look out on the boundless ocean.[42]

4

Image of Eternity

the famous shout on Mount Teches
is mistakenly interpreted by sentimental poets
they simply found the sea that is the exit from the dungeon
                              Zbigniew Herbert, 'Anabasis'

If, as the Rev. M.G. Watkins claimed in 1875, all young men of earlier generations would register their feelings when they first saw the sea by calling out
'Thalatta! Thalatta!', what had prepared their minds for this supreme
moment? Watkins himself provided an answer to this question:
'Wordsworth's advocacy of mountain and sea scenery', which had been
followed by 'all the poets of the reflective school', and Sir Walter Scott's
'painting of nature'. Watkins could well have added *Childe Harold's
Pilgrimage*, where Byron saluted the 'glorious mirror, where the Almighty's
form / Glasses itself in tempests', 'boundless, endless, and sublime – / The
image of Eternity'. But while young men may have been prepared by
Wordsworth and Byron for the sublime spectacle of the ocean, they would
not have been encouraged to shout 'Thalatta! Thalatta!' by reading these
poets. Perhaps Watkins should also have looked across the sea to the poetry
of Heinrich Heine. Heine opened his second *North Sea* cycle (*Die Nordsee*),
first published in 1827, with a 'Sea-Greeting' ('Meergruß') that started with
a ringing echo of the Ten Thousand's shout:

> Thalatta! Thalatta!
> Greetings to you, o eternal sea!
> Greetings to you ten-thousandfold
> From jubilant hearts
> As once you were greeted
> By ten thousand Grecian hearts
> Battling adversity, yearning for home,
> Grecian hearts of world renown.

Heine did not just greet the sea in the authentic Xenophontic manner, he also
went on in the next stanza to recreate Xenophon's great scene:

4. Image of Eternity

> The waters were rolling,
> Were rolling and roaring;
> The sun poured fleetly downward
> Its frolicking rosy lights;
> The sudden-startled files of seagulls
> Flapped away shrilling and squealing;
> The horses were stamping, the shields were clashing,
> And still it rang out like a victory cry:
> Thalatta! Thalatta![1]

Heine's greeting to the sea was a cry of liberation. Dissatisfied by the study of law, unsuccessful in a business venture set up by a wealthy uncle, forced to convert to Lutheranism to have any chance of one of the university posts which were closed to Jews, he had earlier sought to escape from the sham of society by travelling to the mountains of Germany. In his *Harz Journey* (*Die Harzreise*), he offered a farewell to the 'polished drawing rooms' with their 'Neat black coats and silken stockings, / Spotless cuffs and social arts':

> To the hills I shall ascend,
> Where the huts are meek and low,
> Where the breast expands in freedom,
> And the breezes freely blow.

He painted an idealized picture of life in a mining village in the mountains – the life that gave rise to the German fairy-tale, the life of an 'ancient, tremulous woman' whose 'thoughts and feelings are interwoven with every corner of the stove and every carving on the cupboard' near which she sits. Before long Heine again sought release from the city by travelling to the island of Norderney, and it was there that he wrote his poems on the North Sea. He also expressed his sense of liberation from civilized hypocrisy in a prose piece, also entitled *The North Sea*, where he wrote admiringly of the inhabitants' primitive simplicity and their sense of community – both of which were endangered by the island's growing popularity as a bathing resort. And he claimed that he had found for himself the communion with nature that he had earlier pictured in that old woman in her mountain village: 'I love the sea as my own soul. I often feel as if the sea were really my soul itself.' No wonder he could greet the sea 'ten-thousandfold'.[2]

In his poem 'Sea-Greeting', Heine extended the parallel with the Ten Thousand by imagining his own return to the sea as a return home: the plashing of the sea's waters was 'like voices of home' for one who had 'languished in foreign wastelands', while the flickering lights of the sea were 'like dreams of childhood', arousing again 'memories of old'. He went on in the next stanza to describe the feeling of oneness with nature that he had also expressed in his prose writing: the trees are rustling and flowering, the blooms look at him with 'dappled sweet-scented eyes', and 'all's sweet with fragrance and humming, exhalations and laughter, / And in the blue sky the birds are singing – / Thalatta! Thalatta!'. Here, as in the second stanza, Xenophon's shout forms an emphatic close. But now the syntax is more ambiguous. Is 'Thalatta! Thalatta!' what the birds are singing? Or is it just that his communion with nature makes the poet break out with another Xenophontic shout? It scarcely matters. The joy is the thing.

Heine deflates this exultant build-up in the final stanza of 'Sea-Greeting'. He now addresses his 'valiant heart in retreat', and reveals that he is fleeing to the sea pursued by a quasi-Amazonian array of women:

> How often, how terribly often
> Were you beset by the North's barbarian women!
> From big, all-conquering eyes
> They shot forth their burning arrows;
> With twisted double-edged words
> They threatened to cleave the heart in me ...
> In vain did I raise my shield in defence,
> The arrows whistled, the blows crashed down,
> And by the North's barbarian women
> Was I driven to the sea.

The poet's retreat from the 'all-conquering eyes' ('siegenden Augen') contrasts with the Greeks' 'victory cry' ('Siegesruf'). It is with some relief, then, that Heine ends by greeting 'the kindly, lifesaving sea' with a final cry of 'Thalatta! Thalatta!'.

Or rather, it is not Heine himself who utters that cry, but Heine's narrator. It becomes more and more clear that it is a poetic persona speaking, and Heine is far too artful and evasive for us to be able to identify that persona with the poet himself. Even at the start of the poem, 'the equation of the persona with Xenophon's Ten Thousand (all of them!) establishes exactly the kind of heroic posture the poet is after'. That heroic posture changes later in the poem, and the vision of the sea changes with it. And both are further modified in the course of the cycle of poems which 'Sea-Greeting' starts.[3]

The cycle describes a journey of sorts – an 'epic voyage' even. As the poet launches out to sea, he first has to face a thunderstorm, and is then 'Shipwrecked': 'Hope and love! all crumbled to ruins!'. He can still assert a romantic identification with nature, but now he identifies himself with the clouds which toil to haul water up from the ocean before they dispatch it back to the ground, 'a cheerless and tedious job / And useless as my own life'. He can still turn his thoughts to the past, but now he remembers past romances rather than his childhood. He asserts that his maiden loves him, but his boasts are met by the seagulls' 'cold and ironical snickering'. He then probes the sea with questions: 'Oh solve me the riddle of life, / The tormenting primordial riddle.' But his questions are not answered: 'The waters murmur their eternal murmur, ... And a fool waits for an answer.' The sea is now eternally indifferent.[4]

Heine's ecstatic initial refrain of 'Thalatta! Thalatta!' is dimmed not just by the shifting significance of the sea in the later poems of the cycle, but also by the emergence of a more sceptical vision of the classical past. In 'Thunderstorm', lightning can still be described as 'Swiftly flaring and swiftly vanishing / Like a flash of wit from Zeus's head', while 'High prance the white-maned horses of ocean / That Boreas himself begot / On Erichthon's beautiful mares'. But in later poems Heine presents the shoddy image of the sun's bickering marriage with the old god of the sea; he is himself abused for his foolish fancies by the daughters of Ocean, who had comforted Prometheus in his suffering; and he has a vision of the clouds on a moonlit night as the gods of Greece 'displaced and departed', supplanted as they had themselves supplanted the Titans: 'I have never loved you, you ancient gods! / For the Greeks are repulsive to me / And even the Romans are hateful.' Yet he pities these ancient gods, he still likes their sensuality, he is still prepared to take 'the side of the gods that were vanquished', even though they had always taken the victor's side.[5]

Heine's cycle of poems has moved a long way from its joyous identification with the victorious Greeks. With 'The Phoenix', it does briefly become more upbeat: 'heaven and ocean and my own heart / Rang out with the echo: / "She loves him! she loves him!" ' (an erotic rewriting of the earlier refrain). But the cycle ends with a retreat from the sea: 'Happy the man who has reached port safely / And left behind him the sea and its tempests.' The poet is sitting in a pub, no longer seeking answers from the sea, but rather enjoying the world 'reflected / In a brimming drinking glass's mirror'.[6]

So Heine's *North Sea* sequence is 'the record of a liberation that failed'. His literary journey has taken him from the plain air of the Harz Mountains to the wide sarcastic sea. Yet the movement towards disenchantment in the *North Sea* cycle relies on the liberating power of the initial shout of 'Thalatta! Thalatta!' itself – on a romantic reading that could all too easily extract that shout from its place within the cycle and preserve its aura, free from Heine's withering irony; a romantic reading that it was all too easy for later, and lesser, writers to follow.[7]

*

The temptation to read Xenophon's greeting to the sea romantically was too great for the Rev. Samuel Longfellow and the Rev. Thomas Wentworth when they edited 'the first American anthology of poetry devoted entirely to the subject of the sea'. The book was published in Boston in 1853, at a time when the eastern coast of the United States was being domesticated as a holiday destination. Its title? *Thalatta: A Book for the Sea-Side*. The collection was heralded by a contemporary reviewer as 'just the book to put into your pocket when you go to the cool, refreshing water places, and have so much idle time to saunter away'. 'Roaming along the magnificent beaches so abundant in New England' or 'lying at full length on the rocks of Nahont or Cohosset', you would be delighted first by a sentence of Xenophon (no surprise which), and then by Heine's 'Sea-Greeting'.[8]

The popularity of Heine's reading of Xenophon also emerges from a novel by 'S.' first serialized in 1862 in *Fraser's Magazine* under the title *Thalatta! Thalatta! A Study at Sea*, and published in the same year in book form as *Thalatta! or The Great Commoner: A Political Romance*. The author wrote in a preface that the title indicated 'the motley character of the contents': 'the hardy sea-life of the north, and – English politics'. All the same, a reviewer could complain that the novel was 'somewhat ambitiously entitled': for all its 'sharp, briny breezes', it was rather lacking in romance. There was much more politics. The hero, Miles Warrender, has a brief spell in parliament. And his cousin, 'the Great Commoner' of the title, who is overtly modelled on Canning and Disraeli, becomes Prime Minister and dies. Stretched out around this slim story are rambling reflections on political life and picturesque accounts of the simple life of a northern sea village. The romance was more or less confined to a scene where the hero and another (female) cousin go yachting off the north-east coast of England and find themselves caught out in a gale. Providentially saved, he realizes that he and his cousin are in love with each other.[9]

It is in this romantic yachting scene that the appeal of Heine's poetry makes itself felt: 'Miles had brought a volume of poems by Heine with him, and Corry never tired of hearing Miles read. They were strange poems – the utterances of one who had lived upon the stern North Sea, and learned to interpret what the Norse gods said to each other while the North wind blew.' Corry looks 'ever and ever across the water to make sure that the German poet spoke true; and she found that the words were as true as Gospel words'. And Miles also thinks that Heine spoke true: 'that greeting of the sea – "Be thou greeted, thou infinite sea!" – shows how he loved it. That's the one I like best.' The hero's favourite poem is 'Sea-Greeting' – the poem that starts 'Thalatta! Thalatta!'.[10]

Xenophon's exclamation is itself evoked towards the start and end of the novel. First, Miles and a friend are shooting on the twelfth of August – the glorious twelfth, the start of the shooting season:

From the top of the knoll you look down upon the sea – three, four, five miles away. Thalatta! Thalatta! Still it startles you, as it startled the Greeks of old, with a glad surprise. Blue or grey or silvery, I know not which; but alive at least. Therefore it is that we who are gifted with a fatal immortality greet the sea. It, too, has inherited the unhappy prerogative of our house. The earth dies and is buried; the sea, which is its soil, endures for ever.

The cry is repeated at the start of the final chapter – where an old and blind village woman who, less fortunate than her aristocratic neighbours, had lost her lover in a storm at sea, listens to the waves and waits to die: '*Thalatta! Thalatta!* We are once more beside the ancient sea. Still it murmurs solemnly and peacefully upon the "ribbed sea-sand" of the moon-like bay, – solemnly and peacefully, as if a great man had not died, and an historic empire perished.'[11]

These allusions to Xenophon's shout seem incidental. It is as if the author is just groping for the literary touch. In that final chapter ('We are once more beside the ancient sea'), one may perhaps catch an echo of a famous line in *Childe Harold's Pilgrimage*: 'Yet once more let us look upon the sea.' But 'Thalatta! Thalatta!' does not seem to be the key symbol that it was in, say, Mrs Baillie Reynolds' novel '*Thalassa!*'. For all that, it plays its part in the author's celebration of the sea – and of Tory politics. The book asserts, as one reviewer noted, 'the transcendental influence of "the sea" over character'. The hero at one point claims that he has 'never heard of a man who did anything great, who had not known the sea'. The narrator seems to agree: it was 'the scent of the sea in the blood' that had enabled the Warrender family 'to withstand ... the levelling influences of modern organisation'. His final message is: 'I have no confidence in measures; I believe in men.' And men seem to be better if they have been bred by the sea and shouted 'Thalatta! Thalatta!'.[12]

'S.', the author of this piece of Tory hero-worship, was Sir John Skelton, also a historian and a frequent contributor to Victorian periodicals. Some of the obsessions revealed by his novel *Thalatta!* had appeared already in an article on 'Long Vacation Reading' that he wrote (under the pen-name 'Shirley', after Brontë's heroine) for *Fraser's Magazine* in December 1859: 'Books are rather a bore during the holidays. The Long Vacation should be devoted to finer uses and better ends. The first brace of grouse one knocks over on the 12th ... are worth a wagonload of the classics.' Yet it was on the glorious twelfth that 'Thalatta! Thalatta!' first intruded in Skelton's novel. 'Shirley' went on to acknowledge that books may be necessary on wet and windy days – yet 'even on a stormy day like this the sea-side is not altogether destitute of out-door interest. A ship in sight! Let us put away our books and hurry down to the pier. *Thalatta! Thalatta!*'. Xenophon's shout, it seems, could survive an onslaught on the classics. It was sturdy enough to serve as a paean to outdoor life at the seaside while also gratifying the cultural sensitivities of the growing readership of the Victorian periodicals.[13]

*

71

Sir John Skelton was not the only writer in the nineteenth or early twentieth century to attempt to infuse Xenophon's shout with something of Heine's spirit. Many poets attempted to match the delights of Heine's address to the sea. Everyone has a poem on the sea in them, and the increasing number of periodicals in the Victorian era gave more and more people an excuse to publish them. All the more reason, then, to make one's own offering stand out a bit. 'The Sea' was a decent enough title for Keats. Others preferred something a bit more reminiscent of Xenophon. Mortimer Collins, well-known in his day as a man of letters, now a mere name in the *Dictionary of National Biography*, was one of those to pen a poem with the title 'Thalatta': 'O wide sea! O hills that lie / Beneath a glowing golden sky!'. The Byronic and bisexual Hon. Roden Berkeley Wriostheley Noel, a godchild of Queen Victoria, also penned a poem with that title – and with a metre suggested, he wrote, by the sound of the sea:

> When Love is fading from thy path, a faint remembered gleam,
> Whose wondrous glory crowned thy crest in youth's triumphal morn;
> ... Then, poet, seek alone resounding hollows of the sea,
> And plunge thy sullen soul in ocean's grand immensity!

There was also a poem 'Thalatta' written by an American writer of juvenile adventure stories, Willis Boyd Allen ('Far over the billows unresting forever / She flits, my white bird of the sea ...') and a song 'Thalatta' by Harry Reginald Spier ('I am going home to the sea').[14]

A fully Xenophontic title would make a poem stand out even more:

> In my ear is the moan of the pines – in my heart
> is the song of the sea,
> And I feel his salt breath on my face as he showers
> his kisses on me.

That was how the Canadian poet John Reade started his 'Thalatta! Thalatta!' (included in a collection of his works published in 1870). There followed wildly screaming gulls (as in Heine) and sails glistening 'like gems / on the breast of a bride' – but nothing about Xenophon. The same title was given to a religious poem by Joseph Brownlee Brown, to an ode by J. Perry Worden celebrating the visit of the King and Queen to Bristol in 1908, and to a rowing poem written by James Lister Cuthbertson, a teacher at Geelong Grammar School, near Melbourne, for the school magazine:

> Still ring the merry oars, and looking aft
> We leave the harbour of the friendly shore,
> Churn the clear wavelets into seething foam
> On the loved waterway that brings us home.[15]

If one could not manage Xenophon's own 'Thalatta! Thalatta!', there was always 'Thalassa! Thalassa!'. Two poems with that title (in Greek) were published in 1875 (the year Roden Noel's 'Thalatta' came out in *Gentleman's Magazine*): one was in a collection by Henry Ellison, while the other appeared in *Blackwood's Magazine*. Its author, 'J.R.S.', must be Julian Russell Sturgis, an American by birth, educated at Eton and Balliol, and author, among other things, of the libretto for Sir Arthur Sullivan's 'Ivanhoe'. Sturgis' poem is a long and strange affair: 'On sweeps the brave Greek galley, and the main / Resounds with the rhythmic beat of oar and song. / Who rules the waves but we?' We seem to be on an Athenian ship sailing off the coast of Italy, with glimpses of nymphs and a herdsman (or is it Phoebus?) in the nearby hills, and a prophecy of a new race and 'new scholars for the Greek' beyond far western seas. For some reason or other, this poem was not included in the collection Sturgis published in 1894.[16]

A poem entitled 'Θάλασσα, θάλασσα' that was published in 1884 was even more unusual. It described the poet's delight at fleeing Ireland for the smell of the shore he adored and for the sound of the language that had bewitched him. The shore the poem was greeting was the southern shore of France – the same shore that drew a Xenophontic shout from the undergraduate T.E. Lawrence. And the bewitching language was the language of Provence – the language in which the poem was written (hence its subtitle: 'Cridamen di Gré dins l'*Anabàsi* de Xenefoun'). Equally striking was the identity of the author: William Bonaparte-Wyse, a scholarly Irishman who played a leading role in the nineteenth-century Provençal revival – and who was, for good measure, a grand-nephew of Napoleon. Bonaparte-Wyse closed his hymn to Provence with a shout – but not quite the shout of the poem's title: 'like a cock at dawn I cry "Cacaraca!" '.[17]

The appeal of the plainer 'The Sea, the Sea' was rather less strong than the full Xenophontic onslaught – though D.H. Lawrence did succumb to it (but only when he had already written one poem on 'The Sea'). The English phrase was much more common within poems than as a title. 'The sea, the sea in the darkness calls', Henry Wadsworth Longfellow wrote in his short poem 'The Tide Rises, the Tide Falls', and 'the sea, the sea' called to many other poets. But nowhere was 'the sea, the sea' more popular than in a song called 'The Sea' first published in 1832, with words by Bryan Waller Procter ('Barry Cornwall') and music by Sigismund Neukomm (a pupil of Haydn). 'The sea, the sea, the open sea! / The blue, the fresh, the ever free': how could that opening couplet not become famous? The start of the second stanza was equally memorable: 'I'm on the sea! I'm on the sea! / I am where I would ever be.' No surprise that these lyrics were sung in a nautical drama by C.A. Somerset that was itself named 'The Sea!' after the song. The preface to the published play could even claim that that song has been 'ground in our ears by every barrel-organ within the bills of mortality, chaunted by every itinerant chorister, and swelled the horn of every omnibus'. No surprise, either, to find that song parodied in one of J.R. Planché's popular mythical extravaganzas, *The Deep, Deep Sea; or, Perseus and Andromeda* (1833), where the god Neptune sings 'I rule the sea! I rule the sea! / But happy there I can never be'; or in an 1837 burlesque by Joseph Graves, *Cupid*, where the eponymous hero sings 'Psyché! Psyché! my own Psyché, / The pretty, fair, and ever free!'; or again in a song 'The Gin: An Out-and-out Parody on "The Sea" ': 'The Gin! the Gin! Hodge's Cordial Gin! / It fairly makes our heads to spin.' Even if Xenophon did not inspire Procter's song, this famous tune could perhaps impart to the experience of reading the *Anabasis* a brief and unexpected burst of lyricism.[18]

There were, then, many poems with titles that could tempt thoughts of Xenophon published in the century after Heine's 'Sea-Greeting'. So many poems, in fact, that it may seem surprising that poets before Heine had not thought to cite 'Thalatta! Thalatta!' – and even more surprising that the simple English repetition 'The Sea! The Sea!' does not seem to have attracted earlier poets much. There was much earlier English poetry of the sea: exuberant and sentimental critics may even see a continuity from the Anglo-Saxon poem 'The Sea-Farer' onwards. But whether in the Greek or in translation, Xenophon's shout was almost totally ignored by poets before the nineteenth century. Young men in earlier generations had not registered their feelings at the sight of the sea by calling out 'Thalatta! Thalatta!'. Before the nineteenth century, historians of Greece would sometimes quote that shout when they gave their own descriptions of the great scene on Mount Theches. What is telling is that they mostly quoted it in English – and that they did not take it for granted: John Gillies commented on 'the repetition, "The sea! the sea!" ', William Mitford on 'the reiteration of the cheering words "the sea! the sea!" '. That repetition did not seem so strange to people who had read the romantic poets or listened, say, to Procter's popular song. Later historians would not stress the repetition. They would simply quote the famous phrase – and perhaps in its Greek form or even with Greek letters.[19]

The growing use of Xenophon in the classroom and the rush to the seaside for holidays doubtless played their part in encouraging Victorian poets to emulate the great Heine and echo Xenophon's shout. But mere familiarity with Xenophon and the sea was not enough. Xenophon's simple shout of the sea had also to be transformed by the mistaken interpretations of sentimental poets infused with new romantic ideas about the sea. Heine himself, first and foremost of these poets, was not all sentiment. But Heine's touches of darkness were lost in poems like Henry Ellison's 'Θάλασσα! Θάλασσα!':

4. Image of Eternity

Once more, oh once more have I sight and sense
Of thee, thou boundless Ocean! Once again
Thy sound is in my ears, that mighty strain
Of multitudinous waves in one immense
And boundless utterance of omnipotence.
The sense of freedom seems to fire my brain,
And fill my heart with joy almost to pain,
A tongueless rapture, wordless and intense.
Up the stern cliff the wave comes bounding still,
Like a great shaggy hound that leaps to kiss
His unregarding master's hand, and ill
Denial brooks. O God! methinks it is,
'Mid the worn years and hollowness that kill,
And blight Man's life, like the remembered bliss
Of Hope and Youth's indomitable will!

'Once more, oh once more': Ellison is picking up from where Skelton left off ('*Thalatta! Thalatta!* We are once more beside the ancient sea. ...'). His extravagant opening reads like an acknowledgement that he is writing a type of poem that had become all too familiar three quarters of the way through the nineteenth century. He is standing on Byron's shoulders as he looks out on the sea. At the same time, he feels the immediate presence of the sea with the same urgency found in Heine's recreation of Xenophon's great scene.

Ellison assaults Xenophon's sea with the full romantic weaponry. The sea is 'boundless', unlimited in scope, much as it is unlimited in time (Heine's 'eternal sea', Byron's 'image of eternity', Skelton's 'ancient' sea that 'endures for ever'). This ancient sea nonetheless inspires thoughts of the aspirations of youth – as it did for Heine, or for S.H. Kemper's middle-aged businessman poet, or Mrs Baillie Reynolds' disgruntled hero. The sea is also a domain of freedom – and irresistibly so for those composing English rhyming couplets: think of Procter's famous song ('the open sea ... the ever free'), or the poem that leaps to the mind of Kemper's businessman ('the sound and scent of the sea ... the leap of the spirit made free'). 'Spirit of Freedom, thou dost love the sea / Trackless and storm-tost ocean wild and free', wrote Henry Nehemiah Dodge. Loftier poets too could be tempted by the rhyme: Wordsworth in his address to Milton ('Thou hadst a voice whose sound was like the sea, / Pure as the naked heavens, majestic, free'), Byron in the opening lines of his *Corsair* ('O'er the glad waters of the dark blue sea, / Our thoughts as boundless, and our souls as free').[20]

Ellison's Xenophontic title 'Θάλασσα! Θάλασσα!' turns out to be an invitation to enjoy a litany of romantic conceptions of the sea. But why does Ellison allude to Xenophon in his title when he does not allude to Xenophon in his poem? He does not even shout himself as he sees the sea: what he feels is 'a tongueless rapture, wordless and intense'. Perhaps we should note that he stresses the sense of the sea as much as the sight: 'Thy sound is in my ears, that mighty strain / Of multitudinous waves.' Nineteenth-century poets were obsessed with the noise made by waves. Longfellow wrote a sonnet on 'The Sound of the Sea', and Wordsworth compared Milton's voice with the sea. The same obsession can also be found in more popular culture: in *Clayhanger*, a novel of Midlands life in the late Victorian age, Arnold Bennett conjured up a pub scene where some men sing a 'classic quarter, justly celebrated from Hull to Wigan and from Northallerton to Lichfield, "Loud Ocean's Roar" ' – with one man doing 'the yapping of the short waves on the foam-veiled rocks', another 'the long and mighty rolling of the deep'. To an age fascinated by the sound of the sea, it was not least the sound of Xenophon's shout that made it so appealing.[21]

*

The sound of 'Thalassa' and 'Thalatta' ('the former or the latter?') was appealing to punsters like Ronald Knox and Harry Flashman, but there was more to those words than that. 'Thalassa, Thalassa', the classical scholar Richard Jenkyns has written, is known to 'every schoolboy' because of 'the unforgettable sound of the words, the sound of the sea itself'. Not even the pronunciation of Greek favoured by the English public schools could spoil the sound of those beautiful words.[22]

Jenkyns' romantic claim can be supported by a scene at the start of the Irish-Canadian writer Brian Moore's 1971 novel *Fergus*. The story starts with its main character, Fergus Fadden, an Irish writer, at his home on the Californian coast, looking out of the window:

> There, as always, was the sea, the long Pacific breakers beginning their run two hundred yards from shore. *Thalassa, Thalassa, the loud resounding sea, our great mother, Thalassa.* Although Fergus knew no Greek, he liked to say these words over to himself: he had a weakness for sonorous syllables.

Thalassa, Thalassa – sonorous syllables indeed. Moore's own alliteration perhaps hits on one reason why so many people have called 'Thalassa! Thalassa!' to mind more readily than Xenophon's own 'Thalatta! Thalatta!'. Those sibilants are appealing – especially when they evoke the sea.[23]

The 'loud resounding sea' that Fergus hears is also a Homeric sea. 'Loud resounding sea' was a familiar translation of the wonderful Homeric phrase *poluphloisbos thalassa* – a phrase which had the good fortune to appear near the start of the *Iliad*, where the priest Chryses, dismissed angrily by Agamemnon, 'went in silence along the shore of the loud resounding sea'. That epithet 'poluphloisbos' exerted a considerable spell on men like Samuel Taylor Coleridge and the famous Victorian classical schoolteacher and scholar, T.E. Page, who would ask whether it 'represents by its sound the roaring of ocean or the lisping of waves'. James Joyce presumably had the first of those interpretations in mind when he coined the phrase 'those polyfizzyboisterous seas'. But nowhere was the romantic appeal of that Homeric sea exploited better than in Henry David Thoreau's posthumous *Cape Cod*. Thoreau there described his admiration for 'the roaring of the breakers, and the ceaseless flux and reflux of the waves' which 'did not for a moment cease to dash and roar': 'We were wholly absorbed by this spectacle and tumult, and like Chryses, though in a different mood from him, we walked silent along the shore of the resounding sea.' Thoreau then quoted the line of Homer in the Greek – explaining that he 'put in a little Greek now and then, partly because it sounds so much like the ocean, – though I doubt if Homer's *Mediterranean* Sea ever sounded so loud as this.' He added a footnote on the Homeric epithet: 'We have no word in English to express the sound of many waves, dashing at once, whether gently or violently, *poluphloisboios* to the ear'. And he reverts to the Homeric phrase in a striking anthropomorphism: 'The attention of those who frequent the camp-meetings at Eastham is said to be divided between the preaching of the Methodists and the preaching of the billows on the backside of the Cape … On that side some John N. Maffit; on this, the Reverend Poluphloisboios Thalassa.' A shame to point out that Thoreau mistook the Greek declension (he should have written 'Poluphloisbos').[24]

Xenophon's shout of 'Thalatta! Thalatta!' profited from the resonances of the alluring Homeric sea – even if it was distorted to 'Thalassa! Thalassa!' in the process. The distortion to those sibilant syllables came all too easily in the second half of the nineteenth century – an era that saw the start of a cult of Thalassa. You could read a book by an oceanographer, J.J. Wild, with the title *Thalassa* (so much more sensuous than the sub-title, *An Essay on the Depth, Temperature, and Currents of the Ocean*). You could listen to a cantata 'Thalassa' by Charlotte Sainton-Dolby. You could sing a yachting song 'Thalassa', with words by Edwin Arnold put to music by Miss M. Lindsay (Mrs J. Worthington Bliss): 'Who cares on the land to stay, Wooing the wilful May? … With the winds and the wild clouds and me, The low shore soon, Will be down with the moon, And none on the waves but we, And none on the waves but we!'. You could stay on shore, and read the volume on *Yachting* in the Badminton Library, published in 1894, where you could enjoy a chapter written by 'Thalassa' and also discussing a yacht *Thalassa* that had been built for Colonel John Townsend Bucknill in 1887. If you were in the know, you would even realize that the writer 'Thalassa' was Colonel Bucknill himself. Come the new century, you could read in *Scribner's Magazine* a poem 'Thalassa' by Rosamund Marriott Watson: 'Last night I dreamed once more I saw the sea' (a haunting premonition of the opening of *Rebecca*). In the year before the Great War started, you could listen to

'Thalassa', a symphony by Arthur Somervell, or read a poem 'Thalassa' by the French critic and friend of Joyce, Valéry Larbaud, invoking the great poets of epic: 'O Homère! ô Virgile!'.[25]

*

The cult of Thalassa was also an erotic cult. In the course of the nineteenth century, the seaside increasingly became a place where amorous feelings were aroused. Beaches created and channelled desire by promising the sight of bare flesh: 'the mere contact of a bare foot on the sand', Alain Corbin has written in his masterful study of the discovery of the seaside, 'was already a sensual invitation and a barely conscious substitute for masturbation' (though, as Frank Kermode comments, 'we are not told, in any of the very numerous notes, where this information comes from'). And the sea itself was a site for romance where traditional restraints could break down. It was at sea, as he recited Heine, that Skelton's hero fell in love. When the glorious surge of the sea and the joyful cries of strong men fill the dreams of the elderly spinster in Blanche Willis Howard's story 'Thalatta', the eroticism is barely suppressed. And many others would share with Philip Glazebrook's would-be adventurer, Tresham Pitcher, a 'longing' for the sea that had an almost erotic intensity. No surprise, then, to come across sentiments like those expressed by W.J. Henderson in a poem 'Thalassa' published in 1892 in the *Century Illustrated Monthly Magazine*: 'If I might ... feel the snow-white summits of thy breast, / ... Rock slow beneath me, slow and deep and strong.' Lewis Piaget Shanks, a scholar of French literature, offered some more eroticism in another 'Thalassa' poem, published in 1928 in *The American Bookman*: 'As a pale silken wanton lies, with luring scarves and glistening sash, / The sea lolls, and her jewels flash their opalescent fiery eyes.' A few years later, as you devoured the new Rosamond Lehmann, you could read of a girl dancing with a partner, terribly exciting, with her long blue chiffon skirts swirling out, enough to make anyone hold their breath, and 'her name on the programme was Thalassa' (and that name would doubtless seem all the more alluring if uttered with a slight erotic lilt).[26]

The erotic potential of Xenophon's shout was fully realized by the popular novelist Robert W. Chambers (famed now for his horror classic *The King in Yellow*) in a story serialized in the 1920s with the title *Thalassa*. Chambers' story told of a young man and woman trying to outwit a gang of villains as they hunt for some treasure buried during De Soto's great march through the wilds of Florida. As the hero and heroine set out to sea from New York, ' "Thalassa!" came her triumphant cry', and she suddenly seems to become more attractive to her companion (a butterfly-collector turned adventurer): 'The sea seemed to have wrought in her a radiant metamorphosis. ... He saw it when the old Greek cry, "Thalassa!" saluted him from her eager lips. "The

Sea!" And with that clear, triumphant paean ringing in his ears he had witnessed her utter transfiguration.' The consummation comes when, mission accomplished, they sail out from the Florida marshes to the open sea:

> She lifted her head; the growing perfume freshened; the boat began to rock, slightly.
> 'Is it the sea?' she asked her lover.
> 'We are passing the inlet. Listen!'
> Through infinite obscurity came the far thunder of surf.
> 'Thalassa!' she whispered.
> Slowly the mounting fragrance of the sea filled the darkness. The girl trembled in his arms and nestled closer.
> 'You must love me enough,' she said, 'and leave no emptiness in my heart for the sea to creep in and fill. ... I fell in love with it before I fell in love with you. ... The Sea ... Thalassa! —'

And on that word Chambers ends his novel. The novel has nothing whatever to do with Xenophon apart from 'the old Greek cry, "Thalassa!" '. Nonetheless, when he closes his story with that old Greek cry, Chambers is exploiting its Xenophontic aura. It is a cry of passion and triumph. The cry uttered by Xenophon's Greeks when they caught sight of the sea stands here for an erotic fulfilment – the sort of triumph also felt by the hero and heroine in Mrs Baillie Reynolds' novel *'Thalassa!'* as the moon suddenly breaks through the clouds and illuminates the sea beneath them. To shout 'Thalassa' is to have found what one desires, to have escaped from the desert, to have discovered that there is more than Mirage to life – unlike the poor friend of Nancy Mitford's narrator in *The Pursuit of Love*, an 'explorer in the sandy waste' who 'had seen only another mirage'.[27]

*

Xenophon's shout could also come to stand for other sorts of fulfilment in the course of the nineteenth century. Mortimer Collins, one of the Victorian poets who wrote a 'Thalatta' poem, also used this shout in a slightly earlier poem, 'The Pilgrim of Art', where he pictured a man setting forth 'weary of life in cities, and the sound / Of endless commerce' and 'pining to tread the distant Alpine ground' – but seeking instead 'for beauty and for life' in the sea. This 'Pilgrim of Dreams' then imagines a beautiful scene from a distant age – Ionian girls with girded breasts beside white columns and the tossing sea:

> Then let us shout *Thalatta*! Beauty bright
> And life and power blend in that thought divine.
> There pause, tired Pilgrim! The fresh wind's delight
> Breathes icily from the eternal brine.

79

The sea that is greeted here is allegorical: just as the sea meets the gaze of this weary pilgrim, so too, Collins promises,'Undying Art' will find him in his 'wanderings wild and lone'. Collins is giving an aesthetic turn to a favourite moment of religious rapture: pilgrims would often shout as they caught sight of the end of their quest – rather as the crusaders shouted when they first saw Jerusalem from the heights they named Mons Gaudii (the Mountain of Joy). But it is not just because the pilgrim's spirits are restored by the sight of his goal that Collins bids us join him in a shout of 'Thalatta!'. His aesthetic fantasy also plays on the growing fascination that the sea itself had for the religious imagination of the nineteenth century.[28]

For Collins' Victorian audience, to hear the sea (Thoreau's 'Reverend Poluphloisboios Thalassa') and still more to look out on its endless expanse was to contemplate the power of God and the prospect of an afterlife. Philip Gosse, fundamentalist Christian and expert on marine life, could start a work on *The Ocean* by describing how the religious spirit was stirred by the sight of the sea: 'Standing on some promontory whence the eye roams far out upon the unbounded ocean, the soul expands, and we conceive a nobler idea of the majesty of that God, who holdeth "the waters in the hollow of His hand." ' A glimpse of this religious feeling is offered even by Jane Austen in her unfinished final work, *Sanditon*. This amusing satire on the social pretensions of the newly popular seaside resorts suddenly strikes a different note when the heroine, 'looking over the miscellaneous foreground of unfinished Buildings, waving Linen, and tops of Houses', catches sight of the sea, 'dancing and sparkling in Sunshine and Freshness': 'the vision, perhaps, of a dying woman – Austen's dream of a horizon', one critic has written, 'but also, arguably, the most transcendent passage she ever wrote'. Staring at the waves would be how other fictional heroes waited for death: the young Paul Dombey in Dickens' *Dombey and Son*, the blind village woman at the end of Skelton's novel. If death was like putting out to sea, then life itself could be imagined as a stream rising in the hills and flowing down to the sea (as in the closing lines of Matthew Arnold's poem 'The Buried Life') or else as a journey (in Tennyson's phrase) 'from the great deep to the great deep'.[29]

Small wonder that other nineteenth-century poets were tempted to give a religious colouring to the sea that was the end of Xenophon's march. Joseph Brownlee Brown, an American transcendentalist who also translated the *Iliad* into hexameters, succumbed to the temptation in a poem entitled 'Thalatta! Thalatta!: Cry of the Ten Thousand':

> I stand upon the summit of my life:
> Behind, the camp, the court, the field, the grove,
> The battle and the burden; vast, afar,
> Beyond these weary ways, Behold! the Sea!

Even from afar, the poet can feel the freshness of the sea 'whose mighty pulse is peace'. He gives the order: 'Cut loose the bark'. What awaits is: 'Eternity!—deliverance, promise, course! / Time-tired souls salute thee from the shore.' Like Mortimer Collins, Joseph Brownlee Brown here makes the sea an image of eternity that promises respite for the weary traveller. But the respite it offers is not mediated through a sensuous image of dancing Greek girls. The respite is rather the solemnity of salvation – the salvation promised in Wordsworth's 'Intimations of Immortality from Recollections of Early Childhood': 'Though inland far we be / Our Souls have sight of that immortal sea, / Which brought us hither.'[30]

The religious attractions of Xenophon's shout were most fully grasped by a woman called Jocelyn Hodgson in a short memoir published in 1944 with the title *Thalassa, Thalassa*. Hodgson (who wrote only this one book) cites Xenophon's sight of the sea in Greek on the title-page – and then re-interprets the cry of the sea by quoting the famous lines from Wordsworth's 'Intimations of Immortality'. In the memoir itself, she makes no mention of Xenophon. But her Xenophontic title is in line with the key image through which she interprets her life: the sense of discovering religion as a journey home.

Hodgson starts by describing her Edwardian childhood in Yorkshire. She developed a love for the sea at an early age, thanks to regular holidays in Whitby (like Mary McHugh leaving her childhood haunts in the West of Ireland, she would always look out of the window of her railway carriage for a last glimpse of the sea). But she was lonely and unhappy. She hated her father, and her mother died when she was an undergraduate at Cambridge. After her father's death, she was well enough off to lead a comfortable life in London – yet 'I was far from home, though I did not know it'. She sees in her own life and in the lives of her friends an unsatisfied quest. She finds home by abandoning her religious scepticism: 'home is that lovely world I see in glimpses, and long for every moment of my life, because I am exiled from it and am only a homeless wayfarer here.' And as she finishes writing her memoir, it is no longer spring, but autumn, and she is 'starting … on the one journey that has no end, the one journey that is worth while'.[31]

The journey which Hodgson wants to complete is figured as a journey to the sea. Her longing for a return to the sea is conveyed most deeply when she tells of a recurrent dream in which she imagines herself wandering along cobbled streets and dark alleys:

> I am alone in one of these mysterious passages. I cannot find the way out. I hear the sea beating on the distant shore, I hear my mother's voice calling to me, and the seagulls' loud cry, but I am lost for ever. Then I wake up in my narrow London bedroom, and the sea has gone, the seagulls' cry is stilled, and I have lost her, too, with my vanished youth.

Here the voice of the sea is the voice of the lost mother, and we see a hint that Hodgson's death-wish, her desire to complete her journey back to the sea, derives from a longing to recapture her vanished youth, to return to her mother. It is a muted expression of Swinburne's desire to go back 'to the great sweet mother, / Mother and lover of men, the sea'.[32]

The longing for a return to the sea could as easily be interpreted from a secular perspective. The German expressionist poet Gottfried Benn often used oceanic images to express a craving for the annihilation of individuality and a return to a primal state of unity. In his 1927 poem 'Regressive', he wrote that there is nowhere 'for your darkness to find rest' – except sometimes

> in smells
> from the beach, in the colours of corals,
> in fissions, breakdowns
> you raise the heavy eyelid of night:
>
> On the horizon, the ferry of mist,
> stygian blossoms, sleep and poppy,
> the tear burrows into the seas –
> for you: thalassal regression.

Here the triumph of a return to Xenophon's 'Thalassa' lies in the fulfilment of a death-wish – with no promise of personal salvation.[33]

Gottfried Benn's oceanic imagery could itself find parallels in the new discipline of psychoanalysis. The erotic attractions of the sea would naturally attract the attention of Freud: the heroes of those romantic novels triumphantly shouting 'Thalassa!' were experiencing something like the 'oceanic feeling' discussed in the first section of *Civilization and its Discontents*. A friend of Freud's, the writer Romain Rolland, had told him of 'a particular feeling of which he himself was never free … a feeling that he was inclined to call a sense of "eternity", a feeling of something limitless, unbounded – as it were "oceanic" '. While Rolland thought that this 'oceanic feeling' was 'the real source of religiosity', Freud himself thought that it sprang from the collapse of the boundaries built up in childhood between the ego and the world, and that this breakdown of the distinctions between internal and external was erotically driven. Gottfried Benn himself was particularly influenced by one of Freud's disciples, the Hungarian Sandor Ferenczi, who elaborated in his 1924 work *Versuch einer Genitaltheorie* the concept of the 'thalassal regressive trend': 'the striving towards the aquatic mode of existence abandoned in primeval times.' Ferenczi's thesis was that the trauma of humankind's original separation from the sea is transmitted across generations. The fate of the individual human being repeats the fate of the human race: 'ontogeny repeats phylogeny.' We all suffer from what some of Ferenczi's followers have called a 'thalassa complex' – and when Ferenczi's treatise was translated into English, the title it was given was not the literal and scientific *Attempt at a Theory of Genitality* but the eminently romantic *Thalassa*.[34]

*

The great popularity that Xenophon's shout acquired in the nineteenth century and continued to hold in the early decades of the twentieth century reflects a new feeling for the sea that developed in the Romantic era and was promoted by poetry like Heine's. This new feeling for the sea arose from a complex interplay of desires and fears: from a sense of distance from the sea, from a sense of alienation and loss, from an emptiness that needed to be filled. Xenophon's shout of the sea could become a religious cry of triumph as readily as it could stand for erotic fulfilment or for the unconscious desire to return to the mother, the womb, the sea. What might seem to be a cry of individual fulfilment and triumph expresses instead a yearning for the submersion of individual consciousness – a yearning for salvation figured as a return to the depths of the sea.

But why did this yearning for reunion with the primal sea come to be attached to the shout uttered by the Ten Thousand when they saw the sea? The very form of that shout made it a peculiarly fitting way to express a sense of yearning. The repetition 'Thalatta! Thalatta!', 'The Sea! The Sea!', seems to intimate a desire for the sea that has been aroused but that can never be satisfied, a romantic restlessness, a *Wanderlust*. A yearning as futile as Chekhov's three sisters longing for 'Moscow! Moscow!', the home of their childhood, and we know that they will not escape the wastelands of the provinces. A yearning felt also by the 'Birds of Passage' in a poem by the nineteenth-century Swedish poet Esaias Tegnér: 'Seized with desire for the land of our birth / We get in formation: the North! to the North!' ('Mot Norden! mot Norden'). But soon they cry 'all Southward away' ('Mot Söder! mot Söder!') – knowing all the same that they will 'wish once again for the Northland ere long'.[35]

The repetition of 'Thalatta! Thalatta!' could seem even more emotionally compelling in the context of Xenophon's powerful description of the scene on Mount Theches. By telling how he heard the shout of 'The Sea! The Sea!' as he rode forward to give support, Xenophon lets us share in the pleasure of discovery. What Xenophon had taken to be the noise of battle was in fact a cry of joy at the sight of the sea. Any reader who has followed Xenophon to the summit, and seen the soldiers embracing each other and weeping and setting up a great cairn, can understand why the critic George Saintsbury, while conceding that ' "fire" and "energy" are not exactly Xenophon's strongest points', still insisted that 'the famous "Thalatta" episode, with the

Euxine bursting on the eyes of seafarers by blood and custom after months in the plains of Mesopotamia and the rocks and glens of Kurdistan, can hardly be said to be lacking in either'. It was doubtless this passage that was in George Gissing's mind when he attributed to his fictional persona Henry Ryecroft the perception that the *Anabasis* is 'fresh with the air of mountain and of sea'. Most revealing is the way the geographer James Rennell responded to the great 'Thalatta' scene in his 1816 work on the route of the Ten Thousand: 'No one, we presume, (and indeed hope,) can read it without emotion. What a number of tender ideas must have crowded at once into their minds! The thoughts of home, wives, children, friends ... it was a prospect of DELIVERANCE; like an opening view of HEAVEN to DEPARTING SOULS!'. From Rennell's enthusiasm, we can grasp how easy it was to give 'Thalatta! Thalatta!' a metaphorical turn and make it stand for a religious or even an erotic fulfilment.[36]

Xenophon's account may be fresh and fiery, but some readers have searched in vain for some sign of a proper romantic sensitivity. When the blind Joseph Pulitzer listened to his secretary reading out Xenophon's account, he was greatly disappointed by its brevity. Xenophon had left something to the imagination. He did not show the Euxine bursting on the eyes.[37]

Another reader who greatly admired Xenophon, yet seems to have been disappointed by the scene on Mount Theches, was John Ruskin. That at least is what one might infer from a passage in *The Stones of Venice* (1851-3) where Ruskin criticized what he saw as the Greek tendency to reduce the irregularity of nature to a repetitive pattern. He based his polemic on a claim that the common Greek architectural decoration of spirals was a symbol of the sea:

> [Nature] will never hit her mark with those unruly waves of hers, nor get one of them into the ideal shape, if we wait for her a thousand years. Let us send for a Greek architect to do it for her. He comes – the great Greek architect, with measure and rule. ... He sets himself orderly to his work, and behold! this is the mark of Nature, and this is the thing into which the great Greek architect improves the sea ...

> Θάλαττα, θάλαττα: Was it this, then, that they wept to see from the sacred mountain – those wearied ones?

Ruskin here flatters his readers by presuming at least some knowledge of Greek and also a quite detailed acquaintance with the text of the *Anabasis*. It would not perhaps have been so hard to work out that 'those wearied ones' were Xenophon's Ten Thousand. But the oblique allusion to Mount Theches as 'the sacred mountain' could well have been baffling. At any rate, Ruskin's flattery is designed to further his argument. Ruskin is evoking the sort of sentimental readings of 'Thalatta! Thalatta!' which must have been familiar to his readers, and implying that he felt the force of those sentimental readings himself. But he also reacts against those readings by using a dull architectural motif to undermine the romance of Xenophon's shout. 'Was it this, then ...': the complicity Ruskin builds up with his readers strengthens the shared sense of deflation and disappointment. Yet readers might well object that Ruskin's argument is rather weak. He assumes without any evidence that the decorative motif of spirals both represents the sea and reflects a broader Greek perception of the regularity of the sea. It is only thanks to those two unwarranted steps that Ruskin can attribute to Xenophon's Greeks much the same feelings that Philip Glazebrook attributed to his young adventurer-to-be, Tresham Pitcher, as he looked out on the dull, monotonous waves: 'And this was supposed to be the sea! The Θαλασσα of Xenophon's poor soldiers!'.[38]

Xenophon's lack of romantic ardour has disappointed some readers, but others have found his account magnificent precisely because it is so simple. Sir Alexander Grant, writing twenty years after the publication of Ruskin's *Stones of Venice*, saw in Xenophon's description 'that Greek reserve and concentration of style which forms so great a contrast to the Gothic sentimentalism of modern times, and which led Xenophon to narrate the march through so many wild and impressive mountain-passes without a word of allusion to the grandeur of the scenery'. Grant's praise of Xenophon is a hit at Ruskin and his followers. Grant seems to be agreeing with Ruskin that the Greeks had a simple view of the sea, but while Ruskin censures that simplicity, Grant prefers it to Ruskin's Gothic sentimentalism.[39]

However absurd the claim that the Greeks reduced the vagaries of nature to mere regular patterns, Ruskin was right to sense that the sea that the weary Greeks saw from the sacred mountain was not quite the same as the sea that appealed to sentimental poets in the nineteenth century. The Ten Thousand were not aficionados of Heine, but a group of tough mercenaries. When they agreed to serve with Cyrus, they did not know that they would be led so far from the sea. But after they found themselves cut off in Mesopotamia they did at least fight their way back to the sea, and when they saw it they were glad, because the sea felt like home; it signalled a return to the familiar, the promise of renewed contact with fellow Greeks, and perhaps even an easy voyage along the Black Sea coast; and goodbye to all those mountains that Xenophon describes with a similar lack of aesthetic awe. The very simplicity of the Ten Thousand's joyful shout of 'Thalatta! Thalatta!' makes it a potent emblem of the Greeks' feeling for the sea. Other

Greeks did not have to bother shouting 'Thalatta! Thalatta!': the sea was all around them. When they looked out on the sea from the shore, they would more often be reminded of the sea's dangers than filled with awe or pleasure at its sublimity. If they did feel joy at the sight of the sea, it was more likely to be the pleasure described by the Roman poet Lucretius in a famous celebration of Epicurean detachment: 'Pleasant it is, when on the great sea the winds trouble the waters, to gaze from shore upon another's tribulation: not because any man's troubles are a delectable joy, but because to perceive what ills you are free from yourself is pleasant.' The joy of Xenophon's Greeks was more like the pleasure of sailors catching sight of the land – or Heine's pleasure as he takes refuge from the sea in a pub.[40]

When they shouted 'The Sea! The Sea!', Xenophon's Ten Thousand were expressing not a yearning for the primal sea, but a simple joy at their escape from the perils of the Asian interior. Perhaps, indeed, their shout was not 'The Sea! The Sea!' at all, but just 'Sea! Sea!' – as the 1947 translation by Rouse has it, and as the traveller Ainsworth had glossed it a century earlier; or 'Mer, Mer' – as the historian Charles Rollin had written a century before Ainsworth. To shout 'The Sea! The Sea!' is to address the sea whose romantic associations have been with us since childhood. To shout 'Sea! Sea!' – well, it is slightly odd English, but for all that it perhaps conveys better than the conventional translation the Greeks' simple and urgent excitement at the prospect of safety. A shout of 'Sea! Sea!' is like the 'Water! Water!' of Rider Haggard's heroes struggling through the arid wilderness of the African interior in *King Solomon's Mines*; or like the 'De l'eau! de l'eau!' of Jules Verne's adventurers journeying to the centre of the earth, after they have pressed on into the unknown, Columbus-like, despite a desperate thirst.[41]

However one translates the Ten Thousand's shout, it is the very simplicity of 'Thalatta! Thalatta!' that has rendered that shout open to a plethora of exotic elaborations. There are no signposts in 'The Sea! The Sea!': that shout has been an empty space onto which later readers can project the desires that the image of eternity fires in them. It is precisely because Xenophon leaves so much to the imagination that his description of the joyful scene on Mount Theches has had so rich an afterlife. When James Rennell, for instance, compared the Ten Thousand's sight of the sea with 'an opening view of HEAVEN to DEPARTING SOULS', he was giving a religious colouring to the undeniable sense of salvation imparted by Xenophon's account. In her 1872 *History of Greece for Children*, Caroline Ada Norton imported a different religious conception by imagining the first man to see the sea kneeling in gratitude (rather as Balboa is said to have knelt when he first saw the Pacific). It is not that the sense of salvation in Xenophon is totally secular: rather as pilgrims elsewhere sometimes raise a heap of stones when they first see their goal (a custom noted, for instance, by Vita Sackville-West when she travelled in Persia), Xenophon describes how the Ten Thousand

1. The cover of a Swiss artist's Second World War memoir
– a sinking ship drowning out dreams of freedom.

2. 'Perhaps we can soon celebrate with the classic greeting Tallata Tallata': Nansen's ship, the *Fram*, trapped in the ice in 1895.

3. The advance on Akaba (1917), photographed by T.E. Lawrence: 'If "Thalassa, Thalassa" was not on his lips, it was in his thoughts.'

4. 'Again Xenophon supplied a precedent': Kurds swimming on inflated goatskins awakened memories of the schoolroom for soldiers in the Middle East in the First World War.

5. Agatha Christie (*far left*) surveying her husband Max Mallowan's excavations at Nimrud in the 1950s – and the ziggurat Xenophon had noticed twenty-three centuries earlier.

6. Between the woods and the water: Dirk Bogarde plays Patrick Leigh Fermor leading a kidnapped German general across the mountains of Crete in *Ill Met by Moonlight* (1957).

7. 'Westward Ho!': the English attachment to the sea was fostered in childhood by tales of adventure – and paintings like John Everett Millais' *Boyhood of Raleigh* (1870).

8. The artist as romantic hero – Benjamin Robert Haydon, 'a tempestuous and luckless blend of idealism, megalomania, and paranoia'. Portrait by Georgiana Zornlin (1825).

9. The triumph of High Art: Haydon's painting of *Xenophon and the Ten Thousand on First Seeing the Sea from Mount Theches* (1829-31).

10. Theodore Géricault's *Raft of the Medusa* (1818-19), the most famous of all romantic shipwreck paintings.

11. A mountain of the mind: the scene on Mount Theches conjured up for Edwardian children.

12. The death of High Art: Haydon depicts himself as the Roman hero Marcus Curtius sacrificing himself for his city in *Marcus Curtius Leaping into the Gulf* (1836-42).

13. The romance of eastern travel: Francis Rawdon Chesney travelling on the Euphrates by raft.

14. The novelist and scholar Valerio Massimo Manfredi admires the cairn set up by the Ten Thousand.

15. 'A sight to awaken thrilling feelings of delight': Trabzon guide Tenir Demirbulut points out the view of the sea enjoyed by the Ten Thousand.

16. 'Still the towers of Trebizond, the fabled city, shimmer on a far horizon ...': Trebizond in the 1890s, before the factories arrived.

17. 'The snotgreen sea. The scrotumtightening sea. ... *Thalatta! Thalatta!*': the Martello tower from whose battlements Buck Mulligan declaims as he looks out over Dublin Bay.

18. 'When we see the ocean, we figure we're home, we're safe': the Warriors, back home on Coney Island, confront their false accuser in *The Warriors* (1979).

"THALATTA! THALATTA!"

*General chorus (as the children's excursion nears its desti-
nation).* "Oh, I say! There's the sea! 'Ooray!!"
Small boy. "I'll be in fust!"

19. A *Punch* cartoon links the shout of the Ten Thousand with a party of school-children on a trip to the sea.

set up a cairn on Mount Theches and offered some dedications on it. But Xenophon has no notion of the religious sea that inspired Rennell's flight of fancy.[42]

James Rennell was also offloading his own desires on to Xenophon's understated text when he imagined the Ten Thousand thinking of 'home, wives, children, friends'. Many others have pictured the scene in similar terms: the historian John Gillies wrote that 'a sight so long wished in vain ... recalled more distinctly the remembrance of their parents, their friends, their country, and every object of their most tender concern', while the traveller and artist Sir Robert Ker Porter pictured 'the hardiest veterans' bursting into tears and embracing each other 'in the fond hope of soon returning to their wives and children'. The Polish poet K.M. Górski injected the same vein of romance into his poem 'Thalatta' by imagining the soldiers' wives at home, 'staring at the waves yearning' (but he closed with the picture of slave women sitting at the fire and spinning). This romantic vein is not altogether alien to the world of the Ten Thousand: Xenophon does mention that they longed for their parents and wives when their position seemed hopeless after the murder of the generals. But he allows the Ten Thousand no such thoughts of home when they see the sea: he leaves it to his readers to imagine what the soldiers were thinking – and they have obliged.[43]

Xenophon also fails the romantic test by not paying adequate attention to the sea. 'You are Greeks no longer, three months' march from the sea,' a Persian horseman tells the Ten Thousand – not in Xenophon's account, but in Stephen Marlowe's *The Shining*, a historical novel about the Ten Thousand. This Persian horseman's words are parasitical upon the fame of the shout of 'Thalatta! Thalatta!'. That shout dominates the thoughts of later storytellers as they recount the earlier stages of the Ten Thousand's march. They feel compelled to offer their readers little nudges to remind them of the great climax to which the narrative is leading. In Xenophon's original, by contrast, there is no build-up to the sight of the sea – beyond their guide's promise that he would lead them in five days to a spot from which they could see the sea.[44]

Xenophon is as restrained in his description of the sea itself as he is in the run-up to the great scene on Mount Theches. Later writers have made up for Xenophon's apparent shortcomings. In his 'Sea-Greeting', Heine filled the gaps in Xenophon's account by providing a much more immediate engagement with the sea – a picture of the waters rolling and roaring and the seagulls shrilling and squealing. The popular novelist Blanche Willis Howard followed Heine's lead in her story 'Thalatta' when she imagined a vast expanse of rocky coasts, and the sea surging gloriously, and a group of strong men hailing it with cries of joy. Equally stirring was the scene on Mount Theches pictured by the Austrian dramatist Franz Csokor as he travelled down to the Mediterranean coast in 1938: 'the smell of salt in a clear sky and the shrieking of gulls, a rolling and clapping as if from an unseen battle, and then there it was – the Sea!'. Vivid scenes such as these might have made more satisfying listening for the blind Joseph Pulitzer. But even if Xenophon had had the sensitivity of a Heine, the Greeks were much too far from the sea to see the waves or hear the gulls. Five days' march away, they would have seen just a distant streak, but that was enough for them after all their days in the desert and the hostile hills.[45]

By hoisting on to the Ten Thousand's great shout of 'The Sea! The Sea!' the fantasies and desires roused in them by the sight and sound of the sea, Heine and his followers have done much to increase the pleasure of reading Xenophon. Whether or not they have increased understanding of the *Anabasis* itself does not matter. It is precisely because of the freedom they have taken with 'Thalatta! Thalatta!' that they have secured its place in the modern consciousness.

But can Xenophon do anything for the sea in return? Perhaps he can. It is refreshing to return to the simplicity of Xenophon after the almost Wagnerian death-yearnings of Gottfried Benn's 'thalassal regression'. As the American historian Samuel Eliot Morison, biographer of Columbus, and no mean lover of the sea, said in an address to a college audience, 'it is in the simple things of life, like the primitive sport of sailing, that the ancients enhance the joy of living'; and just as 'at each new landfall our hearts leap a bit higher from the memory of that spirited passage in the *Aeneid* when Italy is first sighted', so too 'the sea itself we love the better for the shout that swept through Xenophon's Ten Thousand at the sight of it so many centuries ago.' Morison was speaking three months before the outbreak of the Second World War: before too long, the shout that swept through the Ten Thousand would not just be inspiring a new generation of college students to relish the freedom of the sea but standing for a nation's will to preserve its freedom.[46]

5

The Sea is English

May 1940. As the soldiers retreated towards the coast, they would pass charred corpses, burnt-out farmhouses, flattened villages, women and children pushing their belongings in prams, not knowing where they were going. There were other sights they would recall later – four colleagues carrying a wounded young soldier in a blanket for mile after mile, a soldier resting against a sack until one came closer and saw that half his head was blown away. If they were luckier they might find some champagne to drink in an abandoned cellar. As they drew nearer to the sea, they would see more and more vehicles abandoned by the road side, some damaged by enemy aircraft, others disabled by their own men. Often they would have to march in single file – and even then they would often have to break off to seek cover in a ditch whenever they saw a Stuka dropping like a stone to release its bombs. Finally they had to destroy their own gear, even the cases of champagne they had pilfered in the retreat. And all the time they would look across the flat and marshy land towards the north, straining to catch the smell of the sea, or even a glimpse of the sea itself in a gap in the dunes. But even from a distance there had been one sight that had dominated everyone's view: 'as we approached the coast,' one officer recalled, 'the clear blue of the sky on the horizon was darkened by an immense pillar of black smoke that stood up straight from the ground. Someone said it was Dunkirk.'[1]

The last ships left Dunkirk in the early hours of 4 June. Later that day Winston Churchill told the House of Commons that 'we shall fight on the beaches, we shall fight on the landing grounds, we shall fight in the fields and in the streets, we shall fight in the hills ...'. Churchill's words grabbed the world's attention. But what met the eyes of readers of *The Times* that day? Turning to the editorial page, they would have seen that the main leader was headed 'ANABASIS'. This leader sought inspiration from an ancient Greek army which never surrendered:

> Just a week has passed since the sudden defection of KING LEOPOLD of the BELGIANS struck a chill of apprehension into English and French hearts, lest an admittedly grave strategic reverse should develop into something much more terrible – the destruction of an army. Such an outcome must at that moment

The Sea! The Sea!

have been the natural expectation of the German High Command; that the danger should have been wholly diverted in a week of the fiercest fighting in the history of war is the measure of the feat of arms that has been achieved. The source of the power that has made it possible, and the nature of the enemy's miscalculation, are apparent in the naive propaganda sheet that he has attempted to distribute among our troops. In it they are invited to surrender on the ground that the Allied army is 'encircled'. It is a natural mistake for a people whose record of fighting successes is confined to the land. Such men will regard an army that has been forced back to the coast – 'driven into the sea' is probably the phrase they use – as rats caught in a trap. But that is not how Englishmen think of the sea; and no British army is encircled if a way to the sea is open or can be forced. British soldiers look on blue water as did the Greek army of XENOPHON, whose cry of θάλαττα, θάλαττα! was the climax of the Anabasis, and marked the successful completion of the most famous march of the ancient world.[2]

It was only when the officer had arrived at the immense pillar of black smoke that he gained his first glimpse of the sea. He later described the sense of relief that he felt as an Englishman: he was now as good as home. He remembered peacetime Dunkirk as a pleasant enough place, and was now at least hoping for some breakfast and a bath, and then a morning crossing. It was only after he had caught this glimpse of the sea that he heard about the bombing, and realized that the pillar of smoke came from the burning oil tanks. He did not look at the sea for long. Soon he was taking refuge in a cellar with sixty other men. But at least it was a rich man's cellar, and foie-gras and champagne formed the staple food and drink, and someone even gave a stray dog a taste of the foie-gras, but the dog vomited it out in a corner.[3]

In the rich sentences of the *Times* editorial, contemporary events were endowed with the superlative stature of epic: a week of 'the fiercest fighting in the history of war' bears comparison in some sense with 'the most famous march of the ancient world'. One might quibble about both claims. 'A week of the fiercest fighting'? Perhaps. 'The most famous march'? Alexander the Great's murderous progress through Asia seems to have been forgotten. One might quibble, too, about the comparison between the retreat to Dunkirk and Xenophon's March to the Sea. The force that retreated to the coast at Dunkirk was much larger, travelled a much shorter distance, and faced much less severe terrain and weather but more intensive fighting. The German invitation to the British to surrender on the grounds that they were 'encircled' does, however, suggest two further reasons for the comparison between the two retreats: Xenophon's Greeks had been encircled by hostile rivers, mountains, and peoples, and they too had rejected a demand to surrender and hand over their weapons, and successfully evaded capture.

Whatever the similarities between the two retreats, thoughts of 'Thalatta!

Thalatta!' were fitting at a time when the English claim to look on the sea as their own was itself being bolstered by the way the evacuation from Dunkirk was portrayed: 'There in the sea were England and her ships / They sailed with the free salt upon their lips / To sunlight from the tomb.' 'Thalatta! Thalatta!' suited the tale of heroic redemption that the British built out of the disaster in France. That exclamation had often sounded to later ears like a cry of victory ('wie Siegesruf', in Heine's poem) – a victory snatched out of defeat. It was not that the Greek contingent had been defeated at the battle of Cunaxa. It had, Xenophon assures us, been a victory where the Greeks were fighting, and it was only Cyrus' impetuous attack on his brother that had lost the day. But they had been in a tight spot after Cyrus' death, and they had got out, and it was that getting out of a fix that was so admirable – that retreat that seemed to John Ruskin 'more honourable than a hundred victories', that retreat 'whose glory not the prime / Of victories can reach', as James Thomson had written in his poem *Liberty*. Even before Dunkirk, the British had been attached to displays of courage and endurance in adversity. No surprise, then, that Xenophon's cry of victory – or rather, his celebration of a retreat better than a victory – was also appealing when the myth of Dunkirk itself was being created. That cry conveyed a longing for freedom – and the conviction that the cause of freedom would triumph.[4]

*

It was not just one London newspaper that yielded to the temptation to draw comparisons between the Ten Thousand and the British Expeditionary Force in France. Xenophon's shout was also celebrated in the aftermath of the Dunkirk evacuation in a short book on *The Battle for Flanders 1940* written by Ian Hay, well-known author of school stories and of a First World War best-seller, *The First Hundred Thousand*. Hay's Dunkirk book was propaganda of a more official sort. It was based on Lord Gort's Official Dispatches, and issued in a series 'The Army at War' by the War Office, where Hay was then working as Director of Public Relations. The campaign was solemnly described as a 'tragedy'. But it was 'redeemed by a heroic, superhuman conclusion'. And the title of the final chapter of this quasi-religious tale of redemption? 'Thalassa, Thalassa!'[5]

One of the British officers at Dunkirk was struck by another similarity between the ancient Greek and the modern British army. Recalling how at the start of the battle of Cunaxa Cyrus told Clearchus to move the Greeks away from the right flank, by the River Euphrates, and to have them charge directly against the Persian king, he compared Clearchus' position 'with that of Lord Gort in 1940, when he had to decide whether to stick to the French or stick to the sea'. Just as Lord Gort decided to stick to the sea, so too Clearchus decided to disobey Cyrus' order and stick to the Euphrates. They were both afraid of finding themselves encircled. Yet the British were allies of the French, not mercenaries in their pay. And it seems forced to compare the key British decision to strike back to the sea with a decision made when the Greeks were still in Cyrus' pay and there was not yet any question that they would find themselves stranded and forced to retreat by themselves to the sea. Perhaps this comparison would not have occurred to this British officer (Lieutenant-Colonel M.C.A. Henniker, D.S.O., O.B.E., M.C., R.E.) had not Xenophon's account 'lurked in the back of my mind ever since I heard at Dunkirk the words, "The sea! The sea!" ripple through the ranks of the soldiers'. It was that intense moment that led him, ten years later, to write an article on ' "The Sea! The Sea!" ' for the *Army Quarterly* (thanks to some leave at a hotel where 'a lady of fabulous scholarship' was staying).[6]

Churchill himself felt the same desire to see history in Xenophontic terms. When he wrote his account of the British withdrawal from France and Belgium for his *History of the Second World War*, he called one chapter 'The March to the Sea'. That heading, with its slight evocation of Xenophon, was much more dignified and heroic than, say, 'The Run for the Coast' (the chapter title in one modern account debunking Dunkirk as 'a necessary myth'). Indeed, it is the emotional appeal of the March to the Sea that explains the slightly paradoxical heading of that *Times* leader on Dunkirk. The term 'anabasis' should properly be applied to a march up country, away from the coast. Here it is applied to a retreat to the coast – to use the proper Greek term, a 'katabasis' ('going down', 'descent'). The March to the Sea has usurped the name of Cyrus' march up country: it is somehow assumed that the title of Xenophon's work should refer to the famous part of it. And Anabasis seems more uplifting than Katabasis.[7]

*

Both the British pride in their resilience and the British feeling for the sea were at stake when, a year after the retreat to Dunkirk, Xenophon was again used to impart an uplifting message in a short radio play *The March of the Ten Thousand* written by Louis MacNeice for the BBC. The play was MacNeice's first drama for radio (he joined the BBC staff shortly afterwards). He wrote the script (which is still unpublished) during a trip to Oxford in March 1941, in a flat in Oriel Square, and perhaps, his biographer Jon Stallworthy suggests, under the influence of his friend E.R. Dodds, Regius Professor of Greek at Oxford. The play was broadcast on the General Overseas Service on 16 April, with the script slightly compressed to fit into fifteen minutes: it was a much shorter and slighter piece than some of MacNeice's later and more famous radio plays like *Christopher Columbus* and *The Dark Tower*.[8]

Why did MacNeice choose to adapt Xenophon's story for his first radio drama? MacNeice's writings contain many other allusions to Xenophon, but even without knowledge of those allusions the date of the radio play tells its own story. A play in April 1941 about a Greek retreat to the sea, a triumph over adversity, could hardly fail to recall the British retreat to Dunkirk a year earlier.

It would not have been hard for listeners to pick up the contemporary resonances of MacNeice's play. There was some anachronistic language: a soldier tells how 'the Kurds sniped' at them with arrows. The soldiers' into-nation would also have had a modern feel: the script specifies that the Spartan Clearchus should speak with a Yorkshire accent. The most poetic part of the work, a verse prayer to the North Wind, would perhaps remind listeners that the British forces stranded at Dunkirk had been helped by divine intervention after a nationwide service of prayer (or so the *Sunday Dispatch* claimed at the time, noting that the 'notoriously rough' English Channel 'became as calm and smooth as a pond' while a fog shielded the troops from the air). Above all there was the play's retrospective narrator, whose commentary was interspersed with flashbacks to the march itself (a technique found in several of MacNeice's later radio plays). The narrator sets the scene for the march: 'It was after the great war – the war between Athens and Sparta.' The impact of that phrase 'the great war', with a pause before the explanation, is obvious enough. Later the narrator notes that some put the blame for the defeat at Cunaxa on Clearchus' refusal to follow Cyrus' instructions to lead the Greeks against the king: 'he *would* stick to the rules – last war methods, you know.'[9]

The identity of this narrator is surprising – and another hint of the contemporary overtones of MacNeice's play. It is not Xenophon, as we might expect. It is not even one of the Greek mercenaries. The narrator is simply 'The Lady' – a flute-girl accompanying the expedition who had also been the girlfriend of Clearchus. And yet the very title of the play, *The March of the Ten Thousand*, seems to exclude women along with the other camp followers – the people who sold or made food, the people who carried baggage, the slave boys some of the soldiers slept with. It was all too easy to forget that there were such camp followers battling along with the merce-naries through the passes of Kurdistan: Thomas De Quincey wrote in an 1837 essay that the presence of Greek women on the march was 'singular ... and not generally known'.[10]

Why did MacNeice highlight the experiences of the women on the march? Dunkirk, a myth of male endurance, does not provide the right context. Perhaps MacNeice's 'Lady' should rather be explained by the Blitz. Women were exposed as much as men to the bombs that were falling on London and Coventry and other cities from the air. MacNeice himself stressed the sufferings of female civilians in a radio series aimed at the United States, 'The Stones Cry Out': his first contribution for this series, a programme on Dr Johnson's House broadcast three weeks after his play on the Ten Thousand, included 'an indomitable old lady represent[ing] war-time Londoners'.[11]

While the frame of MacNeice's play may involve some chattering women, the flashbacks are entirely devoted to soldiers. And it is through the words of these men that MacNeice's political message comes across most strongly. They do not want to 'fight for any lousy dictator'. They want to get back to a 'free country' – to Greece, where there is 'freedom to say what you like and live the way you want to – that's what there is in Greece, and that's what I want'. The freedom they want is democratic. So it was not just because they had triumphed over adversity that these freedom-loving Greek soldiers appealed to the British at the time of Dunkirk. They stood both for freedom against foreign threats and for freedom at home.

It is in portraying these soldiers that MacNeice makes his most striking departure from Xenophon's story. Whereas Xenophon focuses on the generals, MacNeice focuses on the common soldiers. The Yorkshire accent of Clearchus ('a real brute', his girlfriend affectionately recalls) is heard only once, and Xenophon never speaks at all (he is alluded to just once – as 'an Athenian, bit of a highbrow'). It is not that MacNeice glorifies the Ten Thousand extravagantly: they are a 'rough bunch of fellows' doing 'just a job of work'. All the more telling that this ordinary bunch rises to the challenge. It is the common soldiers who refuse to surrender when the Persian king sends his demand for the Greeks to surrender ('Speaking from Persia, three times' is scrawled in the margin of the script, with a 'B.B.C. voice': presumably we should imagine 'This is Persia speaking …'). And it is one of the common soldiers who makes a proposal that Xenophon attributes to himself: 'We'll *elect* a new lot of generals. Eh, mates?'. As the Lady remarks: 'What you might call democratic.' And in the prayer to the North Wind the soldiers assert that 'now in the face of the vast / Negations of the east we are all of one mind – / A walking city in the face of death.' The play as a whole celebrates this walking democracy with its homely portrayal of soldiers battling against the odds.

MacNeice included in his original script some passages drawn from Xenophon which showed the Ten Thousand in a more brutal than homely way. There was talk of a soldier who tried to bury alive a wounded comrade, and of how the Greeks burnt out some of the natives who would not sell food, and attacked a mountain fortress, and the native women started throwing themselves and their children down a cliff-face – 'a shocking sight'. All of these passages were cut from the final version: they would have undermined the sense of triumphant conclusion.

How was the triumphant conclusion conveyed? First, a flashback to the soldiers as they approach the sea: 'Soon you'll see the sea. Soon you'll be home.' In the verse ode to the North Wind, more on the lure of the sea: 'there you feel alive, with the salt in the air, / Salt from the sea to sharpen

the wits / And to keep you from sinking away into any mirage of dreams.'
We then follow the rearguard: first, joy as they are promised that they will
soon be able to see the sea. But doubts emerge: 'Didn't you hear the news?
The sea is all dried up.' And then (as in Xenophon's own account) some
confused noises in the distance – 'some more blasted savages' ('natives',
MacNeice first wrote, but that word was changed throughout to 'savages').
The shouting grows louder and louder, and at the same time clearer and
clearer – 'THALATTA! THALATTA!'. And one of the soldiers is heard: 'It's the
sea, brother, it's the sea.' At least that is what MacNeice's typescript has.
But the shout was changed – to 'The sea, the sea!'. Greek was fine for *The
Times*, but not for the radio.

MacNeice's short adaptation of the *Anabasis* makes Xenophon's tale part
of an English story. But it was not just an English story that MacNeice was
telling. His play was produced at a time when the Germans were invading
that free country, Greece: a few months later, MacNeice would look back to
another ancient paradigm, the three hundred Spartans at Thermopylae, in a
feature on 'The Glory that is Greece' commemorating the first anniversary of
Greece's entry into the war. By then, his play's implied comparison with the
British retreat to Dunkirk had gained a new resonance. The Germans struck
with such speed that they cut off a section of the British army in Northern
Greece, under Mount Olympus, and, like the British Expeditionary Force,
these men had to be rescued by sea.[12]

Further in the future when MacNeice wrote his play was another joint
Greek-British enterprise that invited comparison with Xenophon. After the
German occupation of Crete and the humiliating British withdrawal, two
British soldiers who remained on the island helping the Cretan resistance,
Billy Moss and Patrick Leigh Fermor (later famous for his travel books),
dressed in German uniform and held up the car of General Kreipe, the
German divisional commander, as he was being driven home one evening.
The kidnappers left the general's car by the sea and made across the moun-
tains for the southern coast, evading their German pursuers with local help.
As the sun hit the snowy peak of Mount Ida one morning, General Kreipe
was moved to quote the start of Horace's Soracte ode – and gratified when
Leigh Fermor finished the quotation. Another classical quotation was apt
some days later. Kreipe was close to collapse as the party made its way up
another hill ('Cheer up, sir, soon be dead,' Moss encouraged him). As some
Cretan soldiers at the head of the line crested a hill, their shout was heard by
the men in the rear: 'Thalassa! Thalassa!'. 'What is it?' Billy Moss asked – and
Leigh Fermor was at once able to tell him: 'It's the sea.' Or that, at least, is
how the scene was portrayed in *Ill Met by Moonlight*, a film about the
escapade made in 1957 (a year after 'the last retreat' – the humiliation of
Suez) by Michael Powell and Emeric Pressburger (with Dirk Bogarde
playing the part of the erudite and Byronic Leigh Fermor: see Plate 6). In the

book by Billy Moss that gave the film its title (except, at least, in the United States, where the less Shakespearean *Night Ambush* was preferred), it was misty and towards evening when the group crossed the peak that should have given them a view of the sea. A more visually appealing scene was required for the big screen – and what better way to restore British (or for that matter Cretan) military honour than a shout of Xenophontic joy?[13]

*

How did Xenophon's exclamation acquire the link with the British feeling for the sea and for national freedom that it had gained by the time of the Dunkirk evacuation? The story starts with James Thomson's poem *Liberty*, first published in 1735-6.

Thomson's poem (spoken by the goddess Liberty herself) describes the origins of liberty at Sparta and Athens, and then its spread to the other Greek states. It praises the fighting strength that liberty gave the Greeks, and illustrates this by recounting briefly the battles of Thermopylae and Marathon and then the Retreat of the Ten Thousand Greeks. This order breaches chronology (the heroic resistance of the three hundred Spartans at Thermopylae was ten years after the Athenian victory at Marathon), but matches the earlier progression of liberty that Thomson traced from Sparta to Athens and then to the rest of Greece. The sequence closes with a ringing repetition of the Ten Thousand's famous shout – a repetition that seems all the more resonant when one recalls that that shout was echoed by scarcely any other poet before the Romantic era:

> The Sea at last from *Colchian* Mountains seen,
> Kindhearted Transport round their Captains threw
> The Soldier's fond Embrace; o'erflow'd their Eyes
> With tender Floods, and loos'd the general Voice
> To Cries resounding loud – *The Sea! the Sea!*

Thomson then describes how the arts flourished among the ancient Greeks until they fought amongst themselves and lost their liberty; and how liberty arose again first in Rome and then in Britain. In other words, he incorporates Xenophon's March to the Sea in a pointed historical development culminating in the rediscovery of Liberty in modern Britain.[14]

Thomson makes the Ten Thousand part of the story of Greek liberty by aligning them with the heroes of the Persian Wars, the heroes who resisted the Persian invaders by land and sea. The Ten Thousand only saved themselves by their retreat to the sea, but many others have thought that the spirit of Marathon and Salamis, the victories of Greek liberty in 490 and 480 BC, was revived in them. In an address on the value of a classical education delivered before he became President, Calvin Coolidge wrote that 'there is a glory in the achievements of the Greeks under Themistocles, there is an admiration for the heroes of Salamis, there is even a pride in the successful retreat of the Ten Thousand'. He could have spared that 'even': James Thomson devotes nineteen lines to the Ten Thousand in *Liberty* – while the battles of Thermopylae and Marathon together receive only seven.[15]

Thomson's alignment of the Ten Thousand with the heroes of the Persian Wars sits uneasily alongside his later analysis of Greek decline. In keeping with neo-classical political thought, Thomson saw Greek history as following a familiar cycle: 'need engenders virtue and courage, courage results in aggression, leading to success and prosperity; prosperity leads to the self-indulgence of luxury, eventual enervation, and final defeat.' He contrasts the time when arms were 'only drawn / For common GREECE, to quell the *Persian* Pride' with the time 'when GREECE with GREECE / Embroil'd in foul Contention, fought no more / For common Glory', and when Sparta and Athens appealed to Persia for help, 'to be venal Parricides'. By 'Barbaric Gold', the Persian King 'Effect'd what his Steel could ne'er perform': that is, he corrupted the Greeks by luxury. Thomson claims, then, that internal discord cost the Greeks the liberty preserved in the Persian Wars and in the march of the Ten Thousand. Yet the war between Sparta and Athens which saw the Greeks embroiled in contention in fact preceded the Ten Thousand's retreat. And the Ten Thousand had themselves been attracted by barbaric gold (Thomson omits to explain how they came to be stuck so far from home in the first place).[16]

Why then does Thomson pay even more attention to the Ten Thousand than to the soldiers who defended Greek liberty in the Persian Wars? Perhaps because the Ten Thousand were 'by the SAGE-EXALTED CHIEF / Fir'd and sustain'd'. That is, they were led and inspired by a man who had been taught by Socrates. Xenophon's Socratic connection was especially stressed in the eighteenth century by influential ethical thinkers like Shaftesbury, who put him on a par with, if not above, Plato. Thomson himself goes on to hail 'the great ATHENIAN SAGE' as the sun 'From whose white Blaze emerg'd each various Sect / Took various Teints' – including 'the bold Poetic Phrase / Of figur'd PLATO' and 'XENOPHON's pure Strain'. Slightly odd this, since Xenophon was not normally regarded as the founder of a separate philosophical school like Plato's Academy. Thomson's stress on Xenophon the philosopher-general is particularly pointed because he emphasizes elsewhere that mental freedom is the foundation of political freedom. 'Yielded Reason speaks the Soul a slave,' and the Greeks themselves were first enslaved in the mind, by '*Persian* Fetters' (that is, Persian money), before they were enslaved in the flesh by Philip of Macedon.[17]

Thomson's praise of the Ten Thousand was also influenced by one of his main sources for ancient history, the recently published *Histoire ancienne* by

Charles Rollin, with its 'naïve and popular presentation of ancient history in terms of civic virtue and republicanism'. Devotion to liberty was the key part of this civic virtue. Rollin presented the Ten Thousand as supported by 'the warm desire of preserving their liberty', and he described the retreat itself as 'the boldest and best conducted exploit to be found in antient history'. But the desire for liberty that Rollin and Thomson praised is something very different from the freedom that MacNeice's soldiers want. Whereas MacNeice's freedom was a specifically democratic freedom, Rollin and Thomson were not admirers of Athenian democracy. Thomson himself was part of Whig opposition to Robert Walpole, and a supporter of the Prince of Wales, to whom the poem *Liberty* was dedicated. For the Whigs, liberty meant the constitutional and religious protection gained in the 'Glorious Revolution' of 1688. Thomson can admire Sparta's mixed government while applying to Athens the nautical imagery typical of opponents of democracy: 'rash *Democracy* at Athens was checked by Solon who 'allay'd the Tempest' and fixed the state with the 'Anchor' of 'two Senates' (the Areopagus and the Council).[18]

While the seeds of the celebration of the Ten Thousand in the aftermath of the Dunkirk evacuation lie in the eighteenth-century celebration of Greek liberty and of Xenophon himself as a great culture hero, what of the feeling for the sea shown in their exultant shout of 'The Sea! The Sea!'? No wonder that shout appealed to Thomson – the man who a few years later wrote the words of 'Rule Britannia'. Greeks who had never been slaves were saluting the waves that the British now ruled. Thomson makes their triumphant cry a timeless assertion of the Greek and British devotion to liberty and to the sea.

And yet the rest of Thomson's celebration of Greek liberty makes it seem slightly odd that he closes the retreat of the Ten Thousand with the grand climax of 'The Sea! The Sea!'. Elsewhere Thomson fails to make much of the Greeks' devotion to the sea. He picks two famous land battles from the Persian Wars, and not the great naval victory at Salamis. And it is mercantile Phoenicia, not Athens, that is an 'Earnest of BRITAIN'. Could it then be that Thomson echoed Xenophon's shout simply because he was imitating the plain style of a historian like Rollin? 'As he approached nearer, the cry of *the sea! the sea!* was heard distinctly, and the alarm changed into joy and gaiety, and when they came to the top, nothing was heard but a confused noise of the whole army crying out together, *the sea! the sea!* who could not refrain from tears, or from embracing their generals and officers.' That was Rollin's version, and like him Thomson follows Xenophon's grammar of the emotions – tears, embraces, the shout itself. Perhaps Thomson was simply stirred by the profound simplicity of Xenophon's artful artlessness.[19]

*

5. The Sea is English

The temptation to follow the grand historical narrative of James Thomson's *Liberty* became stronger in the aftermath of the Napoleonic Wars. But now the Ten Thousand came to be celebrated for another sort of freedom. Whereas James Thomson had held up for admiration the liberty won through Xenophon's Socratic reason, it now became more common to praise the spirit that animated the Ten Thousand as a whole rather than just that one Athenian general – and also to see it as a distinctively Athenian spirit. James Rennell implied as much when he drew the epigraph for his 1816 geographical work on the *Anabasis* from Pericles' Funeral Oration in Thucydides – a celebration of the Athenian character. In the work itself, Rennell praised the Greeks' comradeship, above all as it was revealed when they catch sight of the sea: 'Military discipline was dissolved in an instant; and the SOLDIER was lost in the MAN.' But he also stressed the institutional framework within which the Greek army – 'a kind of Republic' – operated, electing its own generals, much as the troops in the recent Lewis and Clark expedition across North America had done. Here we see the roots of Louis MacNeice's stress on the Ten Thousand as a democracy, 'a walking city'. MacNeice was there echoing a familiar refrain in criticism on the *Anabasis*. The French philosopher Hippolyte Taine had called the army a 'travelling republic which deliberates and acts, which fights and votes, a sort of Athens wandering in the middle of Asia'. The comparison with Athens was also taken up by Edith Hamilton in a chapter added in 1942 for the second edition of her popular work *The Greek Way* (which later became *The Greek Way to Western Civilization*). Hamilton described the *Anabasis* as 'the story of the Greeks in miniature':

> Ten thousand men, fiercely independent by nature, in a situation where they were a law unto themselves, showed that they were pre-eminently able to work together and proved what miracles of achievement willing co-operation can bring to pass. The Greek state, at any rate the Athenian state, which we know best, showed the same. What brought the Greeks safely back from Asia was precisely what made Athens great.[20]

The most influential proponent of this democratic vision of the Ten Thousand was George Grote in his great *History of Greece* published between 1846 and 1856. Grote wrote his history as an unashamed spokesman for Athens and democracy. A follower of the utilitarian philosophy of his friends Bentham and Mill, Grote had himself been an active supporter of political reform earlier in his career, and elected to the reformed Parliament in 1832. His history was written at a time when the lessons to be learnt from the rise and fall of the Athenian democracy were much debated: it was in a review of this work that Mill famously claimed that the Battle of Marathon was a more important event for English history than the Battle of Hastings.

Grote said nothing as fanciful as that about Xenophon's account of the Ten Thousand, but he did find much there to support his advocacy of democracy; and this political message perhaps explains the extraordinary detail with which he retold a story that in a sense has little claim to be part of the history of Greece. He stressed in particular the political organization of the army: Xenophon, he argued, 'insists on the universal suffrage of the whole body, as the legitimate sovereign authority for the guidance of every individual will'. And he also brought Athens to the fore whenever possible by stressing the advantages of Xenophon's upbringing – 'accomplishments belonging in an especial manner to the Athenian democracy and education' – even though he thought that Xenophon himself viewed Athens with 'the positive antipathy of an exile'. While James Thomson had highlighted Xenophon's links with Socrates, Grote gave most weight to Xenophon's rhetorical training. It was no accident that his long treatment of the Ten Thousand followed on from the two famous chapters on the Sophists and Socrates, where he rehabilitated the sophistic mode of education reviled by most historians and philosophers since that great opponent of Athenian democracy, Plato.[21]

*

Once the stigma of the Platonic attack on Athens' naval democracy had been cast aside, it became much easier to see Athens rather than Phoenicia as the 'earnest of Britain' and to think – as *The Times* put it in 1940 – that the British 'look on blue water as did the Greek army of Xenophon'. That thought had already occurred to a reviewer in the *Dublin University Magazine* in 1855: ' "The Sea, the Sea," sings the Englishman – "Θάλασσα, Θάλασσα," shouted the old Greeks, when they first caught sight of its blue waves, after fighting their way from the heart of the Babylonian empire towards their own sea-girt homes.' It seems unlikely that this glib assertion of similarity between the modern Englishman and the old Greeks would have made many readers pause. Both nations shared an everyday familiarity with the sea: just as the English lived on an island, the Greeks, for the most part, lived either on islands or in strips of cultivated land between the mountains and the sea. For the English, as for the Greeks, to return to the sea (no matter which sea) was to return to security, to the promise that one could sail home unmolested, to the pleasure of a domain that was somehow one's own.[22]

The comparison between the English and the Greek feeling for the sea made in the *Dublin University Magazine* was drawing on, and expanding, a long-standing English claim: in the words of the seventeenth-century poet Edmund Waller, 'Others may use the ocean as their road, / Only the English make of it their abode'. The sea was also what kept the English safe: as one early nineteenth-century poet wrote,

5. The Sea is English

Britannia needs no bulwarks,
No towers along the steep;
Her march is o'er the mountain-waves,
Her home is on the deep.

The same claim was more memorably expressed in an 1878 essay on 'The English Admirals' written by a Scot, Robert Louis Stevenson: 'The sea is our approach and bulwark; it has been the scene of our greatest triumphs and dangers; and we are accustomed in lyrical strains to claim it as our own. ... We should consider ourselves unworthy of our descent if we did not share the arrogance of our progenitors and please ourselves with the pretension that the sea is English.'[23]

The reviewer in the *Dublin University Magazine* was pleasing his readers with the pretension that 'The Sea! The Sea!' is English too. The only surprise would have been that the book under review was *The Physical Geography of the Sea* by the American oceanographer M.F. Maury, discoverer of the Gulf Stream. Or rather, a classical allusion in a scientific review seems surprising from a modern perspective. For the reading public of the mid-nineteenth century, the very familiarity of an allusion to 'Thalassa! Thalassa!' would ease their path into the more daring world of marine science.

Reflections on Xenophon and national identity came as readily to the writer of another scientific article about the sea in the 1850s. He started by expressing his longing for the sea: he felt like a lion which has tasted the flesh of a man – a lion that has 'supped with the gods, and Homeric rhythms murmur in his ears,' and it is no longer happy with anything else. So too he smacked his lips 'at the prospect of man-beef'. That is, the sight of the sea would satisfy him as human flesh satisfied that lucky lion. And so he travelled down to the Scilly Isles, picturesque islands, with healthy, gentle, and dignified inhabitants – but not enough meat. But Xenophon comes to the rescue:

Was not the mere sight of the sea a banquet? Xenophon tells us that when the Ten Thousand saw the sea again, they shouted. No wonder. After their weary eyes had wandered forlorn over weary parasangs of flat earth, and that earth an enemy's, wistfully yearning for the gleams of the old familiar blue, they came upon it at last, and the heart-shaking sight was saluted by a shout still more heart-shaking. At the first flash of it there must have been a general hush, an universal catching of the breath, and the next moment, like thunder leaping from hill to hill, the loosened burst of gladness ran along the ranks, reverberating from company to company, swelling into a mighty symphony of rejoicing. What a sight, and what a sound! There was more than safety in that blue expanse, there was more than loosened fear in their joy at once again seeing the dear familiar face. The sea was a passion to the Greeks; they took naturally to the water, like ducks, or Englishmen, who are, if we truly consider

101

it, fonder of water than the ducks. We are sea-dogs from our birth. It is in our race – bred in the blood.

Once more we see how thoughts of Xenophon bring in their train the same set of allusions: those weary parasangs, so familiar to weary schoolboys; that romantic landscape of desert and sea; and of course the shout of the sea itself. For the true Englishman, the sea that was greeted by that famous shout can make up even for a lack of that most English dish, roast beef.[24]

And all this in a scientific work on the seaside – or at least a work that was designed to help visitors to the seaside enjoy and study the marvels of ocean life. The 1850s were the decade when the British developed an obsession with marine life thanks to the writings of Philip Gosse – and also thanks to the author of our cannibalistic fantasy. His identity is as intriguing as the setting for his belletristic musings: G.H. Lewes, best-known now as the common-law husband of George Eliot. This article was one of a number that were published together as a book, *Sea-side Studies at Ilfracombe, Tenby, the Scilly Isles, and Jersey* – a 'curious amalgam of magazine chatter … and exceedingly detailed descriptions of species and their habits' which was a commercial success and also a 'pet book' of George Eliot's.[25]

*

The pretension that 'The Sea! The Sea!' is English was even more pleasant to the English because they had come to see themselves as the military heirs of Athens. Just as the Athenians had freed Greece from the menace of Persia, the English had freed Europe from the menace of Napoleon. The Battle of Waterloo could itself be conceived as the equal of the great Athenian victory at Marathon. When E.S. Creasy made Marathon and Waterloo the first and last of his *Fifteen Decisive Battles of the World* (one of the most popular history books of the nineteenth century), he was building on a tradition already found in Wordsworth's optimistic lines anticipating an architectural resurgence in England after the Napoleonic Wars:

> Victorious England! bid the silent Art
> Reflect, in glowing hues that shall not fade,
> Those high achievements; even as she arrayed
> With second life the deed of Marathon upon Athenian walls;
> So may she labour for thy civic halls.

The new spirit was marked architecturally by the Caryatid porch of St Pancras Church (1819-22); by the design of the new building for the British Museum, begun in 1823; and by the thankfully incomplete replica of the Parthenon on Edinburgh's Calton Hill. Most important of all was Lord

102

Elgin's transportation of the Parthenon sculptures to London: the painter Benjamin West told Elgin in a letter that he had 'founded a new Athens for the emulation and example of the British student', and when the Marbles were bought for the nation in 1816, the purchase was celebrated by a medal for the marbles paired with a medal for Waterloo.[26]

So strong was the British confidence in the aftermath of Waterloo in the freedom they had secured for themselves and for others that they could adopt 'Thalatta! Thalatta!' as a symbol in other nations' battles for freedom. Xenophon's account of the Ten Thousand seeing the sea was closely echoed by a British historian recounting how the Prussian army under Blücher felt at the first sight of the Rhine as it drove Napoleon's French army back across the river: 'When these brave bands, having achieved the rescue of their native soil, came in sight of this its ancient landmark, the burden of an hundred songs, they knelt, and shouted, *The Rhine! the Rhine!* as with the heart and voice of one man. They that were behind rushed on, hearing the cry, in expectation of another battle.' The sense of unity, the rearguard's mistaken perception of what was happening ahead of them, the repeated shout itself – all are clearly taken from Xenophon. Even in this oblique allusion, national identity and freedom are at stake: the historian gratefully borrows from Xenophon's great scene to express his sympathy with the Prussian defeat of a common enemy. The allusion to Xenophon was spotted and developed by Mary Shelley: in her *Rambles in Germany and Italy* she offered a paraphrase of the passage (which she would have come across in the *Hand-book for Travellers on the Continent* published by John Murray), but added that the shout of 'The Rhine!' was 'accompanied by tears of ecstasy' – the tears shed by the Ten Thousand.[27]

The appeal of the Ten Thousand was also felt during the Greek War of Independence. They were used as an example by Mary Shelley's husband, Percy Bysshe Shelley, in one of his last works – the play *Hellas*, written in 1821 and inspired by the Greek revolt against Ottoman rule:

> Repulse, with plumes from Conquest torn,
> Led the Ten Thousand from the limits of the morn
> Through many an hostile Anarchy!
> At length they wept aloud and cried, 'The sea! the sea!'

That Shelley should have drawn inspiration in this play from the Ten Thousand is slightly surprising, since the play as a whole derives its shape from Aeschylus' *Persians*, a celebration of the Greeks' victory in the Persian Wars. While Aeschylus' play is set in the court of the Persian king Xerxes, Shelley's is set in the sultan's court. And while in Aeschylus' play reports of the Greek victory at Salamis are conveyed to the Persians, in Shelley's play mixed reports from the Greek War of Independence arrive. Shelley makes his debt to Aeschylus plain by having his chorus sing of the Greek victories in the Persian Wars. The only other event of ancient Greek history that the chorus celebrates is the retreat of the Ten Thousand: once more we see how the Persian Wars provided the easiest frame of reference for understanding Xenophon's achievement.[28]

But for Shelley, as for MacNeice, contemporary and classical Greek struggles for independence were also emblematic of a wider struggle for liberation from tyranny. 'We are all Greeks now', and Greece stands for an idea:

> Greece and her foundations are
> Built below the tide of war,
> Based on the crystalline sea
> Of thought and its eternity.

The Ten Thousand's shout of 'The Sea! The Sea!' is also a celebration of that 'crystalline sea' – of the eternal values for which Greece stands, values that endure through the ebb and flow of war between east and west.[29]

While Shelley made 'The Sea! The Sea!' a universal cry of freedom, most other Englishmen were less generous. They preferred to regard themselves as the sole heirs of Greece and of Athens in particular. And they clung to this claim because they viewed the sea as a realm to be controlled. While both the English and the Athenians liked to think that they helped the oppressed, they also gloried in their imperial and mercantile control of the waves. Indeed, it was because Athens' empire was based on naval domination that the British often looked back to it as a precedent for their own empire.

The pleasure felt by the English at their control over the sea explains why 'Thalatta! Thalatta!' struck J. Perry Worden, of the American Consulate, as an appropriate title for a poem to honour the visit of the King and Queen to open the King Edward Docks at Bristol in July 1908. Worden – who had fifty copies of his single-page poem printed – started by quoting Xenophon in the Greek as an epigraph, and then took over himself: 'As thus of old the Greeks acclaimed, *The sea*! / The sea, O Bristol, hail!'. The comparison seems odd. Bristol had always been in a position to hail the sea – unlike Xenophon's Greeks, who had been stranded hundreds of miles inland and fought their way back. But the point is that it was hoped that the opening of the new docks would restore to Bristol the prestige it had as a port up to the early decades of the eighteenth century, and not least as a gateway to the Americas. That is why Worden goes on to invoke the name of Sebastian Cabot, the Bristol-born explorer and map-maker in Elizabethan times, and to tell Bristol to receive 'Thy gracious King and Queen, whose worth, I vow, / Two nations great, not one, do honor now!'. The Greeks' cry has here been transformed from a shout of relief at the sight of the sea, or at most a shout of victory over all the land they had traversed, to a shout of domination over

what lay before their eyes. A member of the American consulate was gratifying his host nation by appealing to 'Thalatta! Thalatta!' in the same spirit
in which *The Times* invoked that cry at the time of Dunkirk. Britons ruled the
waves. Britons would never be slaves.[30]

*

Despite the British tradition of identifying with Xenophon's Greeks that
reaches its culmination with the retreat to Dunkirk, it would be absurd to
restrict the personal appeal of Xenophon to the freedom-loving British. A
number of other campaigns where national identity and freedom have been
at stake have also prompted comparisons with the long march of the Ten
Thousand – expeditions during the U.S. War of Independence, for instance,
or the more aggressive American invasion of Mexico. At the close of the First
World War, a comparison with that long march even had some practical
consequences: the Czech claim for a nation state was strengthened by the
Anabasis of the Czech Legion – an army stranded in Russia that rejected
Bolshevik demands that it disarm and set off instead across Siberia towards
Vladivostok.[31]

It would also be an arrogant pretension to claim that 'The Sea! The Sea!' is
English. That shout has helped other peoples to tell stories about themselves
– stories as laden with political implications as the English appropriations of
Xenophon. Xenophon's shout is exploited, for instance, in a recent
Macedonian poem 'Descent to the Sea' by Vlada Uroševik, a Professor of
Comparative Literature at Skopje University. The poem tells how the Slavs,
'driving down / to the south, towards Ulysses' fatherland', catch sight of
something blue in the distance, and then encounter an old man carrying an
oar on his shoulder. They ask the old man: 'Isn't this a flail for grain?' The old
man is blind Tiresias, the seer, who has lived the life of a man and the life of
a woman. Confused, he greets them: 'Traveller, are you returning again?'

> But those who had asked
> were already far away, shouting,
> like once the Ten Thousand:
> 'Thalassa! Thalassa!'
> but in another language.[32]

Uroševik's poem presents a distorted version of a story found in Homer's
Odyssey. When Odysseus journeyed down to the Underworld, Tiresias proph-
esied his future to him: he would return safely to Ithaca, but he would have to
leave Ithaca again and travel inland carrying an oar until he came to people
who knew nothing of the sea and mistook his oar for a winnowing fan; then
he should plant his oar down, offer a sacrifice to Poseidon, and return home.

Uroševik has Tiresias taking the place of Odysseus: it is Tiresias who carries the oar and is asked what the oar is. That is, the Greek seer still appears to be stuck in the past, rehearsing his old prophecy to Odysseus, perhaps even travelling inland in search of Odysseus himself. The Slavs blithely sweep past him, appropriating from the Greeks a different emblem of arrival: the Ten Thousand's shout of 'Thalassa! Thalassa!'. The Slavs have arrived at a new home, a home where they cannot ignore the traces of the Greek past, but where they can at least meet them on their own terms. However delicately it adapts the Greek cultural tradition, Uroševik's poem enters deep political waters. It would not go down well in modern Athens or Thessaloniki, where any hint of a Macedonian claim to the sea is apt to rouse suspicion.

Uroševik's use of Xenophon's shout is especially striking because that shout has been adopted as an emblem of Greek freedom. It was not just Shelley in his play *Hellas* who drew inspiration from 'The Sea! The Sea!'. For the modern Greeks, too, that shout has become part of the rhetoric of Greek nationalism. Even after one area where Greeks lived had won independence in 1829, other Greeks remained under the Ottoman yoke – including the Greek inhabitants of the south coast of the Black Sea (or Pontus), an area where Greeks had already been settled for some three hundred years when the Ten Thousand arrived there. These Pontic Greeks developed a new sense of national identity in the nineteenth century, and their stronger consciousness of their Greekness was reflected in a new awareness of Xenophon. As the Byzantine historian Anthony Bryer notes, a local schoolteacher 'christened his son Pericles and sent him to Athens, whence he returned after 1842 to teach Xenophon and classical Greek at the Trebizond Phrontisterion'; and local Greek children 'invariably discovered that it was in their very village that the Ten Thousand had shouted "Thalassa, Thalassa" '.[33]

Xenophon's shout acquired a stronger emotional significance for the Greeks of the Pontic region when the Ottoman Empire was dissolved at the end of the First World War. The Pontic Greeks now pushed for an autonomous Greek enclave, and sent delegates to the 1919 Peace Conference. These delegates hoped that Xenophon would go down well in Paris. Stephen Bonsal, an American delegate at the conference, tells in his memoirs, published thirty odd years later, how he received a visit from 'three of the strangest looking men' – 'representatives of the Overseas Greeks, as yet "unredeemed", of the Euxine Pontus (better known in the western world as the Black Sea)':

Soon they were telling me the story of the fate of their nation, alas, for so many centuries submerged by the unspeakable Turks.

'We represent the oldest overseas Greek colony in the world, several centuries older than Marseilles; of course, to us the French port is a mere parvenu,' they insisted. 'Our noble city of Trebizond [on the Black Sea], the

Attic atmosphere of which none of the barbarian hordes has been able to destroy, should really be called Xenophonopolis. Now this is why: When Xenophon brought his men back from the Persian campaign with Cyrus and once again they were all cheered by the sight of the Pontus, "Here," he said, "I want to found a great city, a home for the overseas Greeks, a bulwark of Hellenism against the barbarians on the dark shores of the Great Sea." At first the plan was warmly applauded; with trained oxen the confines of the city that was to be were being drawn when – ah! that was terrible, I should not tell it' –

Bonsal insists, and the story comes out. A soothsayer, Silanus of Arcadia – 'All three delegates spat in unison' – put out a story that Xenophon was planning to lead them back into the deserts of Asia – and also rigged the entrails. ' "So the great plan was defeated, or rather postponed for several generations." ' One of the delegates then objected (rightly) that there had been a Greek city at Trapezus when the Ten Thousand reached the coast. But he made the foundation centuries too early: ' "Ours has been a noble city, a Greek colony since the dawn of history, long, long before Troy." ' Bonsal closes the argument by stating that 'by going back to Xenophon their claims would have priority over all other colonial adventurers'.[34]

The Pontic Greeks achieved nothing at Versailles. For the Greek Prime Minister Venizelos, the Greeks living in Thrace and on the Aegean coast of Turkey were the priority. He tried to put a great idea of his own into force by invading Asia Minor. But the Greek army was rebuffed by the Turks, militarily resurgent under Mustafa Kemal Ataturk. They endured a humiliating retreat back to Smyrna – and the sea acquired a different resonance for the Greeks of Smyrna as the triumphant Turkish army burnt the city, and the boats of the foreign powers looked on at a scene of helpless civilians being pushed into the sea and at a harbour full of floating bodies – the scene 'On the Quay at Smyrna' that Hemingway placed at the start of his collection of stories *In Our Time* as an emblem of the political turmoil of the world in the aftermath of the Great War. There followed the exchange of populations between Greece and Turkey, and the Greeks had to abandon Trebizond for ever, that city where the Ten Thousand had reached the sea, the city that had also been the seat of the Comnenes after the Latin sack of Constantinople, and for eight years the last outpost of the Byzantine empire. They had to move 'home' to Greece – just as more recently other Pontic Greeks who emigrated to Russia in the nineteenth century have followed them 'home' in what Anthony Bryer has called 'the present great *Anabasis* from the Soviet Union'.[35]

*

'The Sea! The Sea!' could symbolize a desire for freedom and for the resurgence of national greatness for many other people besides the English and the Greeks. We saw in Chapter 2 that a German soldier thought of Xenophon's shout when he caught sight of a railway line during a retreat through Macedonia at the end of the First World War – a retreat that he ennobled by calling it a 'German anabasis', an anabasis that heralded the regeneration of the German spirit after their ignominious defeat. We saw, too, that an Afrikaner soldier during the Boer War compared his commando shouting 'The Sea! The Sea!' with Xenophon's Greeks – and here too something more than personal freedom was at stake. Denys Reitz wrote his account of his raid into the Cape in part as a lament for the Boers' lost liberty – as he suggested by his epigraph, the Roman poet Lucan's cutting words on Caesar's victory over the republicans in the Roman civil war: 'the conquering cause had the gods on its side, the conquered had Cato.'[36]

Yet we can also see that 'The Sea! The Sea!' was not quite the same for Boer or German troops as it was for the English. What Englishmen and Greeks felt about the sea was what Germans felt about railways – or about the Rhine, the Rhine (see p. 103). And Denys Reitz was describing the excitement of farmers who (like the Slavs in Uroševik's poem) had never seen the sea. Those soldiers were celebrating a heroic march through the Cape Colony: there was no sense that they were at home when they saw the sea. Indeed, Reitz at once goes on to mention a couple of soldiers elsewhere who had ridden on to a beach and fired at an English cruiser lying at anchor: 'Their bullets pattered harmlessly against the armoured side of the warship, and when the crew turned a gun on them they made haste to disappear into the sandhills, but, on their return to their commando, they boasted that they had fought the only naval action of the war.' The sea, it turns out, was English after all.[37]

'Thalatta! Thalatta!' has achieved an international fame, but no one else has shown quite such a fondness for it as Englishmen – whether they are travellers like Alexander Kinglake and Peter Fleming, or Victorian poets writing their odes to the sea, or an English vicar importing that shout into Jules Verne, or a leader-writer for *The Times* during the Dunkirk crisis. The French critic Hippolyte Taine acknowledged as much when he glossed the 'Thalatta!' scene with the observation that 'the Greeks, like the English, thought themselves at home when they saw the sea'. And the English attachment to Xenophon's sea is also attested by paintings of the *Anabasis*. While scenes from other parts of the work (the retreat through Kurdistan and Xenophon making a sacrifice at his estate in Scillus) have been depicted by artists from France and Italy, it took, as we shall see in our next chapter, a supremely ambitious and patriotic English painter to rise to the challenge of 'Thalatta! Thalatta!' itself.[38]

6

A Stray Genius

Ten days after it had celebrated the British withdrawal from Dunkirk with a leading article headed 'Anabasis' and a shout of 'Thalatta! Thalatta!', *The Times* printed a letter from a Greek man with the heroic name Leonidas, after the Spartan king who had led the three hundred Spartans in the defence of Thermopylae against Xerxes' vast Persian army. He had been reminded by the editorial of his birthplace, Trebizond, the town where the Ten Thousand reached the sea. But he had also been reminded of a distinctively English character – the historical painter Benjamin Robert Haydon. What had happened, he wanted to know, to Haydon's famous painting of *Xenophon and the Ten Thousand on First Seeing the Sea from Mount Theches* (Plate 9)?[1]

It would have pleased the patriotic and self-important Haydon that his *Xenophon* was remembered at this time of crisis. He would have relished, too, the original invocation of Xenophon's great march. In the catalogue for the original exhibition of his painting, he described the retreat of the Ten Thousand as 'one of the most immortal and undaunted actions in the records of human energy'. And in the same Churchillian tone he went on to anticipate the appeal that Xenophon's retreat would have at the time of Dunkirk: 'there is no man of ordinary energy even, but would rather have been the leader and conceiver of it, than have commanded in any of the greatest battles that ever have been fought for empire!'.[2]

It was March 1832 when Haydon first exhibited his *Xenophon* – more or less halfway between the 'immortal dinner' in December 1817, when he entertained a party of his friends, among them Wordsworth, Keats, and Lamb, and the sultry month of June 1846, when he committed suicide, worn out by years of unrewarded devotion to High Art. Much can be learnt about the appeal of Xenophon's sea since the start of the nineteenth century by following the fortunes of this noble failure. For friends like Keats, Haydon was one of London's great spirits, a lively conversationalist, an incessant campaigner, always ready with a letter to a newspaper, or a pamphlet, especially if there was a chance to abuse the Royal Academy and promote state support for the great moral cause of history painting. His pictures are not much in fashion nowadays (Aldous Huxley's view that he was a man with 'absolutely no artistic talent' still prevails): they were not that much in fashion in his own lifetime. But we can get a vivid sense of Haydon the man from his writings – his *Autobiography* and above all his incomparable journal, first published in full in 1963.[3]

In his *Autobiography* Haydon described his childhood in Plymouth, where he was inspired by reading Reynolds' *Discourses*, and his early years in London, where he was inspired still more by the newly arrived Elgin Marbles, but quarrelled with the Royal Academy when his *Dentatus* was moved by Benjamin West from the Great Room to a poorly lit spot in the Ante-Room at the Academy's annual exhibition at Somerset House. He took his memoirs up to 1820, when he was thirty-four. He had finished his enormous painting of *Christ's Entry into Jerusalem*, and was starting on *The Raising of Lazarus*. That ending may have expressed his own later hopes for a symbolic rebirth. But the seeds of his tragedy were already sown. He was considerably in debt, and he would never make up the rift with the Royal Academy (at that time still considered the guardian of artistic taste and respectability) that doomed his professional career. What happened in the years that followed made it a more than personal tragedy: marriage to Mary Hyman, a widow, in October 1821, and children, more debt, more children, more debt.[4]

Haydon emerges from his writings as a 'tempestuous and luckless blend of idealism, megalomania, and paranoia' – but a strangely engaging character all the same (not unlike Gulley Jimson in Joyce Cary's *The Horse's Mouth*). And it is as a writer that he now stands out. Already Thackeray, in a review of Haydon's *Lectures on Painting and Design* published three days before his suicide, wrote that 'Mr Haydon's literary performances contain many a page ... that is likely to outlive works which *one* man in England considers perfect.' That assessment was repeated when his autobiography and extracts from his journals were first published in 1853, and has been echoed often since: 'his genius is a writer's', Virginia Woolf wrote. And it is Haydon the writer who lays bare the irresistible appeal of Xenophon to the nineteenth-century imagination.[5]

*

'Poor little soul! She has not much taste for High Art or high poetry. She and her mother came to see my "Xenophon", which they did not understand, but laughed heartily at my "Reading the *Times*". So much for the prospects of historical Art at Court just now.' So Benjamin Haydon wrote to Wordsworth in 1837, describing one of the visitors who had attended the private viewing of his *Xenophon* exhibition five years earlier. At that time she had been a twelve-year-old princess: now she was Queen.[6]

What was it that Victoria failed to understand? As she gazed at the large canvas (eleven and a half feet by nine and a half) she would have seen, in the bottom left of the painting, a rocky ledge, with a weary, slightly effete,

110

young man lying on it. Beside the ledge a path rose up with various figures grouped along it. The path was partly obscured by the ledge and also over-shadowed by two vast rocks looming over it. The figures moving up the path between the ledge and the rocks seemed to be emerging from a dark pit. At the right edge stood a trumpeter, holding a (rather Roman) standard and blowing his trumpet vigorously out of the picture. To the left of the trumpeter was another slightly odd image: a young soldier carrying a grizzly old man on his shoulders – his father, Haydon explained in his cata-logue. But we hear nothing of fathers and sons in Xenophon's account – except for the fathers at home from whom some soldiers secretly slipped away to join Cyrus. We can allow Haydon some artistic freedom. But what was Cyrus doing hiring a man as old as that? Xenophon does at times state that the older men were given special roles during the retreat (guarding a stronghold, for instance, while the other troops moved out to bury some dead). But these are merely men 'over forty' or 'over forty-five'. Haydon could also have noted that Xenophon does once describe men 'carrying the wounded'. But Xenophon also says that others were carrying their weapons. Why is the old man still wearing his heavy breastplate?[7]

Victoria would perhaps have been even more startled by the figures to the left of the old man and his son, dominating the centre of the picture: a striking white horse, ridden by a man with a muscular back, and carrying in his arms a young woman, her flesh a pure white like her drapery, an image gleaming against the hellish gloom of her surroundings. We might have expected Haydon to follow the masculine traditions of military painting, and portray only a group of men battling with the forces of geography. As it is, his picture accords with the scene he described in his exhibition cata-logue: as the army approached the top of Mount Theches, 'men, women and children, the veteran, the youth, the officer, the private, beasts of burden, cattle and horses, broke up like a torrent that had burst a mountainous rock, and rushed, head-long, to the summit.' This description (Homeric simile and all) derives as much from Haydon's imagination as from the *Anabasis*, which does not at this point have any women or children.[8]

While the young princess was doubtless intrigued by some of these figures, she would perhaps have found the general design of Haydon's painting the hardest thing to understand. The canvas was meant to be showing a famous sight of the sea, but where was the sea? To the left of the heroic horseman, another soldier was looking up to the right towards some men shouting above him, as if straining to see something; behind him another man lay deathly sick in a wagon, and a trumpet firmly rose to the right. Had she lingered over the top part of the painting, Victoria would have seen a smaller figure on horseback on top of the rock – a figure identi-fied in the catalogue as Xenophon himself. He was waving his helmet aloft and pointing with his right arm towards something shimmering in the distance, while some cavalrymen were rushing down towards this streak of light in the top right corner of the picture. As her eyes followed the horsemen's charge to that corner she would finally have seen it – a thin blue streak of sea merging with the horizon. The sea was there after all. But why was it squeezed into a corner?

We can sympathize, then, with the young princess baffled by Haydon's *Xenophon*. The painting has all the virtues and some of the faults of Haydon's work. It is full of energy, but its undeniable vigour threatens to be undercut by the slight unevenness of the composition. 'Grouping without confusion' was, in Haydon's view, one of the elements of greatness in painting, yet the figures in his *Xenophon* do not convincingly interact. The picture runs the danger of seeming more a collage of heroic endeavour than a fully realized whole. Perhaps the *Xenophon* was in the mind of the reviewer in the *Illustrated London News* who complained some years later that Haydon's larger paintings, 'however excellent they may be in parts, are generally so overloaded with prodigalities of academic drawing and unchastened exuberances of fancy, that little more than the intention of the story is manifest.'[9]

*

On 26 March, two days after the private viewing, Haydon opened his exhibition to the public – but, he wrote next day in his diary, 'the novelty is over. I felt less interest; so seemed others, though all was praise.' His thoughts turned back twelve years, to the time when he had shown his vast painting of *Christ's Entry into Jerusalem* at the same venue – William Bullock's Egyptian Hall in Piccadilly, 'London's most famous hall of miscellaneous entertainment'. Since that 'celebrated private day', he reflected, 'how many have died' (he thought of his early patrons Sir George Beaumont and Lord Mulgrave). Others seemed so much older – 'But I never remember I must be old myself – feel so I certainly do not'. He must also have reflected how, on that earlier private day, he had been exhibiting just that one painting, lit up theatrically against a rich velvet backdrop. He had spent the day of the private view full of anxiety, until there was an epiphany – the celebrated actress Mrs Siddons appeared and pronounced the head of Christ a complete success. Now Haydon was showing a rather smaller historical composition, and he was showing it with a number of smaller pictures. At the opposite end to *Xenophon* was the *Mock Election*, an anecdotal, Hogarthian piece which had been bought by George IV and lent by his successor. Haydon also exhibited some smaller genre scenes, the sort of picture that the public liked to buy – and many indeed were marked in the catalogue as already sold. But these were not the sort of painting that Haydon liked to paint, not the sort of painting that would revive British art.[10]

While Haydon himself was in low spirits as the exhibition opened, the epigraph of his catalogue gave a hint of how he wanted to be perceived: 'Yet once more on the Waters, / Yet once more!'. Haydon was quoting (or rather, slightly misquoting) a line from the start of the third canto of *Childe Harold's Pilgrimage*: 'Once more upon the waters! yet once more!'. Byron's restless hero was there describing himself moving away from land – and from Haydon's beloved England at that: 'I depart, / Whither I know not; but the hour's gone by, / When Albion's lessening shores could grieve or glad mine eye.' Nonetheless, the Byronic stance was appropriate for Haydon. The third canto of *Childe Harold* had been published in 1816, four years after the first two cantos. Byron's 'once more ... yet once more' was a way of hailing a (poetic and actual) journey renewed – with an echo of Henry V's speech at Agincourt that must have appealed to Haydon as a patriotic lover of Shakespeare: 'Once more unto the breach, dear friends, once more.' Byron's response to the journey must also have appealed to Haydon. Though the waves bound beneath him, Byron bids 'Welcome to their roar!', and insists that, 'Though the strained mast should quiver as a reed, / And the rent canvass fluttering strew the gale, / Still must I on.'[11]

Byron's line could also be applied to the experiences of Xenophon and the Ten Thousand. That sense of repeated toil, with no end in sight, mirrored the Greeks' feelings as they laboured through the mountain passes and plains of Kurdistan and Armenia. 'Yet once more ...': that was exactly what Xenophon felt when he heard some strange shouts ahead, where the vanguard had just got to the top of yet another hill. More trouble in front, he thought, more of the enemy to fight off – Persian, Armenian, it hardly mattered which. Until the shouts became clearer. The sea, the sea, we have made it ... Could Haydon possibly realize the goals of his youth this time?

*

'Mr Haydon by dint of telling the world he is a great painter has made them believe it', Thackeray wrote in his diary after seeing the *Xenophon* exhibition: he himself found the main exhibit 'so so'. The edge to his remarks doubtless sprang from the good reviews the painting was receiving: it was 'a well-conceived and highly-spirited production' (*London Literary Gazette*), 'a stirring scene, full of energy and excitement, and depicted in a masterly manner ...one of the finest works that Mr. HAYDON or any other British artist has produced', showing proof of 'his genius and energy' (*Spectator*). Its execution was awarded 'almost unqualified approbation' – except for the unusual length of the hind part of the horse, 'which to account for we must imagine the figure to be seated close upon its neck' (*Morning Post*). Other critics were equally sharp-eyed: the *Gentleman's Magazine* faulted Haydon for cutting off the top of Xenophon's helmet. The reviewer in the *Morning Post* also carped that Haydon had not been true to Xenophon's text:

Xenophon should have been with the rearguard, not up towards the front, ahead of all those figures still toiling towards the peak. If the critic, who referred to 'their retreat of 215 days', had read Xenophon's account even more closely, he would have noted that Xenophon rode ahead when he heard the strange shouting above.[12]

For Haydon, conscious of his own genius, this generally warm reception was not enough. 'Xenophon is not failing, but it is not succeeding,' he wrote during the exhibition. But at least he had an excuse to hand: 'The times are so exciting they call off attention' (the opening of the exhibition coincided with the final debate on the Reform Bill). He was still disappointed when he closed the exhibition at the end of August and rolled up the picture: 'would any man believe that the whole body of Academicians have declared Xenophon a failure?' But again he could console himself: it had been pronounced a 'great work' by his artist friend David Wilkie, with whom he had visited Paris eighteen years earlier, at a time when the city was packed with really great works looted from Italy.[13]

When Haydon was preparing to exhibit his *Xenophon*, he had been looking to make a profit from the shilling admission charge – or at least to cover his costs. In the event he lost just over three pounds on the exhibition. But his main anxiety had been for the fate of the painting: while Haydon's contemporaries were fond of the idea of his great heroic paintings, they were rather reluctant to have them hanging at home.

When he exhibited a sketch for the painting in 1830, Haydon announced that he would raffle it for five hundred guineas when it was finished. When he exhibited the finished painting two years later, he upped the sum to eight hundred guineas – but he needed a good few more subscriptions to reach that sum. In the event, Haydon received subscriptions totalling eight hundred and forty guineas – the most he ever received for a painting. But the raffle took place four years after the exhibition: it had been a strain to get enough subscribers, and Haydon felt compelled to respond to an allegation in the *Morning Post* that he was only raffling the painting because he could not sell it. As that slight suggests, raffling was conceived as second best to a commission or a straight sale, but Haydon offered a robust defence: raffling was 'the most English way in the world', since 'it gives every man, from the King on the Throne to the humblest tradesman, a chance and an interest'.[14]

Most of the subscribers to the *Xenophon* were none too humble: among them were one King (William IV), two Her Royal Highnesses (Victoria and her mother), five Dukes, two Marquises, ten Earls, seven Lords, six Knights, and six Members of Parliament. Haydon had particular reason to remember Victoria's subscription. He believed that he offended her by sending her a ticket of admission to the raffle, 'instead of asking her Royal pleasure', and that this insult was why she later chose the lamentable George Hayter as her historical painter rather than Haydon himself. After her marriage to Albert,

Haydon resented what he saw as the increasing German influence over art in Britain. Hence the bitterness of his later recollections of Victoria's visit to the exhibition. But Haydon was not against all things German. He thought it 'an immortal honour' when Goethe, who had earlier bought cartoons of the Elgin Marbles drawn by pupils in Haydon's school, agreed to buy a subscription for the *Xenophon*.[15]

The raffle itself was held in the club room of the Society of Dilettanti in the Thatched House Tavern on St James's Street (Haydon's friend William Hamilton was secretary of the Society, and the Duke of Bedford, whose support Haydon had singled out in an earlier pamphlet, was also a member). The raffle was a great sporting occasion, with many onlookers. The Duke of Sutherland took the chair when enough subscribers had assembled, and the throwing began. The subscribers went through three rounds throwing two dice for every share, with the painter himself throwing for those who were absent – including Goethe, who was long dead by the time the raffle was held. After nearly an hour's throwing, the painting was narrowly won (with throws of 8, 11, 11) by the Duke of Bedford – to everyone else's joy, but 'to his evident perplexity', Haydon's son later wrote. The evening came to an end with a speech from Haydon himself – when he forgot in his excitement to mention the Duke, until prodded.[16]

The scores and subscriptions were reported in full in *The Times*, and a waggish sub-editor seized the chance to show off his cleverness. Immediately below a brief notice on the raffle was the news that 'an English steam-boat had commenced running between Constantinople and Trebisond' – a service that the soldiers in Haydon's painting would not have minded when they arrived at the sea.[17]

After his victory, the Duke did not take the painting to Woburn Abbey, but presented it to a family concern, the Russell Scientific Institution in Great Coram Street. The buoyant Haydon did not take it amiss that the Duke had not hung the painting at home. When he saw it in the library of the Russell Institution in August 1836, he found it 'well lighted & up', with a 'very grand' inscription: in contrast, he was doubtless thinking, to the Academy's bad lighting of his *Dentatus*. And the following month he mentioned the Duke's donation in a letter to the *Spectator* proposing that the Government should give annual commissions for historical paintings to be hung in similar institutions.[18]

The Russell Institution ceased to exist in 1897, and what happened to the painting afterwards was not known to Haydon's biographers or to W.B. Pope, the editor of his diary. They had not even seen a reproduction of the painting. How, then, to set about finding Haydon's painting? The letter to *The Times* from the modern Leonidas in June 1940 provided a clue. His request for information about the painting did not draw a blank. Three days later, a reply indicated that it had been placed in the Russell Hotel at its establishment in 1907. But an enquiry at the hotel soon revealed that Haydon's painting was not there any more. Where could it be? Rolled up in an attic or cellar, long forgotten? Destroyed even? Here the records of the Courtauld Institute of Art came into their own. They revealed that Haydon's painting was sold at Sotheby's in London on 11 April, 1991. It fetched nineteen thousand pounds – just below the lower end of the expected price: Huxley would have felt himself vindicated.[19]

Who had bought the painting? While Sotheby's would not reveal this information directly, they were at least prepared to send on a letter to the purchaser. But no response came. The proud owners, it seemed, wanted to maintain their right to anonymity.

Or so I thought. But one day in September 2003, when the draft of this book was already finished, a letter came out of the blue. Sotheby's letter, it appeared, had been mislaid, and the owner was happy to let me (and even my partner and three-month-old baby) see the great Haydon. The location where Haydon's painting has found its home was a surprise. It is hanging not in the large dark drawing room of a Victorian mansion, but in an extension to a moderate farmhouse in the rolling woodland of East Sussex. And there, dramatically placed at the far end of a well-lit orangerie, gazing down on a marble table and some rather more modern paintings and sculptures done by the owner herself, Haydon's *Xenophon* looks surprisingly good – surprisingly good, that is, for anyone who has imbibed the condescension of Huxley and Haydon's other critics.

*

What had painting the *Xenophon* meant to Haydon? We can follow his progress through his diary and exhibition catalogues. His thoughts seem first to have turned to Xenophon in January 1827, when he had lunch with William Hamilton. As they walked up and down Hamilton's room, looking at his books and examining his collection of Greek helmets (Hamilton had formerly been agent for Lord Elgin and minister at Naples), they talked about some of Haydon's pet topics – Government support for Historical Painting, the Elgin Marbles ... Xenophon must also have cropped up, because when Haydon left Hamilton lent him 'Reynell's Retreat of the 10,000' (he meant Rennell, the geographer).[20]

It was two months after his lunch with Hamilton that Haydon's journal first mentions the idea of a picture of Xenophon. At this time he was finishing off a picture of the young Alexander taming his horse Bucephalus, and had already started sketching the story of Eucles, who collapsed and died as he announced to his fellow Athenians that their army had defeated the Persians at Marathon. Haydon wrote on 20 March: 'Sketched Xenophon. Unsettled which to do, Eucles, Alexander & the Lion, or Xenophon.' In the event, Haydon painted Eucles before Xenophon, and only got round in 1842 to the tempting story of Alexander's combat with a lion. The range of topics he was painting or pondering at this time still points to something significant about Xenophon. Marathon, the Retreat of the Ten Thousand, Alexander: the familiar trinity of conflicts between Greeks and Persians.[21]

As he worked on *Eucles*, Haydon planned the design of *Xenophon* and made some preliminary sketches. He would make occasional notes on Greek armour or the landscape near Trebizond, and jot down details from Xenophon's text ('After remaining 30 days at Trebisond, they embarked all their sick, old men, women, & children': significant details for his composition, as we have seen). One day he read 'Thornton's Turkey & Spelman's Xenophon & got through the whole with a devouring pleasure'. He also showed small sketches for the *Xenophon* at his exhibitions in 1828 and 1829, and a more detailed sketch at the Western Bazaar in March 1830, when the finished *Eucles* was first exhibited. The *Morning Post* questioned his judgement in 'exhibiting these incipient and crude plans', but the *Spectator* praised Haydon's 'magnificent sketch of a design for an intended picture'.[22]

Haydon began the painting of Xenophon in earnest at the time of the *Eucles* exhibition. He was 'beginning after the bustle of Exhibition to verge towards painting like a lover to his mistress', and some passion is evident in his conception of the painting:

> My mind teemed with expressions: the enthusiasm of Xenophon cheering on his men, with his helmet towering against a sea sky! – a beautiful woman leaning on her husband's breast exhausted, in his arms, hearing the shout of '*the Sea! the Sea!*' languidly smiling and opening her lovely eyes! (good God! What I could do if I were encouraged!) – a wounded & sick soldier raising his pale head, & waving his thin arm & hand, in answer to the cheer of his Commander, – horses snorting & galloping, – soldiers cheering & huzzaing! – all struggling to see the welcome sight. I'll read all the retreats – Napoleon's, Charles XII's, Moore's, Antony's, &c. &c.

Here is Haydon at his most enthusiastic – the Haydon who would stride round his room, 'imitating the blast of a trumpet, my cheeks full of Blood, my heart beating with a sort of glowing heat', and exclaim, 'O, who would exchange these moments for a Throne!'. Here, too, is the man Virginia Woolf called 'the best read' of all painters, the man who would turn to books to fire his imagination for painting. Reading Spelman's translation of Xenophon is not enough, he has to read 'all the retreats' (not 'read about' the retreats: the books *are* the retreats). Haydon could even admit that he prefers reading to (one sort of) painting: 'I would rather blaze with Homer – I really would – & give my imagination the reins for hours! than paint a cheek like Vandyke'.[23]

A big decision was still to be made: how large to make the painting? A big decision indeed for a man in debt, with a wife and children to support, and without a commission. He made the painting large, as we have seen: 138 inches by 114. But this was not that large by Haydon's earlier standards. It was only a little over a third the size of earlier works like *Christ's Entry into Jerusalem* (228 inches by 192), to which he had devoted six years, or *The Raising of Lazarus* (168 inches by 229), which took him three years. Haydon had lost something of his earlier grandeur. He could no longer afford to give over three, four, five years to a picture no one wanted. And he even needed his wife's selfless encouragement to paint the *Xenophon* as large as he did: 'Took down a large canvas & looked with longing eyes. At last I thought it no harm to draw in Xenophon with chalk … & while I was deliciously abstracted, in walked my Love, and said, "Why do you not do it that size?" "Shall I?" "Yes," she said, "I know you are longing." I only wanted this hint; so I will risk it at any rate.' The younger Haydon would not have needed the hint.[24]

While he was working on the *Xenophon*, Haydon did at least try to support his family by painting a few portraits. But he hated having to put his *Xenophon* out of the way while he finished 'a rascally Portrait … - a poor, pale faced, skinny creature, who was biting his lips to make them look red': 'I could not help looking at the nape of the heroic neck I finished on Sunday with the back ground & trumpets & scenery. My breast swelled! my heart beat, & I nauseated this bit of miserable, feeble humanity!'. A few months later, he confesses that he has no inspiration for a portrait, and 'often scrawled about my brush & did nothing, while I was studying Xenophon through the openings of my easel!'. Haydon here encapsulates a constant theme in his writings: the superiority of historical painting to the portrait painting that was then both fashionable and profitable. It was because he saw the Royal Academy as a phalanx of petty portrait-painters that he attacked it with such vigour. Portrait painting was, at best, mere imitation, and, at worst, shameful flattery. History paintings, if executed with the genius they required, educated the public in the highest form of art, and encouraged the masculine virtues of courage, self-reliance, and independence. And that was why the Government, Haydon argued, should be encouraging historical painting, and not handing over control of resources to an effete monopoly. (It is ironic that Haydon is now best known for his portrait of Wordsworth on Helvellyn, in the National Portrait Gallery.)[25]

As he toiled for the public good, Haydon was distracted not just by the need to paint the odd portrait to support his family, but also by a sense of futility. His mind may have been teeming one day as he pondered his sublime composition, but he would soon give way to despondency. 'Worked hard these three days, but for what purpose? To die & leave my children starving, for that will be the end.' And as he continues with his painting, a contrast starts to emerge between the world of his paintings, where Haydon can absorb himself in thoughts of heroism and manly independence, and the outside world, with all its fuss, all the petty demands brought on by marrying a widow with two children and by begetting children of his own:

> I am not adapted for the World. I could live for ever in my own. I want no other. But alas, with a large family, how often is my own World broken in on. I lose sight of it for days – illness, pleasure, worrit, the wants of a wife & 8 children, all take their turns of harrass, and make me weep when I lock myself into my painting room & gaze at my Xenophon! Why did I marry?[26]

Haydon's progress was impeded by more than merely thinking about his problems. He had been imprisoned for debt for a few weeks in 1827, and now, as he worked on the *Xenophon*, he was imprisoned again, between 19 May and 20 July 1830. This was all part of the 'singular destiny' that attended his historical pictures: 'The Crucifixion just rubbed in, was seized, I ruined ... *Eucles* just rubbed in – an Execution & imprisonment. ... Xenophon – just finished the female head – arrested & imprisoned.' So he reflected some years later, when he had been arrested again while at work on *The Maid of Saragossa*.[27]

Haydon could bounce back from the worries that oppressed him. The day after he was pondering the sorry state in which he would leave his children, the world of Xenophon triumphs over the world of worry: 'Went into my Painting Room, and felt my heart swell at the look of Xenophon. An overwhelming whisper of the Muse urged me again & again to *go on*.' And after some rubbing in: 'Oh, I was happy, deliciously happy!'. He has 'all my old feelings of glory', and as he enters the room the next day, 'the effect of Xenophon is absolutely *irresistible. Go on I will*.' A few days later he is looking at his picture 'with longing eyes', and then running back from his lawyer 'with all the freshness of youth'. Years later, when he had once more 'escaped from the immediate danger of executions', he would tell Elizabeth Barrett Browning that he had 'always had a brilliant beam in my brain, with "go on" in a star, shining in the midst'. Aldous Huxley caught something of Haydon's tone when he took Haydon as model for the doomed artist Casimir Lyppiatt in *Antic Hay*: 'People mock me, hate me, stone me, deride me. But I go on, I go on.'[28]

For all his resolution to go on, Haydon could still be touchingly hesitant: 'I actually tremble at the thought of concluding it, with my family & no encouragement. ... Let me recollect Xenophon after the death of Cyrus, & Cortez in South America.' He was turning for inspiration to the dark night of despondency when Xenophon formed the resolution to lead the Greeks to safety. He would overcome his own despondency and give proof of the moral value of his painting by completing it.[29]

*

We are now in a better position to try to understand the problems Haydon was trying to surmount as he painted his picture of Xenophon and the Ten Thousand on Mount Theches. The shout of 'Thalatta! Thalatta!', the famous scene that Haydon was seeking to capture, is a great moment, and so seemingly amenable to the static medium of painting. Yet it also condenses a narrative structure: first toil and hope, then fulfilment. How could Haydon's visual narrative convey the same sense of triumph as Xenophon's written narrative?

One of Haydon's solutions was to make the sea itself a mere thin line in the distance. This solution would not have come as a surprise to the close reader of Xenophon. The sea was, after all, still five days' march away when the Greeks saw it, and it is emphasized by the movement of hands, eyes, horses, and trumpets in its direction.

More surprising was Haydon's decision to squash the soldiers who can actually see the sea at the top of his painting. The proportions of the *Xenophon* were indeed criticized in some of the reviews of the exhibition. The *Morning Post* complained that 'the whole centre of the canvas is filled with large episodal figures of the artist's own imagination' (though this was only an 'error in name'); while the *Athenaeum* praised the 'fine picture', but thought 'the accessories far too prominent, as the main incident is but a "picture in little" in the remote distance'. Others, too, were uneasy with this aspect of the composition: the painter G.F. Watts complained that Haydon 'missed making the principal incident the most affecting', while Thomas Taylor, the editor of Haydon's journals, thought the painting represented 'rather an episode in the march up Mount Theches than the discovery of the sea from its summit'. Taylor further wrote that 'the distribution of the picture is not pleasing; the foreground figures look too large, owing to the want of a group in the middle distance to connect them with Xenophon and his soldiers on the hill-top in the background.' Haydon's painting is not at all like the illustrations of the scene on Mount Theches that appear in nineteenth-century histories of Greece for children or in more recent adaptations like Havell's *Stories from Xenophon Retold* (Plate 11) or Household's *The Exploits of Xenophon*. The artists in those books simply show a small group of foot soldiers rejoicing on top of a (generally much too steep) mountain top.[30]

Taylor's description seems to align Haydon's work with French paintings of 'an episode' in the French retreat from Moscow. Such paintings (N.-T. Charlet's *Épisode de la retraite de Russe* of 1836 is a good example) typically showed a column of wounded and weary troops trekking through a desolate landscape. Haydon's critics wanted something different. They wanted a more restricted focus on the triumphant scene, with Xenophon much more to the fore. They wanted something like David's famous painting of 1799, *Napoleon Crossing the St Bernard Pass*, where the Emperor is seen on horseback in the centre of the painting against a bleak, rocky backdrop, raising his hand, as his horse rears up, in a gesture of combat with 'the abstract forces of geography and the elements'. They wanted a painting that even a twelve-year-old princess could understand.[31]

What these critics wanted was in fact closer to the first sketch for the *Xenophon* that Haydon exhibited in 1828 and 1829. The sketch itself has probably not survived, but the design is described in Haydon's exhibition catalogues. In the foreground, the focus was already on the family groups and the exhausted. But elsewhere there were some important differences: 'a trumpeter is blowing his trumpet to the rear guard, who are tumultuously rushing up the mountain. Xenophon, on horseback, is on the left, while the soldiers in the middle ground are raising a trophy; the blue distance is the plain, while the Colchian mountains are on the right, & the sea, a long silvery line, in the horizon; the whole showing the horrors of a retreat.' The sketch seems to depict a slightly earlier scene: Xenophon has not yet reached the top, and instead of the advance guard of cavalry riding down, the rear guard are seen rushing up (unless Haydon is imagining what is taking place off picture, to the right – as in the 1832 catalogue, where the trumpeter is described as 'blowing a blast to collect the rear guard which are mounting behind him'). The sea itself is still appropriately distant, but the soldiers raising a trophy in the middle ground suggest a picture that is more static, and also truer to Xenophon's own description of the scene.[32]

The oddness of Haydon's painting is the greater because the scene suggested by its title is itself vividly recreated in his own catalogue:

> As each, in succession, lifted his head above the rocks, and really saw the SEA, nothing could exceed the affecting display of gratitude and enthusiastic rapture! – some embraced, some cried like children, some stamped like madmen, some fell on their knees and thanked the gods, others were mute with gratitude, and stared as if bewildered! Never was such a scene seen!

Perhaps *that* scene was better described than painted. But it would have been easy enough for Haydon to place a less bewildering representation of the triumphant scene at the centre of his painting.[33]

It would also be easy enough to explain why such a scene could have appealed to him. First sights were a key romantic moment, and Haydon's was an eminently romantic sensibility. 'Let me recollect Xenophon after the death of Cyrus, & Cortez in South America': Haydon was evidently thinking of his friend Keats' poem 'On First Looking into Chapman's Homer', where 'stout Cortez' stares at the Pacific, 'Silent, upon a peak in Darien'. In his *Autobiography*, Haydon describes his joy at his first sight of the Elgin Marbles – a reward 'for all the petty harassings' he had suffered in studying anatomy, and almost like love at first sight or a religious conversion: 'when I saw ... the most heroic style of art combined with all the essential detail of actual life, the thing was done at once and for ever.' Haydon had felt equally enthusiastic when he first read Reynolds' lectures on painting ('The thing was done. ... The spark which had for years lain struggling to blaze, now burst out for ever'), when he first dissected an animal, even when he first set eyes on his future wife. Haydon's strong reaction to the Elgin Marbles was shared by two others whom he took to see them: Fuseli, who 'strode about saying "De Greeks were godes! de Greeks were godes!" ', and Keats, who commemorated the occasion with two sonnets, one on the Marbles, the other dedicated to Haydon.[34]

A first sight of the sea had a particular appeal for the patriotic Haydon. For Haydon, the sea was English, and deserved to be marked as such. The sculptor John Flaxman had proposed in 1799 that a statue of Britannia should be set up at Greenwich. In the earliest entry in his journal, where he describes his thoughts as he stands at Shakespeare's cliff near Dover in July 1808, Haydon proposed a different location for a statue:

> here perhaps, I said, Shakespeare has stood, here Lear defied the storm ... For the first time in my life I saw the white cliffs of England, beating back the murmuring surge, and as the Sun shot a last gleam athwart the ocean, I caught a glitter of the distant coast of France – how I felt. There, I thought, is France, the proud enemy of England. ... how grand it would be, it flashed into my mind, if there [were at] the top a Colossal Statue of Britannia, with her Lion at her feet, surveying France with a lofty air.

Haydon's coastal Britannia would be mistress of all she surveyed, a reminder of the recent naval victories against the French.[35]

The sea also had a more personal meaning for Haydon. At the time he was painting, trips to the seaside were becoming more popular for Londoners, and the growth of the city was making such trips all the more desirable. Haydon himself had spent his childhood by the sea at Plymouth, but now he was reduced to painting in small rooms reeking of oil where he would peer at his large canvases with his hopelessly weak eyes. In his *Autobiography*, he looked back to one occasion when he was able to escape to the coast: 'How I gloried in the ocean beating on a wild shore with angry surf. ... There is no expansion of feeling equal to that produced by a sudden opening on the sea after being for months shut up in a street in London.' But this was a luxury he could not often afford. When, at the end of August 1831, a few weeks before completing his *Xenophon*, he went with his family for a week to Ramsgate and Margate, he noted in his diary that he had twice been imprisoned since his last trip to the sea, five years earlier: 'The steady blue sea, the glittering sail, the expansive & canopied sky, were treats that literally overpowered one's eyes & faculties, after being pent up in brick walls!'.[36]

We could have readily understood Haydon's painting if it had merely depicted the famous first sight of the sea. Haydon instead shows both the toil upwards and the triumph. He suggests a narrative by the movement within the painting from the languid youth lying inert in the bottom left to the sea which the Greeks have been longing to see glimmering in the top right. This implied narrative harmonizes with the account of the retreat Haydon offered in his catalogue, where he focused on two episodes – the night of despair after the Greek generals have been murdered, when the surviving Greeks are lying about like that languid youth, and the scene on Mount Theches when the Greeks see the sea. And this narrative of toil and triumph is further reinforced by two of the figures that seem a bit strange at first: the soldier blowing his trumpet out of the picture hints at the troops struggling behind, while the wife lying in her husband's arms foreshadows the delights that await the soldiers at home. The oddness of Haydon's painting comes from his attempt to transcend the limits of pictorial repre- sentation – to show a whole narrative in one painting. It seems to confirm Aldous Huxley's claim that Haydon was 'a man to whom painting was but another and less effectual way of writing dramas, novels or history'. But why this story?[37]

*

As a narrative of toil and triumph, but above all of toil, Haydon's painting gains particular interest when it is read against other narratives of toil: the toils of the British in their wars against Napoleon, and Haydon's own private toils.

'Have not the efforts of the nation ... been gigantic?', Haydon wrote on the day he heard of the victory at Waterloo. As he went on to paint works like the *Eucles* and the *Xenophon*, Haydon was looking back from one heroic age to another. The *Eucles* itself was, as a modern art historian has noted, 'a fitting production for a society that saw itself, in the continuing euphoria of victory, as the heir to Athens after the Persian Wars'. The *Xenophon* may not have had so narrowly Athenian a context, but it could offer the British an image of their toils to free Europe from the tyranny of Napoleon.[38]

The vision of the British as heirs to the Greeks of the Persian Wars was reinforced by the artistic style Haydon was striving for. He modelled his style on the Elgin Marbles – as G.F. Watts recognized when he said that in Haydon's expressions of anatomy he felt 'a direction towards something that is only to be found in Phidias'. When Haydon had first seen the Marbles, he had at once repainted the heroic figure in his *Dentatus* to gain the combina- tion of the heroic and the natural that he thought was the hallmark of the classical Greek style. From that time on, he keenly advocated the artistic merit of the Marbles against doubters like Payne Knight, and agitated for their purchase by the nation. He even included the Parthenon in the background

123

to his *Eucles*, even though (as he was well aware) it had been built several decades after the battle of Marathon (the anachronism enabled him to draw a contrast in his catalogue between Athenian and English patronage of art: London was not after all quite the new Athens). The Phidian touch can also be seen in the *Xenophon* – in the woman's drapery and the horse's head, in the reclining male (modelled on the torso of Dionysus on the east pediment of the Parthenon, a figure Haydon had often drawn), and above all in the procession of horses at the top, transposed from the Parthenon frieze. There are also other glimpses of the antique: the muscular back of the cavalryman, for instance, resembles the Belvedere torso, which Haydon could have seen on his visit to Paris in 1814. Haydon had written in the catalogue for his 1828 exhibition that 'if historical painting were encouraged … I believe that the genius of this great country would spring forth in a strength unsuspected as yet, and produce works which would make Grecian art a miracle no longer'. Even without that public encouragement, he was still striving in works like the *Xenophon* to rival the Greeks.[39]

Haydon saw his own attempt to match the miracles of antiquity as a fitting counterpart to the military successes of the British. To the glories the nation had won at Waterloo, 'she only wants to add the glories of my noble art to make her the grandest nation in the world.' And he thought that he had succeeded: his *Judgement of Solomon* was 'hailed as a national victory', his *Jerusalem* was 'a national triumph'. 'What are individual heads & small Pictures to me? – disgusting. I am adapted for a great national work, to illustrate a National triumph or moral principle.' That was his mood in June 1829, nine days before starting the *Xenophon*.[40]

Haydon's artistic campaign was particularly directed against the French. He could have taken the young man lying weak and lifeless on the ledge at the bottom of the *Xenophon* from a French orientalist painting. And the painting as a whole was an optimistic remake of Géricault's *Raft of the Medusa* (Plate 10). Géricault's painting was exhibited at the Egyptian Hall in 1820, at the same time as Haydon's *Christ's Entry into Jerusalem* was being shown in the same building. Haydon himself does not refer to Géricault's painting in his journal, and it has even been suggested that the most unfavourable British review of the *Medusa*, in the *Annals of Fine Art*, was written at Haydon's instigation. For all that, Géricault's painting has several points of contact with the *Xenophon*. In Géricault's painting, a ship can be seen in the distance in the top right, just as the sea can be seen in Haydon's. An arm gestures in its direction, like the arms and trumpets in the *Xenophon*. The mountainous rock in Haydon's painting strangely echoes the sail of Géricault's raft. And in both paintings, there are sickly bodies occupying the bottom left. By quoting from the *Medusa* Haydon was, it seems, following the romantic temptation to think of the Ten Thousand lost in the desert as shipwrecked (the French painter Fromentin similarly transferred the arm raised to the horizon to a desert setting in his *Land of Thirst*, 'in dehydrated memory of Géricault'). And the broad similarities point up the key differences. While Géricault shows an old man grieving, with a deathly young body slumped across his legs, and his back to the promise of salvation, Haydon shows a son heroically carrying his father. (In the sketch exhibited in 1830, Haydon had even made the languid youth an exhausted son, wounded and bleeding, being dragged by his sturdy father.) Géricault depicts a moment of uncertainty (is the ship sailing away from the raft or towards it?), and an event that was a famous national scandal: the *Medusa* had run aground owing to the incompetence of the captain, an aristocrat appointed by the restored Bourbon monarchy, and the raft had then been cut loose from the boats that were meant to be towing it. Haydon depicts an unambiguous triumph.[41]

There was another triumph at the time of Haydon's *Xenophon* exhibition. 'The times are so exciting they call off attention': the debate over the Reform Bill was reaching its climax when the exhibition opened, and Haydon found himself caught up in it. Like many others, he hoped that reform of the electoral process would lead to a new era in political life. He even wrote letters to *The Times*, signed 'Radical' or 'Radical, Junior', which he pasted in his journal (beneath one he later added the note: 'I glory in these letters. I'll imprint them on my tomb-stone').[42]

But it had been a struggle to get the bill passed. It had been defeated in the House of Lords the previous autumn, when Haydon was finishing off the *Xenophon*. At that time, he was 'never so excited since the battle of Waterloo about Politicks' – and even distracted from his own great object: 'At work and improved the Xenophon still – but much excited about this Reform.' He also found time to paint the picture that delighted Princess Victoria when he exhibited it along with the *Xenophon*: *Waiting for the Times, the Morning after the Great Reform Debate, 8 October 1831* (now in the offices of *The Times*). That picture showed two men sitting at a table, one of them fully concealed behind a paper, the other anxiously waiting for his chance to read the report of the debate. His impatience to see the newspaper mirrors the widespread impatience for the bill that had just been blocked in the Lords. The painting was a humorously pessimistic counterpart to the *Xenophon*, where a longed-for sight is finally seen.[43]

The presence of even that small painting would give a political colouring to Haydon's exhibition. There were political overtones, too, in contemporary responses to the exhibition: broadly speaking, newspapers that favoured the Reform Bill gave him much better reviews than those that opposed it. And evidently Haydon's painting of heroic endeavour could itself be politically suggestive – as he himself perhaps realized: 'It is the dowry of Englishmen', he wrote in the month before the Lords debate, 'to contest & vanquish impossibilities. If this reform bill passes whose breast will not *broaden*, &

heart swell, who will not go down on his knees and thank God he was born in England?' Vanquishing impossibilities: the Xenophontic touch.[44]

Haydon was particularly in favour of the heroic struggle for political reform because he hoped that it would inaugurate a new era of state support for art – and an end to the monopoly of the Royal Academy. It was easy to see analogies between the Academy and rotten boroughs: a reviewer of the *Xenophon* exhibition in the *Observer* suggested that 'the R.A.'s are amongst the patrons of rotten boroughs, & ... will ... hold to the filthy lucre to the last. We have not the power either to reform or shame them as a body.' And when the review was reprinted in the *Morning Chronicle*, a correspondence on Haydon and the Royal Academy went on for a month. The letters offer a good taste of the artistic quarrels of the time. First 'R.A.' accused Haydon of puffing himself up and of writing his own reviews. 'Moderator' returned to the rotten boroughs analogy, while arguing that Haydon deserved a place in the Academy on merit. Haydon himself then wrote to promise that he would rebut 'R.A.''s charges if he publicly substantiated himself a Royal Academician. In the days that followed, 'Neuter' had a hit at 'Royal Cad', and, since 'Royal Anonymous' had not risen to the challenge, 'Amicus' denied on Haydon's behalf that he ever wrote reviews of his own work. 'Neuter' wrote again, convinced by 'the letter of Mr Haydon, or *Amicus*, who is, indeed, his *umbra*', and adding more abuse of the Academy – while also recommending that Haydon should spend his time painting instead of writing. And finally 'A Reformer' laid into the 'Boroughmongers in art' who obtained their seats 'by as sinister means as in *another great* house'. The painting of *Xenophon* had served merely as an occasion for venting long-standing grievances.[45]

The original review of the *Xenophon* had gone on to conceive the struggles of the artist as a form of heroic toil:

> In art, as well as in everything else now-a-days, it is more profitable to be base and grovelling than to pursue the rugged path, and 'live laborious days' in that ambitious strife with fame which denotes a noble and generous nature. *Sic visum* – the manufacturing of Heads tells best into the Exchequer, and it seems well to the little, little Gods of the R.A. so to work out their being ... In the mean time, a stray genius or so, through good or evil report, keeps steadily on, and gives to Art in this country its greatest glory. Haydon among these is first.

'Pursue the rugged path': the reviewer was seeing the artist's position in Britain as a Choice of Hercules – a choice between a life of 'laborious days' (the quotation is from Milton's *Lycidas*) and a life of ease and pleasure. And when he went on to imagine Xenophon's 'heroic but exhausted army' feeling 'the reward of their all-enduring toil', he was suggesting that the artist's pursuit of the rugged path mirrored the scene that Haydon had depicted.

The same meaning is implicit in Haydon's own writings. He often conceived of his campaign for artistic reform as a rough journey against the obstructions placed in his way by the Royal Academy. While he was working on the *Xenophon*, he published a pamphlet entitled *Some Enquiry into the Causes Which Have Obstructed the Advance of Historical Painting for the Last Seventy Years in England*; and he later rebuffed Charles Eastlake's suggestion that he 'should have borne every indignity from the Academy' by replying that 'I found the great object I had in view could never be obtained while the great obstacle, their monopoly, remained in power.' Haydon also hinted in his exhibition catalogue for the *Xenophon* (which was criticized in *Gentleman's Magazine* for its 'quackery, conceit and bombast') how the painting could be interpreted. In his praise of the Greeks' celebrated retreat, he showed, as we have seen, the typically English admiration for triumph over adversity, for turning defeat into victory. He then explained how the Greeks had won through: 'hope, hope, was their great support! – They dwelt on the sea, in imagination, by day, they dreamt of it, if they slumbered but a moment by night.' The romantic Haydon is here moulding the Greeks in his own self-image. The restrained Xenophon never mentions their longing for the sea, but Haydon himself constantly dwelt on his own grand artistic ambitions. He ended with an optimistic assertion of his own 'unabated energy' and his conviction ('if it please God to spare my life as he has hitherto mercifully done') that he would 'see all the great objects of "High Art" triumphantly carried'.[46]

*

There was a more personal side to Haydon's struggle for artistic reform. It was a struggle not just for institutional reform, but for personal survival as he pursued in isolation an unpopular mode of painting. Haydon's painting can also be interpreted as a dramatization of his own artistic struggle. In his diary, Haydon describes the difficulties and joys of advancing and reaching an end – of a picture that is itself a dramatization of an end obtained.

At times Haydon's difficulties could threaten the very powers he was celebrating in the painting: 'Owing to the plague of Exhibition, to the worrit of a subscription, the harrass of a large family, my interruptions have been terrific. It is impossible to go on so. ... My mind fatuous, impotent ... Voyages & Travels no longer exciting – all dull, dreary, flat, weary, & disgusting. ... I look at my own Xenophon, & wonder how I did it.' Once more we glimpse Haydon's bookish imagination: just as he cannot respond to the stimulus of books, so he cannot comprehend his own artistic powers. But now this inability seems to be a threat to his manhood. Earlier he had been looking at his canvas with 'longing' eyes, and verging towards painting 'like a lover towards his mistress'. Now we find his 'impotent' mind 'drewling over Petrarch – dawdling over Pausanias – dipping into Plutarch'. And all is dreary and flat. He is lost in the desert, not up to the struggle over heights that promises the erotic fulfilment of the sea.[47]

Haydon's occasional confessions of despondency bring out all the more his heroic response to these difficulties. One day in September 1831, he is 'out the whole day on money matters. ... I am nearly through Xenophon, but with not a shilling for the Winter, & my children literally in want of stockings for the cold.' He goes on: 'Triumph I shall. It is the dowry of Englishmen to contest & vanquish impossibilities' (it is here that he speaks of his heart swelling at the thought of Reform). 'Impossibility is the element in which he glories', Hazlitt wrote of Haydon – a remark Haydon himself quoted in his diary the year before his death.[48]

Especially resonant for the *Xenophon* is Haydon's conception of his toils as a journey uphill or an escape from pressing dangers. 'Was it not uphill work for Alexander, Caesar, Napoleon and Wellington?' was how he dismissed objections to his campaign for public support for art. A modern scholar has written that Haydon 'struggled alone like Sisyphus rolling the vast stone of history painting up the hill of indifference'. Haydon phrased it better in a letter to Elizabeth Barrett: 'Homer should have painted a Man in Hell as an historical painter in *England*! You know the line[s] in the Odyssey – Sisyphas [*sic*] would have been a joke to him.' Often in his journal he writes of himself as 'driven up in a corner' or 'threatened on all sides'. He was using these terms already on the last day of 1812, when he prayed to God not to desert him, 'surrounded as I am with difficulties and dangers'. Things became much worse when he had a family. He spent a day in April 1826 'in excruciating reflections what to do! with five children & surrounded with difficulties'. Haydon describes his financial problems in the same way as Xenophon describes the Greeks after the murder of the generals, surrounded by hostile tribes, mountains, and rivers. That was the scene Haydon recreated in his own narrative of the retreat in his exhibition catalogue, and it was to Xenophon's behaviour during that crisis that Haydon looked for inspiration.[49]

Haydon's struggles to support his family help to explain the two odd couples in the painting: the son carrying his father and the husband carrying his wife. Haydon seems to have been striving for pathos, as in many of his other paintings where he included family groups. In his *Raising of Lazarus*, for instance, he showed the mother and father of Lazarus, even though they are not in the biblical story – an 'intrusion' seen as 'a great mistake' by the Academician C.R. Leslie. For his *Eucles*, Haydon even sought the guidance of the Professors of Greek at Oxford and Cambridge on an apparent ambiguity in Plutarch, the source of the story: did Eucles die at the 'first' house he came to, or at the house of the 'first' men in the city? Far better, he decided, to paint Eucles dying in front of his wife as she held their young child in her arms, with his aged father and his oldest son watching. Young children are also something of a Haydon leitmotif. In his first sketch for the *Xenophon*, he had shown the woman carrying a newborn child, and his first plan for a picture of *Nero Burning Rome* had 'a young husband escaping through the flames with a beautiful wife from recent childbirth, pale, exhausted, and lovely ... the nurse behind holding the newborn infant'. But pathos was not everything. The son carrying his father is a model of family piety. We should not look to Xenophon's text for his source: he is taken from another of the most famous scenes of ancient literature, Virgil's account of Aeneas carrying Anchises away from the ruins of Troy. As for the woman carried in her husband's arms, it is scarcely insignificant that she was modelled (like several of Haydon's women – including the goddess Venus) on his wife Mary ('I don't think Cleopatra or Aspasia, Thais, or Phryne, could beat her beauty'). Haydon was presenting the ideal of manliness to which he aspired: an image of himself carrying his family triumphantly out of danger.[50]

*

'There is nothing like danger! I could not live if I had not always the sensation of a precipice at my feet!' So Haydon wrote to Elizabeth Barrett some years after completing the *Xenophon*. The *Xenophon* itself suggests that he was addicted to heroism. The figures struggling uphill are far more forcefully realized than the blurred line of horsemen at the top, who have lost their identity in their shared triumph. The exception is 'Xenophon cheering on the point of a rock', a figure Haydon described as 'the finest composition I ever saw': 'How mysteriously I was impelled to begin it! – an urging on the brink of ruin!'. Xenophon 'on the point of a rock' matches the artist 'on the brink of ruin': this painting about the triumph of High Art, the triumph of Haydon's ideals, is also a painting about Haydon's own need for heroism.[51]

An autobiographical reading of Haydon's *Xenophon* may seem outmoded. Art critics have moved away from the concerns of the individual artist and towards the concerns of patrons and of society at large. Haydon, however, was not painting what patrons wanted, but what he wanted them to want. And we do have access to the aspirations and anxieties that he expressed in his journal.

There is in any case a public dimension to the virtues that the painting celebrates. It has to do with an image of England as well as with an image of Haydon. And even without any knowledge of Haydon's writings, the viewer can easily enough decode the painting. The *Xenophon* is a profoundly patriarchal image. Consider again that woman in her husband's arms. Haydon, we have seen, at one time planned to make her exhausted and languid. Later he changed his mind: 'it came in my head to make her a spirited, fine creature, with sparkling eyes at the sound of trumpets; in short, such a creature as would follow her lover through peril of land and water. I think I have succeeded.' Yet the painting is not far off the iconography of rape: the man with his wife in his arms looks like a god carrying off a helpless woman or Paris seizing Helen. The strong muscles on his back are clearly visible, and he is the only one of the Greeks not wearing hoplite armour. Haydon is following the convention of heroic nudity, familiar from antique sculpture and vase painting, and from David's painting of the Spartans at Thermopylae ('there is not enough of the Naked for me', Haydon moaned to Elizabeth Barrett when he succumbed to the early Victorian penchant for paintings of medieval chivalry). This is the sort of history painting that reinforces the 'masculine virtues of independence and self-restraint'. 'If the march of the Ten Thousand was a feat, the march of the women was a marvel', one historian has commented. In Haydon's painting, it is the man with his wife in his arms who is the marvel.[52]

*

'The happiness of History Painting', Haydon once wrote after three delightful days reading in the British Museum, was that 'Dentatus acquainted me with the Romans; Solomon & Jerusalem & Lazarus with the Israelites & Eastern nations; Pharaoh with the Aegyptians; & Alexander with the Divine Greeks.' Following Haydon's attempt to portray Xenophon's first sight of the sea has led us to engage at some length with Haydon and his struggles. It is only fitting to see those struggles through to their end – and to a final, and extremely poignant, evocation of the noble retreat, the heroic extrication from difficulties that Haydon celebrated in his *Xenophon*.[53]

When Frederic Wordsworth Haydon, Haydon's third son, published a selection of his father's *Correspondence and Table-Talk* in 1876, he chose as epigraph some lines from *Childe Harold's Pilgrimage* – the poem which Haydon had used in his *Xenophon* catalogue. They were printed in capital letters, like an epitaph:

> HAVE I NOT HAD TO WRESTLE WITH MY LOT?
> HAVE I NOT SUFFERED THINGS TO BE FORGIVEN?
> HAVE I NOT HAD MY BRAIN SEARED, MY HEART RIVEN,
> HOPES SAPPED, NAME BLIGHTED, LIFE'S LIFE LIED AWAY?
> *   *   *   *   *   *
> BUT I HAVE LIVED, AND HAVE NOT LIVED IN VAIN.[54]

'Hopes sapped': the phrase was all too applicable to Haydon. The painting of *Xenophon* expresses Haydon's hopes for the triumphant realization of all the objects he had in view. But triumphs continued to elude him. He still went on and on, until finally, fourteen years after his *Xenophon* exhibition, he committed suicide. His suicide came as a surprise to those who knew him: Leigh Hunt found it 'astonishing', for he had 'looked upon him as one who turned disappointment itself to a kind of self-glory – but see how we may be mistaken'. What went wrong? Why could Haydon no longer cling to the myth of Xenophon?[55]

Haydon was firstly frustrated of the satisfactions of narrative. Already a few days after finishing the *Xenophon*, he was feeling discomfort: 'I feel the want of a great work to keep my mind excited.' 'A great work' was what he needed 'between me & adversity – I feel protected before a great Canvas or Wall.' As Huxley noted, 'he was only interested in the literature of painting; he needed a subject to stimulate his imagination.' Yet he knew that he would never attain the triumph of completion: 'I was never satisfied with anything till I forgot what I wanted to do.'[56]

Haydon's hopes for artistic recognition were also disappointed. His paintings did not take him out of difficulties. A reviewer in the *Spectator* may have written that his *Xenophon* exhibition 'vindicates his claims, as a historical painter, to public and national patronage', but he secured only the odd commission – the *Reform Banquet* for Lord Grey, for instance, which at least meant that Haydon could make all the prominent reforming politicians listen to his ideas about patronage as they sat for him. Time and time again he would dash off small paintings of *Napoleon Musing at St Helena*: there were always buyers for this image of the Emperor standing on a cliff top and looking out at the sea, with a scroll at his feet inscribed with the names of his transient victories. But when there was at last a major state project (paintings for the Houses of Parliament, rebuilt after the fire of 1834), Haydon did not win a prize in the competition. 'What is "High Art" in England', he wrote early in 1843, a year after a British army had come unstuck in Afghanistan, 'but a long Kyber Pass? with the misery of a passage in, but not a passage out.' So much for all the hope implied by his painting of those Greeks troops who had found a passage out.[57]

Haydon's enthusiasm for political reform also waned. The new parliament proved to be not too dissimilar from the old one, and within a few years Haydon would write that 'I *do certainly* regret the part I took about the Reform Bill. ... what have we got? – black-guards in the House, and what did all the chattering Reformers do who got in?' Characteristically he added a note two years later, retracting that statement of regret. He had perhaps been most distressed that the extra copy of the *Reform Banquet* which he had expected to paint was cancelled and that his exhibition of the picture made a large loss.[58]

All this time there was his constant failure to support his family – and the sight of child after child dying. The first, Fanny, died in November 1831, a month after he finished the *Xenophon*. And the years that followed saw

Alfred die in 1833, aged seven; Harry the next year, aged three; Georgiana the next year, a few weeks before her second birthday; and Newton in 1836 (a week after the *Xenophon* raffle), aged just nine months. ('After a time one loses count of the births and deaths', Huxley wrote.) His wife also had to endure the death of one of her children by her first husband. She was worn out and ill – no longer the spirited creature shown in the *Xenophon*. Not even the sea could offer much consolation for all these troubles: 'Went to Dover & swam & shouted & dived. ... I have had no recreation for 3 years, & swimming always braces me, but then comes this calamity – Life.'[59]

But Haydon continued to paint and exhibit. In 1842, he finished *Curtius leaping into the Gulf* (Plate 12), a painting in which he depicted himself as the Roman hero Marcus Curtius sacrificing himself for his city. In this 'painting about the death ... of High Art', as a modern critic has called it, Haydon negated the uplifting message of the *Xenophon*, with its image of weary troops emerging as if from the dark pit of death. His self-image was as heroic as in the *Xenophon*, but now he was offering a dramatic image of his own self-sacrifice for the cause of art. Whereas earlier Haydon/Xenophon stood waving his helmet at the sea, triumphant, now Haydon/Curtius leapt down a crevasse.[60]

Yet even after the *Curtius* Haydon still went on – for a few years more at least. He might not have won the commission for parliament, but he would draw the pictures anyway. And so to his final exhibition in 1846, which showed drawings of *Nero* and *Aristides*. The vigour and energy present in the *Xenophon*, and even in the *Curtius*, seem absent from these works: Dickens wrote in a letter after Haydon's death that he 'went to that very exhibition at the Egyptian Hall of which he writes so touchingly in his Diary', and found the *Nero* 'quite marvellous in its badness'. Whatever the quality of the paintings, Haydon was once again making political points. The evils of despotism were illustrated by Nero, and the evils of untrammelled democracy by Aristides (an Athenian hero from the wars against Persia who was subsequently exiled). He was also making a point about art by portraying Aristides with a face similar to his own. Like the Athenians, the English did not value their best men. He also recycled the anachronistic backdrop of the Parthenon which he had used for the *Eucles*: at least the Athenians had valued public art.[61]

Haydon's exhibition was no match for a competing attraction in the room next door: P.T. Barnum's famous dwarf, General Tom Thumb. Scarcely anyone came to see Haydon's pictures, but the crowds poured in to visit the dwarf, and Tom Thumb's imitations of the musing Napoleon added to Haydon's distress. His disgust found relief in an advertisement (if it can be called that) in *The Times* on 21 April: '*Exquisite Feeling of the English People for High Art* – GENERAL TOM THUMB last week received 12,000 people, who paid him £600: B. R. HAYDON, who has devoted 42 years to elevate their taste, was honoured by the visits of 133½, producing £5. 13. 6.' The ½, which *Punch* found 'touching', was a little girl.[62]

'Yet once more on the waters, yet once more.' But never again. Haydon closed down the exhibition on 19 May, humiliated, and even more in debt. In the days that followed, his mental balance was further affected by a prolonged spell of sultry weather. On the morning of 22 June, he wrote the last entry in his diary, then shot himself. When he failed to kill himself with this grand gesture, he cut his throat. His daughter found his body later in the day. That evening, the weather broke with a great storm.

A month earlier, as he cleared out the exhibition, Haydon had aligned himself with two great Athenian leaders who were rejected by the people they had served so well. And it is here that we catch a faint hint of Xenophon as Haydon makes his final invocation of the noble retreat: 'Removed Aristides & Themistocles, & all my drawings. Next to a Victory is a Skilful retreat, & I marched out before General Thumb, a beaten but not conquered exhibitor.'[63]

In the Tracks of the Ten Thousand

The famous first view of the sea, which aroused the enthusiasm of the weary soldiers, was, even independently of the circumstances under which it was seen, a sight to awaken thrilling feelings of delight. Though we cannot speak with confidence of the exact spot where the scene which Xenophon describes occurred, yet for a considerable distance along the mountain ridges in this part the impression would be the same. Here from a height of between 7,000 and 8,000 feet above the sea, the eye which has been accustomed to the treeless uplands and monotonous plains of Armenia looks down upon forest-clad mountains and delicately cut ridges, separated from one another by ravines, and gradually descending towards Trebizond; while, away to the north-east, cape after cape is seen extending into the Euxine, backed by ranges which run up to the snow-topped mountains of Lazistan, and the whole is completed and harmonized by the soft blue expanse of water. The entire view, from its delicacy and multiplicity of form, and its combination of sea and mountains, strikingly resembles the coasts of Greece. When suddenly presented to the eye of a Greek, it must have spoken to him of home in every line.

H.F. Tozer, *A History of Ancient Geography*

A couple of months before Benjamin Robert Haydon started to sketch his picture of *Xenophon and the Ten Thousand on First Seeing the Sea from Mount Theches*, he borrowed from his friend William Hamilton a copy of James Rennell's *Retreat of the Ten Thousand*. His jottings in his journal show that he read Rennell's work as he began his planning: 'The Greeks, after passing the mountains, descended a valley well *wooded & watered*, & reascended after some days march to the *Eastward of Trebisond* the *Colchian Mountains*. Rennell, Page 308.' Haydon was evidently hoping that Rennell's investigation into the route of the Ten Thousand would help him convey the great scene on Mount Theches. Yet he could just as easily have taken these notes from Xenophon's own account – and these notes could in any case only have helped him with the background to his painting. Neither the soldier Xenophon (who had been there) nor the modern geographer Rennell (who had not) would offer Haydon any help with the landscape of Mount Theches itself.[1]

Haydon would have been helped much more by the picturesque description that the learned Oxford scholar, the Rev. Henry Fanshawe Tozer, gave of the view from the mountains above Trebizond. By the time Tozer was writing, at the end of the nineteenth century, many books and articles had been written by committed scholars and casual travellers having their say in the great debate thrown up by Xenophon's account (where exactly among those mountain ridges was Mount Theches?), or else just nodding appreciatively at those heroic predecessors who had passed through the tough but strangely attractive terrain that irresistibly recalled the Swiss Alps. Indeed, Tozer himself was one of the scholars who had travelled along part of Xenophon's route. When he imagined how the harmonious view towards the Black Sea must have seemed to a Greek, he was describing a view he had seen himself and feeling an instinctive identification with the army whose tracks he had followed.[2]

Why did travellers like the learned Tozer suddenly start following Xenophon around in the nineteenth century? Why did the geography of the *Anabasis* become a concern for scholars and non-scholars alike? Like Benjamin Haydon, we can conveniently start our own investigation with James Rennell's grandly titled work of 1816, *Illustrations, (Chiefly Geographical,) of the History of the Expedition of Cyrus, from Sardis to Babylonia; and the Retreat of the Ten Thousand Greeks, from thence to Trebisonde and Lydia.*

*

James Rennell was the foremost geographer of his day. In his later years, when he devoted himself to literary topics like the geographical system of Herodotus and the route of the Ten Thousand, his home in London was a well-known gathering place for travellers venturing themselves to Xenophon's Middle East and elsewhere. But even though he had not been to Eastern Turkey, he was no armchair topographer. He started in the navy at the age of fourteen, but rose to become Chief Surveyor in India. He was also an expert on water currents – the 'founder of the science of oceanography'.[3]

Rennell's work marks the end of an era in the investigation of Xenophon's route. In antiquity, the historian Arrian had followed Xenophon's footsteps, for a while at least, and claimed that he had seen the Black Sea with pleasure from the same place as Xenophon. No one since Arrian had made the same claim. 'The Ancients ... knew these Countries much better than we do,' Reinhold Forster complained when he wrote the geographical notes for Spelman's 1740 translation of the *Anabasis*, and with some reason. Forster was relying on the reports of travellers like the German physician and botanist Leonhart Rauwolff, who travelled in the Levant between 1573 and 1576 – the first European to note (in print at least) the strange oriental habit of drinking coffee, and also one of the first to claim that the modern Kurds are the same as Xenophon's Carduchi. Forster was also using the writings of some more recent travellers like the French jewel trader Jean-Baptiste Tavernier and Joseph Pitton de Tournefort, a famous botanist and antiquarian who led an expedition sponsored by Louis XIV through Greece and Turkey at the start of the eighteenth century. In Tournefort's series of letters from the east Forster could read a notable discussion of the Pontic honey that poisoned the Ten Thousand, but he would learn little about the intricacies of Xenophon's geography.[4]

Rennell was in much the same position as Forster as he tried to reconstruct Xenophon's route from the works of the classical and Arabic geographers. A few travellers had ventured along the path of the Ten Thousand since Forster's day, but Rennell was still wrestling with the reports of Tavernier (where was the village named Halicarcara at which Tavernier had stopped?), and still following Tournefort's circuitous route from Trebizond to Erzerum (after passing through that wooded Macronian valley, he would reason, the Greeks must have ascended the Colchian mountains 'at the opposite side of that ridge, which M. Tournefort ascended, on the third day from Trebisonde'). But Rennell was not content with the state of knowledge as it was. The title of his book also promised *An Appendix, Containing an Enquiry into the Best Method of Improving the Geography of the Anabasis &c.* Here Rennell used his own vast experience to offer practical advice to travellers setting out to follow Xenophon's route. He wanted more of the sort of data offered by travellers like W.G. Browne, the 'melancholy tale' of whose murder by banditti between Tabriz and Tehran was still ringing in his ears as he wrote, but who had at least discovered the elevation of Erzerum in his last journey.[5]

No part of his geographical investigation of Xenophon interested Rennell more than discovering the precise spot from which the Greeks had seen the sea. It was Rennell who expressed the hope that no reader could read Xenophon's description without emotion, and compared the first sight of the sea with 'an opening view of HEAVEN to DEPARTING SOULS!'. But he did not just wax lyrical about Xenophon's descriptive brilliance. He also drew attention to the routes followed by earlier travellers in the vicinity. And he drew particular attention to a key clue offered by Xenophon's account: the cairn that the Ten Thousand had raised on Mount Theches – 'as a monument of antiquity … nearly as curious as the *Tumulus* of Hector: and with those who disbelieve the story of the Iliad, much more so'. 'It would be curious alone,' he added, 'to see what quantity of vegetable earth has been collected on it, in the course of 22 centuries.'[6]

*

James Rennell's romantic positivism reached its zenith in a comparative geography of Western Asia. Two volumes of this grand project were published posthumously in 1831. Had he got as far as the section on the route of the Ten Thousand, he would have been able to take account of the first travel book to engage in detail with Xenophon's route rather than just mention it in passing. This book, published just two years after Rennell's earlier enquiry into the geography of the *Anabasis*, was John Macdonald Kinneir's *Journey through Asia Minor, Armenia, and Koordistan, in the Years 1813 and 1814, with remarks on the Marches of Alexander and Retreat of the Ten Thousand*. 'The excellent Kinneir', as the great expert on Anatolia Louis Robert dubbed him, was one of the growing number of British soldiers who found life in the Middle East congenial: he had earlier travelled widely in Persia as a member of Sir John Malcolm's embassy in 1808-9, and he was later to serve as the East India Company's envoy at Tabriz, where (now Sir John) he died in 1830.

Kinneir made his journey through Asia Minor, Armenia, and Kurdistan en route to India. He had set out early in 1813, intending to travel through Sweden and Russia to Constantinople, but Napoleon's retreat from Moscow made a more direct route possible. Kinneir joined the headquarters of the Emperor Alexander in pursuit of Napoleon, and then turned back at Dresden and made his way via Vienna to Constantinople. After visiting Southern Turkey and Cyprus, he returned to Constantinople, where he met a fellow East India Company officer, William Chavasse. Together, as the *Gentleman's Magazine* put it, they 'fatally resolved, instead of performing their journey to India by the accustomed route, to explore, from their over-sanguine ardour, the tract described by Xenophon'. They made their way along the coast to Trebizond, and south through Armenia and Kurdistan. It was here that their resolution proved fatal. They were briefly imprisoned in a dungeon by a Kurdish chief, their hopes of tracing further the retreat of the Ten Thousand were destroyed by a report of robbers on the road ahead, and Chavasse caught a fever and died during their enforced detour. After burying his companion by the banks of the Tigris, Kinneir moved on to Baghdad, and from there down to the coast and by sea to India.[7]

Kinneir's book, presented in the form of a journal, set the terms for many later accounts of journeys in the footsteps of Xenophon. The appeal of the Ten Thousand was acknowledged both in the title and in frequent allusions in the text. He notes, for instance, that the river at Gemishkhana answers Xenophon's description of the tree-lined river on the border of the Macronian country, and as they approach Erzerum he confesses that 'the chief object of our wishes was to trace the retreat of the Ten Thousand'. Near the end of his account, when he has reached Baghdad, not far from the battlefield where Cyrus fell, he even devotes a whole chapter to 'Remarks on the Retreat of the Ten Thousand'. All this was part of his professed aim of contributing to the 'general stock of geographical knowledge'. The cause of utility was also served by several appendices: twelve pages of inscriptions, together with full details of latitudes and of bearings taken on the Tigris.[8]

Kinneir also wrote in his preface that he hoped the account would 'not prove altogether uninteresting'. That claim was designedly understated: he added at once that many of his routes led through 'countries never traversed by any European since the days of Alexander the Great', and his account does indeed prove to be spiced with danger. More than one later traveller would echo Kinneir's heroic stance when he insists that only those who have travelled along Xenophon's route can fully appreciate the *Anabasis*: 'as the retreat of the Ten Thousand often occupied my thoughts in my journies across the sultry wilds of Irak, Arabia and the rugged mountains of Koordistan, I could never reflect without a feeling of admiration and wonder on the difficulties which that heroic body had to overcome.'[9]

Kinneir was exploring the regions through which Xenophon had travelled at a time when they were of pressing political concern to the British. Kinneir was one of the first heroes of the Great Game, gathering geographical information with an eye on the threat to British India that could be posed by a new Napoleon or by the growth of Russian power. Like Xenophon, he was looking at the landscape of the east from a military perspective. But whereas Xenophon was re-telling his own experiences as a soldier marching through Kurdistan and Armenia, Kinneir's eyes were on the future. Noting, for instance, that Xenophon describes a proposal to cross the Tigris on inflated skins, Kinneir comments that 'the plan might be improved upon, and might be of considerable use to our army'. Elsewhere he writes that the plain of Erzerum is well calculated for assembling a large force 'in the event of any European power ever undertaking the invasion of Persia or India'. And he closes his book with a 'Dissertation on the Invasion of India', where he warns that one of Britain's enemies could convey an army by sea from Constantinople to Trebizond, and then up through the mountains to Erzerum and across to Persia and the east. Kinneir had in fact planned to explore more routes to India himself – 'the north-eastern parts of Persia, and the vast plains which stretch beyond the Oxus towards the confines of the Russian empire' – but he was prevented by illness and a sudden recall to Madras. All the same, the threat to India that Kinneir conjured up was enough to grab readers' attentions. Even the Rev. John Williams, a mere armchair explorer, could express in his 1829 work on the routes of Xenophon and Alexander the 'faint hope' that events in Persia – 'an object of deep interest to every patriotic Britain' – would make his enquiry 'as interesting as a description of the latest discovery of an ice-bound island within the arctic circle or of a desert-environed tribe in the centre of Africa'.[10]

The excellent Kinneir proves disappointing in one respect. Even though he followed the route of the Ten Thousand in reverse as he travelled up from Trebizond through the mountains to Gemishkhana and Erzerum, likening peaks to a stormy sea, he is brief and vague when he comes to mention the peak from which the Ten Thousand saw the sea: 'There is a mountain near Gemishkhana which answers the description of that of Theches, inasmuch as the Black Sea is visible from its summit on a clear day.' It looks as if Kinneir simply gained this information second-hand, perhaps from a guide. Or at least if he did follow the tracks of the Ten Thousand on to this mountain with no name, he failed to respond with the same emotional intensity that James Rennell could display from his house in London.

Kinneir's travels in the vicinity of Mount Theches did, however, enable him to criticize an earlier French geographer. Jean-Baptiste D'Anville had placed the town of Gymnias (from where a guide led the Ten Thousand to Mount Theches in five days) at 'the large village of Ginnis or Khinis', but Kinneir showed that this was much too far away from the mountain. By his polemic Kinneir again set the tone for later discussions of Xenophon's geography: just three years later a French traveller would complain, in a footnote stretching over three pages, that Kinneir had mistakenly aligned the village of Khinis with D'Anville's 'Ghinis' – which was an altogether different village called 'Djennès'. Tricky names, it seems, were another of the difficulties facing the pioneer explorer in Xenophon's Armenia.[11]

*

The Frenchman who took issue with Kinneir was Pierre-Amédée Jaubert, an orientalist who had been an interpreter for Napoleon on his Egyptian campaign and was then sent as an envoy to the Shah. Like Kinneir and Chavasse, Jaubert experienced the dangers of eastern travel: on his way out to Persia, he was shut in a dry cistern for four months by the pasha of Bayazid, and as he hastened back through Armenia to Trebizond, he fell seriously ill. His route did at least give him one advantage over Kinneir: since he was following the tracks of the Ten Thousand down towards the coast, he could report that he finally saw the sea at a place 'close without doubt to that of the retreat of the Ten Thousand' (and he recalled that Arrian had seen a statue of Hadrian erected there). The sickly Jaubert also entered imaginatively into the experiences of the Ten Thousand when he pictured himself 'in the same position as the Greek of whom Xenophon speaks' who wanted to return to Greece stretched out on deck 'like Ulysses'. Yet this remark is more an elegant display of wit and learning than a sign of any deep identification with Xenophon. Indeed, Jaubert can praise the 'animated' Arrian as much as Xenophon himself: a judgement that would have baffled most nineteenth-century readers. And even Jaubert's Xenophontic sighting of the sea is deceptive. Had he been more deeply versed in the geography of the *Anabasis*, he would have seen that, when he saw the sea a few miles from Trebizond, he was not in fact that close to the site of Mount Theches, which was still five days' march away from the sea.[12]

The first traveller who seems to have responded passionately to Xenophon's account of the scene on Mount Theches was Sir Robert Ker Porter, author of a large and beautifully illustrated account of his *Travels in Georgia, Persia, Armenia, Ancient Babylonia, &c. &c., During the Years 1817,*

1818, 1819, and 1820. Porter first trained as an artist in Britain, where his early works included a great panorama one hundred and twenty feet long depicting the storming of Seringapatam; he then moved to St Petersburg, painted for the Czar, and married a Russian princess. It was under the auspices of the Russian Academy of Science that he travelled in the Middle East, drawing the great Achaemenid and Sassanian reliefs, but alert, too, to the classical past. As he describes his journey through Armenia, Porter drools over Xenophon's account of the scene on Mount Theches ('few passages in history are more affecting') and evokes the Greeks' 'shouts and cries of *The sea! the sea!* calling him up', and 'the hardiest veterans' bursting into tears 'in the fond hope of returning to their wives and children'. But even though Porter presents himself seeking the spot where the Ten Thousand crossed the Araxes and the Euphrates, 'riding over the same country with his volume in my hand' while comparing geographical positions with the descriptions of Xenophon, he did not go out of his way to trace the site of Xenophon's affecting scene.[13]

The delight forgone by Robert Ker Porter was first tasted by a British soldier, Francis Rawdon Chesney, later famous as leader of the ill-fated Euphrates expedition. Chesney first travelled to Constantinople in 1829 to help the Turks in their war against Russia. When he arrived too late, he travelled south, where he established the practicality of a canal to Suez and explored the lower reaches of the Euphrates (Plate 13). It was then that he determined to examine the Upper Euphrates and the bordering country. He describes in his autobiography, written more than thirty years later, how he set off for Trebizond, proposing to himself, 'though as a secondary object of interest', to follow the march of the Ten Thousand. As he passed through Ghūmish Khaneh (Kinneir's Gemishkhana), he diverged (so he thought) from their path and ascended the great mountain barrier to the village of Zingani and down again through 'romantic and beautiful' scenery reminding him of the Alps in grandeur. He then 'caught sight of the sea from some of the windings of the valley' as he approached 'Trebizonde', where 'the last evening of 1831 was happily spent, under the hospitable roof of Her Britannic Majesty's Consul, Mr Brant' (himself a contributor of pieces on Armenian topography to the journal of the newly formed Royal Geographical Society). Chesney abandons this relatively restrained tone when he describes how he left Trebizond again a fortnight later. He 'entered the wild mountains, which have been so graphically described by the Father of (especially) Military History', and as he came to a valley 'closely shut in by wild precipitous hills' he recalled Xenophon's 'graphic description': 'every step now identified his well-known localities, and proved the faithfulness of his descriptions of those natural features on which time has made but little change.' With a sudden shift he turns to the site of the best known of Xenophon's localities:

7. In the Tracks of the Ten Thousand

The sea is visible from three lofty mountains in this vicinity – from that of Zingana, from the higher Karagool, and from the Gaiur Tagh, or 'Infidel Mountain'. I waded through the deep snow to the summit of the 'holy mountain of Theches', and on reaching it, I felt inclined to exclaim, with Xenophon's patient followers, 'The sea! – The sea!' I came to the conclusion that this was the very spot where all their anxieties and uncertainties had been brought to a close by the sight of the sea at a short distance from them.

While Pierre-Amédée Jaubert had satisfied himself that he was seeing the sea somewhere near where Xenophon had seen it, here for the first time – two months before Haydon exhibited his picture of the Ten Thousand on Mount Theches – we have a traveller not satisfied by mere proximity, but determined to manufacture the authentic experience. Or this at least was how Chesney described his experience as he looked back on his youthful travel more than three decades later. In his grand official account of the Euphrates expedition (so grand that he was only able to complete two of the projected four volumes), he offered a less personal description and a more tentative identification of the site of the Mount Theches. And even in his memoir Chesney did not go all the way. He only felt inclined to exclaim 'The Sea! The Sea!': that shout did not actually burst from his lips.[14]

On his return to England, Chesney lobbied hard for an expedition to test whether the route to India could be quickened by steam navigation of the Euphrates. He was finally given funds, but the expedition itself met with disaster: the *Tigris*, one of the two ships that had been dragged in pieces across from the Mediterranean, sank in a hurricane, twenty of the participants were drowned, and Chesney was left to encourage his disconsolate followers at Is Geria in a speech where, as a modern historian has written, he 'unconsciously echoed similar harangues by Xenophon and Julian in their Mesopotamian campaigns'. Before that calamity, the participants had enjoyed a library packed with the historical classics and frequent stops for hunting and historical research. Among the participants was the exotic William Elliot, who was born in Calcutta to an English soldier and an Indian mother, and had converted to Islam and learnt Arabic. Elliot (also known as 'Dervish Ali') had earlier been employed by Colonel Taylor, the British Resident at Baghdad, to trace Xenophon's route. His researches were not without incident: once, after he had cured a native woman of ophthalmia, she was offered to him as wife, 'but he exchanged her for a donkey, the latter being more useful in following the footsteps of the Greeks'. Elliot himself died young, travelling in the desert between Damascus and Baghdad: the only writings he left behind were a few notes.[15]

Another participant in the Euphrates expedition was William Ainsworth, whose own *Travels in the Track of the Ten Thousand* lay in the future. Ainsworth made his first trip to Kurdistan after the end of the expedition, searching for coal to power the steam boats that Chesney hoped to establish on the Euphrates. He went back on a longer expedition sponsored by the Royal Geographical Society and by the Society for Promoting Christian Knowledge. He was looking for two rather different sorts of relics: the route of the Ten Thousand and Chaldean Christians (whose rites were thought to have scarcely changed since the early centuries of Christianity). The book this expedition produced was the first full-length study of Xenophon's route by someone who had covered most of it himself. It came at a price – to the Royal Geographical Society: 'the trouble caused by the travellers borrowing money on the credit of the Society and their insistent demands for help in extricating them and their dependants from difficult positions ran up the bill the Society had to pay to a total of £1850.'[16]

In the course of his travels, Ainsworth found himself at the Turkish defeat by the Egyptians at the battle of Nazib in 1839. The subsequent Turkish retreat upset Ainsworth's travel plans, but he did get the chance to meet Helmuth von Moltke, future victor of the Franco-Prussian war, who was then working as surveyor and adviser to the Ottoman army. Moltke himself was one of the most significant writers to contribute to the romance of Xenophon's Orient. In his much-reprinted *Letters from Turkey* he pictured himself standing on a starlit night on the ruins of the old Roman castle of Zeugma:

> The Euphrates glittered below in a rocky chasm, and its rushing filled the still-ness of the evening. There Cyrus and Alexander, Xenophon, Caesar and Julian stepped past in the moonshine; from this same point they had seen the kingdom of Chosroes [a Parthian and Sassanian royal name] on the other side of the stream, and seen it exactly so, because Nature is here made from stone and does not alter.

This epiphany is striking enough, but Moltke created a further Xenophontic moment when he caught sight of the Black Sea as he returned to Constantinople: 'From a ridge we saw finally the glistening sea and broke out like Xenophon's Greeks into a loud cry of joy.' Moltke's fanciful feeling for the past could compensate for the fact that he was himself several hundred miles west of the spot where the Greeks shouted 'Thalatta! Thalatta!'.[17]

As the nineteenth century advanced, travel became slightly easier than it had been for the likes of John Macdonald Kinneir and Robert Ker Porter, and more and more travellers would feel the urge to add an allusion or two to Xenophon as they wrote up their hefty accounts of their Turkey trips – to note, perhaps, like the American missionary Horatio Southgate, that the modern place name Tekeh, or Tekíyeh, could be a corruption of Theches. From May 1836, one could even travel by steamer from Constantinople to Trebizond. One of the passengers in the first month of the new service was the geologist William Hamilton (son of the Hamilton who lent Haydon his copy of Rennell), doing the fieldwork for his two-volume *Researches in Asia Minor, Pontus and Armenia* – researches that included a solid dose of anti-quarianism. Hamilton's boat stopped further along the coast to take on board 'a detachment of riflemen on their way to Persia, under the command of Captain Wilbraham' – a British officer who would himself write an account of how he spent a winter following Xenophon's footsteps in Kurdistan and Armenia when he was not allowed to accompany the Persian army to Herat. The fine points of Xenophontic geography were also of interest to other military advisers and surveyors employed by the Persians or Ottomans, among them Wilhelm Strecker and the great cartographer Heinrich Kiepert (one of Moltke's colleagues), both answering the call of a German traveller in Armenia who had exhorted his fellow countrymen not to leave all the research on the spot to the English. (A French traveller to the region also commented on the abundance of travel books written by the English – but dismissively wrote that they merely aroused the reader's desire without satisfying his curiosity.) The tradition of soldier scholars continued even to the First World War, when a British participant in the Mesopotamia campaign published at Basra a short pamphlet on the topography of the battle of Cunaxa.[18]

Following the Ten Thousand would also amuse those who were simply travelling for pleasure. 'This is pre-eminently the age of touristism,' it was claimed in *Fraser's Magazine* in 1856, and parts of Xenophon's route were now in reach for the more enterprising of the tourists. The burgeoning travel book industry was leading to alarm in some quarters. In 1859 one critic bemoaned the perception that travel books were easy to write, and wondered why the public had such an appetite for these books even though they would feel distaste for a boring travel companion. What was needed in the good writer, he thought, was something of the Childe Harold spirit and of Kinglake's subjectivity.[19]

Amidst this proliferation of travel books, the most widely read work to discuss the route of the Ten Thousand did not come from the pen of a new Kinglake, but from a writer who could lure readers with the promise of exciting archaeological finds. This book was Austen Henry Layard's *Discoveries in the Ruins of Nineveh and Babylon* (1853). Layard had first travelled to the east en route for Ceylon, but he got only as far as Persia, where he had an adventurous time with the nomadic Bakhtiari. He returned to Mesopotamia at a time when Paul Botta, French Consul at Mosul, was beginning to dig in the great mound of Kuyunjik across the river. With funds from Sir Stratford Canning, at that time Ambassador in Constantinople, Layard did some digging himself nearby at Nimrud (which he mistakenly took for the biblical Nineveh). It was when he set out in 1849 for a second expedition (this time to dig at the mound across the river from Mosul – the proper site of Nineveh) that Layard decided to follow in Xenophon's footsteps. He recorded in his popular account of the spectacular finds of that expedition how he sailed by the English steamer from Constantinople to Trebizond, and then went by land through Armenia and Kurdistan, attracted by the geographical and political interest of the route. After arriving at Mosul, he treats his readers to 'a few words' (in fact six pages) on the route of the Ten Thousand 'during their memorable retreat, the identification of which had been one of my principal objects during our journey'. He had himself been following it in reverse, but now he takes the readers back through the Greeks' route, identifying rivers along the way, and ending with a tentative proposal for the location of Mount Theches – 'between Batoun and Trebizond, the army having followed the valley of the Tcherouk'. The romantic associations of antiquity were alluring and melancholy for those travelling in the Near East themselves, but those obscure and alien place-names ('Batoun', 'Tcherouk') perhaps help us to understand why it took actual discoveries like Layard's great finds in Assyria to sugar the pill of Xenophontic topography and offer any sort of competition to the polar and African explorers.[20]

The growing popularity of travel to Turkey was marked by the appearance of guidebooks. The 1840 *Hand-book for Travellers in the Ionian Islands, Greece, Turkey, Asia Minor, and Constantinople* published by John Murray seems to have been the first to include Eastern Turkey. Among the routes it proposed for the adventurous traveller one went through Gumichkhaneh (another transliteration of this splendid place-name) and Erzerum to Van, and another from Gumichkhaneh to Trebizond. Both of these routes led along part of Xenophon's path, but the guidebook did not tempt travellers with that thought. Indeed, it did not suggest any routes at all along the path that Xenophon must have taken through Kurdistan, to the west of Lake Van. By contrast, the *Handbook for Travellers in Turkey* published by Murray in 1854 (the earlier guide now having been split into two) advertised that Route 61 was 'interesting as being that of the 10,000 Greeks', and gave an 'outline of their perilous march ... serviceable to the traveller who may wish to trace it in his progress' (with data mostly taken straight from Layard's recent work). And the new Murray *Handbook for Travellers in Asia Minor, Transcaucasia, Persia etc.* that came out in 1895 would even give you the proper nudge as you crossed the Zigana Pass: 'Over this pass, perhaps, the remnant of the "Ten Thousand" marched, and from one of the rocky peaks hard by possibly arose that shout of "Thalatta", "Thalatta", which must have filled the hearts of the weary soldiers with fresh life and hope.'[21]

*

In the course of the nineteenth century, then, more and more travellers thought of the Ten Thousand as they crossed the high range of mountains behind Trebizond and saw for themselves the Black Sea. Some of them would even convince themselves that they were looking down on the sea from the same spot where 'Thalatta! Thalatta!' had first been uttered. But how could they convince those who had not stood on the spot themselves? The sceptical reader could see that the Black Sea is backed behind Trebizond by a long range of mountains. Some travellers would report that as you approach Trebizond from some directions you only catch your first sight of the sea when you are quite close to the city. But here and there amidst the mountains were several peaks offering a more distant view. Which one of these was Mount Theches itself? Travellers who wanted to persuade others that they had successfully located the mountain could have turned for advice to that geographical guru, James Rennell, and tried to find the cairn that the Ten Thousand had set up. They could have been further helped by the Rev. John Williams, who adduced evidence that, he claimed, had not been noticed before. His new evidence was in fact the passage to which Jaubert had drawn attention – Arrian's mention of some altars and a statue of Hadrian at the spot where Xenophon first saw the sea. Williams thought it not improbable that 'Trapezuntine tradition, together with the cairn of stones' could have safely conveyed knowledge of the site down to Hadrian's time.[22]

The cairn that the Ten Thousand set up on Mount Theches was finally discovered in 1996 (Plate 14). The sensational find was made by a former naval officer, Dr Timothy Mitford, and hailed by the archaeological correspondent of *The Times*: 'Xenophon's resourcefulness in extracting his force has now been matched by a British scholar.' Readers would feel the pleasure of being transported back to the great days of British exploration – until they read on and discovered that the resourceful Mitford 'quite literally stumbled on the cairn', and only then because he was led there by a local man, Celal Yilmaz, whose father and grandfather had for many years gone to the mountains for the summer pasture. When he described his discovery for an academic journal in an article entitled, naturally, 'Thalatta, Thalatta', Mitford suggested a more modest similarity with Xenophon: 'like Xenophon's guide', Celal offered to take him to the first spot from which the sea could be seen. What he then found was a 'broad, gradual ascent' (suitable for horse riding) leading up to 'a stupendous vantage point', with space around the rim for perhaps 400 men shoulder to shoulder – and, to clinch it, 'a circular base, evidently of a huge pile of stones 12m in diameter'. But all he could see that day was 'a sea of clouds a thousand feet below'.

The Rev. Williams would have been pleased that Xenophon's cairn was discovered thanks to Arrian. It was while Mitford was studying the Roman road system in Eastern Turkey (the route that Arrian would have taken) that Arrian's description made him curious about the site of Mount Theches. Yet 'of Hadrian's altars and statue', he noted, 'there is no trace'.[23]

At this point the Italian scholar Valerio Massimo Manfredi came to Mitford's rescue. Manfredi is the most recent traveller to have followed Xenophon from sea to shining sea – though he is more famous, perhaps, as the writer of airport bestsellers about Alexander the Great. The three expeditions that Manfredi led between 1978 and 1985 resulted in the appearance in 1986 of *La Strada dei Diecimila*, the most technically advanced work yet published on the route of the Ten Thousand: since then Iraq and Kurdistan have been too dangerous for further research. When Manfredi read of Mitford's discovery, he was inspired to return to the trail of Xenophon. He contacted Mitford and arranged that they visit the site together in the autumn of 1999. There Manfredi came to the view that what Mitford described as 'the ruins, Greek or Ottoman' of 'a rounded shelter for animals', measuring some eighteen metres by twenty, may be the base of the statue of Hadrian – and perhaps formed from stones taken from the Greeks' cairn (or rather their cairns: Manfredi believes that a later source which speaks of more than one cairn derives from a variant eyewitness tradition).[24]

Had Mitford in fact discovered the cairn (or pair of cairns) erected by the Ten Thousand? Arrian's description needs to be looked at more carefully:

> To Trapezus we came, a Greek city, as that Xenophon says, settled on the sea, a colony of the Sinopeans, and the sea we saw with gladness from the same place as Xenophon and you. The altars have now been erected, but from rough stone, and so the letters are not clearly cut ... As for your statue, it has a pleasing pose (for it points to the sea), but it is not well crafted, nor does it resemble you. So send a statue worthy to bear your name in this same pose: for the place is most suitable for an everlasting memorial.

Perhaps this passage is a red herring. Arrian's comment that he saw the sea from the same spot as Xenophon and Hadrian is parenthetical: the location of the statue of Hadrian is fixed by Arrian's initial statement that he arrived at Trapezus. The statue of Hadrian was not perched on a remote hill, but in the city of Trapezus, pointing at his new harbour in a gesture of domination appropriate to the edges of the Roman empire. It is Arrian who twists this imperial message by hinting that Trapezus deserves the everlasting memorial of Hadrian's statue because it was where Xenophon reached the sea. Arrian also goes on to say (as Jaubert noted) that there are temples of Apollo and Hermes in the same place as the statue. So anyone disposed to look for the base of Hadrian's statue and altars on a mountain top had better find a couple of temples there as well.[25]

Even without the support of Arrian, Mitford's location of Mount Theches is still convincing. It lies on the only high-level pass in the area, and it is supported by the general lie of the land and by the cairn itself. But Mitford was not the first explorer to discover a cairn in this area. William Ainsworth noted in 1844 that some have sought for the monument 'at Kárá Kápan where there is a positive pile of stones', and added that Colonel Chesney, his companion on the Euphrates expedition, assured him 'of his being acquainted with the position of the actual monument' in a location that would suit his own view of the route. Two years earlier, the geologist William Hamilton had described how, six miles south of 'Karakaban', he had seen on a rising knoll a mile to the west 'a large block of stone, standing upright on the summit, apparently surrounded by a mass of smaller ones'. 'A hasty traveller', Hamilton continued, 'might easily have taken it for the cairn erected by the soldiers of Xenophon' – but he himself carefully argues that Xenophon's cairn must lie further inland. But perhaps he was being overly cautious: his cairn is not in fact so far from Mitford's.[26]

Do any of these other heaps of rock have a better claim than Mitford's to be the cairn set up by the Ten Thousand as they looked down on the Black Sea? It is hard to tell, since it is almost impossible to work out just what it was that these earlier travellers saw. Was the pile of stones that Ainsworth notes at 'Kárá Kápan' the same as the stones that Hamilton saw six miles south of 'Karakaban'? Where was the cairn that Colonel Chesney came across? Chesney himself did not allude to it in his own autobiography (and his own preferred site for Mount Theches is quite some distance from Ainsworth's). The difficulty of interpreting these early travellers' accounts is exacerbated by the roughness of the maps that were then available (and that the travellers themselves provide in their books). And not even the technology of the twentieth century has removed all of these problems. Gustav Gassner, who was based at Trabzon for several years in the 1930s, and also collated many earlier travellers' claims for the location of Mount Theches, found and photographed two cairns near the Zigana Pass (slightly to the west of Mitford's). Half a century later Valerio Manfredi also found and photographed a cairn in the same area that he tentatively identified as one of Gassner's, but the upright stone had disappeared in the meantime.[27]

It is not just the lack of clarity in early travel accounts that makes it hard to pick the right cairn. Xenophon himself scarcely made things easy for the modern explorer. He did not describe how large the cairn was – except with the single word 'big'. And even if Xenophon had been more precise, we would still not know how big the cairn is now: Rennell's idea of an untouched pile of stones gradually gathering soil is a fantasy. Another reason why it is hard to come to a firm judgement about the site of Mount Theches is that travellers have often relied on second-hand reports about whether the sea can actually be seen from a particular peak. Most of the year, there is just the sea of cloud that Mitford saw: mist rising up from the Black Sea tends to condense into thick clouds as it meets the steep sides of the mountains above Trabzon. Indeed, modern pollution along the Black Sea coast has altered for ever the levels of visibility in the region: you can't see the same sea twice.

It is refreshing to take refuge from these uncertainties in the panache of P. Briot, a Frenchman who worked as chief engineer at Trebizond in the 1860s. Briot could make the confident claim that 'no one has either recognized or visited Mount Théchés since the passage of the Ten Thousand' – until he did so himself, that is. He described how he visited the summits of the chain of Vavoug-Dagh, where he found 'little pyramids of loose stones which took the form of a semi-circular shelter'. No fool he: these were 'the work of shepherds'. He lost all hope – but to satisfy his conscience he decided to scale another group of hills. He found there some more heaps of stones – but these 'were nothing more than dykes of porphyritic rock'. Off to another summit, a kilometre and a bit away. At the first summit, 'a mound of stones', and then, 'by a slight curvature of the ground at 150 or 200 metres further on, I arrived at another summit; it was there I had found the mound raised by the Ten Thousand'; and as he looked out to the north-west there 'plunged deeply the valley of Khorsat, at the bottom of which it struck me that I saw the sea'. Briot celebrated his discovery by taking breakfast and pouring out 'libations on the mound in memory of the Ten Thousand'. And he would even have proposed to erect a statue of Xenophon at Trebizond and name the main square after him – 'if the Mahometans were not iconoclasts'.[28]

Perhaps Briot had hit the jackpot? He had 'no fear that the honour of my discovery would be taken from me, because Mount Théchés is in a position upon which one is continually tempted to turn one's back'. Or was that a problem? An English geographer objected that Briot's cairn was not 'situated on some principal road' (as Rennell had required). But then perhaps their guide led the Greeks off the direct route to fulfil his promise that he would show them the sea in five days. A bigger objection to Briot's cairn is that it is too far from the sea. But as it turned out the biggest threat to his honour came from his own handwriting. Briot sent his French manuscript to the Royal Geographical Society, and an English translation was published in its journal – under the name 'Rorit'. Briot also sent his manuscript to the leading geographical societies in Berlin and Paris (the *Gesellschaft für Erdkunde* and the *Société de Géographie*). Though neither of these societies published Briot's gripping narrative in their journals, they both took some account of his communication. The *Zeitschrift* of the German society reported his claims in a sceptical piece by that old Turkey hand, Kiepert – who gave Briot's name as 'Borit'. And at the same time, a few weeks before the German siege of Paris began, the *Bulletin* of the *Société de Géographie* carried the news that the geographical scholar Vivien de Saint-Martin reported on a letter from 'Borit' at one of its meetings. Saint-Martin shared Kiepert's scepticism: 'Borit', he complained, had not had access to recent books (his only citation was Kinneir), and his cairn was so far away from the coast that he could only have seen vapours and not the sea itself. So poor 'Borit' and 'Rorit' received a bad press at the hands of the learned scholars in the capitals of Europe.

And his real name was only revealed thirteen years later, when Kiepert, communicating some fresh geographical news from Strecker, mentioned that he had met Briot in Constantinople.[29]

*

What was (and is) at stake in the attempt to pin down the place where the classic shout 'Thalatta! Thalatta!' was first uttered? Honour for the gallant Briot, doubtless. But there was more to it than that. As Philip Glazebrook has noted in his *Journey to Kars*, discussions of Xenophon's route also gave the travel writer the chance to 'flatter his own and his reader's scholarship' – no matter whether the writer displayed Chesney's enthusiasm or Hamilton's caution. There was no great call for the scholarship to be all that reliable. Indeed, Gustav Gassner, the writer who has offered the most complete overview of earlier views on the location of Mount Theches, is wrong on several counts (he says, for instance, that Hamilton located Theches at Karakaban – even though Hamilton explicitly argued against a site several miles from there). But those travellers who failed to play the classical game could find themselves criticized. As early as 1830, a reviewer in the *Athenaeum* took the French naturalist Fontanier severely to task for his lack of reverence towards Xenophon:

> The very name of Trebizond would have called up in the mind of a classical scholar, or of anyone for whom heroism and the spirit of adventure have any charms, recollections of that glorious little army, to whose labours and wanderings this city put an end, in affording to it the means of transporting itself to Greece by sea. But M. Fontanier ... is not a Hellenist, and thinks he does the Ten Thousand sufficient honour in once or twice alluding to Xenophon in this part of his work.

Yet Fontanier had not in fact done too badly for a non-Hellenist: he had copied down a Greek inscription and observed that Xenophon's description of the town of Sebasta did not quite correspond to modern Sivas.[30]

Philip Glazebrook's refreshing critique of scholarly posturing and the petty polemic of the footnote is the more striking because it is itself made in a travel book. *Journey to Kars* describes a trip through Turkey that Glazebrook made when he was preparing for his novel about the world of the nineteenth-century traveller in Ottoman lands, *Captain Vinegar's Commission* (discussed in Chapter 3). The travel book treats many of the same themes as the novel: it analyses how Xenophon was part of the school learning that could only be put to use by journeying into the east, and also part of the cultural stock that imparted a sense of authority to writer and reader alike. Glazebrook's own journey was a quest for the impulses which

149

drove Victorian travellers to endure 'discomfort, danger, illness, filth and misery ... in lands which, at best, reminded them of Scotland', and this self-consciousness makes *Journey to Kars* a very different sort of travel account from those we have met so far. Whereas the nineteenth-century travellers were fond of criticizing factual errors, Glazebrook criticizes, or at least seeks to understand, a cast of mind.[31]

It was not just through learned discussions about the site of Mount Theches that travellers could put their knowledge of Xenophon to use. Xenophon shaped their experiences in other ways – much as he shaped the experiences of travellers in other parts of the world (Alexander Kinglake labouring through the Egyptian desert, or G.H. Lewes travelling by train to the Scilly Isles, or the British prisoners from Kut on the run in Turkey). He could supply the heroic aura that Glazebrook's Tresham Pitcher had yearned to feel – an aura that could light up briefly even a solid work like H.F.B. Lynch's two-volume *Armenia: Travels and Studies* published in 1901 (an important source for the state of the country before the First World War massacres).

Lynch had a career similar in many ways to that famous earlier traveller, Alexander Kinglake: Eton and Cambridge, a brief spell at the bar, then eastern travel, and later some time in parliament. But Lynch was a more serious student of the east. He came from a remarkable family of travellers: two of his uncles had served on Chesney's Euphrates expedition (one of them went down with the *Tigris*, the other led a second expedition); and his father – who married a daughter of Colonel Taylor, the Resident at Baghdad – and another uncle had founded the Euphrates and Tigris Steam Navigation Company, generally known as Lynch Bros. (His father, for good measure, also translated the piece by 'Rorit' for the Royal Geographical Society.) Lynch himself was senior partner of the family company and responsible for establishing a new trade route to Persia. But he also found time for his Armenia book, where he described two journeys to the Russian and Turkish provinces in the 1890s. His reasons for travelling had been both sentimental and practical: it looked as if the great Eastern Question would be resolved in Armenia (where the first massacres of Armenians were then taking place). Lynch also knew how to draw his readers in by flattering, or patronizing, them: 'What does my reader know about the ancient history of Armenia? At least he remembers the wonderful march of Xenophon ...'. And he reverted to that wonderful march when he described the end of his first trip. He had set off from Trebizond, hiked up Ararat, and done the rounds of Armenia and Kurdistan, before returning to Trebizond – which he reaches in a chapter entitled 'Return to the Border Ranges – Θάλαττα, θάλαττα!' (Plate 16). Here too Lynch flatters his readers' knowledge of Greek while also adding some gloss to his own journey. So too one of the Turkish prisoners in the First World War, E.H. Keeling, would use Xenophon's shout (again in Greek) as a title for the chapter where his escape party first saw the Black Sea. Unlike Keeling, however, Lynch makes no allusion to Xenophon within the chapter. After the earlier lesson in ancient Armenian history, the simple heading was enough.[32]

What Lynch merely implied was made explicit by a traveller thirty years earlier, John Ussher, at the end of his *Journey from London to Persepolis*. Ussher's book seems to hint at the anxieties of adding to the crowded market of travel books halfway through Victoria's reign. He insists, for instance, that he only ventured to lay his (seven hundred page) account before the public when it was suggested that a description of his route 'might be useful to future travellers in such comparatively untrodden countries': by this time, the plea of utility, the thrill of the new, must have sounded a bit hollow. Ussher could boast the initials 'F.R.G.S.' after his name, but he still insists that he and some friends only travelled for pleasure – the pleasure, for instance, of astonishing the locals by playing cricket in the Mesopotamian desert. At the same time, he alarms his readers by closing one chapter with a dark reminder of politics ('at no distant time the head-quarters of a Russian general will in all probability be established in the palace of the Shahs at Teheran'). He also makes the authority of a Fellow of the Royal Geographical Society felt whenever he mentions that he crossed or followed the path of the Ten Thousand. He hints at his own learning by citing the view of 'most authorities' – but he could easily have gleaned all the details from his copy of Murray's guidebook. These allusions to Xenophon provide, at any rate, fitting preparation for Ussher's account of his feelings as he approaches Trebizond on his return journey: 'the sensations we ourselves experienced on beholding the calm water, made us easily realize the feelings of the harassed, exhausted, and toil-worn Greeks, when ... they at last beheld the sea, the termination to their sufferings.' Ussher even closed his book with his arrival at Trebizond – an odd place to end an account of a trip from London to Persepolis. We might have expected him to end with an account of the exotic Persian ruins – or else back in foggy London. After all, as Paul Fussell has written, 'somehow we feel a travel book isn't wholly satisfying unless the traveler returns to his starting point: the action, as in a quest romance, must be completed. We are gratified – indeed, comforted, by the "sense of an ending", the completion of the circuit.'[33]

Why did Ussher fail to give his readers the security of a return to London? In many travel books, the return to the sea is figured as a return to civilization from the barbarism of the benighted interior. That is not quite what Charles Doughty made of Arabia Deserta, but his great work does end when he arrives back at Jidda and is 'called to the open hospitality of the British Consulate'. Similarly Samuel Baker (who discovered, or at least named, Lake Albert N'yanza) takes us from the interior of Africa to the British hotel at Suez, and on finally to the British mail at Cairo. For the Englishman, a return to the sea is a return home, a completion of the quest. So too for Ussher Trebizond marked the close of his adventures in the interior. From there he could catch the steamer to Constantinople, and, as Thackeray wrote, 'wherever the steamboat touches the shore adventure retreats into the interior, and what is called romance vanishes'. But Ussher was also striving to assert a link with Xenophon by ending his book at Trebizond. Just as the sufferings of the weary Greeks terminated when they saw the sea, so too Ussher could safely conclude the narrative of his own adventures with a dignified ending at the city where the Greeks reached the sea. How better to gratify his readers, who could conclude (like the reviewer in *The Times*) that 'Mr Ussher is a gentleman, and he merited his success and this splendid monument of his travels and pleasant explorations'?[34]

Trebizond was also the endpoint of the *Journeys in Persia and Kurdistan* by the most famous and formidable of female travellers in the nineteenth century, Isabella Bishop Bird. Bird undertook this ride across some two and a half thousand miles of tough terrain when she was nearly sixty. As she told the story of her journey up from the south through Kurdistan with 'M.' (Major Sawyer, an Intelligence Officer in the Indian Army), she followed her (male) predecessors by throwing the usual Xenophon references into her account. Finally, as she described her approach to Trebizond at the end of the book's penultimate paragraph, she again turned to Xenophon – except here she gave a twist to the usual tale: 'unfortunately for the traveller, the admirable engineering of the modern waggon road deprives him of that magnificent view of the ocean from a height which has wrung from many a wanderer since the days of the Ten Thousand the joyful exclamation, "*Thalatta*! *Thalatta*!".' The steamboat may remove the romance of the coast, but here the technology brought by foreign engineers like Briot threatens even the romance of the approach to the coast. But a restless traveller like Isabella Bishop Bird was not in any case likely to share in the relief at a journey's end felt by softer men. Bird may close her book with her arrival in Trebizond, but she 'would willingly have turned back at that moment to the snowy plateaux of Armenia and the savage mountains of Kurdistan'.[35]

*

While travellers could cross other points along Xenophon's route conscious only that those points gained a particular interest from the classical connection, it was when they got to the pass from which the Ten Thousand saw the sea that the urge to interpret their own experiences in the light of these heroic predecessors was strongest. And no traveller felt that urge with more intensity than a German officer, E. von Hoffmeister, as he rode up towards the Zigana Pass in May 1910. He had only one thought in his mind as he approached the pass through a 'sea of cloud': can one see the sea? 'Here the

Greeks must have marched, from here they must have shouted "Thalatta, Thalatta" ...'. But then – a dark ridge appeared to the north, blocking the view. Disappointment. What was he to do? Turn back to Baiburt and try another route? A policeman stationed at a post on the pass came to his rescue. There was one spot in the whole range, he revealed, where one could see the sea on a clear day – and it was clear that day. It was a three quarters of an hour climb up through the snow and ice (and remember that this was May). But von Hoffmeister had no choice. He clambered up with the policeman guiding him – up to one peak, down again, and up to a second peak, broader and more spacious. His guide ahead called back, 'There it is' – and

in an instant all fatigue vanished: a couple of leaps, and I stood at the top. Icy wind, glittering snow, the white sky above me, fluttering cloud below – and right to the north a hazy blue streak. Quickly I took up my glasses: with the best will I could make out nothing other than this hazy streak; but the gendarmes pointed to it again and again and repeated, 'It is the sea, sir, it is the sea!' Frankly speaking I was rather disappointed ...

He had hoped to see steamers and sails. But yes, they are right. It can only be the sea. 'And here, perhaps even by the path I had taken, the scout had led them, here they stood and saw, embracing each other, deliverance from their sufferings, the sea: "Thalatta! Thalatta!".' A cloud suddenly comes up: half an hour later and he would have seen nothing. He has to make his way down the icy slope through the mist – but he is helped down by his triumph. And no trace of his initial disappointment remains as he reaches the coast and draws his account to a close by evoking a famous myth: 'Once, in legendary times, there came audacious seafarers, the Argonauts, to the land of Colchis, to fetch the golden fleece; I too went there, found a golden fleece, held it fast, and brought it home: it is the Thalatta, Thalatta! of the Greeks.'[36]

With the extravagant von Hoffmeister we have reached ourselves the peak of heroic identification with the Ten Thousand and their shout of the sea. As von Hoffmeister stands on a summit, as he comes to realize that yes, this is the place, as he overcomes his initial disappointment, as he constructs in retrospect an Argonautic fantasy for himself, he experiences the fulfilment for which Glazebrook's Tresham Pitcher was longing when he looked out on a bleak seascape in Wales and asked whether this could really be the 'thalassa' of Xenophon's soldiers.

But even von Hoffmeister disappoints us. Not even this enthusiast says that he actually shouted 'Thalatta! Thalatta!' as he stood on that snowy peak and found his golden fleece. T.E. Lawrence may have echoed Xenophon's shout when he caught sight of the Mediterranean, Mrs Baillie Reynolds' romantic heroine may have gasped 'Thalassa!' as the moon came out from behind a cloud, but did any travellers echo Xenophon's shout when the

Black Sea burst upon their eyes? Harry Lynch contented himself with a chapter entitled 'Thalatta! Thalatta!'. Francis Rawdon Chesney merely felt an inclination to echo that shout. And Isabella Bishop Bird does not name any travellers who actually shouted 'Thalatta! Thalatta!' in the days before modern technology deprived them of the pleasure.

Perhaps it was more common to echo that shout internally? The Belgian historian Franz Cumont implied as much when he described his own descent towards the Black Sea: 'There is no traveller, who, on descending towards this coast, has not heard ring within himself the joyous cry of the Ten Thousand at the sight of the sea.' (He too would make Trebizond the close of his account of 'this attractive country, one of the most romantic of all those still peopled by children of the Greeks'.) Already in antiquity at least two travellers had shared in Xenophon's pleasure at the sight of the Black Sea: Arrian and the emperor Hadrian. But while Arrian imitated Xenophon in nearly everything else, he does not say that either he or Hadrian imitated Xenophon's shout. It was left to one of Hadrian's modern biographers to speculate, in a romantic footnote, that Hadrian shouted 'Thalatta'.[37]

But it was not just in the minds of other travellers and writers that Xenophon's shout was echoed. The Ten Thousand's joyful exclamation did escape the mouths of at least two travellers in Eastern Turkey in the nineteenth century: the Rev. Henry Tozer, the Winchester and Oxford scholar who gave so picturesque an account of the mountain scenery above Trebizond, and his regular travelling companion, Thomas Crowder, a Major in the Oxford Militia and Bursar of Corpus Christi College, Oxford. Tozer and Crowder travelled to Turkey together during the long summer vacation in 1879. They took the steamer from Constantinople to Samsoun, and then rode into the interior as far as Bitlis and Van before descending to Trebizond. The journey took up the whole vacation, from June to the start of October, but at least Tozer got a publication out of it – a book on *Turkish Armenia and Eastern Asia Minor*. 'The veteran traveller', *The Times* review noted, was observing an area that was 'now succeeding to European Turkey as an apple of discord' – but 'the reader will find more of Xenophon than of the Eastern question in these pages'. And the key Xenophon question was Mount Theches. It was in a chapter with 'Thalatta! Thalatta!' as one of its sub-titles that Tozer recalled their first view of the Black Sea as they returned towards the coast: 'we had not proceeded far before our eyes were gladdened by a most welcome sight. "Thalatta! Thalatta!" we both exclaimed, for it was indeed the sea; and it must have been from a point somewhat corresponding to this that Xenophon and his soldiers first saw it.' But Tozer has no sooner asserted his communion with Xenophon than he undermines it: 'Their exclamation has become a household word, and only those who have fought their way for months through an enemy's country, and have often passed the night on fields of snow, as they did, could realize what it meant to them.'

Not even Tozer himself, it seems, can appreciate that famous shout. But he can at least enjoy the view: 'even the ordinary traveller, who has journeyed, first along the arid, uniform levels between Ararat and Erzeroum, among villages either ruined or at the best resembling mud-heaps, and afterwards over the chill bleak mountains which separate Armenia from the coast, could feel the inspiring effect of this view. And such a view! we had seen nothing equal to it in our whole tour ...'. There followed much the same description that he later gave in his *History of Ancient Geography*.[38]

And so it was that the Rev. Tozer and Major Crowder did what so many travellers ought to have done, and shouted 'Thalatta! Thalatta!' in more or less the same spot as Xenophon's Greeks twenty-three centuries earlier. Or did they? Thomas Crowder also kept a record of their long vacation tour, and his account (which has never been published) is rather different:

> Very shortly after starting the leading Zabtieh [policeman] pointing at a cleft in the mountains to our right exclaimed, 'Deniz', the Sea, and vividly was Xenophon's Θάλαττα, Θάλαττα brought before our minds as he beheld it under similar circumstances and probably from a very similar spot. There sure enough it was far away N.N.E., a hazy expanse, and our first view of the sea for ten weeks.

Tozer has them shouting 'Thalatta! Thalatta!', Crowder has them merely thinking it. And Tozer has them observing the sea themselves while Crowder has a guide pointing it out to them – and shouting in Turkish himself. Who was right – the clergyman don or the bursar? We might expect Crowder's unpublished journal to be more accurate. Tozer was writing what consumers of travel books wanted to read. By omitting the active role played by the native guide, he was following a common practice among travel writers. Yet Turkish guides seem to have known what travellers liked to hear: already in the 1840s George Grote was informed that guides on the peak of Karakaban point out the view of the sea 'with great animation'. It would be rash, however, to take Crowder's own account as simple truth. He was writing after the event, in leather bound volumes, with page numbers, running titles ('View of the Sea'), footnotes, and sketches – eminently literary volumes which were available for consultation in Oxford. He even goes beyond Tozer when he asserts that Xenophon saw the sea 'under similar circumstances' (and in fact he first wrote 'under very similar circumstances', but then crossed out 'very').[39]

It matters little whether Tozer or Crowder was more accurate. Either way, this was the greatest moment of what Crowder called 'one of the grandest long vacation Tours that was ever attempted'. For Crowder, too, it was 'one of the most magnificent scenes' he ever saw in his life – a scene 'of a Greek character', a 'heavenly view': 'We were suddenly plunged into fairy land after ten weeks experience of treeless aridity.' 'Thalatta, Thalatta', Greece, heaven, fairyland, all rolled into one: Crowder's instantaneous pleasure seems to exceed even the joy felt by that modern Argonaut, von Hoffmeister. But then, September is a better month than May for trekking through the mountains of Eastern Turkey.

*

It is not just nineteenth- or early twentieth-century travellers who have displayed their learning and indulged their emotions by evoking Xenophon. When he died in 1916 aged eighty-seven, the Rev. Tozer was hailed as 'the last and not least distinguished of the classical tourists'. Nonetheless, later and less distinguished travellers to Eastern Turkey have kept the tradition going in their own way – even when they are travelling down to the coast by bus. The Eton-educated historian and journalist Neal Ascherson, for instance, cannot help observing in his 1995 book *Black Sea* that his bus journey from Ankara to Trabzon takes him along the route used by Xenophon as it winds down to the sea. Indeed, like the Victorian travellers analysed by Philip Glazebrook (another to make the journey from Eton to Trabzon), Ascherson even offers reflections on the site of Mount Theches: 'where exactly they were when the soldiers saw the blue band on the horizon ahead of them, and cried out "*Thalassa*! The sea!", cannot be known. Some think that it was near the port of Ordu, about a hundred miles west of Trebizond, others that they filed down a little further east.' Ascherson does not enter the morasses of Xenophontic topography just to show off (and in fact it is clear enough that the Ten Thousand were above Trebizond, and nowhere near Ordu, when they saw the sea). His point is that, no matter where they were, 'when the soldiers shouted "*Thalassa*!", the local people understood them.' Ascherson, it turns out, is simply using the Ten Thousand to introduce an enquiry into what 'home' meant for the Greeks of the Black Sea region: travelogue serves as a vehicle for reflection on their sense of nationhood. Like Glazebrook's *Journey to Kars*, Ascherson's *Black Sea* is partly a quest into the past, an exploration of a national consciousness that became particularly intense in the nineteenth century. But while Glazebrook was concerned with the self-fashioning of the European traveller, Ascherson's profound study arouses empathy for the peoples those travellers observed and often despised. Even though he starts with the location of Mount Theches, his perspective turns out to be far removed from the nineteenth-century adventurers in Ottoman lands.[40]

Philip Glazebrook's perspective in *Journey to Kars* is closer to the nine-teenth-century travellers whose tracks he was following, but the persona he presents himself is very different from the heroic chivalry of those earlier travellers. Glazebrook's much more cautious character emerges clearly from the passage where he ponders the nineteenth-century obsession with

Xenophon. It is as he travels by bus from Kars to Trabzon, and starts his descent, that his thoughts turn to the *Anabasis* – which he has 'never thought … a particularly enthralling work'. He moves away from his worries about whether 'they lost as many travellers off the footpath in those days as they lose in bus-smashes now', and ponders why the 'Thalatta' scene appealed so much to those earlier travellers keen to wrap themselves and their readers in a mantle of scholarship. It is as if the burden of those past narratives makes Glazebrook himself dismissive of Xenophon – and unable to describe his own feelings as he first sees the Black Sea. But in fact it is just that he is travelling at night. And when he follows his excursus by writing that 'I was very glad to reach the Black Sea myself after a journey of seven and three quarter hours', he does suggest a comparison of sorts between his own experiences and Xenophon's – a comparison that suits the cautious persona he constructs for himself in studied contrast to earlier travellers. His own excursus, moreover, merely reinforces the traditional value set on the 'Thalatta' scene – while also flattering his readers' feeling of superiority to those inauthentic Victorians.[41]

Glazebrook's own travels in the tracks of Xenophon reflect all the same a significant change of sensibility. The sort of heroic posturing that absorbs Glazebrook's interest had been rendered old-fashioned by travellers in the mould of Peter Fleming. Indeed, Glazebrook's more detached and self-conscious tone can already be found in a travel book from 1932 – *A Tower of Skulls* by Gerald Reitlinger (later a historian of Hitler's extermination of the Jews). As Reitlinger gets to 'Gumush Khaneh', he notes that it 'may be a place mentioned by Xenophon in his account of the march of the ten thousand' (i.e. Gymnias). He 'had struck their trail already at Ashkalé, and the line taken by the Russian-built road is approximately that of the anabasis.' He then pauses to consider how George Grote 'attached much importance to Xenophon's line of march, and particularly the place where the cry of "Thalassa! Thalassa!" was raised', and had 'read exhaustively the account of every traveller who had been into northern Anatolia, for the benefit of his footnotes'. Less dismissive than Glazebrook, he finds such research 'far the most agreeable of any that can be made, and … more innocent than most'. But like Glazebrook he is not concerned to promote an image of his own bravado. He gives his chapter the deflating sub-heading 'Staggering in Xenophon's Footsteps' (the Fleming touch), and is cautiously aware of the dangers of even the modern road: 'Two stranded lorries marked the spot where the cry of "Thalassa! Thalassa!" must have been raised.' But he is not tempted to echo that great cry: 'to-day there was no sea to be found: a heavy mist hid everything, as is usually the way with such historic viewpoints.'[42]

Yet Reitlinger does achieve a moment of identification with Xenophon. As they turn a corner near Trabzon, 'then came shouts of "Kara Deniz! Kara Deniz!" the *Thalassa! Thalassa!* of my anabasis'. But this is a vicarious identification, achieved via his Turkish guides, as vocal as their nineteenth-century counterparts. And what did they see? 'Before us was a thin slip of grey like the mouth of the Thames at Southend.' So much for the romantic rapture expected from Xenophon's shout of the sea. Like the heavy mist that hid everything at Xenophon's actual viewpoint, the thought of a grey English resort lowers the tone before we take Reitlinger's posturing too seriously.[43]

*

The most splendid realization of Glazebrook's anxieties about travel writing comes not in a travel book, but in a novel published in 1956: Rose Macaulay's *The Towers of Trebizond*. The narrator Laurie (the androgynous name is typical of Macaulay: her sex only emerges in the final few pages) is travelling in Turkey with two eccentric missionaries: her aunt Dot (who speaks the famous opening words – 'Take my camel, dear' – as she returns from High Mass) and the very Anglo-Catholic Father Hugh Chantry-Pigg. While aunt Dot is preparing a book on the position of women in Turkey, the priest is in the grip of the past: he follows St Paul's steps at Alexandria Troas with an optimistic plan in hand, and duly looks up in the *Anabasis* all the places that they pass on the Black Sea coast. Like many earlier travellers, Father Chantry-Pigg seems to be intent on a rather sterile display of learning. But the younger narrator is likewise only too happy to absorb herself in textual minutiae. She knows that the geologist William Hamilton proposed moving the site of Cerasus nearer to Trebizond because Xenophon could not possibly have made it there in three days – 'but what with this rearranging the sites of ancient cities … and the number of heavy stones that geologists have to pick up and travel about with … this Hamilton must have been a slow traveller'. Laurie's learning is at least more quirky than Father Chantry-Pigg's. And it is allied to a yearning romanticism about the past. She dreams (with the help of a potion from a sorcerer at Trebizond) that she has landed at Cerasus with the *Argo* and she sees the natives acting just as Xenophon said they did eight hundred years later ('they were still having loving intercourse with women in public as they lay about the woods, and I thought, this would never do if it was Hyde Park').[44]

Macaulay's novel is not just peopled with characters hooked on the Turkish past, it is also full of reflections on the production of travel books. Her narrator has lots of friends busy 'writing their Turkey books', two of them, David and Charles, 'somewhere by the Black Sea, following Xenophon and Jason about' (the novel also has a character called Xenophon and a yacht called the *Argo*). What are all these friends writing about? 'The usual things, I suppose. Antiquities and scenery and churches and towns and people, and what Xenophon and the Ten Thousand did near Trebizond.' The plagiarism endemic to travel writing is nicely exposed when Charles is eaten by a shark,

and David publishes under his own name a piece his friend had written on
'The Lure of Trebizond' – as Laurie knows, since she had earlier found a
draft in a hotel drawer (and she had spotted then that Charles had got a lot
of it from earlier travellers like Lynch). Travellers are also liars, of course. A
BBC van travels through Turkey and bribes village people to sing for it, and
when Laurie comes to write her own Turkey book, she invents a Byronic
swim across the Hellespont for herself and her safely dead friend Charles.[45]

This connoisseur of travel writers could scarcely have failed to observe
their fondness for Xenophon's great shout. So when Laurie finds herself
following Xenophon once more on the way back to Trebizond with her
Turkish friend Halide (aunt Dot and Father Chantry-Pigg have disappeared
across the border in the Soviet Union, drawn by the thought of Armenian
churches and Caucasian mares), she reaches after a couple of days the spot

> where it is proper for travellers sighting the Black Sea to cry 'Thalassa' (or if
> they prefer it 'Thalatta') like Xenophon's army, but we were too dispirited to
> do this, and anyway Halide, who despised this Greek army, would not have
> copied its ways, either in crying Thalassa or in making herself sick and mad
> with honey from the local rhododendrons, which she was now sure that the
> camel had done, if not aunt Dot and Father Chantry-Pigg too.

It may be 'proper' to shout 'Thalassa' or 'Thalatta' ('the former or the latter'?)
– but perhaps it is harder after this gentle parody. Or is the thought that it is
'proper' to echo Xenophon's shout itself a tribute to the self-awareness of the
nineteenth-century travellers? As we have seen, it is in fact much more
common for those earlier writers to evoke the appeal of 'Thalatta! Thalatta!'
than to say that they shouted it themselves.[46]

The narrator's quirky wistfulness is not the only note struck in
Macaulay's novel. The allusions to Jason and Xenophon, and their modern
followers, are not just pleasant asides: they reinforce the thematic contrast
which Macaulay sets up between secular and religious quests. Byzantine
Trebizond stands in the novel (as Macaulay herself wrote in a letter) for an
'ideal and romantic and nostalgic vision of the Church' – the church that the
adulterous narrator has abandoned. (Macaulay herself had been sundered
from the Church owing to a long love affair with a married man, but she had
returned to it by the time she wrote the novel.) Trebizond starts to acquire
this symbolic force when Laurie first approaches it from the sea: it is Whit
Sunday, and Laurie and Chantry-Pigg are seeking their first sight of the city,
and he asks her how long she will shut herself from God. This symbolic force
becomes stronger as Laurie feels a mysterious sense of loss as she explores
Trebizond: 'I felt as if I had come not home, not at all home, but to a place
which had some strange hidden meaning.' Later, in Jerusalem, she has a
vision of 'the Trebizond of the world's dreams, of my own dreams, shining

towers and domes shimmering on a far horizon, ... yet the only reality, a walled and gated city ... standing beyond my reach, yet I had to be inside, an alien wanderer yet at home, held in the magical enchantment'. And at the end of the novel, when she has killed her lover through her own impetuous driving: 'Still the towers of Trebizond, the fabled city, shimmer on a far horizon, gated and walled and held in a luminous enchantment.' But Laurie is shut out of the city, doomed to stay spiritually in modern Trabzon – with its 'squalid' beach, a city 'that scarcely knew or remembered lost Byzantium ..., blind and deaf and not caring any more, not even believing, and perhaps that was the ultimate hell'. All the more appropriate, then, that when Laurie was first approaching Trebizond from the interior she was too dispirited to cry 'Thalassa' and share with the Ten Thousand in that almost religious sense of salvation and homecoming.[47]

Other recent writers have exploited in rather simpler terms the disparity between past Trebizond and present Trabzon that becomes so potent a spiritual symbol in Rose Macaulay's novel. In *The Scholar and the Gypsy*, a book in which two travel companions offer alternating accounts of a trip to Eastern Turkey, Nigel Ryan describes how he wakes up in Trabzon – 'the fabled city where the Argonauts stepped ashore, where Xenophon rested on his great march home, where Hadrian built a harbour, where Comnenus founded an empire that outlived Byzantium'. The point of this parade of learning is that he finds himself 'in a dilapidated seaside resort in the off-season', a Blackpool to the Venice of ancient Trebizond. And so he sets off with his friend on his travels, and on to an incongruous juxtaposition: 'We came to a place where a recent landslide had buried a line of cars and a busload of tourists. We passed the spot where Xenophon's Ten Thousand ... cried out in unison "*Thalassa! Thalassa!*".' The mood here seems redolent of travellers like Reitlinger and Glazebrook, similarly fixated by the dangers of the modern road. But while we do not feel any specific allusion to other travellers at this point, we are not surprised to hear from the scholar, James Howard-Johnston, that, as they approach Trabzon a second time, his companion is reading *The Towers of Trebizond* – the bit, of course, where Rose Macaulay's characters are approaching Trebizond.[48]

Even guide books can offer reflections, of sorts, on the difference between now and then. 'The something you should know' about the Zigana pass is that it is where Xenophon's men shouted 'Thalassa! Thalassa!'. But 'modern travelers here tend to let out rather less celebratory shouts as the road ascends in dizzying hairpin turns, inches away from precipitous drops into deep gorges' (those same anxieties again ...). And sheep often occupy the road, so that 'it is quite possible that they were shouting "The sheep! The sheep!"'.[49]

*

7. In the Tracks of the Ten Thousand

We have followed a number of modern travellers along the tracks of the Ten Thousand, and seen how some of them were tempted to find the spot where 'Thalatta! Thalatta!' was first shouted or even to echo that shout themselves. But we have also seen that some more recent travellers have had reasons for resisting that temptation. They have struck a more detached and ironic note that seems to mirror cultural trends since the First World War. To write that 'every British schoolboy knows' that the Greeks shouted 'Thalatta! Thalatta!' was always hyperbolic. Now it would be grotesquely so. Few schoolboys (or schoolgirls) learn Latin or Greek, and not many of them (at least in Britain) start on Caesar or Xenophon – 'incurably tedious authors', E.R. Dodds argued in 1920, who 'should be expelled from the school curriculum'. Increasingly they have been expelled: they are deemed too redolent of the world of men and war, too boringly moralistic. There has also been a greater reluctance to look to the ancient world for models of exemplary behaviour. It is not just that the feats of Cato or Brutus have become less familiar. It is also that the modern world seems to provide greater paradigms – if not of virtue, at least of suffering. After these great shifts in social and educational values, how could 'Thalatta! Thalatta!' still be an incontestable symbol of happiness gained? Yet 'Thalatta! Thalatta!' has retained its hold on the modern imagination precisely by virtue of the fact that its value as a symbol of triumphant return has been openly contested. The responses of these more recent travellers are more than matched, as we shall see in our next chapter, by the extraordinarily varied and productive use of Xenophon's shout by other writers in the twentieth century.[50]

8

The Snotgreen Sea

'la mer, la mer, toujours recommencée'
Paul Valéry, 'Le Cimetière marin'

'The sea, the sea, always renewed': in 1922, the year that Paul Valéry's poem about a graveyard by the sea was published in his collection *Charmes*, Xenophon's shout of the sea was renewed again in another book published in Paris – James Joyce's *Ulysses*. Joyce's novel starts with 'stately, plump' Buck Mulligan emerging with his shaving equipment into the mild morning air on the parapet of the Martello tower overlooking Dublin Bay which he shares with some friends (Plate 17). Mulligan calls Stephen Dedalus, talks to him as he shaves, and then wipes his razor on Stephen's handkerchief as he looks out on Dublin Bay: ' "God," he said quietly. "Isn't the sea what Algy calls it: a great sweet mother? The snotgreen sea. The scrotumtightening sea. *Epi oinopa ponton*. Ah, Dedalus, the Greeks. I must teach you. You must read them in the original. *Thalatta! Thalatta!* She is our great sweet mother. Come and look." '[1]

It may seem surprising to find Xenophon's shout echoed on the third page of one of the iconic works of twentieth-century literature. That shout had been evoked in a great variety of settings and registers in the Victorian and Edwardian eras. But how could 'Thalatta! Thalatta!' stand up in the wake of the Great War, in a more fragmented world, in an age more sceptical of grand narratives? How could a classic cry of homecoming retain its appeal in an era when exile could be seen as a hallmark of the modern condition? The Xenophontic shout with which Buck Mulligan greets Dublin Bay at the start of *Ulysses* seems to be mockingly undermined by the autobiographical seal with which Joyce closes his novel: '*Trieste-Zurich-Paris*, 1914-1921.'

Parody is one way Xenophon's shout could endure in the modernist imagination. When he describes Mulligan casting his gaze over Dublin Bay at the start of *Ulysses*, Joyce is playing on hackneyed descriptions of the joy experienced at the sight of the sea. 'Thalatta! Thalatta!' is here cited at the beginning of a book and of a new day, after a short anabasis up a flight of stairs. It is not a climactic cry of triumph after a long struggle. It is telling, indeed, that it is not the quieter and more refined Stephen Dedalus who hails

162

the sea, but the blustering Mulligan. Throughout the opening scene of *Ulysses*, Mulligan comes across as a bit pretentious, a bit extravagant in his devotion to Hellenism. His greeting to the sea is all a bit too much, especially first thing in the morning, with a shaving bowl in his hand.

Joyce's initial parody also signals the extraordinary transformation of the literary canon undertaken in the novel as a whole. Just as Joyce plays with a Homeric text, the *Odyssey*, so too Mulligan plays with the Homeric sea: 'snotgreen sea' is a variation on 'winedark sea', a traditional translation of the Homeric formula he quotes, *epi oinopa ponton*. The variation marks Joyce's move from the grandeur and nobility of Homeric epic to the everyday Dublin of Dedalus and Bloom. 'Come and see': we are being invited to look at, and rejoice in, Joyce's sea of cryptic allusion. Paradoxically, 'Thalatta! Thalatta!' becomes the joyful shout of the modernist release from literary convention.

Joyce makes further use of Xenophon's sight of the sea later in *Ulysses*. Here it is Simon Dedalus (Stephen's father) talking: 'And Xenophon looked upon Marathon, Mr Dedalus said, looking again on the fireplace and to the window, and Marathon looked on the sea.' The father at least has obeyed Mulligan's injunction to the son to look on the Xenophontic sea. He is re-interpreting Xenophon through an allusion to some famous lines from 'The Isles of Greece', a pastiche of Greek patriotic songs inserted by Byron in *Don Juan:*

> The mountains look on Marathon –
> And Marathon looks on the sea;
> And musing there an hour alone,
> I dream'd that Greece might still be free.

By transferring Xenophon's sight of the sea to Marathon, Simon Dedalus is suggesting that the achievement of the Ten Thousand in reaching the sea is parallel to the Greek victory in that earlier engagement with the Persians. Or rather, Dedalus (or Joyce) is playing on that traditional way of celebrating the retreat of the Ten Thousand, and playing, too, on the sounds of words – Xenophon, Marathon; and even (or so one modern scholar claims) Xenophon, xenophobia .... Dedalus' 'pseudoantique jingle' may also be due to his 'desire to parade a smidgeon of misinformation about ancient Greek history'. If so, he has perhaps succeeded. A modern critic, contrasting the sea of Camus' *La Chute* (which leads to 'the stagnation of frustration, cowardice, self-mortification and despair') with the Greeks' 'cry of victory and achievement', has written: '*Thalassa, thalassa*, cried the Greeks, returning from Marathon.'[2]

The great shout on Mount Theches is not the only familiar part of the *Anabasis* to find its way into *Ulysses*. At the end of the 'Oxen of the Sun' episode (the chapter set in a maternity hospital which charts the development of English prose style through nine months of gestation), Joyce abandons the controlled pastiche found in the earlier parts of the chapter and mingles together for several pages snatches of colloquial speech and other odds-and-ends: 'En avant, mes enfants! Fire away number one on the gun. Burke's! Thence they advanced five parasangs.' In this 'afterbirth' section, as thoughts turn naturally enough to the pub ('Burke's' was a bar near the hospital), Joyce recycles the formula Xenophon used for describing the Greeks' progress through the Persian empire (and five parasangs a day was indeed their most common march). It is as if those parasangs are so familiar from Xenophon's use in the schoolroom, so much a part of the cultural stock, that they force themselves into the Joycean stream of words – even though (or precisely when) his characters are just thinking of moving down the street.[3]

It would be easy to read Joyce's use of motifs from the *Anabasis* as a mere literary play with overfamiliar motifs. But such an approach would be overly reductive. Ideas of national identity have often been at stake in the use that has been made of 'Thalatta! Thalatta!', and such ideas are also at stake in Joyce's parody of a rapturous salute to the sea at the start of *Ulysses*. When Mulligan calls the sea 'snotgreen', that epithet is inspired by the handkerchief he has borrowed from Stephen Dedalus: 'The bard's noserag. A new art colour for our Irish poets: snotgreen.' The snotgreen sea that Mulligan hails is a distinctively Irish sea. But as he hails this Irish sea Mulligan holds up a mirror that Dedalus bitterly calls a 'symbol of Irish art' – 'the cracked lookingglass of a servant'. Even though Mulligan has appropriated a classic Greek shout that came readily to English tongues, the subservience of the Irish to the English is stressed by that mirror. Or perhaps Mulligan's overheated 'Thalatta! Thalatta!' is precisely a sign of that subservience? At any rate, the dominance of the English is reinforced by the setting of this opening scene. The Martello tower in which Mulligan and Dedalus live is one of the watchtowers built by the English for protection against a French invasion. And another of their housemates is indeed an Englishman, Haines – 'the seas' ruler'.[4]

Joyce's engagement with the meaning of Irishness at the start of *Ulysses* is strengthened by the religious associations that the snotgreen sea acquires. After hailing again 'our mighty mother', Mulligan turns to face Stephen Dedalus: 'The aunt thinks you killed your mother. … to think of your mother begging you with her last breath to kneel down and pray for her. And you refused.' His words make Stephen think back to her death: 'he saw the sea hailed as a great sweet mother by the wellfed voice beside him. The ring of bay and skyline held a dull green mass of liquid. A bowl of white china had stood beside her deathbed holding the green sluggish bile which she had torn up from her rotting liver by fits of loud groaning vomiting.' This view does not hold the promise of religious salvation – a promise with which other writers could invest Xenophon's shout of the sea. The snotgreen sea is aligned instead with the bile his dying mother vomited when Stephen refused to pray for her. It stands for Stephen's rejection of Catholicism, and so for Joyce's own flight from his native land and his native religion.[5]

Mulligan's shout of 'Thalatta! Thalatta!' opens up, it seems, some surprising vistas of its own. In Joyce's hands, Xenophon's shout becomes both a dreary repetition of a cliché and a celebration of Joyce's own creativity; and the sea that Mulligan greets is an Irish sea that must be welcomed despite the ambivalent presence of the English and at the same time rejected, however strongly it continues to loom in the exile's imagination.

The complexity of the Xenophontic allusions in *Ulysses* is more than matched by Joyce's experiments with Xenophon in *Finnegans Wake*. 'Catastrophe and Anabasis' and 'Xenophon' are among the marginal annotations in Joyce's final work – the latter accompanied by the appropriate enough thought that 'Delays are Dangerous. Vitavite!'. There is also an isolated appearance of the inevitable 'parasangs'. But most telling are the mocking echoes of Mulligan's Xenophontic moment that form part of the happysteamylogical fanseas of *Finnegans Wake*: 'Galata! Galata!' and 'kolossa kolossa!', for instance; or 'The latter! The latter!' (the same pun that occurred to Ronald Knox and Flashman); or again 'The letter! The litter!' (this with reference to the mysterious letter that plays so large a part in the 'plot' of *Finnegans Wake*); and later (in a nicely aquatic context) 'ye seal that lubs you lassers, Thallassee'. The most demanding echo of Xenophon's shout – and so the one most at home in Joyce's notoriously difficult text – is 'raptist bride is aptist breed (tha lassy! tha lassy!)'. Those words are a cryptic allusion to the famous story of the rape of the Sabine women told by Livy. Livy's account is, in part, a sort of 'Just So' story, explaining the origins of the Roman marriage cry of 'talassio, talassio' (which was sometimes written 'thalassio, thalassio'). A young Sabine woman of great beauty, Livy explains, was seized by some men from the household of a Roman named Thalassius, and 'in reply to the many questions about whose house they were taking her to, they, to prevent anyone else laying hands upon her, kept shouting, "Thalassius, Thalassius!"'. That, at least, is how Livy's account is translated in the Penguin edition: Livy's Latin has the name just once. It is as if the translator has been swayed by Xenophon's teasingly similar shout – or by Joyce.[6]

Another rich example of Joyce's punhellenism is 'Galata! Galata!'. This echo occurs in a passage where HCE – the father figure in the dream of *Finnegans Wake* – tells how he founded a city:

> I bade those polyfizzyboisterous seas to retire with themselves from os (rook-wards, thou seasea stamoror!) and I abridged with domfine norsemanship till I had done abate her maidan race ... Heaven, he hallthundered, Heydays, he flung blissforhers. And I cast my tenspan joys on her, arsched overtupped,

from bank of call to echobank, by dint of strongbow (Galata! Galata!) so streng we were in one, malestream in shegulf.

Taken in isolation, 'Galata! Galata!' seems to evoke milk (Greek *gala*) – and so the idea of the sea as mother. It hints, too, at Galatea, the sea-nymph beloved of the Cyclops, and at the Galatians, a tribe associated with the Celts that migrated into Asia Minor in antiquity. Taken in context, 'Galata! Galata!' is even more resonant. HCE is envisaging the act of founding a city as an act of bridging and as a sexual conquest. So when he exclaims 'Galata! Galata!' he is evoking the Galata bridge across the Golden Horn in Istanbul (the association is prepared in 'blissforhers', punning on Bosporus, and continued in 'dampfbulls' and 'constantonoble'). He is also evoking the modern use of 'Thalatta! Thalatta!' as a cry of erotic fulfilment: it is bliss for him too. At the same time, even though the Galata bridge does not cross the Bosporus, the channel dividing Europe and Asia, we can hardly fail to think of Istanbul's symbolic role as a meeting point of east and west when we encounter a pun based on the *Anabasis*, a key text in the opposition of Persia and Greece. Indeed, in his gazetteer to *Finnegans Wake*, the Joyce scholar Louis Mink has sought an even stronger link: 'Retiring from the Anabasis, Xenophon's troops cried "Thalassa! Thalassa!" when they reached the Bosporus across from Galata.' Mink has moved Xenophon's shout several hundred miles west of its actual setting in the mountains above Trebizond. He has been confused by Joyce's pun – much like the Camus scholar who thought the Greeks' shout took place on their return from Marathon. Or rather, Mink is trying to make Joyce's pun cleverer than it actually is. Or does Joyce's cleverness lie in his inviting precisely this confusion?[7]

There is another hint of Xenophon in an earlier phrase in HCE's monologue: 'rookwards, thou seasea stamoror!'. Joyce is here recalling the legendary scene of King Canute bidding the seas retire. His phrase 'seasea stamoror' suggests 'sissy stammerer', and 'stamoror' can also be taken as a Latin phrase: 'stop, I delay'. That translation seems appropriate for a stammerer – and the preceding repetition 'seasea' itself enacts a stammer. At the same time, 'seasea' evokes 'sea sea' – the shout of Xenophon's Greeks. Joyce here reduces both the loud sounds of the Homeric 'polyfizzyboisterous seas' and the Ten Thousand's great shout of 'The Sea! The Sea!' to a weak stammer.

That shout is heard in its full force in the monologue spoken by Anna Livia Plurabelle (the river Liffey) as she runs out through Dublin towards the sea that is her father: 'Sea, sea! Here, weir, reach, island, bridge. Where you meet I.' The echo is the more forceful because it occurs near the end of the fourth and last book of *Finnegans Wake* – rather as 'Thalatta! Thalatta!' is found near the end of the fourth book of the *Anabasis* (though the four-part structure of *Finnegans Wake* owes much more to Vico than to Xenophon). That Anna exclaims 'Sea, sea!' rather than 'The Sea! The Sea!' is not just a sign of Joyce's linguistic sensitivity. 'Sea, sea!' can also be heard as 'See, see!' (evoking the earlier motif 'Look, look') – or again as 'Sea, see!' and 'See, sea!' In two words Joyce brilliantly conveys the essence of Xenophon's exclamation. At the same time, Anna's cry of 'Sea, sea!' also looks backwards. The end of *Finnegans Wake* is as much a beginning as an end: the final sentence flows back syntactically to the opening sentence. The cry of 'Sea, Sea!', however, looks back not to the start of *Finnegans Wake*, but to the opening scene of *Ulysses*. This cry, a less pretentious version of Buck Mulligan's 'Thalatta! Thalatta!', reverses the emotional disharmony of the earlier scene: 'Stephen's pain at separation and alienation from his mother is turned into its opposite, reconciliation figured as return to the womb.'[8]

*

Two later emigrant Irish writers, Brian Moore and Louis MacNeice, have followed Joyce's lead by using Xenophon's shout to negotiate their relationship to their Irish past. Moore evokes Xenophon at the start of his 1971 novel *Fergus*, where the main character, Fergus Fadden, an Irish writer living in California, looks out from his house towards the sea:

> there, as always, was the sea, the long Pacific breakers beginning their run two hundred yards from shore. *Thalassa, Thalassa, the loud resounding sea, our great mother, Thalassa.* Although Fergus knew no Greek, he liked to say these words over to himself: he had a weakness for sonorous syllables. Now he said aloud 'Thalassa! Thalassa!' and in that moment saw his father again.

Xenophon's shout here ushers in the central theme of the novel: the burden of the past, represented by the return of Fergus' dead father. Fergus suddenly starts seeing other figures from his past as well – his mother, an aunt, his sister and brother, old teachers: figures who somehow seem more real than a beach house somewhere outside Los Angeles. These various figures from Fergus' past come together at a surreal nighttime beach party, where Fergus roams among the uninvited guests struggling to recall a wrong that he has done in the past. The novel ends with Fergus surviving a heart attack, and dawn coming up in the east, and breakers slamming on the morning shore, 'monotonous as a heartbeat', and Fergus walking back toward the house. While Moore leaves it open whether Fergus has gained any redemption from his confrontation with the past, he underlines the impossibility of escape from the past. The exile is still defined, still haunted, by the land and the religion from which he tried to escape. There is some irony, then, in Fergus' initial cry of 'Thalassa! Thalassa!': that cry of freedom and escape is instantly answered by the presence of the father, the return of the inescapable past.[9]

When Brian Moore has Fergus say aloud 'Thalassa! Thalassa!' as he looks out over the Pacific, he is also conjuring up another father: James Joyce. The Xenophontic allusion at the start of *Fergus* (like the description of the sea as 'our great mother') is stolen from Buck Mulligan's speech at the start of *Ulysses*. The allusion is the more pointed because Moore himself, like Joyce (and the fictional Fergus), was writing as an Irishman in exile (he emigrated to Canada, took Canadian citizenship, and later moved to the United States). So when Moore describes Fergus seeing his father again just after he has echoed Xenophon's shout, he is acknowledging his debt to Joyce. That debt is shared by Moore's character Fergus: his sister taunts him by setting his literary worth against his 'old hero Mr James Joyce' and even alludes to the setting of the opening scene of *Ulysses*: 'Wouldn't it sicken you, the Dublin people making a shrine out of that blinking Martello Tower he used to live in?' Moore himself acknowledged his debt to Joyce in a short piece 'Old Father, Old Artificer' that he wrote for a Joyce Centenary Issue in the *Irish University Review*. In that article he recalled how he had felt liberated by his first encounter with *Ulysses* – and how he stole the book from a friend's parents. And he concluded by stressing the theme that resounds so loudly in *Fergus* – the necessity of exile from the Irish past that is also a sign of a deep attachment: 'for the rest of us, failed heirs, false heirs, Joyce remains our mentor: he who helped us fly past those nets of home, father-land and church.'[10]

*

When the hero of Moore's novel says aloud 'Thalassa! Thalassa!', he looks back not just to James Joyce but also to another of his literary heroes, Louis MacNeice. MacNeice was another Irish writer who explored his Irish roots through that Hellenic shout. But MacNeice was a different sort of Irishman from Joyce and Moore. He was born in the North to Protestant parents (his father was a distinguished clergyman in the Church of Ireland). He was also an Irishman who did know Greek well – thanks to a traditional classical education in England: he attended Sherborne preparatory school, and then won scholarships to Marlborough and Merton College, Oxford. 'A natural examinee, an intellectual window-dresser', he got firsts in Mods and Greats, the two parts of the Classics course at Oxford, and was then appointed to a Lectureship in Greek at the University of Birmingham. MacNeice was also an Irishman who returned to Europe from the United States at the start of the Second World War – and returned not to neutral Ireland but to the London of the Blitz.[11]

It was in the London of the Blitz that MacNeice wrote for the BBC his radio play on *The March of the Ten Thousand*, with its triumphant close on the Greeks' shout of 'The Sea! The Sea!'. MacNeice also alluded to the sea where

8. The Snotgreen Sea

'Xenophon crusted with parasangs' knew he was home in the poem we encountered in Chapter 3, 'Round the Corner'. Those notorious parasangs were the other aspect of Xenophon's account that particularly appealed to MacNeice. Along with the shout of the sea, they form a single constellation of ideas that recurs in several of his other works: parasangs connote the Ten Thousand's tough retreat through mountains and desert, the retreat that culminated in the sight of the sea.

Xenophon's parasangs first appear in MacNeice's long autobiographical poem *Autumn Journal*, written late in 1938, when war was pending and his own political consciousness had been aroused by a trip to Spain. In one section of his poem, MacNeice looks back to the time of Chamberlain's visit to Munich:

> the crisis hangs
> Over the roofs like a Persian army
> And all of Xenophon's parasangs
> Would take us only an inch from danger.

We can easily imagine why it was hard for MacNeice in the Europe of 1938 and after his experience of the Spanish Civil War to grasp the sense of freedom symbolized by 'Thalatta! Thalatta!'. But in a work published earlier that year, MacNeice did echo Xenophon's shout – or rather he let his father echo it.[12]

The echo of Xenophon appears in *I Crossed the Minch*, a travel book that MacNeice was commissioned to write about a trip to the Hebrides. MacNeice padded the book out with some parodies and poems, and also mixed in a fair amount of personal reminiscence. In one passage, he looked back eleven years to his first visit to the West of Ireland:

I drove in a saloon car with my father, and as we came over a hill, still some miles from the coast, my father, who had not been back there for many years, leaped in his seat under the constricting roof and cried like Xenophon's troops 'The Sea! The Sea!' I looked over his shoulder and saw, where the land dipped far off, a regular leap of white like the flash of an animal's teeth.

The father shouts, but it is the son who interprets the shout by invoking Xenophon. And what the son is trying to express by that allusion is the father's sense of return to the land where he grew up (his family lived on a small island near Clifden in Connemara).[13]

For all his 'highbrow' status, MacNeice here seems to be exploiting Xenophon's shout of the sea in a fairly simple way. That shout seems to be a stock image, a sentimental expression of his father's nostalgia, not unlike the longing conveyed by *Thalassa*, the title of Mary McHugh's memoir of her

169

childhood in the West of Ireland. For MacNeice imagining his father, as for McHugh, Xenophon's shout conveys a yearning for the scenes of childhood.

MacNeice's recollections of that trip to the West of Ireland are also connected with one of the deeper themes of his Hebrides travelogue. He explains that he had gone to the Hebrides 'partly hoping to find that blood was thicker than ink – that the Celt in me would be drawn to the surface by the magnetism of his fellows'. As he travels to the North of Scotland, his identity as an Irishman is at stake – for he is now an Irishman living in England, separated from his countrymen. Not only that. He is seeking in the Hebrides his father's Ireland, the Ireland he never had himself: 'I hoped to find them like the West of Ireland.' MacNeice's quest for a shared sense of identity is also tied up with his perceptions of the sea. Straight after he relates his father's Xenophontic shout at the sight of the Atlantic, he explains that he 'thought the Scotch sea would be like that too. ... I took it that when I went in Scotland north and west I should find the same pleasant changes as when in Ireland going west and south'.[14]

MacNeice hoped to feel something in common with the Celts of the Hebrides, to be able to identify with the father, but, as he admits at the outset, that was 'a sentimental and futile hope'. The reader is faced with 'a tripper's book written by someone who was disappointed and tantalized by the islands and seduced by them only to be reminded that on that soil he will always be an outsider'. And that sense of alienation is measured by MacNeice's response to sea. He later tells how he visits North Uist and goes on a 'desolate walk' in a 'desolate landscape' of 'vast unbroken dampness': 'I walked sadly up the road and down a lane towards the sea. But not really the sea. That which in English is called SEA, in German MEER, and in Greek θάλασσα, has nothing whatsoever in common with the dreary sewer that lies between Claddach and Kirkibost Island. A mere vomit of a sea ...'. MacNeice fails to respond as his father had responded to the Atlantic. He is in the position rather of Stephen Dedalus when Buck Mulligan's 'snotgreen sea' brings back memories of the bile his mother vomited up on her deathbed.[15]

No surprise, perhaps, that in the poem with which he closed the book MacNeice returned to fathers and sons. He pictured the islands where

> There is still peace though not for me and not
> Perhaps for long – still peace on the bevel hills
> For those who can still live as their fathers lived
> On these islands.

MacNeice's failure to connect with the Celts of the Hebrides stands at the same time for his failure to follow the path of his father. He had left that path by leaving Belfast and by abandoning his father's faith. He is not at peace, he cannot keep up the continuity of father and son that persists on the Hebrides:

we sense something of his struggle with the impressive, yet distant, figure of his father. But even for those who can live as their fathers lived there is not peace for long, for this is 1938, and the crisis hangs over the roofs like a Persian army, and if all of Xenophon's parasangs will not take us an inch from danger, Chamberlain's piece of paper is unlikely to do much better.[16]

MacNeice reverted to his first trip to the West of Ireland in his vivid autobiographical fragment *The Strings are False*, which was written in 1940, but published only posthumously. Here he developed further the allusion to Xenophon:

> I drove with my family to Connemara: my father had not been back there since settling in the North, so that all the time my reactions to the West were half my father's. That is, I was not seeing the West for the first time; I had been born there sixty years before and this was my homecoming. When we drove over a hill-top and there was the Atlantic gnashing its teeth in the distance, my father rose in his seat and shouted 'The sea!' And something rose inside me and shouted 'The sea' Thalassa! Thalassa! to hell with all the bivouacs in the desert; Persia can keep our dead but the endless parasangs have ended.

The differences between MacNeice's two descriptions of the trip to the West are suggestive. The account in *I Crossed the Minch* is more dramatic in its peripheral parts: it has the father leaping against a constricting roof, and its simile of the sea 'like the flash of an animal's teeth' is replaced in the later account by the more compressed metaphor of the sea 'gnashing its teeth'. The account in the autobiography, by contrast, is more impressionistic and emotional. And it is in this later account that MacNeice gives a much more elaborate description of the sight of the sea.[17]

The accounts differ in several ways at this key moment. In *I Crossed the Minch*, the father makes a Xenophontic shout: he is the one returning home. In *The Strings are False*, the son shouts as well. MacNeice shares his father's emotions: 'I had been born there sixty years before and this was my homecoming.' Whereas earlier the father had not been to the West 'for many years', now it is said to be his first visit there since he had moved to the North – and 'this is in fact inaccurate', as a footnote supplied by MacNeice's sister states. The inaccuracy aligns father and son: for both, the trip is a first of sorts.

It is not just that MacNeice now shares the father's emotions. The father's shout of 'The Sea! The Sea!' is separated out into two separate shouts: first father, then son, shouts 'The sea'. Except that it is not quite the son who does the shouting. While the father 'rose' and shouted, 'something rose' inside the son and shouted. That is, MacNeice did not make a conscious choice to shout: the shout was something that happened to him. We may compare how T.E. Lawrence 'instinctively' shouted at the sight of the Mediterranean. But while Lawrence was escaping from the cold north to the south, to the land of the crusades and of Greek myth, MacNeice is returning to the land of his father. It is his father's voice that shouts through him, his father's voice that is the voice of his subconscious.

A final difference between the two accounts may be noted. While the father had shouted 'like Xenophon's troops', now the allusion to Xenophon follows the son's shout. The Xenophontic shout is not so much shared between father and son as transferred to the son. And the son engages much more intensely with the world of the *Anabasis*, parasangs and all.

To what do these differences amount? In the account published in 1938, MacNeice fails in his quest to identify with his father's race. In the account written in 1940, but not published in his lifetime, the son strongly identifies with the father. In his *Autumn Journal*, 'all of Xenophon's parasangs / Would take us only an inch from danger', but now Thalassa! Thalassa!, 'the endless parasangs have ended'. It is as if MacNeice is battling with that earlier Hebridean failure, and seeking to restore at a private level the security and integration that is no longer possible in the world at large. As we shall see, MacNeice's striving for integration with the father would grow still stronger towards the end of his life.

If MacNeice's struggle with his father has been at stake in his memories of his trips to the Hebrides and to the West of Ireland, what of his mother, who died when MacNeice was five? She too came from the West of Ireland, and she is far more present in the memories of MacNeice's sister Elizabeth. Elizabeth confirmed that the family viewed Connemara as 'a kind of lost Atlantis': 'We were in our minds a West of Ireland family exiled from our homeland.' But whereas the brother associates the West with the father, the sister thinks of the mother: 'My father occasionally told us stories of Connemara, but my mother spoke of it so constantly and with such love and such longing that I think it was she who really made it come alive for Louis and myself.' Why the different perspectives? Partly doubtless because Louis was four years younger and had fewer years to listen to the mother's voice. But that by itself cannot explain why the world of the father dominated Louis' quest for a sense of home – especially when he was travelling to the Hebrides, from where his mother's family probably came.[18]

Perhaps the figure of the absent mother does make itself felt in *The Strings are False*. For MacNeice, the world of the mother was a world of death, captured by the memory of the morning when he heard of his mother's death and crept beneath the coverings of his bed. 'To hell with all the bivouacs in the desert': perhaps there we do catch a hint of this world of death. The desert stands for the wasteland (remember 'the vast / Negations of the east' in his radio play on the Ten Thousand) and for fixedness; and the tents for caves, confinement. The sea, by contrast, stands for life, for flux and variety, for the father. The same co-ordinates may be felt in many of MacNeice's poems where there is no overt allusion to his parents

– for instance, the well-known poem from 1944, 'Prayer before Birth', where the poet imagines the parts he must play when 'the white / waves call me to folly and the desert calls / me to doom'. And these same co-ordinates are there too in *I Crossed the Minch*, where the father 'leaped' in his seat under 'the constricting roof', and MacNeice sees the sea as a 'leap of white'. That is, the father is as alive as the sea, and asserting life against that 'constricting roof' – another image of containment and death. There is more at stake, then, in MacNeice's evocation of Xenophon's shout than nostalgia for the world of his father's youth, 'a nostalgia for somewhere I had never been'. Behind it all looms the figure of the mother, not quite absent: 'Persia can keep our dead.'[19]

*

'Round the corner was always the sea': the poem MacNeice wrote twenty years after his autobiography can now be seen not just as a charming recollection of the simple joys of childhood, but as a deeper search into origins. In that poem 'Round the Corner' MacNeice contrasts the plenitude of childhood with the longing of adolescents, when 'our calf loves yearned for union in solitude somewhere / Round that corner where Xenophon crusted with parasangs / Knew he was home …'. But while 'adolescents', as MacNeice wrote elsewhere, 'are what we all to some extent remain', his poem suggests that the sea of childhood can still return, enriched with new associations:

> Round
> That corner regardless there will be always a realm
> Undercutting its banks with repeated pittance of spray,
> The only anarchic democracy, where we are all vicarious
> Citizens; which we remember as we remember a person
> Whose wrists are springs to spring a trap or rock
> A cradle; whom we remember when the sand falls out on the carpet
> Or the exiled shell complains or a wind from round the corner
> Carries the smell of wrack or the taste of salt, or a wave
> Touched to steel by the moon twists a gimlet in memory.
> Round the corner is – sooner or later – the sea.[20]

The colloquial refrain 'round the corner' has acquired a deeper meaning by the end of the poem. This deeper meaning was partly inspired by some lines from Rex Warner's translation of a poem by George Seferis:

> We knew it the islands were beautiful.
> Somewhere round about here where we are groping,
> Maybe a little lower or a little higher,
> No distance away at all.

When MacNeice reviewed Warner's translation, he commented: 'on a plane just a shade above or below our own or just round the corner which after all is our own corner, so near and yet so far in fact, lies something which might make sense of both our past and future and so redeem our present.' There is always something more, always a residue of hope: as MacNeice wrote of the collection in which 'Round the Corner' appeared, *The Burning Perch*, 'even in the most evil picture the good things, like the sea in one of these poems, are still there round the corner'.[21]

What is it that promises to make sense of our past and future? MacNeice offers some further hints in his autobiographical fragment 'Landscapes of Childhood and Youth', which was written in the 1950s and first published in *The Strings are False*. Here he looks back to his first sight of the Atlantic, during a family holiday at Portstewart, near Portrush on the north coast of Ireland. The family got out at what seemed an inland station, and MacNeice was surprised by the tangy taste of a ginger drink, but then 'walking slightly up hill and round a corner I ran head on into a yet tangier surprise, one which is with me still when the open sea catches me unawares'. He uses the same language when he tells of his first sight of Magilligan Strand, which offered a different visual experience – the sight of the sea outlined against the shore for miles: 'we suddenly came round a corner and there it was, unbelievable but palpably there. Once again, as with my first sight of the Atlantic or the unfelt wind beyond the wall, I had the sense of infinite possibility, which implied, I think, a sense of eternity. … Magilligan Strand was like falling in love.' MacNeice goes on to link these two unexpected sights 'round a corner' with 'what I feel makes life worth living', 'the surrenders – it may be to the life-quickening urge of an air-raid … to a girl on top of the Empire State building … to the first view of the Atlantic or to the curve of a strand that seems to stretch to nowhere or everywhere'. The same thought is expressed in a poem on 'The Sea' where MacNeice writes that the sea is capable

> Any time at all of proclaiming eternity
> Like something or someone to whom
> We have to surrender, finding
> Through that surrender life.[22]

'Like something or someone to whom we have to surrender': in 'Round the Corner', MacNeice also seems to be surrendering to someone, that person 'whom we remember when the sand falls out on the carpet', his (our?) father. 'As "Round the Corner" comes round to the sea,' Jon Stallworthy writes, 'we recognize that the poet has come round to his father.' That father who leaped out of his seat and echoed Xenophon's great shout at the sight of the sea, a shout that MacNeice found himself echoing, in his imagination at least, as he battled against his sense of alienation and exile.

8. The Snotgreen Sea

That father whom MacNeice did find himself following in 'The Strand', a poem written in 1945, four years after his father's death:

> ... my steps repeat
>
> Someone's who now has left such strands for good
> Carrying his boots and paddling like a child,
> A square black figure whom the horizon understood –
>
> My father. Who ...
> Kept something in him solitary and wild,
> So loved the western sea and no tree's green
> Fulfilled him like these contours of Slievemore
> Menaun and Croaghaum and the bogs between.

The father retained his sense of place, he could recapture the fulfilment of a childhood very different from that portrayed in the son's poem 'Autobiography' – a childhood where 'trees were green / And there was plenty to be seen'. Yet the communion with the father was transient:

> It was sixteen years ago he walked this shore
>
> And the mirror caught his shape which catches mine
> But then as now the floor-mop of the foam
> Blotted the bright reflections – and no sign
>
> Remains of face or feet when visitors have gone home.

In 'Round the Corner', by contrast, MacNeice is no longer the exiled shell. Sooner or later round the corner is the sea, the sea which 'has never grown smaller', which is 'the biggest thing this side of God': the sea that stands not just for the father, but also for eternity, for redemption, for the Father.[23]

The sea came too soon for MacNeice, who died of pneumonia aged fifty-five, two years after composing 'Round the Corner'. But in what may be the last poem he wrote, 'Thalassa', he himself came round again to Xenophon's sea – and with it, even more clearly, to the figure of the Father. The poem starts with a preparation for a voyage: 'Run out the boat, my broken comrades; / ... Let every adverse force converge – / Here we must needs embark again.' In the next stanza, as he tells his 'heartsick comrades' to run up the sail, a religious image appears: 'your past life', he tells them, is 'a ruined church, But let your poison be your cure'. This religious colouring is kept up in the final stanza:

> Put out to sea, ignoble comrades,
> Whose record shall be noble yet;

> Butting through scarps of moving marble
> The narwhal dares us to be free;
> By a high star our course is set,
> Our end is life. Put out to sea.

'With its stoical reaffirmation of his underlying faith in life', MacNeice's literary executor, the Greek scholar E.R. Dodds, wrote, the poem 'makes a fitting conclusion to his life's work.' Even though it is not in fact certain that the poem was the last MacNeice wrote (it was found among his papers with no date), Dodds placed it last in his edition of MacNeice's *Collected Poems*. That placement was also appropriate because of the faint echo of Xenophon's climactic cry of triumph – and because there are hints of another sort of faith. Earlier, in *The Strings are False*, by surrendering to Xenophon's sea, MacNeice had found some integration with his father and his roots in the West of Ireland. But now the sight of the sea is not enough. The poet seeks redemption by putting out to sea.[24]

Like the romantic heroes of Mrs Baillie Reynolds' novel *'Thalassa!'*, like S.H. Kemper's obnoxious businessman poet, Louis MacNeice was able to recapture a lost world by looking down on the sea. For MacNeice, however, the sea of his childhood merges with the sea that was the constant companion of his father's youth, and Xenophon's shout of the sea is central to his imaginative engagement with the sea of his father. Paradoxically, 'Thalatta! Thalatta!' comes to express his own nostalgia for the sea of his father's childhood.

*

In their different ways, then, our three Irish writers, James Joyce, Brian Moore, and Louis MacNeice, found 'Thalatta! Thalatta!' a useful vehicle for drawing out the tensions felt by the Irishman in exile – the tensions between yearning for the past and the desire for freedom. The joyful transfer of Xenophon's shout to northern climes in Heine's 'Sea-Greeting' and in Skelton's novel *Thalatta!* (where the hero reads Heine's poem in a yacht) eludes these modern Irish writers. Nor can they feel the ecstasy felt by an earlier Irish writer, William Bonaparte-Wyse, when he applied the Greek shout of the sea to his love for the land and language of Provence.

The difficulty of gaining an unmediated access to the joy of the Ten Thousand was expressed by another northern poet, Rodney Pybus, in his 1994 poem 'Cold Blue':

> Not often but sometimes deepdark
> as blue stout, this northern sea
> is known to cut off breath with

one slash from its chill.
I have seen its distant cousin,
warm, companionable,

from the top of a valley filled
with a tribe of old grey olivetrees;
the drowsy air seemed to bubble

down below, the blue wings of the midday
sky were spread over this familial sea,
so that when memory flutters

and I watch this cold blue
shivering, I want to
shout 'Fly, *thalassa*, fly!'

Pybus, who grew up in the North-east of England, here seems to be separating himself from the rapturous appropriation of Xenophon found in Heine and other romantic poets (an endnote expressly draws attention to 'Thalassa! Thalassa!' as the source of the final line). It is no Homeric wine-dark sea that the speaker watches, but a stout-dark sea. This dark northern sea does not offer the sort of escape that the Black Sea promised Xenophon's Greeks. The only escape it offers is the flutter of memory, the thought of the seas of the south. This northern sea must itself be called on to take wings – 'Fly, *thalassa*, fly': an appropriate image for a poem in a collection called *Flying Blues* which is full of birds and butterflies. Far from laying claim to a Hellenic identity, the poet emphasizes a sense of cultural distance. And it is precisely because Xenophon's cry of narrative triumph has come to be an assertion of personal and political liberation and of national pride and independence that it helps Pybus – as it helped Joyce and his successors – to explore the tension between belonging and alienation so powerfully.[25]

Rodney Pybus triggers another allusion to Xenophon's shout in his ambitious epistolary poem 'Words of a Feather' (published in the same collection as 'Cold Blue'). This poem tells the story of an English accountant who finds liberation when he is sent to work in Mauritius and starts an affair with a local woman:

Our cries of love, the old *carmen* of sex,
... are not always those
of travellers coming at last to the ocean,
shouting their *thalassa*'s of amorous arrival.

'*Thalassa*'s of amorous arrival': Pybus has caught well the erotic potential of Xenophon's shout that was realized by earlier writers – even though there is no reason to think that he had himself come across the romantically Xenophontic titles used by Mrs Baillie Reynolds and Robert Chambers. Indeed, the allusion is particularly apt because the dramatic date of Pybus' poem is the 1930s – closer in time to those romantic writers than to his own present. But Pybus' character feels detached from the joy of travellers coming at last to the ocean – from the conventional world of romance that their amorous *thalassa*'s symbolize. It has become as hard to feel the pleasure of an erotic 'Thalassa!' as to adopt Xenophon's sea as a symbol of cultural belonging.[26]

Several other poets have exploited Xenophon's erotic shout with the same inventiveness and the same air of alienation found in Rodney Pybus' poems. One of these poets is Sean O'Brien, well-known for his descriptions of working-class life and the urban landscapes of Northern England – including the 'sex landscape' of 'railway land': 'The old come here to walk their dogs, the young to fuck each other, the middle-aged to fuck their dogs.' It is in this incongruous setting (in a prose poem 'The Railway Sleeper', from O'Brien's 2001 collection *Downriver*) that Xenophon's shout makes a surprising appearance: 'Desire is a street opening for the first time as you walk: gasholder, graveyard, pie-shop, cobbler's, church, the ribbed fishermen's terraces climbing back into black and green woods. *Thalassa! Thalassa! Railways! Railways!*'. Where does this baroque juxtaposition come from? O'Brien's words strangely recall the German soldier who thought of Xenophon's shout when he caught sight of a railway line on his retreat through the Balkans. But it is doubtless more relevant to note that the narrator has just depicted himself lying in bed, listening to 'the sound of waves, of trains'. Yet that auditory experience scarcely prepares for the gloriously unexpected exclamation: '*Thalassa! Thalassa! Railways! Railways!*'. Perhaps that exclamation springs from the poem's reflections on desire: like the sea, trains are often emblems of desire (and not just for Freudians: 'queer,' as one of Rosamond Lehmann's characters reflects, 'how a train journey throws up images, applies some stimulus to memory and desire …'). And this connection with memory and desire links railways and the sea more intimately than the mere physical collocation of railway line and coast. Readers of O'Brien's works may well think back to the epigraph to one of his earlier collections – a letter written by Debussy: 'My memories go back to the time I was six. I remember the railway passing in front of the house and the sea stretching out to the horizon. You sometimes had the impression that the railway came out of the sea or went into it – whichever you like.' Perhaps it is in part the way railway lines stretch out into the horizon and arouse the pathos of distance that links them with the sea, that image of eternity. At any rate, Xenophon's shout once again applies some stimulus to memory and desire ….[27]

The romantic transformation of Xenophon's shout is itself transformed with even more virtuosity by the modern Estonian writer Jaan Kaplinski in his poem 'Dust. I Myself'. The speaker of the poem – who may be 'a speck

of dust, or its voice, another speck of dust', or else 'its longing to be something else' – turns to address 'you, spermatozoon, semen':

> You, too, received your longing from somewhere, your longing for the
> warm, dark primal fluid
> in which your, my, ancestors, once swam, divided, and united again.
> The sea. *Thalassa. Thalatta.*
> The sea, of which so little now remains.
> Sometimes it is memory, sometimes our own blood.
> Sometimes sea water, which in Norway during the war was used for
> blood transfusions, when there was not enough blood.

The speaker, whoever it is, seems to have taken on board the theories of the
Hungarian psychoanalyst Sandor Ferenczi. The description of our longing to
return to the primal sea, the primal unity from which we are now splintered,
closely resembles Ferenczi's notion of the 'thalassal regressive trend'
(discussed in Chapter 4). At the same time, the pairing of 'Thalassa' and
'Thalatta' evokes the shout of the Ten Thousand – as well as the alternation
between those two Greek forms in the modern reception of that shout.
Kaplinski's own distortion '*Thalassa. Thalatta*' is itself eloquent – especially
when it cuts off 'the sea' from 'the sea, of which so little now remains'. A
shout of 'The Sea! The Sea!', 'Thalatta! Thalatta!', could be seen as a step
towards recovering primal unity, but we are now divorced even from the
plenitude of Xenophon's time, from the Ten Thousand's harmony as they
shouted together. We can recover that earlier sense of wholeness only in our
memory – or through the sea that is in our blood (a romantic image – but is
it actually true that sea water was used for blood transfusions?).[28]

The most sustained use of Xenophon's shout as a romantic symbol in
modern poetry is to be found in an intense and intriguing work *Thalassa
Thalassa* by the Australian poet Javant Biarujia (a name adopted from the
private language he invented). The poem, published in 1983, is a reflection
on the narrator's relationship with his addressee, Riwan, who lies sick in bed
('Your name means "dream" in Arabic – it is a flower in the shape of male
genitalia – or male genitalia in the shape of a flower'). It consists of fragmented and dreamlike clips of scanned and unscanned verse that the reader
struggles to integrate into a coherent narrative. Along with romantic motifs
(blood, flowers, the desert), the sea, and Xenophon's sea in particular, is one
of the recurrent images in the poem:

> as i drifted to sleep i caught some of your words
> a silent *bruit de voix*
> a disquisition on oceanography
> and Xenophons *Anabasis* –
> thalassa thalassa

Later we catch dream-like images of the Ten Thousand:

> beneath the photic layers of dream *insolite*
> having left the bars
> i wandered the seedy streets
> gloomy and fetid alleys where
> old women defecated
> squatting like children
> i passed Xenophons soldiers each one seeking
> his own pleasure

And Xenophon himself shares in the poem's homoeroticism:

> Xenophon too was
> troubled by the perfect physique
> of early manhood
> of sturdy young athletes[29]

Some direction is given to the weltering imagery of Biarujia's poem by its form. The three parts of the poem are made up of fifty-one numbered segments, each the same length as the equivalent segments in the other parts of the poem, and further linked by the repetition of words and themes. The place where most direction is given to the poem is the closing section of each part – where the poem's title, *Thalassa Thalassa*, is explained by further echoes of Xenophon's shout. The first echo appears at the end of the second part:

> a husk of passion
> you stood between fire and water
> longing for a storm
> we forgot god on the day of our births
> the sea the sea

This echo corresponds with the Greek phrase at the end of the third part:

> 'let every moment renew your vision' (Gide)
> a husk of passion
> forget god from the day of your birth
> and whom I love hear the soldiers chorus
> thalassa thalassa

And these two Xenophontic echoes help in turn to fill in an absence in the corresponding section in the first part:

8. The Snotgreen Sea

1. a dusk like silk fuses the day
   a dusk of tropical fruit
   a husk of passion
2. a topaz forest bends to drink at the sea
3.

We can see in retrospect that the poem has moved along a path away from the blank line at the end of the first section towards the fulfilment of the Greek shout. And a final section in prose offers some explanation of the title: 'Darling Riwan, ... I love you, I chose the exulting cry of the general's men to signify our love in the love of the sea on your part, and the sea in my blood on mine'. But Xenophon's soldiers are excluded from the erotic fulfilment of their shout: their story dates 'from an epoch before the sea was truly beheld and love beholden'. The narrator has no wish to identify with their sordid pleasure-seeking amidst defecating old women.[30]

*

Many modern writers, it seems, have skewed the romantic and nationalistic uses of 'Thalatta! Thalatta!' – while also paying a homage of sorts to that inherited set of associations. It is another thing to wrench Xenophon's shout away from its expected frame of reference altogether. So violent a wrenching calls for something even more surreal and cryptic than Javant Biarujia's erotic elegy. It calls for 'The Deconstructed Man' – a poem by James Laughlin, publisher and friend of William Carlos Williams and other avant-garde writers. Laughlin's poem boasts the happy couplet 'I am the deconstructed man / I do the best I can'. And the best the deconstructed man can do, it seems, is scatter isolated poetic allusions and other bits-and-bobs:

> the sea was not my mother but my mother took me to the sea
> the old Cunarder Mauretania and Bill the sailor
> who showed me how to splice a rope
> and Jack turned green when we were beating through the chop above Grenada
> avoid the Indian Ocean you can die of heat
> posh P & O boats are like baking ovens
> the sea the sea cried Xenophon after his weary march
> O mother sea our bodies turn to dust our hearts return to thee.

Laughlin's fractured poem seems at this point to be merely a series of nautical observations. Yet even here we can see a hint of the romantic equation of Xenophon's sea with the sea that is our mother, the sea to which we all return, and a hint, too, of the contrast between the dust of the deathlike desert and the fluid life of the sea. And Laughlin further undercuts the

181

poem's apparent aspiration to a free play of signification by the poised beauty and balance of the final line, with its internal rhymes.[31]

The story of Xenophon's weary march is more radically disturbed so as to fit the requirements of nonsense verse in the 1990 poem 'dwang parasang' by the Dutch poet Ben Zwaal (from a book itself entitled *dwang parasang*):

> the antics
> blow their noses
> a satrap
> closes his empire
> with a handkerchief
>
> the ten thousand
> break out
> through the sneezing sea
> with troubles
> hachoo thalassa
>
> the moon sleeps
> no more with Endymion

Zwaal seems here to be trying to rival the linguistic playfulness of James Joyce. The surprise 'hachoo thalassa' ('hatsjie thalassa' in the Dutch original), for instance, is a reaction against the romantic suggestion that the sibilant 'Thalassa, Thalassa' simulates the sound of the sea. Xenophon's shout has become a mere sneeze: so much for all the Greeks' toils through Asia. Many of Zwaal's other effects are lost in translation. Behind the unexpected image of sneezing antics there lies a pun on 'strapatsen' (used in Dutch of extravagant antics, but the German sense 'toils' can also be felt) and 'satraap' ('satrap'). And even the punning title of Zwaal's poem is hard to convey in English. 'dwang parasang' – literally 'force parasang' – suggests both the arduous march of the Ten Thousand and schoolchildren's forced march through the Greek text. 'Xenophon covered with his men daily a few parasangs', the blurb on the back cover explains, 'and still the pupils in a Gymnasium are forced to chew and re-chew and swallow almost vomiting his monotonous account written in unintelligible characters.' At the same time, by a self-referential twist, the title hints at the compulsion to write poetry, the urge to create new verbal associations out of the familiar stock of images (and few words spring more readily to the mind of any reader of the *Anabasis* than 'parasang').

Reading the whole of Zwaal's poem gives a fuller meaning to the pun 'hatsjie thalassa'. Zwaal's sneezing sea recalls the 'snotgreen sea' greeted by Buck Mulligan at the start of the great modernist text, *Ulysses* (where Zwaal's playful parasangs are also anticipated). But Zwaal is also hinting at one of the great scenes earlier in the *Anabasis*. When Xenophon rouses the dejected troops after the murder of the Greek generals, someone sneezes in the middle of his speech, and the sneeze is taken as a good omen. By having 'hatsjie thalassa' close the part of the poem that seems to deal with the Ten Thousand, Zwaal is also playing on the closural force that 'Thalassa! Thalassa!' has acquired. But he follows that distortion of Xenophon with two lines of 'fine' poetry, alluding to a famous piece of classical mythology – the moon's passion for Endymion and Endymion's eternal sleep. More specifi-cally, he alludes to a famous image made of that story by Shakespeare's Portia: 'The moon sleeps with Endymion, / And would not be awak'd!' – a lyrical way of saying that the moon has gone behind a cloud. Zwaal's piece of classical learning seems haunting and beautiful, but the effect is undercut by its apparent lack of connection with what precedes (unless there is a bilin-gual pun in the moon sleeping 'nooit meer' with Endymion – 'no more', but also 'no sea'?). But even the allusion to the moon is making fun of a stock romantic scene – lovers gazing at each other (and perhaps at a stretch of water) under a moonlit sky: recall the climactic scene in Mrs Baillie Reynolds' *'Thalassa!'*, quoted in Chapter 3, and also Shakespeare's Lorenzo and Jessica in fabulous Belmont, the lovers to whom Portia's words are also drawing attention.[32]

It would be rash to treat Zwaal's extravagant wordplay as if it could be divorced from the *Anabasis* itself. Like Joyce and some of the other writers we have met earlier, Zwaal is distinctly modernist in his move away from content to a playful fascination with words for their own sake. But why does 'Thalassa! Thalassa!' have such an appeal? It is not just that Xenophon's shout – like his parasangs – is part of the cultural quarry that modern writers mine. It is also that it has often been taken as the culmination of a narrative of fulfilment and triumph. Most of the literary texts which allude to 'Thalatta! Thalatta!' remove it from its narrative context and allude to it as a great moment that condenses in itself one of the most basic narrative struc-tures: first toil (all those parasangs ...), then hope, and finally fulfilment. Indeed, several times in this book Xenophon's exclamation has cropped up because it has been used as a chapter heading (in a romantic novel and an English translation of Verne, in narratives written by an escaped prisoner of war and at the time of the Dunkirk evacuation, or again in several travel accounts) – at times without any reference to Xenophon in the text itself. It is as if the mere heading is enough to evoke a narrative of struggle and success. So the way in which writers allude to 'Thalatta! Thalatta!' can be seen as a commentary on narrative itself – a reflection on our desire for a final revelation of meaning.[33]

Even though one of the hallmarks of modernism is often held to be its resistance to the satisfactions offered by the traditional narrative form, Xenophon's shout has nonetheless retained its appeal in the modern age.

Indeed, it preserves its traditional closural force at the end of *Finnegans Wake* (Anna Livia Plurabelle's cry of 'Sea sea!'), and in Javant Biarujia's homo-erotic poem, and even, in a sense, in Rodney Pybus' closing 'Fly, *thalassa*, fly'. In other modern works, however, 'Thalatta! Thalatta!' is evoked in isola-tion from any strong narrative context: remember Jaan Kaplinski's poem 'Dust' ('*Thalassa. Thalatta*'), for instance, or James Laughlin's 'The Deconstructed Man', or the puns ('Galata! Galata!', 'tha lassy! tha lassy!') scattered through *Finnegans Wake*. Zwaal's poem seems closer to these works in its subversion of narrative expectations. It does not just mock Xenophon's cry of triumph, it also follows 'hachoo thalassa' with those two apparently irrelevant lines about the moon's passion for Endymion. Yet while they twist and play with mythological motifs, the modernist texts we have met so far also seem to recuperate those motifs for a fragmented world. Even to sneeze 'hachoo thalassa' is not to reject Xenophon's sea outright.

*

One way 'Thalatta! Thalatta!' can be rejected outright – or at least made a more ambivalent symbol of escape and liberation – is by questioning what lies beyond the apparent 'happy ever after' of the sight of the sea. A new ambivalence about that ending can be found in a number of works written since the start of the Second World War, among them a 1943 memoir by the Swiss artist Edmond Bille describing his life as a citizen of a neutral country in a world at war. In his memoir, itself entitled *Thalassa*, Bille quotes Xenophon's 'cry of joy' on the title page, and then reflects in a dedicatory letter on his experiences by the Atlantic shore of Portugal as 'a spectator ... at the terminus of the lamentable Exodus'. There he studied the stream of refugees: 'heroes without panache, hunted but victorious lovers who have remained apart from the resigned herd and from the madness of the pariahs ... Thalassa! The sea! It is *she* who attracted them all, like water attracts suicides. And those men, alas, had only one desire left: TO LIVE.' Against the backdrop of a disordered world Bille focuses on the aspirations of private individuals and on the promise of the New World – a promise symbolized by 'Avenida da Liberdade' ('Avenue of Liberty'), the heading of the last section of his account. He seems to be following the conventional image of Xenophon's sea as an icon of freedom – albeit a freedom that is now only possible for the individual seeking refuge from a maddened world. And yet there are dangers in this sea that seems to promise freedom. The voyage of one optimist across the Atlantic ends in shipwreck. And the threat of ship-wreck is conveyed even more starkly by the cover which Bille drew for his memoir (Plate 1). The cover shows, beneath the title 'Thalassa', a second 'Thalassa' half submerged in waves, and beneath this, a ship sinking into the deep – a sinking ship that drowns out the dreams of the freedom of the New

World, but also stands for the ship of state, the ship of old Europe enmeshed in war. Reaching the sea by the avenue of liberty is not, it seems, the same as securing salvation.[34]

Arrival at the sea is equally fraught with anxieties for the future in a 1959 radio play *Anabasis* by the German dramatist Wolfgang Weyrauch. Weyrauch's play, like the play which Louis MacNeice wrote for the BBC during the Second World War, tells the story of the Ten Thousand's March to the Sea. But whereas MacNeice kept within the bounds of realism, Weyrauch's is a parable play, similar to some of MacNeice's later quest plays. The Ten Thousand's march through Armenia dramatizes the opposition between rational trust in the future and despair. The focus throughout is on whether the Greeks will be able to surmount their obstacles and reach the sea. At the start, they are stuck on a mountain of ice, and the enemy are around them and calling on them to surrender. The soldiers are despondent, but while the Captain, the 'soldier of war', counsels that they defend themselves by attacking, Xenophon the 'storyteller', the 'soldier of peace', insists that they should save themselves by reason and that true courage lies in not using the weapons that one has available. Xenophon is given three days to prove himself right and find the sea. He sends out a flute player and a dumb man, but the first two days they come back without success. As the third day draws to its close, the soldiers start to stone Xenophon. But at last, as Xenophon lies crushed on the ground and close to death, the sound of the flute is heard. It is, however, only the dumb man playing on the flute as he carries on his back the body of the flute player. Suddenly the dumb man recovers his voice and proclaims that he has seen the sea. But when he leads them there and the soldiers do see the sea, the sea looks 'hateful' and its noise drowns their voices. Even Xenophon seems gloomy: 'The sea before us is no sister of the sun. It is related to the night. It is a part of the cloud which hovers over it. It is called the Black Sea.' The cloud hovering over, and merging with, the dark sea perhaps recalls Hiroshima and Nagasaki. It is as if the Greeks have arrived at a sea clouded over by the threat of nuclear war, the threat that the 'soldiers of war', the advocates of the pre-emptive strike, may win the day. But there is still a faint hope for the future: when the Greeks find ships, the shadow of the flute player will somehow remain with them and save them.[35]

The pessimistic close of Weyrauch's radio drama is especially striking because it contrasts with the much more positive play about the *Anabasis* which Weyrauch wrote with Ernst Glaeser in 1932. Glaeser wrote then that 'as witnesses of an especially desperate and morally unstable age, in which each individual seeks to protect himself from a fate that is only to be banished together', they had felt the duty 'to sing the Song of Songs of that human solidarity which alone can protect Europe today from relapsing into a barbarism from which there is no escape. In the "Anabasis" for the first time in known Greek history the masses appear as hero, and proof is offered that the masses, disciplined and bound by a single thought, have more power than the individual.' In retrospect this celebration of the human solidarity of some soldiers who did escape from barbarian lands could seem dangerously close to Nazi totalitarianism. In Weyrauch's new version it is not the masses who are the hero, but the individual leader Xenophon who has always to overcome the despair of the soldiers – and even this Xenophon nearly dies at their hands.[36]

A similar tension between triumph and despair is central to Sol Yurick's gritty 1965 novel *The Warriors*, where the story of the *Anabasis* is transferred to New York. At first sight, Yurick's presentation of the Ten Thousand seems to belong firmly in the celebratory tradition. Yurick tells the story of a juvenile gang, the Coney Island Dominators, that travels up to the Bronx for a night-time meeting of gangs called by a charismatic leader, Ismael, with 'the dreams of an Alexander, a Cyrus, a Napoleon'. But the meeting turns into a brawl, the police move in, Ismael is shot, and the Dominators have to evade the police and make their way home through the turf of other gangs. The Ten Thousand feature in the story as heroes from a children's comic that the youngest member of the gang starts to read when they have found their way to a subway train:

> The Junior took out his comic book and started to read. ... he could follow the whole action from the pictures. It was about ancient soldiers, Greeks, heroes who had to fight their way home through many obstacles, but in the end they made it. He had enjoyed reading it so much that it was the third time he was going through.

The Junior's reading of his comic is then set off against the macho posturing of the rest of the gang: 'Even the Junior had to look up from a panel showing the grinning faces of the Greek heroes as they saw The Sea, The Sea.' During the gang's antics, a page is torn out to wipe away some chocolate – 'it was the panel showing the heroes arriving at the sea'. But The Junior does get to the end: 'The heroes were, The Junior could see, the hardest men in a hard world, admirable, but, he thought, he wouldn't like to be in their place, even though he envied their adventures. He sighed, turned back to the beginning as the train went through the echo-y tunnel ...'. As so often, no sooner is the *Anabasis* evoked than our attention is forced on the scene where the Ten Thousand see the sea – here interpreted through The Junior's eyes as the climax of a triumphant achievement. And the 'Thalatta' passage is made to seem all the more celebratory by its distancing from the puerile bickering to which it serves as backdrop. Greeks who fight their way to freedom seem to have no connection with gangland New York, with a sordid brawl in the Bronx on Independence Day. And The Junior dimly recognizes that lack of connection.

186

He does not know who these heroes are (he recognizes that they are Greeks, but neither Xenophon nor the Ten Thousand are named). But he does know that he would not like to be in their place. Yet he is still continually in need of the satisfactions that his comic offers. He is already reading it for the third time; and he will turn back to its beginning more than once in the night.[37]

While the comic book version of the *Anabasis* seems to point up the limited world of New York gangland, Yurick's novel also invites us to read the exploits of the Ten Thousand through different lenses. Does the *Anabasis* offer the meagre consolations of a comic? Did Italo Calvino hit the mark when he wrote that 'on occasions Xenophon appears to be one of those heroes from children's comics, who in every episode appear to survive against impossible odds'? Or perhaps Yurick is making a self-conscious allusion to the source of his own story by having the story of the *Anabasis* told in a comic, as a sort of *mise-en-abîme*. If so, we can read Yurick as distancing his own transference of the *Anabasis* to New York from other, simpler, and more triumphalist adaptations like that offered by the comic book. And a compelling hint that this is how we should read his novel is offered by an epigraph taken from the *Anabasis* – from a speech made by Xenophon after the Ten Thousand have seen the sea, when their way forward is once more blocked: 'My friends, these people whom you see are the last obstacle which stops us from being where we have so long struggled to be. We ought, if we could, to eat them up alive.' Wanting to eat people raw is the hallmark of savages, of the desperate and disturbed. These are words for hard men in a hard world. Perhaps the world of the Ten Thousand is not so different from the lawless world of the New York gangs. Like those gangs, they have to try to negotiate their way through hostile terrain while keeping their identity as Greeks, as warriors, intact.[38]

It is when Yurick returns to Xenophon's description of the Ten Thousand seeing the sea that he creates the greatest distance between his own story and the simplistic world of the comic book. The Coney Island Dominators do return to the sea, and they do echo (and even cap) Xenophon's 'Thalatta! Thalatta!': 'Hinton smelled the cool sea wind and began to feel a joyful excitement and quickened his step again. ... He began to run. They ran after him, laughing silly, unable to control themselves. ... Hinton pointed and yelled, "The Ocean!" They yelled, "The Ocean, The Ocean!" and they all laughed hysterically.' But after this they return home to the grim apartment block they call 'The Prison', and the story ends with Hinton curled up on a balcony: 'his eyes stared out over the trees and through the laundry lines towards where the sea would be if it wasn't blocked off by a big hotel.'[39]

The end of Yurick's novel goes against conventional expectations about how an escape story should end. At the same time, Yurick continues to thwart any simple equation between the Dominators and Xenophon's Greeks. The Dominators' sense that they have been involved in a great adventure is undercut when the remnants of the gang discover that their original leader (who they thought had been killed) had made it home all by himself. It is as if the Ten Thousand had found Clearchus safe and well when they reached Trapezus. Perhaps we cannot really compare these adolescents out for a night on the town with the heroic Greeks who marched for months across sand and snow.

Xenophon's 'Thalatta' passage is central to understanding not just Yurick's novel, but also the changes made in 1979 when the novel was turned by Walter Hill into a film, also called *The Warriors*. This film – which is rebuked in one film guide for having a 'comic book plot' – alters the original novel in a number of ways, and most of these changes seem to remove the tensions that make Yurick's novel interesting. It replaces the novel's 'more conventional picture of street-gang culture' (a culture of murder and gang rape) with a sort of 'Woodstock exoticism' – a festive array of improbable gang costumes. The comic book disappears, and with it the most obvious source of explicit allusion to the *Anabasis*. But the leader who wants to unify all the gangs is at least renamed Cyrus. A more significant change is that when Cyrus is shot dead, the Coney Island gang – here called the Warriors – is wrongly accused of killing him, and more actively pursued by the other gangs on its way home. So the Warriors are innocents on the run. But they do make it back to Coney Island, and the film ends not with them returning home to a dismal housing estate with no view of the sea, but with them standing on a beach, looking out at the sea: 'When we see the ocean, we figure we're home, we're safe' (Plate 18). Their innocence has been acknowledged, their accusers brought to book, and their heroic status affirmed: ' "You Warriors are good. Real good." "The best." '[40]

Yurick's questioning novel seems to be tamed by the rather more straightforward film. But even in the film there is disillusionment. Already when they arrive back at Coney Island at daybreak, their new leader has asked: 'This is what we fought all night to get back to?' And when the film closes with the gang looking out at the sea, the point is that they are looking *away* from home. In the words of the closing soundtrack, 'In the City':

> Somewhere out on that horizon
> Out beyond the neon lights
> I know there must be something better
> But there's nowhere else in sight.

So both the book and the film versions of *The Warriors* evoke Xenophon's great description of the Greeks' sight of the sea while also inviting us to question the meaning of 'escape'.

*

The gloomy atmosphere of the twentieth century has, it seems, created a tension between admiration for the Ten Thousand's successful retreat to the sea and alarm at the prospect of what lies beyond their arrival at the coast. The reworkings of Xenophon by Edmond Bille, Wolfgang Weyrauch, and Sol Yurick confirm the pattern we traced in a number of soldiers and adventurers in Chapter 2: the move from a strong emotional engagement in 'The Sea! The Sea!' to the irony of Peter Fleming and the suspicion felt by T.E. Lawrence towards attempts to impart a Xenophontic aura to his capture of Akaba. But these various responses all cast a shadow over the brilliance of the 'Thalatta' scene rather than reject it outright. For an outright rejection of Xenophon's sight of the sea, we have to turn to the long poem *Paterson* by one of the most distinguished American poets of the twentieth century, William Carlos Williams. In Williams' American setting, as for some of the Irish writers discussed earlier, Xenophon's sea stands for nostalgia for the past. But it is no longer quite the same nostalgia that it was for James Joyce and Louis MacNeice, or even for Brian Moore when he transferred Xenophon's shout to California. Xenophon's sea now stands for a nostalgia that must be resisted.

Paterson is Williams' most ambitious poem: planned in four books, and published between 1946 and 1951, it is the tale of a city (Paterson, New Jersey) and a man (also called Paterson). While it has the fragmentation typical of modernism (it includes many prose fragments, among them excerpts from the history of Paterson, economic discussions, letters from Ezra Pound and Allen Ginsberg), it also follows the course of the river Passaic down to the falls and finally to the sea.

The shout of 'Thalassa! Thalassa!' is first heard in the third book, 'The Library'. Paterson has sought refuge in the library from the roar of the present. He is pursuing a search for a redeeming language, but his mind roams as he reads:

> Awake, he dozes in a fever heat,
> cheeks burning .   .   loaning blood
> to the past, amazed .   risking life.
>
> And as his mind fades, joining the others, he
> seeks to bring it back – but it
> eludes him, flutters again and flies off and
> again away   .
>
>   O Thalassa, Thalassa!
>   the lash and hiss of water
>   The sea!
>   How near it was to them!
>
>   Soon!
>
>   Too soon   .

189

'Loaning blood to the past', Paterson in the library is in the position of Odysseus in the Underworld (a draught of blood was needed for the ghosts to speak), and the sea ('O Thalassa, Thalassa!') stands for the past that he is attempting to bring back. The Underworld analogy is appropriate, for 'The Library is desolation, it has a smell of its own / of stagnation and death' – an atmosphere Paterson finally finds intolerable: 'I cannot stay here / to spend my life looking into the past.'[41]

Though Paterson manages to resist the call of Xenophon's sea in the library, that call is felt still more strongly in the fourth book of *Paterson*, 'The Run to the Sea'. The book ends with the Passaic flowing down to the Atlantic – just as the fourth book of *Finnegans Wake* ends with the Liffey flowing into the Irish Sea and the fourth book of the *Anabasis* ends with the Ten Thousand reaching the sea. As the river draws near to the Atlantic, the voice of the poet splits into two:

> I warn you, the sea is *not* our home.
> the sea is not our home
>
> The sea *is* our home whither all rivers
> (wither) run   .
>
> the nostalgic sea
> sopped with our cries
> Thalassa! Thalassa!
> calling us home   .
> I say to you, Put wax rather in your
> ears against the hungry sea
> it is not our home!
>
> .   draws us in to drown, of losses
> and regrets   .

The competing voices become still more intense as the sea gets nearer and nearer:

> Listen!
> Thalassa!   Thalassa!
> Drink of it, be drunk!
> Thalassa
> immaculata: our home, our nostalgic
> mother in whom the dead, enwombed again
> cry out to us to return   .
> the blood dark sea! ...
>
> .   .   not our home! It is NOT
> our home.[42]

190

As earlier in 'The Library', so at the end of Williams' poem, the sea (Xenophon's sea) is associated with death, with a return to the primal source. The sea also represents 'the pull of longing toward a lost culture', as Williams indicates by the 'overwrought cry' of 'Thalassa! Thalassa!', a cry that 'seems to parody the longing of a Pound or an Eliot', the longing of those Americans who did seek to recapture that lost culture of Europe.[43]

Williams' poem ends by resisting the grand tradition of narrative closure. Paterson risks death by swimming out to sea, but then he turns back to land. When he reaches the shore, he puts wax in his ears and heads inland with a dog, passing as he goes some girls throwing balls on the beach. The hero of Williams' modern epic resembles Edgar Allen Poe, whose greatness, in Williams' view, was that 'he turned his back and faced inland, towards originality'. So too when Williams has his hero swim in from the sea he affirms the quest over the goal: 'Virtue is wholly / in the effort to be virtuous.' He also asserts the possibility of creativity, the possibility that language can redeem us: as he wrote in a letter, 'the ocean of savage lusts ... is not our home. It is the seed that floats to shore, one word, one tiny even microscopic word, is that which can alone save us.' Williams further asserted the possibility of creativity, the need to resist the pull of the sea, by carrying his poem on beyond 'The Run to the Sea'. Though he had originally planned the poem in four books, he published a fifth book of *Paterson* in 1958, and was working on a sixth when he died.[44]

But even as William Carlos Williams rejects the nostalgic sea he cannot help being defined by the past that he is resisting: 'Thalassa! Thalassa! / Drink of it, be drunk!'. Indeed, he memorably re-inscribes the great emotional pull of Xenophon's sea in the tussling and excited dialogue with which the book concludes. At the same time, the Paterson who resists the call of Xenophon's sea repeats the actions of another Greek hero, Odysseus, as he puts wax in his ears (like Odysseus putting wax in his comrades' ears as they sail past the Sirens), passes girls throwing a ball (like Nausicaa and her friends), and meets a dog more fortunate than Odysseus' dog Argos, which died when it first saw its master again.

*

'Virtue is wholly / in the effort to be virtuous': William Carlos Williams' reluctance to accept 'Thalatta! Thalatta!' as a triumphant shout is matched in other recent readings of the *Anabasis* by a greater stress on the Greeks' toils in the earlier stages of their march. This trend is well illustrated by the poem 'Anabasis' by the Polish writer Zbigniew Herbert. Herbert's poem (as we saw in Chapter 4) deflates overly romanticized renderings of Xenophon's shout of the sea: 'the famous shout on Mount Teches / is mistakenly interpreted by sentimental poets / they simply found the sea that is the exit from the dungeon.' But the poem does not just resist the allure of sentimentality, it also expresses some admiration for Xenophon's own refusal to mythologize or sentimentalize. The poem starts by setting Cyrus' 'foreign legion' in the vastness of the spaces they crossed before they found the sea:

> cunning pitiless and yes they murdered
> two hundred and fifteen daily marches
> – kill us we can't go any further –
> thirty-four thousand two hundred and fifty-five stadia

The exactness of those numbers is a pointed response to the sense of arduous endeavour that Xenophon's account creates (stades, a Greek measure, are a slightly disappointing replacement for the parasangs that have more commonly impressed themselves on readers of the *Anabasis*). And for all the destruction the Ten Thousand cause, there is still something admirable in Xenophon's bluntness:

> festering with sleeplessness they went through savage countries
> uncertain fords mountain passes in snow and salty plateaux
> cutting their road in the living body of peoples
> luckily they didn't lie they were defending civilization

Herbert's poem ends by drawing a universal lesson from the struggles of the Ten Thousand through hostile lands:

> they made the journey without the Bible without prophets burning bushes
> without signs on the earth without signs in the sky
> with the cruel consciousness that life is immense

It is as if the Ten Thousand are existential heroes: their parasangs (or at least their stades) are their thing.

Zbigniew Herbert's response to Xenophon is mirrored in an essay on the *Anabasis* by another great modern writer, Italo Calvino. Like Herbert, Calvino is impressed by Xenophon's blunt refusal to moralize: 'Xenophon has the great merit, in moral terms, of never mystifying or idealizing his or his men's position. … He is aware of being at the head of a horde of parasites in a foreign land, and that the "barbarian" peoples whose lands they have invaded are in the right not his men.' And Calvino is even more explicit than Herbert in his claim that the Ten Thousand are an appropriate symbol of the modern condition:

> The Greek army, creeping through the mountain heights and fjords amidst constant ambushes and attacks, no longer able to distinguish just to what extent it is a victim or an oppressor, and surrounded even in the most chilling

massacres of its men by the supreme hostility of indifference or fortune, inspires in the reader an almost symbolic anguish which perhaps only we today can understand.[45]

Many modern readers share the perception of Herbert and Calvino that the retreat of the Ten Thousand is best defined not by its goal – the triumphant, and all too familiar, 'Thalatta! Thalatta!' – but by the hardships of the journey – soldiers struck by snowblindness as they try to make their way across the Armenian plateau in winter, as their shoes stick fast to their feet, as they lose the will to move on, parasang after parasang, obstacle after obstacle. This shift of sensitivity is reflected in modern anthologies of travel and exploration: two modern editors, Eric Newby and Benedict Allen (both adventurers themselves), have included not the famous scene on Mount Theches but the long walk through the snows of Armenia. The tramp across the snows of Armenia also appealed strongly to the Swedish writer (and Nobel Prize winner) Eyvind Johnson. In an autobiographical novel from 1937, Johnson portrayed his hero thinking of the Greeks' struggles through snow in the Armenian mountains as he makes his way to work through snow. And Xenophon loomed much larger in Johnson's 1957 novel *Molnen över Metapontion* (*Clouds over Metapontion*). Here a Jewish prisoner in a German concentration camp invents for his fellow prisoners the story of Themistogenes of Syracuse (the pseudonym under which Xenophon is thought to have published the *Anabasis*). This new Themistogenes had been a prisoner in the stone quarries at Syracuse before he joined Xenophon on Cyrus' march, and his experiences in the quarries are recalled when the Greeks find themselves cut off in Mesopotamia. The setting for this story, a concentration camp during the Second World War, is itself eloquent of the symbolic force of Xenophon's tale of encirclement and escape, and that symbolic force is strengthened by parallels between the story of Themistogenes and the life of one of the Jewish prisoner's listeners. In the account of the retreat little is made of the great moment of triumph when the Greeks first catch sight of the sea. This is no tale of triumph: 'ultimately there cannot be any such thing as good victors,' one of the characters says. But there is a glimpse of that character urging on his disheartened comrades through the Armenian snows. There are no victories, but there is endurance.[46]

Nowhere is the physical endurance of the Ten Thousand during their long march more bizarrely proclaimed than in 'Rilke's Feet', an intermittently lyrical work by Christopher Middleton, an English academic renowned as both author and translator of experimental poems. Rilke and (metrical and anatomical) feet are the two guiding themes in Middleton's poem. It is feet that are the dominant strand in the eleventh, and penultimate, section of the poem, which starts with a sudden shift to the world of the Ten Thousand:

> Xenophon Xenophon it were fit to include ...
> An echo of your script from Corinth, your
> Fictional grammar of the human foot
>
> Anabasis uh I am tired and my secret
> Reader wonders where we have got
> As did your mob of Greeks thirty years before
> Thirty years before you finally wrote
>
> A bit boastfully about the march to the sea ...
> But hardly anybody cares now
> About the fleetfooted Carduchi ...

The Carduchi also fit into this foot-obsessed poem because they rest the base of the bow on the left foot as they shoot. But the main reason why Middleton dwells on Xenophon's 'fictional grammar of the human foot' (again the endless parasangs seem to lurk in the background) is the march through the snows of Armenia:

> And soon backwards the snow
> Is opening its white tomb
>
> Illshod columns of infantry
> Straggle into Armenian mountains
> Was there no shit they could not bite through
>
> Newly flayed oxenskin
> Froze that night to the footsoles
> Thongs cut into ankle flesh

Middleton then alludes to the snowblindness that afflicted the Greeks before ending the section on the *Anabasis* with a disruptive shift of person: 'Small bags later we tied / To the horse hooves else / In the snow to their bellies they sank.'[47]

'Xenophon Xenophon': we can understand by the end of Middleton's poem why that name is repeated. The repetition replaces the expected allusion to 'Thalatta! Thalatta!'. Readers of this challenging poem are not allowed to hear that shout themselves. They are not offered such an easy escape from the poem's meanderings. 'Anabasis uh I am tired': the narrator shares the weariness of Xenophon's Greeks as they march for parasang after parasang, and soon readers of the poem find themselves assimilated to the Greeks, sharing the symbolic anguish of modernism. With its sensitivity to the pathos of footsoles and ankle flesh, Middleton's poem suggests that T.E. Lawrence anticipated a new way of appreciating the *Anabasis* when he playfully claimed that his thoughts as he rode down to the sea after his long trek through the desert were not on 'Thalassa, Thalassa', but entirely 'on his feet'.[48]

8. The Snotgreen Sea

*

For all the recent fascination with Xenophon's feet, it is still 'The Sea! The Sea!' that has been the strongest temptation for the poetic ranks of modernism. The continual poetic renewal of Xenophon's shout of the sea uncannily confirms Paul Valéry's famous line, 'la mer, la mer, toujours recommencée' – a line that inspired the narrator of Anthony Powell's *A Dance to the Music of Time* to some apt ruminations: 'The poem's emphasis on aqueous reiterations provoked in the mind a thousand fleeting images, scraps of verse, fragments of painting, forgotten tunes, disordered souvenirs of every kind: anything, in fact, but the practical matters required of one.' Powell's words could as easily be applied to the modernist use of that other aqueous reiteration – the Ten Thousand's shout of 'Thalatta! Thalatta!'. But – as Powell also hints – resonant poetic scraps and disordered memories do not satisfy everyone. Some readers have been more concerned with the practical matters required of them. It is not that the modern move away from the goal of the Greeks' march is without any political implications: in their resistance to a strong narrative of triumph, modernist readings seem subversively to undermine conventional certainties. Yet they end with an aporia that can all too easily shade over into reaction. However much it conforms to a traditional pattern. Xenophon's strong narrative does hold more promise for those who want to change the world.

It was Xenophon's strong narrative of struggle and triumph that appealed to Benjamin Robert Haydon as he pursued his struggles for artistic and political reform. It was that same strong narrative that appealed to the British during the Dunkirk evacuation. And that narrative could even, rather oddly, be conjured up by an American judge, Walter Clark, at the end of an address delivered in 1913 to the Federation of Women's Clubs on 'The Legal Status of Women in North Carolina: Past, Present, and Prospective':

> After weeks of daily battles, the head of the column, led by Xenophon, climbing the mountains of Kurdistan, caught sight of the wide waste of waters which would bear them back to Argos, to Athens and to Sparta. They shouted 'Thalatta! Thalatta!' – 'The sea! The sea!' The cry rolled back down the mountain along the struggling columns, cheering the weak, the weary, and the wounded with the hope of home, at last. The women have made a brave and gallant fight, not only for justice to themselves, but, in their unselfishness, for justice and salvation for the little children and for justice to all the poor and oppressed. Your advancing columns have caught sight of that immortal sea of justice which enwraps the globe, and you have seen glimmering upon it, in ever-broadening circles of light, the rosy auroras of the coming dawn, for all mankind, of a brighter and a happier day.

Who could cap that liberating (or patronizing) rhetoric?[49]

One writer who could cap that rhetoric was Sol Funaroff, a communist

195

poet who was born in Beirut in 1911 of Russian parents and raised in the tenements of Manhattan's Lower East Side, and who died at the age of thirty-one of the lung problems that had plagued him since he was trapped in a slum fire as a child. Among Funaroff's works was a 'cinematic poem' called 'What the Thunder Said: A Fire Sermon' which he wrote when he was twenty-one. The poem's title was derived from T.S. Eliot's poem *The Wasteland* – which was also the source for the epigraph: 'Where are the roots that clutch, what branches grow / Out of this stony rubbish?'. Funaroff's poem answers that question with a combination of modernist aesthetics and radical political commitment – a commitment which he himself saw as a reaction against the fragmented and shattered world of *The Wasteland*, the 'most significant expression' of 'the fundamentally political and religious attitudes of negation, frustration, the martyrdom of the individual and the decay of the materialistic world'. Funaroff's 'Fire Sermon' portrays a Russian revolutionary addressing a crowd of workers as a thunderstorm threatens and depicting the triumph of the communists in Russia as a titanic, Promethean struggle, a storming of heaven:

> Yes
> the world is burning
> and the stormwind's big bellows fan the flames
> and the hammer pounds stronger and stronger
> and the anvil rings in answer
> Thalatta! Thalatta!
> and her all-conquering legions
> shout and clash and clang their armor
> and scarlet seas surge
> exultant upon new shores
> flowers of revolution red and gold bursting
> the magniloquent red battlehorses of
> plunging plumes in the thundering wind
> paced with the lightning

'Thalatta! Thalatta!': this is not the romantic sound of the sea, the softly sibilant syllables uttered by Fergus Fadden as he looked out at a beach in California. This is a rough and rugged cry, a hard cry in a hard world, hailing the 'scarlet seas' of the Russian Revolution – hailing seas that Funaroff knew he would never see. As he wrote in another poem:

> I am that exile
> from a future time,
> from shores of freedom
> I may never know,
> who hears, sounding in the surf,
> tidings from the lips of waves

that meet and kiss
in submarine gardens
of a new Atlantis

But this 'exile ... from shores of freedom' still closed 'What the Thunder Said' with a resounding 'yes!' – a politicized rewriting of the final word of Molly Bloom's famous monologue at the end of *Ulysses*.[50]

The same political message was given to Xenophon's shout by another American communist in the 1930s, James Neugass (later an ambulance driver for the International Brigade in Spain). Neugass made 'Thalassa, Thalassa' the title of a poem celebrating a strike by some modern Greek sailors. The poet took as his epigraph a press dispatch: '- twenty-five Greek freighters in the harbor of Buenos Aires ... on strike ... and in spite of the actions of the police and the reformist agencies, and with the assistance of revolutionary trade-unions on shore ... won all demands.' But at the start of his poem he draws the reader away to the romantic world of ancient Greece – a world of 'mariners, seabirds, sailing-ships of the lustrous early annals, / ... Bravers of dragon'd watery abysses beyond the Pillars of Hercules'. This sugary stuff seems surprisingly similar to the outpourings of a Victorian periodical poet like J.R. Sturgis. But the mock-romantic tone is precisely the point. As Neugass goes on, 'that was a long time ago. Ask the professors.' The demands of the present are different: 'Here, in the anchorage at Buenos Aires, are twenty-five sooty / Greek freighters'. Neugass, it turns out, is reacting against the image of 'the old days, yearned after by poets and schoolmasters'. He highlights instead the neglected victims of antiquity:

Butchered by State enemies, on the decks of floating meat-markets,
At the command of State pederasts, the philosophers and priests
– Well, maybe it wasn't all milk and honey, all culture and art,
    O drudges, blindmen, Greeks!
'Romance, travel, adventure.' So what? – saleswords for slavery.
In Buenos Aires, they went out on strike and they went out solid,
They sat on deck and stared at their officers, sang the Comintern.
Two went down under a third-mate's Colt. The sharks got another.
They went out solid, they didn't scab, they stayed out and they won;
For the first time since the first oaken keel slid down the ways,
In our treasured ancient Greece, Greek seamen lifted their arms
Together and for themselves, pitched overboard their lying history,
Struck once and won the first small part of what shall be theirs,
    The Red Internationale of
    Seamen and Harborworkers!

Paradoxically, Xenophon's shout is here celebrated in an explicit rejection of 'romance, travel, adventure' – a rejection of precisely the spirit that 'Thalatta!

Thalatta!' was normally taken to epitomize. It has become instead a celebration of the spirit of Greek workers.[51]

*

The story of 'Thalatta! Thalatta!' in the twentieth century is a story of extraordinary transformations. The various associations – nationalistic, romantic, religious, erotic – that Xenophon's shout had acquired by the First World War have all been picked up by modern poets and novelists and shaped for their different ends – for postmodern pleasure as well as for communist diatribes. The last word on this explosion of creative energy can go, perhaps, to an unheralded forebear of modernism – an unnamed Scottish caddy. The story goes that Sir Peter Scott Lang, Regius Professor of Mathematics, was approaching the green on the High Hole on the Old Course at St Andrews when he caught sight of the estuary at full tide brimming like a sea and exclaimed 'Thalassa! Thalassa!' – at which one of the caddies remarked to another: 'A dinna see onie lassie.' James Joyce may have delighted in punning on the climactic words of Xenophon's narrative, but he never got the chance to upstage a pretentious professor at the home of golf.[52]

9

Thalatta! Thalatta!

This is a great moment, when you see, however distant, the goal of your wandering. The thing which has been living in your imagination suddenly becomes a part of the tangible world. It matters not how many ranges, rivers or parching dusty ways may lie between you: it is yours now for ever. So did those old Barbarians feel who first from the Alpine wall looked down upon the Lombard plain, and saw Verona and its towers and the white river bed below them: so did Xenophon and Cortez, and every adventurer and pilgrim, before them or after.

Freya Stark, *The Valleys of the Assassins*

The goal of our wandering is in sight. We have followed Alexander Kinglake and T.E. Lawrence, Heinrich Heine and Buck Mulligan, Louis MacNeice and Fergus Fadden, and many others, real and fictional, who have looked out over the seas and oceans of the world (Red and Med, North and Irish, Atlantic and Pacific) and shouted or at least thought 'Thalatta! Thalatta!'. We have followed others who have trodden in Xenophon's footsteps and shouted or thought 'Thalatta! Thalatta!' as they have looked down on the Black Sea. We have heard that shout echoed in an extraordinary range of works: in poems as diverse as Henry Ellison's and Javant Biarujia's, in novels as diverse as Mrs Baillie Reynolds' and Sol Yurick's, in war memoirs and travel books, in letters and newspaper editorials. 'Thalatta! Thalatta!' is the shout that has encapsulated the heroic retreat of the Ten Thousand for later readers of Xenophon's graphic memoir – whether they have themselves been lost in a desert for a few hours, or forced to march in his tracks for weeks on end, or just armchair readers, finding in those two words a convenient symbol of liberation and an escape from boredom. 'Thalatta! Thalatta!': Xenophon's shout has proved as varied (I may as well say it) as the sea itself.[1]

But perhaps we should not rush too hastily towards our goal. We should reflect on what we have missed in this journey through relatively uncharted country. An obvious absentee has been Iris Murdoch's novel *The Sea, the Sea* – but then her story owes much more to *The Tempest* than to the *Anabasis*. Indeed, it owes nothing to Xenophon except its title – and even that is inspired more by Paul Valéry's poem 'Le cimetière marin'. The list of absentees also includes several pieces of music inspired by Xenophon – among them a recent song by the Sheffield gothic band Libitina ('Thalatta, Thalatta, the sea in sight, / My soul's heavy load made now light'). And while we have encountered many different voices – Afrikaner and Australian, Polish and Provençal, Estonian and Macedonian, even one or two proud Englishmen – we have not looked at Serbian or Brazilian allusions to 'Thalatta! Thalatta!' or at the 1994 German-Romanian film *Thalassa, Thalassa: Return to the Sea* directed by Bogdan Dumitrescu (a road movie about seven children who steal a car and beat a lawless path down to the sea – the Black Sea, of course).[2]

The goal of our wandering has itself shifted as we have journeyed towards it. In February 2004, the month my final draft was completed, Panos Karnezis published his impressive novel *The Maze*, which draws parallels with the retreat of the Ten Thousand as it charts the progress of a Greek brigade caught up in the withdrawal from Anatolia in 1922. First the brigade is lost in the desert, haunted by the memory of a civilian massacre ordered by its commander, who comforts himself with morphia and Greek mythology. The brigade then reaches a town untouched by the war, where the mayor organizes a scout parade – and one boy whose shirt is missing a button is punished by having to semaphore his patrol leader the complete first page of the *Anabasis*. Later, an alcoholic journalist who has failed to reach the battle-front compares the brigade with the Ten Thousand – but only because he wants to achieve fame as its official chronicler, restoring the nation's lost pride after the humiliating rout at the hands of the Turks. When the brigade leaves the town, the Greek population leaves with it, and the novel ends with the brigadier catching sight of the sea, and some ancient ruins inundated by the waves, and ships and islands in the distance – 'the motherland!'. But his elation lasts only for a moment. Soon he suspects that the sight of the sea is 'an unkind deception of the morphia', and turns back to his lexicon of Greek myths.[3]

Evocative and powerful as it is, Karnezis' novel still suggests that piling on echo after echo, 'Thalassa!' after 'Thalatta!', would not change our general picture much. Karnezis follows the literary tradition by recalling Xenophon's gloomy pedagogic role. And like some other recent writers he suggests that the sea offers no escape from the desert. He overturns the positive associations Xenophon's sea has acquired as an emblem of national triumph, a symbol of accomplishment for soldiers and adventurers, and a cry of romantic exultation at returning to the primeval element. Karnezis even chose 'The Sea! The Sea!' as the epigraph for *The Maze* – an epigraph whose heroic register stands in tension with the darkness of the novel itself. But at proof stage he replaced it with a quotation from Giorgio de Chirico: 'In the shadow of a man who walks in the sun, there are more enigmas than in all religions, past, present, and future.' Why did Karnezis reject 'The Sea! The Sea!' outright? Perhaps because it seemed all too familiar. Or rather, it is its very familiarity that enabled him to reject it. Even without an explicit allusion to that famous shout, we can still read the end of the novel as an ironic rewriting of Xenophon: there is no escape from 'The Sea! The Sea!'.

And yet the familiarity of Xenophon's shout need not have detracted from the power of *The Maze*. The novel's power lies in its self-consciousness about myth – and in its awareness of the fine boundary between myth and cliché. The three sections have the emblematic titles 'The Desert', 'The Town', and 'The Sea'. The brigadier is called Nestor. And there are even footnotes telling the stories of some Greek myths mentioned in the text. If Karnezis was afraid that an epigraph of 'The Sea! The Sea!' was too close to cliché for comfort, that fear can be seen as a last-minute loss of faith – an anxiety that his own voice might remain lost in the maze of cliché.[4]

*

One could spend several pages dissecting a modern novelist's decision not to use 'The Sea! The Sea!' as an epigraph. But this has already been a long enough book about two Greek words – about a second's shout snatched from many months of marching. Rather than looking at further allusions (and non-allusions) to 'The Sea! The Sea!', we should perhaps reflect on the cost of the obsession with that single scene. The range of echoes we have encountered has revealed the different cultural assumptions that have moulded responses to the Ten Thousand's shout of the sea. But has the very fame of 'Thalatta! Thalatta!' hindered the understanding of Xenophon's memoir? It has been all too easy for those drawn by the appeal of that shout to wrest it from its context and to forget what happens in the *Anabasis* – if indeed they have read it in the first place.

Some writers have forgotten that the Ten Thousand were in the mountains of Eastern Turkey when they shouted 'The Sea! The Sea!'. Mary Shelley's Frankenstein and the Welsh poet David Bush have presented them shouting for joy as they catch sight of the Mediterranean. A Joyce scholar has written that they shouted as they arrived at the Bosporus. That critic may have been misled by Joyce's own 'Galata! Galata!': the Heine scholar who made the same mistake had no such excuse. Others have mistaken the occasion of Xenophon's shout as well as its location: the biographer of Iris Murdoch who wrote that the shout was uttered in the Persian Wars, or the Camus scholar who specified that it was on the way back from Marathon, one of the battles of the Persian Wars. We have also seen that the word 'anabasis' has come to be used not of a march up country and away from the sea but of a march to the coast. *The Times* gave its editorial on the retreat to Dunkirk the title 'Anabasis', and the *Spectator*, in a rather different context, noted that 'General Sherman's great anabasis, which *The Times* has at last ceased to call a retreat' had 'ended in his gaining the sea coast of Georgia'. Another Joyce scholar has even written of 'the march up country to the sea by Xenophon's 10,000 heroes'.[5]

Such mistakes tell us even more about modern cultural assumptions than accurate recollections of the scene on Mount Theches. When the title of Xenophon's work is applied to the most famous part of it, we see the grip of the march to the sea on modern readers. When the shout is placed during the Persian Wars, the error is not just due to Joyce's mischievous take on Byron ('And Xenophon looked upon Marathon ... and Marathon looked on the sea'). The great Greek resistance against Persian invaders was a far more appropriate setting for a cry of national triumph than the retreat of a bunch of mercenaries. So too with the location of the shout. The Mediterranean and the Bosporus are much closer to Greece than a remote corner of the Black Sea – and isn't 'Thalatta! Thalatta!' meant to celebrate a triumphant return home?

The celebrity of 'The Sea! The Sea!' has not simply led to confusion about Xenophon's narrative. It has even overshadowed the rest of the scene where that exclamation first rings out. It takes the sensitivity of George Gissing (or rather his persona Henry Ryecroft) to notice that other stories are unfolded in that scene. 'A delightful passage of unsurpassable narrative', he writes, 'tells how the Greeks rewarded and dismissed a guide who had led them through dangerous country.' Gissing does not mention that this is the guide who led the Greeks to their famous sight of the sea on Mount Theches. He does not even mention 'Thalatta! Thalatta!' itself. He focuses solely on this native guide:

> The man was in peril of his life. Laden with valuable things which the soldiers had given him in their gratitude, he turned to make his way through the hostile region ...'When evening came he took his leave of us, and went his way by night.' To my mind, words of wonderful suggestiveness. You see the wild Eastern landscape, upon which the sun has set. There are the Hellenes, safe for the moment on their long march, and there the mountain tribesman, the serviceable barbarian, going away, alone, with his tempting guerdon, into the hazards of the darkness.

Xenophon, some have complained, left a bit too much to the imagination. What those moaners needed was a bit of Gissing's novelistic imagination – an imagination that could admire Xenophon's restraint and respond not to the all too obvious shout of the sea, but to Xenophon's closing cadence.[6]

Gissing also has Ryecroft recall another guide whose encounter with the Greeks proved to be less fortunate:

> Among the Carduchian Hills two men were seized, and information was sought from them about the track to be followed. 'One of them would say nothing, and kept silence in spite of every threat; so, in the presence of his companion, he was slain. Thereupon the other made known the man's reason for refusing to point out the way; in the direction the Greeks must take there dwelt a daughter of his, who was married.'

Once more we may note how much Xenophon's account leaves unsaid. And once more it takes Gissing to elicit the full richness of Xenophon's few words: 'It would not be easy to express more pathos than is conveyed in these few words. … there, in a line or two, shines something of human love and sacrifice, significant for all time.' When George Grote wrote up this scene, by contrast, he mentioned that the Greeks killed the guide – but not why the guide had kept his silence.[7]

Gissing's reading of Xenophon shows that there is much more to the *Anabasis* than a single shout of triumph. His focus on those native guides may indeed make us inclined to read rather differently some of the representations of Xenophon's experience we have come across earlier. Think of that poem which Mrs Baillie Reynolds placed at the front of her romantic novel *'Thalassa!'*. She imagined the Greeks 'in hostile deserts lost', wandering across a 'barren plain', until 'one day, one moment found them unawares': 'Their goal! – Where no man deemed such goal could be … / *"Thalassa!"* was their cry – "The Sea! The Sea!" '. That retelling suited well enough Reynolds' own story of a middle-aged man saved by falling in love. Xenophon's own story is rather different. For one thing, Reynolds reduces the varied terrain that the Ten Thousand faced to the romantic duo of the desert and the sea. Yet when the Greeks caught sight of the sea they had moved on from the desert of Syria and Iraq ('a flat plain like the sea', as Xenophon calls it) through the rough mountains of Kurdistan and the highlands of Armenia and back into rough mountainous country. They only passed through a proper desert on the march out with Cyrus, and they returned by a different route precisely in order to avoid it. The Greeks were not lost in hostile deserts when they saw the sea. Indeed, they were not lost at all. They were led to their vantage-point by a guide – just as earlier they received help from other guides. Xenophon's account, if read carefully, turns out to be a story about the Greeks' difficult dealings with the peoples whose land they have to cross – a story at least as interesting as those romantic narratives of the Greeks suddenly finding salvation in the desert like shipwrecked sailors spotting a sail on the horizon.[8]

It seems, then, that the richness of Xenophon's story has often been lost owing to an excessive and overly romantic concentration on the Greeks' great shout of triumph. What Xenophon tells is a story of tense cultural interaction with haunting vignettes like the murder of that guide who kept silent to protect his daughter. What Xenophon tells is a story to which modern writers like Italo Calvino and Zbigniew Herbert could respond. Both Calvino and Herbert were struck, as we have seen, by the fact that Xenophon presents the Greeks cutting their road through the lands of others without idealizing their position, without lying that they were defending civilization. And both writers were moving towards an almost existential exaltation of the Ten Thousand: Calvino found that Xenophon's Greeks inspire 'an almost symbolic anguish which perhaps only we today can understand', while Herbert wrote that they made their journey 'without signs on the earth without signs in the sky / with the cruel consciousness that life is immense'. These readings seem compelling: Xenophon's Greeks, lost in a moral desert, become fitting emblems of modern humanity.[9]

Yet not even Italo Calvino and Zbigniew Herbert can do justice to Xenophon's story. The Greeks made their journey 'without signs in the sky'? Xenophon himself stresses that they were guided by signs from the gods. Signs like his own dream on the night after Clearchus' murder – a dream that came from Zeus. Or the signs that the Greeks received whenever they sacrificed animals and inspected their entrails. No surprise that when they reached Trapezus they made thank offerings for their safe conduct to Zeus the Saviour and to Heracles and to the other gods to whom they had made vows. Xenophon himself is rewarded at the end of his story when he prays to the right gods – and the peaceful and pious description of his estate at Scillus he gives earlier in the work shows the rewards he enjoyed back in Greece. He emerges as a rather unfashionable figure: a religious optimist.

The modern temptation to attach symbolic weight to the Greeks' painful march across the snow-covered plains and mountains of Armenia leads to an image of Xenophon's story as distorted as those naive celebrations of a triumph over the desert. Both readings sacrifice the rich specificity of Xenophon's account to the concerns of their very different audiences.

Modern readings have distorted Xenophon even more by ignoring what happened to the Greeks after they had seen the sea. What happened first was that they came to a deep ravine where their path was opposed by some men drawn up on the other side. Once more, it seemed, they would have to fight their way through. But suddenly one of the light-armed troops in the Greek army came up to Xenophon: 'He said that he had been a slave at Athens and that he knew the language of these people. "I think," he said, "that this is my own fatherland. If there is no objection, I should like to speak to them." ' The people opposing the Greeks were called the Macronians, and thanks to this former slave at Athens, the army was able to negotiate its way through their land and onwards to the sea.[10]

The Ten Thousand, we are glad to discover, did not always have to cut their road in the living body of peoples. But what was someone who had been a slave at Athens doing in Xenophon's heroic army? The poignant story of the Macronian peltast casts a rather different light on the immortal Ten Thousand. We suddenly hear of a non-Greek slave in their number – and there must have been a good few others like him among the light-armed troops. Xenophon obscures their presence – except in this one scene. And even here he does not reveal what happens to this peltast. For all Xenophon's reticence, this scene does make us think again about the triumphant exclamation that precedes it. If the sight of the sea meant the promise of home for the Greek mercenaries, what did home mean for this peltast when he suddenly found himself back in his fatherland? What did it mean for him to see the sea? Did he shout 'Thalatta! Thalatta!' – in another language?

It is one thing to neglect what happens to the Ten Thousand between Mount Theches and the coast. Far more startling is the way readings of the *Anabasis* have neglected what happens after the army has reached the coast. After devoting four books to the romantic march up country and the daring retreat to the sea, Xenophon goes on to devote a further three books to what happened to the Ten Thousand after they reached the sea. Yet the grip of 'Thalatta! Thalatta!' on later imaginations has meant that far more attention has been paid to the first four books of the *Anabasis* than to the last three.

'The shout of happy thousands rends the air: / "The sea! the sea!" and all is safety there': this snappy couplet, from the poem *The Captive of Stamboul* by Jeremiah Holmes Wiffen (librarian to the Duke of Bedford who won Haydon's *Xenophon*), encapsulates the story of the Ten Thousand that has appealed in modern times. As we have already seen, this was the story told by James Thomson in his poem *Liberty*, by Benjamin Haydon in the catalogue for his *Xenophon* exhibition, and by Louis MacNeice in his radio play on the march of the Ten Thousand. This was also the story told by Stephen Marlowe in his historical novel *The Shining* – which ends with the hero riding up Mount Theches with his girlfriend on his horse behind him (shades of Haydon's painting) and hearing the words 'The Sea! The Sea!'. And this was the story set to verse in the seventeenth century by America's first published poet, the Puritan Anne Bradstreet, in the course of her long historical poem *The Foure Monarchies* – an account of Assyrian, Persian, Greek (or rather Macedonian), and early Roman history. Bradstreet took the story of the Ten Thousand down to Trebizond, where:

> There was of *Greeks* setled a Colony,
> Who after all receiv'd them joyfully.
> Thus finishing their travail, danger, pain,
> In peace they saw their Native soyl again.

Many others have echoed Bradstreet's claim that the Greeks' toils were over when they saw the sea: Victor Frankenstein in Mary Shelley's novel, for instance, or *The Times* leader at the time of the Dunkirk evacuation. Others have seen fit to stop their own toils at that point. Hippolyte Taine simply gave up writing about the *Anabasis* at that point – as did S.S. Van Dine's famous detective Philo Vance, 'a man of cultural ardencies, in whom the spirit of research and intellectual adventure was constantly at odds with the drudgery necessary to scholastic creation': 'I remember that only the preceding year he had begun writing a life of Xenophon – the result of an enthusiasm inherited from his university days when he had first read the *Anabasis* and the *Memorabilia* – and had lost interest in it at the point where Xenophon's historic march led the Ten Thousand back to the sea.' That, after all, is the end of what the French colonel Arthur Boucher called 'the glorious, heroic part of the retreat' – and that is where Boucher wished that Xenophon himself had stopped.[11]

The *Anabasis* has also been rewritten as a March to the Sea in triumphant works written for children such as Witt's *Retreat of the Ten Thousand*, Havell's *Stories from Xenophon Retold*, and Barbary's *Ten Thousand Heroes*. Typical of the tone of these books is Witt's concluding observation that the Greeks held games at the sea 'not far from … the spot where the Argonauts were said to have landed long ago to win the Golden Fleece'. This Argonautic link – which also fired up the German traveller von Hoffmeister – had already been made in antiquity by the Sicilian historian Diodorus. But it is the modern epitomator who makes the point of the parallel explicit: 'there was still a strain of the blood of the heroes in the veins of the brave Ten Thousand.'[12]

Schoolchildren would also encounter Xenophon's tale pared down to a simple retreat to the sea. There is a strong bias in school editions of the *Anabasis* in favour of the first four books: indeed, the two single-volume editions most commonly used in British and American schools (to judge by the number of reprints) cover precisely the first four books. Few of those who read Xenophon in Greek would get beyond 'Thalatta! Thalatta!'.[13]

*

Modern responses to the *Anabasis* both inside and out of the schoolroom seem to have been gripped by a feeling for the shape a story of travel and escape like Xenophon's should have. Many nineteenth-century accounts of journeys to the interior end back at the coast: romance and adventure, as Thackeray observed, did not sit well with steamboats. The sea has proved a tempting way to close other sorts of works too: films like Truffaut's *Les Quatre Cents Coups* or Godard's *Le Mépris*, poems like Derek Walcott's modern epic *Omeros* ('the sea was still going on') and Matthew Arnold's 'The Future'. 'The infinite sea' (the closing words of Arnold's poem) may create a paradoxical sort of ending, but perhaps that is part of its attraction. Mellow, reflective, we confront mortality, or immortality, and dream of escape, the escape promised by Xenophon's own shout of 'Thalatta! Thalatta!'.[14]

But what if we look beyond that shout? What do we lose if we present Xenophon's story as a simple retreat to the sea?

The early American poet Anne Bradstreet, surprisingly, seems to offer some help in answering this question. The first edition of her poem *The Foure Monarchies*, which was published without her knowledge in 1650, *did* have six lines on the Greeks' march along the Black Sea (as well as slight alterations to the immediately preceding and following lines). It was when she revised the poem for the first authorized edition that Bradstreet made Xenophon's story conform to the simpler pattern of an escape to the sea. Her earlier version read:

> These after all, receiv'd them joyfully:
> There for some time they were, but whilst they staid,
> Into *Bithynia* often in-rodes made:
> The King afraid what further they might doe,
> Unto the *Spartan* Admirall did sue,
> Straight to transport them to the other side,
> For those incursions he durst not abide;
> So after all their travell, danger, pain …[15]

Even in her fuller version Bradstreet clings to a positive depiction of the Greeks' action. She has kept the idea of return, but has made it instead a return to Byzantium, to the gates of Greece, to Europe. A different story could be told. What happened when the Greeks arrived at Trapezus? Like the young T.E. Lawrence arriving at the south coast of France, they would have accepted a passage to Greece straightaway. But they did not have the good fortune of the British officers on the run in Turkey when they reached the coast. There were no boats conveniently on hand to take the Ten Thousand back home. Nor did anyone send ships to rescue them. They were forced to surmount further dangers along the coast of the Black Sea. And as they made their way along the coast they proved a nuisance not to the Persians, as Bradstreet claims, but to their fellow Greeks. They clashed with the Greek cities along the coast, and near the city of Cerasus some of the mercenaries attacked some friendly natives who had been selling goods, stoned to death their envoys, and then pursued a market official and some other Greeks down into the sea 'as if a wild boar or stag had appeared', and those who did not know how to swim drowned. Not long after this, Xenophon planned to settle the Ten Thousand in a new city, but his plan was disrupted by the despicable Arcadian soothsayer Silanus – the man at whose name the Pontic Greek envoys at Versailles spat in unison. The Ten Thousand quarrelled not just with their fellow Greeks but also among themselves: at one point an Arcadian group even split off from the main army.

The Ten Thousand did finally arrive back at 'the gates of Greece', but when they got there they found themselves as much at a loss as when they were marooned at 'the gates of the king'. The Persians were, as Bradstreet noted, keen to get them across to Europe (though it was not the Persian king who dealt with the Spartans, but only the satrap Pharnabazus). The Spartans, who were still indebted to Persian gold, were at first all too glad to help. But when they had got the Ten Thousand across the Bosporus they did not know what to do with them. In the days that followed, the remnants of the Greek army almost sacked Byzantium, and then found themselves shut out, with nowhere to turn. The Spartans then plotted against Xenophon, rather as the satrap Tissaphernes had plotted against the Greek generals after the battle of Cunaxa, and Xenophon narrowly escaped with his life. In desperation the army signed up for a Thracian pretender named Seuthes, in many ways a degenerate Cyrus, and helped him to enslave some of his fellow Thracians. Finally, as relations between the Spartans and Persians worsened, they were enlisted by the Spartans, who had earlier accepted Persian money to keep them out of Asia.

What sort of story was Xenophon telling? He was suggesting that the Greek mercenaries moved from relative unity in the face of a common danger to disunity and squabbling after they reached the sea. And the way he presented the dangers they confronted in their march along the Black Sea coast repeatedly hints at links between the army's experiences before and after their arrival at the sea. The Ten Thousand did not just have to escape from the Persians and the tribes blocking their path to the sea. They also had to extract themselves from the political confusion that awaited them when they once more encountered their fellow Greeks. Xenophon's memoir is an escape story that subverts itself, a celebration of Greek achievement that becomes an analysis of Greek weakness.

*

Those modern retellings which have looked beyond the Greeks' return to the sea have tended to follow Anne Bradstreet's lead and tone down Xenophon's increasingly pessimistic story. In his popular work *The Glory that was Greece*, J.C. Stobart did recognize that, after the Ten Thousand had arrived at the sea, 'many more adventures awaited them and they were seldom very welcome visitors'. Yet he rather archly added that 'no fewer than 6000 reached home, and, we trust, lived happily ever after'. Similarly Brian Johnson's *Long March Home* ends with Xenophon returning 'to his native Athens, a rich and famous man', while 'I returned to Athens' are the narrator Xenophon's final words in Geoffrey Household's *Xenophon's Adventure*. Household's ending looks back to the opening words: 'I am an Athenian.' That opening is followed by Xenophon's discussion with Socrates about whether he should go on Cyrus' expedition – an incident told in the *Anabasis* in a flashback when Xenophon first becomes prominent. Household has normalized Xenophon's story not just in his handling of narrative order and person (the real Xenophon spoke of himself in the third person), but also in his ending. Like Stobart and Johnson, he satisfies Paul Fussell's law of travel books by giving his readers the gratification of a completed circuit.[16]

These popular works all misrepresent the ending of Xenophon's story. The comfortable sense of an ending afforded by a homecoming is denied the Ten Thousand. Xenophon hands the army over to a Spartan general, and it sets off for a new war against Persia. The idea of escape has disappeared. Most of the army is still caught up in the cycle of Greek-Persian hostility, and a return to Greece turns into a return to Asia. The circuit is completed, but in an unexpected way. As for Xenophon himself, he did end up rich when he prayed to the right gods and attacked the country estate of a Persian grandee. But it is more likely than not that the closure offered by Household and Johnson is (literally) false. What awaited Xenophon was exile from Athens – an event that he does mention in the *Anabasis*, but so cryptically that it is extremely unclear, and still a matter for debate, when and why he was exiled. Was it for serving with Cyrus against the Persian king, or for serving later with the Spartans? Whatever the circumstances of his exile, Xenophon probably did not return to Athens, but stayed on in Asia with the Spartans.

The same feeling for literary form that explains the tendency to stop accounts of the *Anabasis* at the sea can also, it seems, distort those accounts which have looked beyond the great 'Thalatta' scene. But what else is at stake in such skewed portrayals of Xenophon's story? A hint is offered by the distinguished nineteenth-century scholar J.P. Mahaffy, who regretted that the opening books of the *Anabasis* were the books most read in schools: 'the concluding books ... have perhaps the most interesting and valuable lessons. ... it is here that we obtain our only clear and detailed account of the doings of a mercenary force, when not engaged in actual campaign – of the scourge which such a force was to all the surrounding countryside, and how they were just as likely to plunder a Greek as a barbarian settlement.' This strong countervoice bears out the ideological implications of the way the *Anabasis* was normally presented. One school editor argued that the contents of Book 4 – the book in which the Ten Thousand struggle through Armenia and reach the sea – made it especially good for schools. The later books, by contrast, could seem to some readers 'longer and more banal', with their 'often boring' speeches. Such judgements could be as much ethical as aesthetic. When James Rennell noted that the transactions in the last three books were 'not of a character to interest so deeply', he at once added a moral gloss. Those transactions were not of a character 'to rise so high in our estimation' either: 'For one cannot but be disgusted, at finding those, who had so long figured as heroes, in the former part of the history, degenerate into pirates and buccaneers, towards the conclusion.' Those last books were better forgotten: a scourge to their fellow Greeks was not how most people wanted to imagine the Ten Thousand.[17]

Looking beyond Xenophon's account of the Greeks' first sight of the sea may even make us inclined to read that great scene rather differently. The temptation has always been strong to imagine that the simplicity of

Xenophon's narrative reflects the simplicity of Xenophon himself – but T.E. Lawrence knew better when he described the *Anabasis* as 'cunningly full of writing tricks' and 'pretentiously simple'. We cannot safely isolate the happy scene on Mount Theches from its place in Xenophon's account. The harmonious picture Xenophon gives of the Greeks as they look down on the sea strikes just the note required: all that fellow-feeling is soon to dissolve. Xenophon builds up an impression of unity to strengthen the contrast with what follows.[18]

The breakdown of the Greeks' discipline would seem less surprising if Xenophon had not artfully held back some instances of insubordination in the march through Armenia. At one point in the march along the coast Xenophon has to defend his leadership earlier in the campaign against complaints that he had been too harsh. One soldier complains that Xenophon had hit him. Xenophon recognizes the man – and recalls that he had hit him because he was trying to bury a wounded comrade alive. When the offender objects that the soldier died anyway, Xenophon gives a fine response ('We shall all die: is that any reason why we should be buried alive?') and the Greeks shout out that Xenophon had not hit him enough. Xenophon delays this disturbing episode until the point when he has to defend his earlier action. But how many other such incidents were there in the march to the sea that he does not mention at all?[19]

The more one pries open Xenophon's account, the more one becomes aware of the art that conceals itself behind the facade of simplicity. If we had even one other substantial account of the retreat of the Ten Thousand to read against Xenophon's, we would doubtless have a rather different impression of Xenophon. Perhaps then even the great scene where the Greeks exclaim 'Thalatta! Thalatta!' would lose some of its naive charm.

The difficulties that arise when more than one source is available are only too clear in the case of the magnificently simple cry of 'Land! Land!' shouted from Columbus' ship. That cry has struck several readers of Xenophon as the nautical equivalent of 'Thalatta! Thalatta!' – 'two cries bursting out equally from the heart and answering each other at a distance of twenty centuries, like the two parts of an alternating chant'. But did Columbus or anyone on his ship actually shout 'Land! Land!'? No such shout is mentioned in his 'diario' (not his actual log, but a later transcript, considerably rewritten). In the *Life of Columbus* by his son Fernando it is reported that Pinzón, the captain of the second ship, did cry out 'Land, land, sir! I claim the reward!'. But it turned out that he had only seen squall clouds. Later Columbus tried to 'prevent men from crying "land, land!" at every moment' by decreeing that anyone who 'claimed to have seen land and did not make good his claim in the space of three days would lose the reward even if afterwards he should actually see it'. There was a shout when land was finally seen – but the sixteenth-century historian Oviedo records it as 'lumbre!

tierra!' ('light! land!'). The true sailor's version of 'Thalatta! Thalatta!' is supplied by the later testimony of one of the sailors on board, who reported that one of his colleagues 'saw a white head of sand and raised his eyes and saw the land and fired a lombard and cried out "tierra, tierra", "land, land" '. But this testimony cannot simply be taken on trust. It was given at an investigation by the Spanish crown into Columbus' voyage: there was bitterness that Columbus himself had won the reward for spotting land by claiming that he had seen a light first.[20]

The picture of bickering and discord that emerges from a quick glance at the sources for Columbus' voyage contrasts with Xenophon's portrayal of the Greeks shouting together and embracing one another, ordinary soldiers and officers alike. The Greeks do not argue about who first saw the sea. No officer walks in front to gain the honour for himself – as Balboa is said to have walked ahead to catch the first sight of the Pacific. The only reward is for the guide who led them to their vantage-point.

While the precise shout with which the discovery of the New World was hailed remains unclear, there is no reason to doubt that (some of) the Ten Thousand did actually shout 'Thalatta! Thalatta!'. But even without taking Xenophon's broader narrative of unity and disunity into account, it does not take much reflection to realize that what happened on Mount Theches must have been a lot more complicated, a lot more messy, than Xenophon's account suggests. Any narrative that compresses the experiences and emotions of thousands of men and women into a few sentences can hardly fail to elide differences and present an over-simple picture. Perhaps a few of those tough men even thought of their wives at home, watching the waves and yearning for their return.

*

Just as we may want to question the triumphant narrative closure seemingly implied by the Greeks' shout of 'Thalatta! Thalatta!', so too we should not be too complacent about the comfortable conclusion that this book has reached so far. I have sketched a neat historical development. I have suggested that, for Victorian and Edwardian readers, Xenophon's shout was a fairly simple, unproblematic symbol, and Xenophon's men models of discipline and endurance. And I have contrasted this cosy picture with the unsettling range of responses found in some modern texts. But it would be rash to pretend that the story I have told in this book is the whole story of 'Thalatta! Thalatta!'.

A story of romantic rapture and imperial gung-ho followed by disillusionment and postmodern splintering is simply too neat to be plausible. To posit a now lost golden age for 'Thalatta! Thalatta!' may simply be to impose one myth on top of another. Perhaps it is worth taking another look at some of the earlier adventurers who echoed Xenophon's shout – like Daniel Defoe's mutinous sailors in *Captain Singleton*. Those profit-seeking adventurers shouting out 'the *Sea*! the *Sea*!' as they cross Africa are not a particularly illustrious parallel for the Ten Thousand. Perhaps they are not so far from Sol Yurick's juvenile gang battling its way from the Bronx to Coney Island. And while we cannot be altogether sure that the adventures of Captain Singleton's group were modelled on those of the Ten Thousand, we have also seen that the Ten Thousand did come in for criticism in the nineteenth century and earlier. When James Rennell dismissed them in the later stages of their journey as 'pirates and buccaneers', he was echoing the words of the historian John Gillies (a friend of his). Long before Yurick transferred Xenophon's story to New York, a hostile tradition about the Ten Thousand was well established – especially among writers fearful of untrammelled democracy. Perhaps it is rather the extremely positive image of these mercenaries that demands special explanation – and an explanation for that is at hand in the powerful advocacy of George Grote and Hippolyte Taine.[21]

It is not just who echoes Xenophon's shout that is of interest in *Captain Singleton*, but also when it is echoed. The point about Defoe's pirates shouting 'the *Sea*! the *Sea*!' as they cross Africa is that it turns out they have only seen a lake. They are still stuck in the African interior. So too earlier, when they were sailing from Madagascar to the African coast, they had shouted '*Land*' – when it was only a small uninhabited island they had seen. Defoe does not have them shout '*Land*' when they reach the coast, or 'the *Sea*!' when they have crossed to the other side. He seems to be obeying a law of irony – the same law that Heine obeyed when he started his increasingly pessimistic cycle of North Sea poems with an ecstatic 'Thalatta! Thalatta!'; or that Virgil obeyed when he had Aeneas and his men shout for joy at the sight of Italy, before they are blown across to Carthage.[22]

This law of irony was also followed by the British officers in the First World War who escaped from captivity in Turkey. Two of these officers made a point of saying that no shout like the 'Thalassa! Thalassa!' of Xenophon's Ten Thousand broke from their lips when they caught sight of the south coast of Turkey. But they soon found a boat and crossed to Cyprus. What of the other two officers from Kut whose experiences in captivity we followed in Chapter 2, E.H. Keeling and H.C.W. Bishop? We left them after they had escaped, standing with eyes fixed on the Black Sea, (almost) as elated as the Ten Thousand. What happened next? Their joy did not last long: they were recaptured by the Turks and marched back inland. So the escaped prisoners who recalled Xenophon's joy soon got into trouble – while the ones who did not feel that elation were soon saved.

Xenophon himself was also obeying this law of irony when he described the Ten Thousand's short-lived pleasure at the sight of the sea – but at least it is the sea that they have seen. Paradoxically, however, as soon as we recall that the Ten Thousand's joy was short-lived the irony of the reworkings of Xenophon's shout in the narratives of Defoe, Heine, and the Kut prisoners is dimmed. They rely for their full effect on the sort of simplified reading of Xenophon that was then prevalent.

Even if this law of irony does not cloud our image of Xenophon's shout, it may make us suspect that what those Kut officers are giving us is not 'raw' experience, but something manufactured, something in some sense fictional. This would scarcely be surprising. Perhaps all autobiography, whether written down, or spoken to others, or even to ourselves, is a fiction of sorts – a later ordering and selection of experience that cannot help being fictive, an ordering whose fictiveness may even be faithful to the way we live our own lives. Think of the two very different accounts Louis MacNeice gave of his visit with his father to the West of Ireland. Think also of the two very different accounts given by the Rev. Tozer and Major Crowder of the great Xenophontic moment in their long vacation tour to Eastern Turkey. In the case of the Kut officers, at least, our suspicions of artifice become rather stronger when we observe that the officers who do not feel elation stress that they did not shout 'Thalassa! Thalassa!', while those who are elated are merely reminded of Xenophon. For the first group to have merely said that they did not think of Xenophon would not have been dramatic enough. For the second group, an actual shout would have been too dangerous a step into fiction. At any rate, the stronger our suspicions of artifice, the more 'Thalatta! Thalatta!' loses its naive charm. Yet it can still be objected that life can be like fiction, or even stranger. Take what happened to Keeling and Bishop after they were recaptured. They were ambushed and captured by some brigands. But these brigands turned out to be political outlaws opposed to the Young Turks, and the British officers escaped with them to the Crimea. Their feeling of joy was premature, but only a bit. Maybe those thoughts of Xenophon were their raw experience – or at least part of it, the part they wanted to pass on.

The simple identification with Xenophon seemingly implied by a shout or thought of 'Thalatta! Thalatta!' may be complicated, then, by a sense that that shout comes from a constructed, artificial persona. In the case of the escape narratives of those officers from Kut, we may not feel that this affects greatly our impression of what those texts are trying to achieve. They strive for suspense and excitement rather than for a subtle delineation of character. Rather different questions may be raised by a work like A.W. Kinglake's *Eothen* – with his 'Thalatta! Thalatta!' at the sight of the Red Sea following swiftly from his conviction that, in the wastes of the desert, he himself, and no other, had charge of his life.[23]

At stake in Kinglake's self-presentation is the depiction of the landscape of the east by the imperialist west. His self-assertiveness was not to the liking of Edward Said: 'It is for the comparatively useless purpose of letting

Kinglake take hold of himself that the Orient serves him.' Now while Kinglake has asserted his western individuality in a dominant enough manner before he sees the sea (thirsty, he encounters some Bedouins, and simply walks up to their water-flask and drinks, without asking), afterwards night comes, and he still has not made the sea, and he falls off his camel, and it runs off, and he has to commandeer a donkey from some Algerian refugees. It is deep into the night when he finally gets to Suez and clean sheets. So much for his confident self-sufficiency. Perhaps Kinglake is implying that the Orient fails in its comparatively useless purpose, and telling us more about himself than about the Orient. Or rather, he is telling us about a constructed image of himself. And nothing is more revealing of that constructed image than an ambiguity in his original allusion to Xenophon: 'as I rose in my swift course to the crest of a lofty ridge, Thalatta! Thalatta! the sea – the sea was before me!'. Is 'Thalatta! Thalatta!' what he shouted when he saw the sea? Or what he thought? Or only what he later wrote, to heighten his achievement in finding the right direction and to make his later misfortunes more amusing?[24]

The uneasy self-consciousness of Kinglake's Xenophontic cry was more than matched by the undergraduate T.E. Lawrence as he told his mother about his cycling holiday in France. He set off his exaggerated Mediterranean passion, his instinctive cry of 'Thalassa! Thalassa!', against the bemused response of the French tourists 'hoping to find another of the disgusting murders their papers make such a fuss about' – the tourists for whom the Mediterranean is simply home. The hyperbole of his mythical allusions (his sufferings were a combination of those of Sisyphus, Tantalus, and Theseus), the artlessness of that instinctive shout, the amusingly dark perception of those tourists – perhaps after all we should not expect even a teenage Lawrence to offer too straightforward an approach to understanding Xenophon's appeal.[25]

*

It seems that we should avoid too reductive a determinism, too sharp a division between earlier and more recent responses to Xenophon. In their different ways, the image of 'Thalatta! Thalatta!' offered by Sol Yurick's novel *The Warriors* or by T.E. Lawrence's conception of his exploits in the Arabian desert seemed to be striking a distinctly modern and disillusioned note. We can now see that the note they strike, distanced, self-aware, questioning, can be paralleled in earlier writers, in perspectives that predate the great catastrophes of the twentieth century.

But why should writers in the nineteenth century have wanted to distance themselves from Xenophon's shout? Perhaps because it could already then seem too obvious. The nostalgic association of Xenophon and childhood discussed in Chapter 3 was gently mocked by a *Punch* cartoon headed 'Thalatta! Thalatta!' which showed a group of boys scrambling for a view of the sea from the window of a railway carriage – with shouts of "Ooray!!' and 'I'll be in fust!' (Plate 19). As early as 1822, William Maginn, a prolific writer of light verse, exploited the Greek shout in a poem published in *Blackwood's Magazine*, 'A Twist-imony in Favour of Gin-Twist'. As this comic celebration of alcohol draws to a close, θαλαττα, θαλαττα appears in the side margin as the running title for the third last stanza:

> Although it is time to finish my rhyme,
> Yet the subject's so sweet, I can scarcely desist;
> While its grateful perfume is delighting the room,
> How can I be mute o'er a jug of gintwist?

Maginn's poem has nothing to do with Xenophon or the sea. The celebratory and closural force of Xenophon's shout must even then have been blatant enough to justify this light-hearted pastiche. Later in the century, the satirist Ambrose Bierce evoked Xenophon's exclamation in a more sinister context: 'The Fountain Refilled', a poem about a man who gets 'drunk' on blood. This quasi-alcoholic kills people for their blood, but finds that he cannot kill them in large enough quantities to satisfy his appetite. His supplies start running out, and he becomes distraught – until he has a dream:

> Yes, Hans Pietro Shanahan
> (Who was a most ingenious man)
> Saw freedom, and with joy and pride
> 'Thalassa! (or Thalatta!)' cried.

What this most ingenious man has dreamt up is a steady new source of victims: he buys up the franchises for street cars and feasts on unfortunate pedestrians. Bierce's dark use of Xenophon's shout relies on its conventional association with success and freedom – and also, perhaps, on the romantic link of the sea with blood. At the same time, Bierce plays on the two forms of the Greek word. You say 'Thalassa', I say 'Thalatta': the rather random alternation between these two forms could seem just as ludicrous as an excessive devotion to the shout itself. Bierce anticipates the delight taken in this happy alternative by Rose Macaulay, Flashman, and young Ronnie Knox.[26]

We have come across many others who seemed rather conscious that an allusion to Xenophon's shout could easily be overdone. There was, for instance, the periodical contributor who wrote in 1875 that men in earlier generations who first saw the sea when their minds were formed would register their feelings by shouting 'Thalatta! Thalatta!': a knowing exaggeration that was doubtless meant to be amusing. There was also the Rev. Tozer, writing up his Turkish travels a few years later, and quite aware, even as he claims that he shouted 'Thalatta! Thalatta!', that that exclamation had become 'a household word'. More often travellers following Xenophon's footsteps would simply reflect on the habit of shouting 'Thalatta! Thalatta!', or perhaps merely include that phrase in a chapter title. That expedient could be taken as a mild assertion of heroism – or else as a neat way of tipping one's hat at Xenophon while avoiding an embarrassing effusion of emotion. The scholarly German C.F. Lehmann-Haupt, who was sent out by the Prussian Academy in 1898 to look for Urartian inscriptions, could even include 'Further over Gümüsch-chana and the Zigana range (Thalatta! Thalatta!)' as one of fifty or so sub-headings for a long chapter in his multi-volume book on Armenia. He did not allude to Xenophon's shout in the text proper: he was too busy criticizing the geographical failings of poor von Hoffmeister. He simply left his readers to make what they would of a 'Thalatta! Thalatta!' reduced – or elevated – to a parenthesis within a sub-heading.

Echoing Xenophon's shout in other parts of the world was at least a bit less obvious. But even then travellers like T.E. Lawrence and Louis MacNeice might want to shirk responsibility by saying that they shouted 'instinctively' or that 'something rose' in them. And others were too self-conscious to shout at all. When G.H. Lewes was travelling by train to the Scilly Isles, he reflected on how the Ten Thousand had shouted at the sight of the sea – and 'at that sight I too should have shouted, had not the glorious vision come upon me through the windows of a railway carriage; where my fellow-travellers, not comprehending such ecstasy, might have seized me as an escaped lunatic.' Similarly a father in a periodical story seeing his children yelling with delight at the sea might almost wish that 'some such ebullition' were permitted to his own excited feelings. Perhaps indeed silence was better? When the explorer Samuel White Baker was approaching Lake Albert N'yanza, he arranged to give three cheers with all his men – but when he first saw the lake 'I felt too serious to vent my feelings in vain cheers for victory'.[27]

Some writers even thought twice about adopting Xenophon's exclamation for the title of a work – much as Panos Karnezis recently thought twice about using it as an epigraph. When Sir John Skelton's novel *Thalatta!* first appeared in *Fraser's Magazine* in 1862, it was called *Thalatta! Thalatta! A Study at Sea*. He explained in the preface to the novel that that title had been 'pronounced by the critics to be unpardonably affected'. But even the new title was pronounced by the *Spectator* 'a studied affair, and, let us add, a mistake'. And thirty years later Sir William Fraser in his memoir *Disraeli and his Day* recalled *Thalatta!* as a 'remarkable book' that had been published under a 'fanciful title'. Another thirty years later, and the popular writer Robert W. Chambers published his new serialization about a treasure hunt in the Florida swamps under the title *Thalassa*. But when it came out as a book the title had been changed to *The Gold Chase*. Presumably it was felt that *Thalassa* would not sell as many copies.[28]

*

It is clear, then, that we should avoid too pat a view of the differences between then and now, between the enthusiasms of the Victorians and the ironies of postmodernism. Indeed, we should beware of seeming too superior for another reason too. It is not just that 'Thalatta! Thalatta!' was never that simple. It is also that it can even now be that simple. The example of Sol Yurick's *The Warriors* could be balanced, for instance, by Harold Coyle's 1993 novel *The Ten Thousand*. Here the old triumphalist story is transferred to the twenty-first century, as the Tenth Corps of the U.S. Army, cut off in Central Europe and ordered to disarm and withdraw by a resurgent Germany, resolve to force their way through to the sea – with inspiration drawn from an ancient precedent:

> 'A force of ten thousand Greek mercenaries in the service of the King of Persia was betrayed and left high and dry in the center of what is today Iraq. ... the Greeks closed ranks and marched back to Greece.'
> 'Your memory is good, Scotty.'

Central to this 'bout between the modern German Arminius and ... the American Xenophon' is the refusal to disarm: 'Just as Xenophon knew in 400 BC that it would have been a mistake to disarm his ten thousand and trust the Persian king, every officer in the Tenth Corps knows in their hearts that it would be wrong for us to allow the United States to capitulate in the face of nuclear blackmail.' 'Malin's March to the Sea' is a success – even though the general himself dies. The story ends with the general's body being put in the surf, as each man 'lifted his gaze beyond him to the sea'. There follows a brief epilogue – set at home. So Coyle reclaims the positive value of the myth of the Ten Thousand – while forgetting that they were employed by the rebellious brother of the Persian king, not by the king himself. All the same, his may well be as valuable a response to the *Anabasis* as Yurick's. Xenophon *is* good in a crisis (or so that *Times* leader writer in June 1940 thought).[29]

Can we explain why Yurick and Coyle adapt Xenophon's story in such different ways? Yurick's novel seems to be a response to the breakdown of domestic certainties and the rise of juvenile crime in the years after the end of the Second World War: it is in the mould of novels of teenage gang violence like Irving Shulman's *The Amboy Dukes* (1947) and Evan Hunter's *The Blackboard Jungle* (1954). The paperback tied to the film even advertised the novel as 'the most dangerous book since *A Clockwork Orange*': 'Remember it next time you're on the street alone.' Coyle's depiction of

217

Central Europe seems to be a response to the breakdown of Cold War certainties at the end of the 1980s, a reassertion of American moral and military supremacy in a changed world. Yurick reflects social changes without suggesting any solution: Coyle offers reassurance. That is to say, we cannot explain the differences between their novels. It is just that they are different sorts of people writing different sorts of novel for different sorts of audience.

Different Xenophons can even appear in editorials in *The Times*. At the time of the withdrawal from Dunkirk, the retreat of the Ten Thousand was hailed as the greatest march of the ancient world, a heroic prototype for the British retreat to Dunkirk. A rather different image of this march suited the paper's editorial line in December 1864: 'The "ten thousand" Greeks were led by XENOPHON from the plains of the Euphrates to the shore of the Black Sea, but the enterprise was undertaken by the wreck of an army. The retreat itself is celebrated in history, but it told the world that the invasion of Persia was a ruinous failure.' That editorial was printed when news had just arrived that Sherman had completed his march through Georgia to the sea. *The Times*, a supporter of the southern states in the Civil War, was responding to positive comparisons between Sherman and Xenophon. It was insisting that Sherman had been in as much of a fix as the Ten Thousand, and had narrowly escaped thanks to the desperate measure of cutting a path to the coast. It was wrong about Sherman – but perhaps not so wrong about Xenophon.[30]

How we read 'Thalatta! Thalatta!' is, it seems, not just a question of genres and the differences between genres. It is also politically charged. Indeed, we have seen that the focus on this one shout has gone hand in hand with, if not itself directly contributed to, idealized readings of the text as a whole. And this idealization has evidently had imperial overtones. What is at stake is not just the historical question of how Xenophon is viewed in relation to Alexander. Rather, it is the question of how identifying with the experiences of Xenophon has bolstered the self-image of the 'west' as it has grappled adventurously with the frontier regions of the 'east'; or how it has shaped, if need be, the self-definition of naval peoples, and naval powers, against the landlubber Germans.

It is, in part at least, because of these political overtones that some broad trends in the use of 'Thalatta! Thalatta!' across time can still be heard. It is hard not to read a passage like that leading article in *The Times* at the time of the Dunkirk crisis as the swan-song for one image of the Ten Thousand. The British no longer rule the waves, and Xenophon was always rather an imperial pleasure, and when last did a *Times* leader use Greek font, let alone quote a Greek phrase without translating it? We have also seen that later writers, as one might expect, have playfully modified and undercut the romantic tones that had become part of how that shout was heard. Appropriations like Joyce's 'Galata! Galata!' or Ben Zwaal's 'hatsjie thalassa', 'hachoo thalassa', may not be that 'true' to the original, but they are the more aesthetically rich for that freedom.

There are other unexpected ways in which Xenophon lives on. A quick navigation through the sea of words on the internet throws up some odd treats – like an unexpectedly heroic whisky website: 'like Xenophon's hard-bitten remnant, we too may call out in joy and thankfulness, *Thalassa! Thalassa!*: for to fight and win through to an Islay malt is like the Ten Thousand's survivors reaching the strand at Trebizond.' And the Byzantinist Anthony Bryer writes that 'now that English schoolboys have abandoned Xenophon, Pontic Turkish write to me about Ksenofon'. Presumably no shout like 'Thalassa! Thalassa!' breaks from their lips, but 'The Sea! The Sea!' is still going on.[31]

Notes

Full bibliographical references are given when items are first mentioned, and in the Select Bibliography in the case of items mentioned more than once.

1. The Black Sea

1. Mulligan: J. Joyce, *Ulysses* (Paris, 1922), 5. Once celebrated: C. Tuplin, 'On the Track of the Ten Thousand', *Revue des études anciennes* 101 (1999), 331-66, at 332. 'Thalatta! Thalatta!': *Anab.* 4.7.21-5. Some manuscripts have 'Thalatta!' written only once: it would be intriguing if 'Thalatta! Thalatta!' were an instance of dittography – that is, if this book were tracing the reception of a scribal error.

2. New York: S. Yurick, *The Warriors* (London, 1966; orig. pub. 1965). Germany: H. Coyle, *The Ten Thousand* (London, 1994; orig. pub. 1993). Planet Marduk trilogy: D. Weber and J. Ringo, *March Up Country* and *March to the Sea* (both Riverdale, NY, 2001), culminating in the somewhat less Xenophontic *March to the Stars* (Riverdale, NY, 2003).

3. 'Memorable morning': A.H. Layard, *Discoveries in the Ruins of Nineveh and Babylon: With Travels in Armenia, Kurdistan and the Desert* (London, 1853), 227.

4. Superhuman deed: J. Rennell, *Illustrations, (Chiefly Geographical,) of the History of the Expedition of Cyrus, from Sardis to Babylonia; and the Retreat of the Ten Thousand Greeks, from thence to Trebisonde and Lydia* (London, 1816), 252.

5. Superlative work: A. Grant, *Xenophon* (Edinburgh and London, 1871), 175; J. Gillies, *The History of Ancient Greece: Its Colonies and Conquests, From the Earliest Accounts till the Division of the Macedonian Empire in the East* (Basel, 1790; orig. pub. 1786), iii. 331; W. Mitford, *The History of Greece* (London, 1808-18; orig. pub. 1784-1818), iii. 112.

6. 'Fiction and truth': E. Gibbon, *The History of the Decline and Fall of the Roman Empire* (Harmondsworth, 1994; orig. pub. 1776-88), i. 952 n. 115.

7. Greeks and the sea: e.g. R.G.A. Buxton, *Imaginary Greece: The Contexts of Mythology* (Cambridge, 1994), 99; P. Horden and N. Purcell, *The Corrupting Sea: A Study of Mediterranean History* (Oxford, 2000), 27. Acta Philippi: F. Bovon, B. Bouvier, and F. Amsler, *Acta Philippi* (Turnhout, 1999), i. 96. 'Thalassa, Thalassa' is not found in the longer version of the *Acta Philippi* which was discovered on Mount Athos in 1974 in a manuscript known, after the monastery, as Xenophontos 32. Ancient allusions: Arrian, *Periplus Maris Euxini* 1.1; Libanius 18.79 (Franco Basso alerted me to this passage).

8. 'Thalassa or thalatta': G.M. Fraser, *Flashman at the Charge* (London, 1999; orig. pub. 1973), 236-7, and personal correspondence dated 4 April, 2001.

9. 'Thalatta or thalassa': E. Waugh, *Ronald Knox* (London, 1962; orig. pub. 1959), 28. Knox's niece, the novelist Penelope Fitzgerald, does not mention the story in her biography *The Knox Brothers* (London, 1977). John Taylor told me the Knox anecdote;

Denis Feeney has heard the story told of another precocious youngster, John Stuart Mill – but it suits Ronald Knox much better.

10. *Finnegans Wake*: J. Joyce, *Finnegans Wake* (London, 1939), 100, 93, 324, 551, 547, 328; cf. R.J. Schork, *Greek and Hellenic Culture in Joyce* (Gainesville, Fa., 1998), 29. Hachoo: B. Zwaal, *dwang parasang* (Amsterdam, 1990), 19.

11. 'Britannic character': J.W. Fortescue, 'A Day with Xenophon's Harriers', *Macmillan's Magazine* 71 (1895), 182-9, at 182.

2. Eastern Adventure

1. 'Useguard', 'No shout': M.A.B. Johnston and K.D. Yearsley, *Four-Fifty Miles to Freedom* (Edinburgh and London, 1919), 35, 227-8.

2. 'Scarcely ... more elated': E.H. Keeling, 'An Escape from Turkey in Asia', *Blackwood's Magazine* 203 (1918), 561-92, at 572; *Adventures in Turkey and Russia* (London, 1924), 108.

3. 'Almost as elated': H.C.W. Bishop, *A Kut Prisoner* (London, 1920), 163.

4. Crusoe: E.M.W. Tillyard, *The English Epic and its Background* (London, 1954), 55. New World: cf. H. Taine, 'Xénophon: L'Anabase', in *Essais de critique et d'histoire* (5th edn; Paris, 1887), 49-95, at 50, 54, 55, 61. El Dorado: cf. R. Nickel, *Xenophon* (Darmstadt, 1979), 6. 'Manliness': E.M. Walker and J.H. Freese, 'Xenophon', in *Encyclopaedia Britannica* (11th edn; Cambridge, 1911), xxviii. 885-7, at 886.

5. 'Animated': Gibbon, *Decline and Fall* i. 952 n. 115. 'Knight-errantry': J.A. St John, *The History of the Manners and Customs of Ancient Greece* (London, 1842), i. 343. Boy's own: O. Murray, 'Greek Historians', in J. Boardman, J. Griffin, and O. Murray (eds), *The Oxford History of the Classical World* (Oxford, 1986), 186-203, at 198. Holiday: R.C. Horn, 'The Last Three Books of Xenophon's Anabasis', *Classical World* 28 (1935), 156-9, at 156. Helpful discussions of the nineteenth-century adventure story include M. Green, *Dreams of Adventure, Deeds of Empire* (London and Henley, 1980); P. Brantlinger, *Rule of Darkness: British Literature and Imperialism, 1830-1914* (Ithaca and London, 1988); J. Bristow, *Empire Boys: Adventures in a Man's World* (London, 1991); and R. Phillips, *Mapping Men and Empire: A Geography of Adventure* (London, 1996).

6. Adventurer: *The Times*, 13 May 1930, p. 10. Romantic rebel: W. Jaeger, *Paideia: Ideals of Greek Culture*, trans. G. Highet (Oxford, 1939-45), iii. 156-7. 1745: Grant, *Xenophon*, 24.

7. The east: F. Maclean, *Eastern Approaches* (London, 1949), 16-17. China: P. Fleming, *News from Tartary* (Edinburgh, 2001; orig. pub. 1936), 12.

8. War-correspondent: J.B. Bury, *The Ancient Greek Historians* (London, 1909), 151. On Henty, cf. J. Richards, 'Popular Imperialism and the Image of the Army in Juvenile Literature', in J.M. MacKenzie (ed.), *Popular Imperialism and the Military, 1850-1950* (Manchester), 80-108, at 89-100, who notes the shift from the maritime focus of the adventure stories of Marryat, Kingston, and Ballantyne to the army focus of the late Victorian Henty.

9. Afghanistan: T. De Quincey, 'Affghanistan', *Blackwood's Edinburgh Magazine* 56 (1844), 133-52, at 134; W.F. Ainsworth, *Travels in the Track of the Ten Thousand Greeks* (London, 1844), p. vi. On British myths of imperialism, cf. e.g. R.H. MacDonald, *The Language of Empire: Myths and Metaphors of Popular Imperialism, 1880-1918* (Manchester, 1994), esp. 80-111.

10. 'Britannic character': Fortescue, 'A Day with Xenophon's Harriers', 182.

11. 'Spontaneous allusion': P. Wilson, 'Introduction', in D. Defoe, *The Life,*

Adventures, and Pyracies of the Famous Captain Singleton, ed. S. K. Kumar (Oxford, 1990; orig. pub. 1720), p. xvi. 'The *Sea!*': Defoe, *Captain Singleton*, 103.

12. Frankenstein: M.W. Shelley, *Frankenstein: The Modern Prometheus* (Oxford, 1980; orig. pub. 1818), 204, 205.

13. Cook, Bligh: Rennell, *Illustrations*, 197, 287.

14. Xenophon the explorer: E.H. Bunbury, *A History of Ancient Geography* (London, 1879), i. 357; P.M. Sykes, *A History of Exploration From the Earliest Times to the Present Day* (3rd edn; London, 1950), 12. Out of all the great explorers, Xenophon is Bernard Levin's hero: Levin explains that the image of the first glimpse of the sea 'has brought me closer than anything else I have ever read to understanding, and envying, the spirit that throughout the ages has animated those who have travelled further than their fellows', and even inspired in him the impossible dream of retracing Xenophon's journey (*Enthusiasms* (London, 1983), 113, 114-15).

15. Shouting: J.M. Stuart, *The Journals of John McDouall Stuart* (London, 1864), 407; R. Burton, *The Source of the Nile* (London, 1993; orig. pub. as *The Lake Regions of Central Africa*, 1860), 452; S.W. Baker, *The Albert N'yanza: Great Basin of the Nile and Explorations of the Nile Sources* (London, 1962; orig. pub. 1866), ii. 359; G.F. Lyon, *A Narrative of Travels in Northern Africa, in the Years 1818, 19, and 20* (London, 1821), 335.

16. De Soto: C.M. Harvey, 'The Red Man's Last Roll-Call', *Atlantic Monthly* 97 (1906), 323-30, at 325. '*Ocian in view!*': M. Lewis and W. Clark, *The Original Journals of the Lewis and Clark Expedition*, ed. R.G. Thwaites (New York, 1959), iii. 207 n. 1. 'Like Xenophon's Greeks': J. Bakeless, *Lewis and Clark: Partners in Discovery* (New York, 1947), 278.

17. *Eothen*: A.W. Kinglake, *Eothen, or Traces of Travel Brought Home from the East* (London, 1961; orig. pub. 1844), 55, 94, 98, 139-40, 144, 184-5, 186.

18. Desert as sea: Kinglake, *Eothen* 134, 148, 153. 'In hostile deserts lost': G.M. Reynolds, *'Thalassa!'* (London, 1906), p. vi. 'Boundless wilderness': K.M. Górski, *Wierszem 1883-1893* (Krakow, 1904), 39-40 (trans. S. Sprawski, with modifications by S. West, who first alerted me to a reference to this poem). On the opposition of desert and sea, cf. W.H. Auden, *The Enchafèd Flood, or the Romantic Iconography of the Sea* (London, 1951), 13-42.

19. Antony and Xenophon: Plutarch *Antony* 49.5-6, 45.12, with C. Pelling's commentary (Cambridge, 1988), ad loc. Italy: T. Hutchinson, *Xenophontis de Cyri expeditione libri septem* (4th edn; Cambridge, 1785; orig. pub. 1735), ad loc., citing Virgil, *Aeneid* 3.522-4; cf. joy at the sight of land as an epic simile in Homer, *Odyssey* 23.233-9, of Odysseus and Penelope re-united, and Torquato Tasso's *Jerusalem Delivered*, of the crusaders' first sight of Jerusalem (London, 1962; Ital. orig. 1580), 58.

20. Shipwreck narratives: J.G. Dalyell, *Shipwrecks and Disasters At Sea* (Edinburgh, 1812), iii. 320, 391, 64; J.-B.H. Savigny and A. Correard, *Narrative of a Voyage to Senegal in 1816* (London, 1818; Fr. orig. 1817), 69. 'A sail! A sail!': Defoe, *Captain Singleton* 25-6, 39; G.G. Byron, *The Complete Poetical Works* (Oxford, 1980-93), iii. 153 (*Corsair* i. 83); S.T. Coleridge, *Collected Works*, xvi: *Poetical Works I* (Princeton, 2001), 386; C. Ricks (ed.), *The Poems of Tennyson* (London, 1987), ii. 649; E. Sue, *Romans de mort et d'aventures* (Paris, 1993), 473 ('Une voile! Une voile!' – also the title of the chapter). Columbus: G. Cousin, *Kyros le jeune en Asie Mineure (Printemps 408-Juillet 401 avant Jésus-Christ)* (Paris and Nancy, 1905), p. xxxvi; E. von Hoffmeister, *Durch Armenien: Eine Wanderung und der Zug Xenophons bis zum Schwarzen Meer* (Leipzig and Berlin, 1911), 249; A. Dupouy, *La Poésie de la mer dans la littérature française* (Paris, 1947), 12; the emotions of Xenophon's soldiers and Columbus' followers were already compared by R.J. Thornton, *Medical Extracts: On the Nature of Health* (London, 1797), 861, in a discussion of nostalgia.

21. Tallata: quoted in R. Huntford, *Nansen: The Explorer as Hero* (London, 1997), 348. I am grateful to Nicholas Horsfall for this reference.

22. Boer commando: D. Reitz, *Commando: A Boer Journal of the Boer War* (London, 1929), 214, 296. I am (again) grateful to Nicholas Horsfall for this reference.

23. Finding and losing the *Anabasis*: W.K. Hancock and J. Van der Poel (eds), *Selections from the Smuts Papers* (Cambridge, 1966), i. 409, 431. T. Pakenham, *The Boer War* (London, 1979), 521, perhaps goes a bit far when he writes that Smuts 'turned to his beloved Anabasis' to 'take refuge' from the 'horrors' of the campaign.

24. Mountains: D.C. Gallaher, *A Diary Depicting the Experience of DeWitt Clinton Gallaher in the War Between the States While Serving in the Confederate Army*, ed. D.C. Gallaher, Jr. (Charleston, W. Va., 1945), 5. Tents: H.J. Coke, *Tracks of a Rolling Stone* (London, 1905), 192; *A Ride over the Rocky Mountains to Oregon and California* (London, 1852), 313. Railways: F. von Notz, *Deutsche Anabasis 1918: Ein Rückzug aus dem bulgarischen Zusammenbruch in Mazedonien* (Berlin, 1921), 56.

25. 'La mer!': J. Verne, *Voyage au centre de la terre* (Paris, 1977; orig. pub. 1864), 197. 'The sea – the sea': J. Verne, *A Journey to the Centre of the Earth* (London, 1872), 212 (trans. not named). 'Thalatta! Thalatta': J. Verne, *A Journey into the Interior of the Earth*, trans. F.A. Malleson (London, 1876), 166. Verne himself did include a more Xenophontic shout in a short story 'The Eternal Adam', published posthumously in 1910. The story is set tens of thousands of years in the future, when other lands have been submerged in the sea and a single large continent remains. A container is discovered with a journal describing the great deluge. Some people had been discussing, with some scepticism, the civilization of Atlantis – when the ground started to tremble, and they saw the gardener rushing from his house at the end of the garden: ' "The sea! ... The sea! ..." he was shouting at the top of his voice. Turning towards the ocean, I stood there motionless, stupefied. ... The cliff had vanished, simply vanished, and my garden was sloping down to the edge of the sea' (*The Eternal Adam and Other Stories*, ed. P. Costello (London, 1999), 211-44, at 226-7). With some virtuosity, Verne makes that shout of the sea a cataclysmic cry of horror.

26. Seeking adventure: G. Greene, *Journey Without Maps* (London, 1978; orig. pub. 1936), p. ix. Thalassa: Fleming, *News from Tartary*, 231.

27. Castaways, diver: Fleming, *News from Tartary*, 143, 160, 238. Bathing: Kinglake, *Eothen*, 154.

28. Tartar adventure: Fleming, *News from Tartary*, 9 (dedication), 149 (No Man's Land), 12 (Africa), 11 (skulls), 172 (amateur), 20 (comic), 11 (undeserved), 121 (goose), 29 (trade-name), 234-5 (Cherchen), 243 (Britannia), 187 (picnic). Not showing off: A. Powell, *To Keep the Ball Rolling* (Harmondsworth, 1983), 258.

29. Fleming and Lawrence: Fleming, *News from Tartary*, 318, 331. For Fleming's nostalgia, cf. his praise of the book on the 1891 Hunza-Nagar expedition by E.F. Knight, 'who travelled and wrote in the days when Special Correspondents were not compelled to spend their whole time between the local Foreign Office and a bar' (p. 374).

30. Cycling: T.E. Lawrence, *The Home Letters of T. E. Lawrence and his Brothers* (Oxford, 1954), 64, 66.

31. Xenophon and Lawrence: I. Calvino, 'Xenophon's Anabasis', in *Why Read the Classics?*, trans. M. McLaughlin (London, 1999; Ital. orig. 1991), 19-23, at 21; P. Green, 'Text and Context in the Matter of Xenophon's Exile', in I. Worthington (ed.) *Ventures into Greek History* (Oxford, 1994), 215-27, at 225, makes the same comparison. 'Eastern adventure': T.E. Lawrence, *Seven Pillars of Wisdom* (London, 1935), 276 n. Letter to Shaw: quoted in J.M. Wilson, 'T. E. Lawrence and the Translating of the *Odyssey*', *Journal of the T. E. Lawrence Society* 3.2 (1994), 35-66, at 37.

32. 'March up-country': T.E. Lawrence, *Seven Pillars of Wisdom: The Complete 1922 'Oxford' Text* (Fordingbridge, 2004; orig. pub. 1997), 162. Strategy, 'diathetics', Akaba: Lawrence, *Seven Pillars* 192, 194, 195 (alluding to *Anab.* 1.1.5), 312.

33. Bedouins: L. Thomas, ' "The Uncrowned King of Arabia", Colonel T. E. Lawrence: The Most Romantic Career of Modern Times', *Strand Magazine* 59 (1920), 141-53, at 148; *With Lawrence in Arabia* (6th edn; London, 1925; orig. pub. 1924), 90. On Lawrence and Thomas, see G. Dawson, *Soldier Heroes: British Adventure, Empire and the Imagining of Masculinities* (London and New York, 1994), 167-90.

34. On his lips: B.H. Liddell Hart (ed.), *T. E. Lawrence to his Biographer, Liddell Hart: Information about Himself, in the Form of Letters, Notes, Answers to Questions and Conversations* (London, 1938), 176; *'T. E. Lawrence': In Arabia and After* (London, 1934), 206.

35. L.H.: R. Graves (ed.), *T. E. Lawrence to his Biographer, Robert Graves: Information about Himself, in the Form of Letters, Notes and Answers to Questions* (London, 1938), 181, 182. Liddell Hart did indeed write that Lawrence has 'a claim to historical consideration among those we call the Great Captains' (*'T. E. Lawrence'* 438).

36. 'Bustard': Lawrence, *Seven Pillars* 513. 'March up-country' removed: J. Meyers, 'Xenophon and *Seven Pillars of Wisdom*', *Classical Journal* 72 (1977), 141-3, at 142.

37. 'Fraudulence of adventure': P. Zweig, *The Adventurer* (London, 1974), 237. Xenophon and Caesar: M. Brown (ed.), *The Letters of T. E. Lawrence* (London, 1988), 367; Liddell Hart, *T. E. Lawrence to his Biographer*, 68; Wilson, 'T. E. Lawrence', 37. Cf. also a letter of 1932 saying that the *Anabasis* was one of the familiar Greek books he could read without a crib (H. Orlans (ed.), *Lawrence of Arabia, Strange Man of Letters: The Literary Criticism and Correspondence of T. E. Lawrence* (Rutherford and London, 1993), 254); and for his high opinion of the *Cyropaedia*, cf. Liddell Hart, *T. E. Lawrence to his Biographer*, 133. For Lawrence on Caesar's *Commentaries*, cf. also his letter to George Bernard Shaw – who had compared the two men as writers: 'They are the antithesis of mine: indeed, I suspect that no successful general ever spilled so much of himself on to paper as I did' (J.M. and N. Wilson (eds), *T. E. Lawrence: Correspondence with Bernard and Charlotte Shaw, 1922-1926* (Fordingbridge, 2000), i. 15). Most of Lawrence's allusions to Xenophon are noted in Meyers, 'Xenophon and *Seven Pillars*'. But note that he makes an important slip: he cites the sentence 'If "Thalassa, Thalassa" was not on his lips ...' as Lawrence's own comment on Liddell Hart's draft (p. 143).

38. 'Hardships': T.W. White, *Guests of the Unspeakable: The Odyssey of an Australian Airman: Being a Record of Captivity and Escape in Turkey* (London, 1928), 97.

39. Longest march: Bishop, *A Kut Prisoner*, 79.

40. 'Bitter laugh': E.O. Mousley, *Blow, Bugles, Blow: An English Odyssey* (London, 1931), 198. Mousley's memoir: *The Secrets of a Kuttite: An Authentic Story of Kut, Adventures in Captivity and Stamboul Intrigue* (London, 1921).

41. Tigris, baggage, goatskins: Keeling, *Adventures in Turkey* 20, 29, alluding to *Anab.* 3.3.1 and 2.4.28; photo facing p. 28. Inflated skins: H.C.W. Bishop, 'From Kut to Kastamuni', *Blackwood's Magazine* 203 (1918), 241-61, at 249; *A Kut Prisoner* 52.

42. God: Johnston and Yearsley, *Four-Fifty Miles*, 294. Goatskins: Pte. D. Hughes, in D.L.C. Neave, *Remembering Kut: 'Lest We Forget'* (London, 1937), 163. Nineveh: P.W. Long, *Other Ranks of Kut* (London, 1938), 83-4.

43. Letter to *The Times*: 18 November 1921, p. 6. In parliament: *The Times*, 12 October 1944, p. 8, and 28 February 1951, p. 7 (on prisoners in the Far East and in Korea). Stagnation: M. Proust, *In Search of Lost Time*, trans. C.K. Scott Moncrieff and T. Kilmartin, revised by D.J. Enright (London, 1996; Fr. orig. 1913-27), vi. 365.

44. Officers and slaves: R. Braddon, *The Siege* (London, 1969), 281.

3. Our Friend of Youth

1. 'First Greek sentence': F.S.N. Douglas, *An Essay on Certain Points of Resemblance between the Ancient and Modern Greeks* (London, 1813), 9 (the accent on θάλασσα was printed wrongly).

2. 'Romantic heroes': R. Stoneman, *Across the Hellespont: A Literary Guide to Turkey* (London, 1987), 207. Prominent: J.P. Mahaffy, *A History of Classical Greek Literature* (2nd edn; London, 1883; orig. pub. 1880), ii. 264.

3. On classical education, see M.L. Clarke, *Classical Education in Britain 1500-1900* (Cambridge, 1959), esp. chs 6-7; and for a less factual and more analytical and sociological approach, C.A. Stray, *Classics Transformed: Schools, Universities, and Society in England, 1830-1960* (Oxford, 1998).

4. Greek at three: J.S. Mill, *Autobiography* (Harmondsworth, 1989; orig. pub. 1873), 28.

5. Pusey in bed: H.P. Liddon, *Life of Edward Bouverie Pusey* (London, 1893-7), i. 15, 9-10.

6. 'Unspeakable gratification': T.J. Hogg, *The Life of Percy Bysshe Shelley* (London, 1858), i. 188.

7. Schools: N. Carlisle, *A Concise Description of the Endowed Grammar Schools in England and Wales* (London, 1818), i. 136, 829, ii. 147. (He offers no help about the curriculum at Durham Grammar School: 'Repeated applications have been made for information concerning this school, but no answers have been received' (i. 402).) 'Wretched compilation': a correspondent in H.C.M. Lyte, *A History of Eton College, 1440-1910* (4th edn; London, 1911; orig. pub. 1875), 382.

8. Adams family: C.J. Richard, *The Founders and the Classics: Greece, Rome, and the American Enlightenment* (Cambridge, Mass., 1994), 34, 49.

9. Criticism of Eton: 'Public Schools of England – Eton', *Edinburgh Review* 51 (1830), 65-80, at 73. Interview (composed 1854-8): J.H. Newman, *The Idea of a University: Defined and Illustrated* (Oxford, 1976; orig. pub. 1873), 276-8 (I am grateful to Greg Rowe for this reference).

10. School editions: see the study by A. Rijksbaron, 'The Xenophon Factory: One hundred and fifty years of school editions of Xenophon's *Anabasis*', in R.K. Gibson and C.S. Kraus (eds), *The Classical Commentary: Histories, Practices, Theory* (Leiden, Boston, and Köln, 2002), 235-67, offering a much fuller (though still incomplete) list of school editions than his earlier Dutch version (*Lampas* 34 (2001) 114-39), and useful remarks on Xenophon's role in the educational system in continental Europe.

11. 'Naturally Anabasis': J.H. Hutton, *A Few Words on Private Schools, their Deficiencies, Advantages and Needs, in Special Relation to the Proposals of the Schools-Inquiry Commission* (Brighton, 1870), 33.

12. Prep schools: C.E. Williams, 'The Teaching of Latin and Greek in Preparatory Schools', in *Board of Education Special Reports 6: Preparatory Schools for Boys: Their Place in English Secondary Education* (London, 1900), 187-97, at 193.

13. Lawrence: J. Wilson, *Lawrence of Arabia: The Authorised Biography of T. E. Lawrence* (London, 1990), 41. Dodds: R.B. Todd, 'E. R. Dodds: The Dublin Years (1916-1919)', *Classics Ireland* 6 (1999), 80-105, at 93.

14. Boy's Own: H.J. Lloyd in P. Warner (ed.), *The Best of British Pluck: The Boy's Own Paper* (London, 1976), 136. Xenophon vs. Caesar: W.H. Morris, *Greek versus Latin: Or, The Comparative Value of Greek and Latin in Modern Education* (London, 1870), 13.

15. Good for schools: anonymous preface of Hutchinson's 1785 edition. Boyish appeal: Fortescue, 'A Day with Xenophon's Harriers', 182; W. Wilson, 'Woodrow

Wilson on the Teaching of Caesar', *Classical Journal* 21 (1925-6), 3-4, at 3; cf. Horn, 'The Last Three Books', 156.

16. 'Without any sex': S. Goldhill, *Who Needs Greek? Contests in the Cultural History of Hellenism* (Cambridge, 2002), 289; cf. C.A. Stray, 'Schoolboys and Gentlemen: Classical Pedagogy and Authority in the English Public School', in N. Livingston and Y.L. Too (eds), *Pedagogy and Power: Rhetorics of Classical Learning* (Cambridge, 1998), 29-46, at 44, on the sexless Caesar. (Goldhill surprisingly adds: 'everyone was to know how the Greeks of the March of the 400 shouted "*Thalassa, Thalassa*".') Pederasts: 4.6.3, 7.4.7. Bowdlerization: G.H. Nall, *Xenophon's Anabasis: Book vii, edited for the use of schools* (London, 1895); also the edition of Book 7 in the Rivington's Greek Texts series (London, 1888: no editor named).

17. 'Young ladies': A. Trollope, *An Autobiography* (Oxford, 1999; orig. pub. 1883), 338-9.

18. 'Easy passage': V. Woolf, *The Voyage Out* (Oxford, 2001; orig. pub. 1915), 263. 'Dull': V. Woolf, *The Flight of the Mind: The Letters of Virginia Woolf*, i (London, 1975), 19. Marching through: J.P. Hallett, 'Writing as an American in Classical Scholarship', in ead. and T. Van Nortwick (eds), *Compromising Traditions: The Personal Voice in Classical Scholarship* (London, 1997), 120-52, at 121. Bryn Mawr: C. Winterer, 'Victorian Antigone: Classicism and Women's Education in America, 1840-1900', *American Quarterly* 53 (2001), 70-93, at 85 (I am grateful to Isobel Hurst for the reference).

19. 'Lady-killer': Wilson, 'Woodrow Wilson', 3-4. 'Force-marched': A. Hecht, *Flight Among the Tombs: Poems* (Oxford, 1997; orig. pub. 1996), 60.

20. 'Text for schoolboys': W.W. Tarn, 'Persia, from Xerxes to Alexander', in J.B. Bury, S.A. Cook, and F.E. Adcock (eds), *The Cambridge Ancient History*, vi: *Macedon: 401-301 BC* (Cambridge, 1927), 1-24, at 18, alluding to Juvenal 10.166-7: 'Go on, madman; run through the wild Alps to please boys and become an oration!' ('i, demens, et saevas curre per Alpes / ut pueris placeas et declamatio fias'). 'We loathed Xenophon': cited by G. Highet, *The Classical Tradition: Greek and Roman Influences on Western Literature* (Oxford, 1967; orig. pub. 1949), 490. 'Ungrateful task': A. Pretor, *The Anabasis of Xenophon: Book VII* (Cambridge, 1880), 13, cf. also 25-6. Headmaster: A.N. Wilson, *The Victorians* (London, 2002), 290-1. 'Mountains of Xenophon': F. Will, 'Introduction', in id. (ed.) *Hereditas: Seven Essays on the Modern Experience of the Classical* (Austin, 1964), pp. vii-xiv, at p. xii.

21. 'Feeble interest': W.G. Clark, 'General Education and Classical Studies', in *Cambridge Essays* i (London, 1855), 282-308, at 298. Hardships: G.L. Cawkwell, 'Introduction', in R. Warner (trans.) *Xenophon: The Persian Expedition* (Harmondsworth, 1972), 9-48, at 9. Mutiny: A. Lang, 'Homer and the Study of Greek', in his *Essays in Little* (London, 1891), 77-92, at 81-2. Cf. the remarks in R.O.A. Crewe-Milnes et al., *Report of the Committee Appointed by the Prime Minister to Inquire Into the Position of Classics in the Educational System of the United Kingdom* (London, 1921), 154: 'No author ... has suffered more than Xenophon from the schoolmaster's habit of using him as an exercise book in Greek grammar; no author can be made more living, if the teacher will take the trouble to explain the story in relation to modern experience of marching, of equipment, of desert and mountain scenery, of snow-blindness and the temper of a democratic army.'

22. Parasangs: J.C. Stobart, *The Glory That Was Greece: A Survey of Hellenic Culture and Civilisation* (London, 1911), 201. Allen: lecture reprinted in C. Bridge and I. Spence, 'H.W. Allen's "Xenophon's Greek Diggers" ', *Journal of the Australian War Memorial* 30 (1997).

23. Boredom: Calvino, 'Xenophon's Anabasis', 21.

24. Tresham Pitcher: P. Glazebrook, *Captain Vinegar's Commission* (London, 1987), 31-2, 86, 89.

25. 'Longing': Fraser, *Flashman at the Charge*, 236-7.

26. 'Sunny days': G. Gissing, *The Private Papers of Henry Ryecroft* (London, 1964; orig. pub. 1903), 91-2. Robin Lane Fox first alerted me to this passage.

27. From Lancing to Nimrud: M. Mallowan, *Mallowan's Memoirs* (London, 1977), 17, 262.

28. *Bookman*: 'Mrs Baillie Reynolds', *The Bookman* 32 (1907), 190. Goddesses: P. Braybrooke, *Some Goddesses of the Pen* (London, 1927), 156. Reynolds receives a brief entry in S. Kemp, C. Mitchell, and D. Trotter (eds), *Edwardian Fiction: An Oxford Companion* (Oxford, 1997), 339, but is not covered in the standard reference books on female authors.

29. Quotations from Reynolds, *'Thalassa!'* 79-80, 276-7, 310, 311, 80, 79.

30. *Jane Eyre*: C.F. Taber, 'The Novelty of Plot and Some Recent Books', *The Bookman* (New York) 25 (1907), 179-84, at 181-2; cf. also the review in *Athenaeum* 4110 (1906), 125. Poem: Reynolds, *'Thalassa!'* , p. vi.

31. Poetic businessman: S.H. Kemper, 'O You Xenophon', *Atlantic Monthly* 126 (1920), 39-44, at 39, 40, 44.

32. Dreaming shopkeeper: B.W. Howard, 'Thalatta', *Scribner's Magazine* 22 (1897), 206-15, at 207, 214.

33. Irish childhood: M.F. McHugh, *Thalassa: A Story of Childhood by the Western Wave* (London, 1931), 213, 218.

34. *Childe Harold* (iv. 175): Byron, *Complete Poetical Works*, ii. 183.

35. Seaside holidays: M.G. Watkins, 'At the Seaside', *Cornhill Magazine* 32 (1875), 414-26, at 414. Aristocracy: A. Corbin, *The Lure of the Sea: The Discovery of the Seaside, 1750-1840* (Harmondsworth, 1995; Fr. orig. 1990), 269. Corbin offers a fascinating genealogy of the desire for the sea; for other recent discussions, see J. Walvin, *Beside the Seaside: A Social History of the Popular Seaside Holiday* (London, 1978) and, for more detailed social and economic analysis, J.K. Walton, *The English Seaside Resort: A Social History 1750-1914* (Leicester, 1983); the twentieth-century German experience is treated in an excellent exhibition catalogue, W. Timm (ed.), *Thalatta, Thalatta! Das Strandbild im Zeitalter des Massentourismus* (Regensburg, 1989).

36. Children and the sea: E. Walker, 'A Trip to the Sea', *New Monthly Magazine* 29 (1830), 433-9, at 436; Anon., 'A Family Trip to the Sea-side', *Bentley's Magazine* 32 (1852), 310-18, at 310; R. Doyle, 'At the Sea-side', *Cornhill Magazine* 4 (1861), 582-3, at 583; C. Dickens, *Sketches by Boz* (Oxford, 1957; orig. pub. 1836-7), 344.

37. The sea and adventure: Anon., 'The Sea', *Dublin University Magazine* 45 (1855), 574-86, at 574-5; Watkins, 'At the Seaside', 417.

38. Family holiday: J. Betjeman, *Collected Poems* (4th edn; London, 1979), 157, 159, 160.

39. Railway-carriage windows: R. Hilton, *'Thalatta! Thalatta!'*, *Blackwood's Magazine* 283 (1958), 224-30, at 224. South Wales: D. Bush, 'The Sea, the Sea', *Poetry Wales* 21 (1985), 51-5, at 54-5.

40. 'Round the Corner', childhood: L. MacNeice, *Collected Poems* (2nd edn; London, 1979; orig. pub. 1966), 518, 183.

41. First sight: V.H. Hobart, 'A Chapter on the Sea', *Fraser's Magazine* 56 (1857), 64-71, at 69; reprinted in his *Essays and Miscellaneous Writings*, ed. M. Hobart (2 vols; London, 1885), i. 188-208. 'It's coming': B.R. Haydon, *The Diary of Benjamin Robert Haydon* (Cambridge, Mass., 1960-3), iii. 165.

42. Penalty for travelling young: Watkins, 'At the Seaside', 416.

4. Image of Eternity

1. 'Sentimental poets': Z. Herbert, 'Anabasis', in *Report from the Besieged City and Other Poems*, trans. J. and B. Carpenter (Oxford, 1987), 45 (I owe knowledge of this poem to Stephanie West). First sight: Watkins, 'At the Seaside', 416. 'Image of eternity': Byron, *Complete Poetical Works*, ii. 185. 'Sea-Greeting': H. Draper (trans.), *The Complete Poems of Heinrich Heine* (Oxford, 1982), 145 (I have restored 'Thalatta! Thalatta!' for the translator's 'Thalassa! Thalassa!'; for the original, see H. Heine, *Historisch-kritische Gesamtausgabe der Werke* (Hamburg, 1973-97), i. 394-9: 'Thalatta! Thalatta! / Sei mir gegrüßt, du ewiges Meer! / Sei mir gegrüßt zehntausendmal, / Aus jauchzendem Herzen'). The poem was first published in the second volume of Heine's *Reisebilder (Travel Pictures)*, and then at the end of the collection of his early poems, *Buch der Lieder (Book of Songs)*, where the second cycle had the epigraph 'Motto – Xenophon's Anabasis, IV, 7'; in the second and third editions of *Reisebilder*, this motto was applied to both cycles of North Sea poems.

2. *Harz Journey*: H. Heine, *Selected Prose*, trans. R. Robertson (Harmondsworth, 1993), 33, 46. 'I love the sea': Heine, *Gesamtausgabe*, vi. 150 ('Ich liebe das Meer, wie meine Seele. Oft wird mir sogar zu Muthe, als sey das Meer eigentlich meine Seele selbst'). This prose work, *North Sea III*, was also published in *Reisebilder II*.

3. 'Heroic posture': J.L. Sammons, *Heinrich Heine: The Elusive Poet* (New Haven, 1969), 82.

4. 'Epic voyage': M. Perraudin, *Heinrich Heine: Poetry in Context: A Study of 'Buch der Lieder'* (Oxford, New York, and Munich, 1989), 101. At sea: Heine, *Complete Poems*, 147, 150, 154.

5. Hateful gods: Heine, *Complete Poems*, 146, 148-9, 151, 152-4.

6. Back to port: Heine, *Complete Poems*, 155, 156.

7. Failed liberation: S.S. Prawer, *Heine: Buch der Lieder* (London, 1960), 53.

8. *Thalatta* anthology: J. Flibbert, 'Poetry in the Mainstream', in H. Springer (ed.) *America and the Sea: A Literary History* (Athens, Ga., 1995), 109-26, at 109; review cited by W.H. Bonner, 'Thalassa, Thalassa! Thoreau at Newport?', *Thoreau Society Bulletin* 120 (1972), 7-8, at 8.

9. 'Motley character': J. Skelton, *Thalatta! or The Great Commoner: A Political Romance* (London, 1862), p. vi. Review: 'Novels and Novelists of the Day', *North British Review* 38 (1863), 168-90, at 189.

10. Reading Heine: Skelton, *Thalatta!* 136-7, 138.

11. Thalatta: Skelton, *Thalatta!* 27-8, 358.

12. 'Yet once more': Byron, *Complete Poetical Works*, ii. 183. Influence of sea: *Spectator* 1806 (7 February, 1863), p. 1611; Skelton, *Thalatta!* 299, 26, 371.

13. Books a bore: J. Skelton, 'Long Vacation Reading', *Fraser's Magazine* 60 (1859), 672-83, at 672, 683.

14. 'Thalatta': E.J.M. Collins, *Summer Songs* (London, 1860), 102-3; R.B.W. Noel, 'Thalatta', *Gentleman's Magazine* 17 (1875), 160-4 (reprinted in his *Songs of the Heights and Deeps* (London, 1885), 65-75; wrongly indexed as 'Thalatta! Thalatta!', in W.F. Poole, *An Index to Periodical Literature* (3rd edn; Boston, 1882), i. 1298); W.B. Allen, 'Thalatta', in W.M. Williamson (ed.) *The Eternal Sea: An Anthology of Sea Poetry* (New York, 1946), 284; H.R. Spier, 'Thalatta (The Sea)', words by O. M. Dennis (New York, 1924).

15. 'Thalatta, Thalatta': J. Reade, *The Prophecy of Merlin and Other Poems* (Montreal, 1870), 76-7; J.B. Brown, 'Thalatta! Thalatta!: Cry of the Ten Thousand', in E.C. Stedman (ed.), *An American Anthology, 1787-1900* (Boston and New York, 1900), 305-

6; J.P. Worden, 'Thalatta! Thalatta!' (Bristol, 1908); J.L. Cuthbertson, *Barwon Ballads and School Verses* (Melbourne and London, 1912), 170-1.

16. 'Thalassa! Thalassa!': H. Ellison, *Stones from the Quarry* (London, 1875), 251; J.R. Sturgis, 'Θάλασσα! Θάλασσα!', *Blackwood's Magazine* 118 (1875), 225-7 (in both cases, the title is in Greek, but transliterated in the contents). In the first volume of W.E. Houghton, J.H. Slingerland, and J.L. Altholz, *The Wellesley Index to Victorian Periodicals* (Toronto and London, 1966-89), Sturgis is identified as the author of two articles in *Cornhill Magazine* published under the initials 'J.R.S.'; in the third volume, that attribution was changed to Sir John Robert Seeley (i. 1165, iii. 1010). Sturgis' authorship of our poem is clinched by the fact that a character in the poem, Agathon, also appears in Sturgis' *A Book of Song* (London, 1894), in 'Agathon', a reverie on revisiting Athens ('Away with me to Athens, Agathon!').

17. 'Cacaraca': W.-C. Bonaparte-Wyse, 'Θάλασσα, θάλασσα!: Cridamen di Gré dins l'Anabàsi de Xenefoun', *Revue des langues romanes* 25 (1884), 153 ('Mai subran, i sentour de la costo adourado, / I dardai benfasènt dóu parla que m'enfado, / A l'aubo coume un gau, cante: – "Cacaraca!" ').

18. 'The Sea, the Sea': V. de S. Pinto and W. Roberts (eds), *The Complete Poems of D. H. Lawrence* (London, 1964), 454-5, 197; H.D. Longfellow, *Poems and Other Writings* (Library of America 118; New York, 2000), 658. '... the Open Sea': B.W. Procter, *English Songs and Other Small Poems* (London, 1832), 1-2; C.A. Somerset, *The Sea! A Nautical Drama*, with remarks by D.-G. (London, 1834). Neptune: T.F. Dillon Croker and S. Tucker (eds), *The Extravaganzas of J. R. Planché Esq.* (London, 1879), i. 162. Psyche: quoted by W.D. Adams, *A Book of Burlesque: Sketches of English Stage Travestie and Parody* (London, 1891), 69. Gin: Anon. (London, n.d.).

19. Repetition: Gillies, *History* iii. 365; Mitford, *History* iii. 171. The Greek phrase was quoted in *Additions to the Universal History, in Seven Volumes, in Folio* (London, 1750), 141, with the gloss 'that is, The Sea! the Sea!'. 'Thalatta' in later historians: e.g. G. Grote, *A History of Greece* (London, 1904; orig. pub. 1846-56), vii. 277. Greek font: J.G.A. Holm, *The History of Greece from its Commencement to the Close of the Independence of the Greek Nation*, trans. F. Clarke (London and New York, 1906-11), iii. 5, the English translation of a German history – where the original has 'Thalatta! Thalatta!' (*Griechische Geschichte von ihrem Ursprunge bis zum Untergange der Selbständigkeit des griechischen Volkes* (Berlin, 1886-94), iii. 6).

20. Freedom: Procter, *English Songs* 1; Kemper, 'O You Xenophon', 40; H.N. Dodge, 'Spirit of Freedom, Thou Dost Love the Sea', in W.M. Williamson (ed.) *The Eternal Sea: An Anthology of Sea Poetry* (New York, 1946), 24; W. Wordsworth, *The Poetical Works of William Wordsworth* (Oxford, 1940-9), iii. 116; Byron, *Complete Poetical Works*, iii. 150.

21. Sound of the sea: Longfellow, *Poems*, 634; Wordsworth, *Poetical Works*, iii. 116; A. Bennett, *Clayhanger* (Harmondsworth, 1989; orig. pub. 1910), 93.

22. 'Unforgettable sound': R. Jenkyns, *The Victorians and Ancient Greece* (London, 1980), 160.

23. 'Sonorous syllables': B. Moore, *Fergus* (London, 1992; orig. pub. 1971), 3.

24. 'Poluphloisbos': Homer, *Iliad* 1.34; Coleridge, *Collected Works*, 942-3; F. Fletcher, *Our Debt to the Classics: A Retrospect* (The Presidential Address of the Classical Association; Oxford, 1946), 12; Joyce, *Finnegans Wake* 547; H.D. Thoreau, *A Week on the Concord and Merrimack Rivers, Walden, The Maine Woods, and Cape Cod* (New York, 1985), 894-5. M. Kaimio, *Characterization of Sound in Early Greek Literature* (Helsinki, 1977), 74, suggests that the epithet 'probably does not originally denote loudness, but repetition' ('much-roaring', i.e. 'always roaring').

25. Ocean: J.J. Wild, *Thalassa: An Essay on the Depth, Temperature, and Currents of the*

Ocean (London, 1877). Yachting: E. Arnold, *Thalassa: A Yachting Song* (London, 1862); J.T. Bucknill, 'Small Yacht Racing on the Solent', in E.R. Sullivan (ed.) *Yachting* (London, 1894), 241-319. Poems: R.M. Watson, 'Thalassa', *Scribner's Magazine* 43 (1908), 655 (reprinted in *The Poems of Rosamund Marriott Watson* (London and New York, 1912), 315); V. Larbaud, *Les Poésies de A. O. Barnabooth* (Paris, 1966; orig. pub. 1913), 53-4. I have not seen A.W. Smith, *Thalassa and Other Poems* (Philadelphia, 1893).

26. Surrogate masturbation: Corbin, *Lure* 77; F. Kermode, *Pleasing Myself: From Beowulf to Philip Roth* (Harmondsworth, 2001), 228. Kermode's review also covers Corbin's *The Foul and the Fragrant* – but is entitled 'The Sea, the Sea' (rather than, say, 'The Shit, the Shit'). Erotic: Skelton, *Thalatta!* 138; Howard, 'Thalatta', 207; Glazebrook, *Captain Vinegar's Commission*, 88. 'Thalassa' poems: W.J. Henderson, 'Thalassa', *Century Illustrated Monthly Magazine* 44 (1892), 907; L.P. Shanks, 'Thalassa', *American Bookman* 67 (1928), 157. Dancer: R. Lehmann, *The Weather in the Streets* (London, 1981; orig. pub. 1936), 175.

27. 'Thalassa!': R.W. Chambers, *The Gold Chase* (London, 1927), 87, 90, 252. Mirage: N. Mitford, *The Pursuit of Love* (Harmondsworth, 1949; orig. pub. 1945), 100.

28. Pilgrim: E.J.M. Collins, *Idyls and Rhymes* (Dublin, 1855), 5, 8. Mons Gaudii: J. Morris, *Farewell the Trumpets: An Imperial Retreat* (London, 1998; orig. pub. 1978), 176. The scene was famously described by the sixteenth-century Italian poet Torquato Tasso in his *Jerusalem Delivered*: 'But when the gliding sun was mounted high, / Jerusalem, behold, appear'd in sight, / Jerusalem they view, they see, they spy; / Jerusalem with merry noise they greet, / With joyful shouts, and acclamations sweet' (p. 57) – a passage modelled on Virgil's description of Aeneas catching sight of Italy.

29. Majesty of God: P. Gosse, *The Ocean* (London, 1849), 1. 'Dancing and sparkling': J. Austen, *Northanger Abbey, Lady Susan, The Watsons, and Sanditon* (Oxford, 1990), 340, and p. xxxii of the introduction by T. Castle. Staring at waves: C. Dickens, *Dombey and Son* (The Oxford Illustrated Dickens; London, 1966; orig. pub. 1848), 225-6. Flowing to sea: M. Allott and R.H. Super (eds), *Matthew Arnold* (Oxford, 1986), 155 ('The hills where his life rose, / And the sea where it goes'); Tennyson, *Poems*, iii. 278 (from 'The Coming of Arthur').

30. 'Intimations': Wordsworth, *Poetical Works* iv. 284.

31. Home: L.J. Hodgson, *Thalassa, Thalassa* (London, 1944), 114, 125, 158.

32. Back to the mother: Hodgson, *Thalassa, Thalassa* 51; A.C. Swinburne, *Poems and Ballads & Atalanta in Calydon* (Harmondsworth, 2000), 37 (from 'The Triumph of Time').

33. 'Thalassal regression': G. Benn, *Selected Poems*, ed. F.W. Wodtke (Oxford, 1970), 78 (my trans.). Benn's phrase is 'thalassale Regression': the editor wrongly calls the adjective 'thalassale' a neologism (p. 159) – but see the next note. For general discussion, see C. Eykman, 'Thalassic Regression: The Cipher of the Ocean in Gottfried Benn's Poetry', in A.-T. Tymieniecka (ed.) *Poetics of the Elements in the Human Condition: The Sea (Analecta Husserliana* 19; Dordrecht and Lancaster, 1985), 353-66.

34. Oceanic feeling: S. Freud, *Civilization and its Discontents*, trans. D. McLintock (Harmondsworth, 2002; Ger. orig. 1930), 3. 'Thalassal regressive trend' ('thalassalen Regressionszuge'): S. Ferenczi, *Thalassa: A Theory of Genitality*, trans. H.A. Bunker (London, 1989; orig. publ. 1938), 52; *Versuch einer Genitaltheorie (Internationale Psychoanalytische Bibliothek*, 15; Leipzig, Vienna, and Zurich, 1924), 70. 'Thalassa complex': A. Lingis, 'The Rapture of the Deep', in A.-T. Tymieniecka (ed.) *Poetics of the Elements in the Human Condition: The Sea (Analecta Husserliana* 19; Dordrecht and Lancaster, 1985), 287-97, at 288.

35. Chekhov: in fact 'To Moscow!' thrice, spoken by Irena at the end of the second act of *The Three Sisters* – but often transformed into 'Moscow! Moscow!'. Tegnér: in J.

Moffett (ed. and trans.), *The North! To the North!: Five Swedish Poets of the Nineteenth Century* (Carbondale and Edwardsville, 2001), 9.

36. Heaven: Rennell, *Illustrations*, 250. Fire and energy: G. Saintsbury, 'Xenophon', *The Dial* 80 (1926), 475-80, at 477. Sea-air: Gissing, *Private Papers*, 92.

37. Pulitzer: A. Nevins, 'Not Capulets, Not Montagus' (Presidential Address to the American Historical Association), *American Historical Review* 65 (1960), 253-70, at 264. Is this anecdote true? D.C. Seitz, one of Pulitzer's secretaries, told the same story about Pulitzer's disappointment with Homer's account of the wooden horse (*Joseph Pulitzer, His Life and Letters* (New York, 1924), 31). Nevins may well have transferred the story to Xenophon.

38. 'Those wearied ones': E.T. Cook and A. Wedderburn (eds), *The Works of John Ruskin* (London, 1903-12), ix. 408-9 (quoted and discussed by R. Jenkyns, *Dignity and Decadence: Victorian Art and the Classical Inheritance* (London, 1991), 155-6).

39. Magnificently simple: Dupouy, *Poésie de la mer*, 12. 'Greek reserve': Grant, *Xenophon* 50-1.

40. 'Pleasant it is': Lucretius 2.1-4, trans. W.H.D. Rouse and M.F. Smith, *Lucretius: On the Nature of Things* (Loeb Classical Library; Cambridge, Mass., and London, 1992), 95.

41. 'Sea, Sea': W.H.D. Rouse, *The March Up Country: A Translation of Xenophon's Anabasis into Plain English* (London and New York, 1947), 124, cf. p. xi; Ainsworth, *Travels* 187; C. Rollin, *Histoire ancienne des Egyptiens, des Carthaginois, des Assyriens, des Babyloniens, des Mèdes et des Perses, des Macédoniens, des Grecs* (Paris, 1740; orig. pub. 1730-8), ii. 586 – the English translation had 'the sea, the sea' (*Ancient History* (London, 1734-9), iv. 116); so too J.L. Le Cointe, *Commentaires sur la retraite des dix-mille de Xénophon; ou Nouveau Traité de la guerre, à l'usage des jeunes officiers* (Paris, 1766), ii. 122 (presumably taken from Rollin). 'Water! Water!': H.R. Haggard, *King Solomon's Mines* (Oxford, 1989; orig. pub. 1885), 82; Verne, *Voyage* 169.

42. Salvation: Rennell, *Illustrations* 250. Greeks kneeling: e.g. C.A. Norton, *History of Greece for Children* (London, 1872), 77; M.C. Ford, *The Ten Thousand* (London, 2001), 363, picturing the troops 'kneeling in the mud, their arms encircling each other's shoulders, praying to the gods'. Balboa: see the 1546 account by Oviedo quoted in K. Romoli, *Balboa of Darién: Discoverer of the Pacific* (Garden City, NY, 1953), 158-9. Cairns: V. Sackville-West, *Passenger to Teheran* (London, 1991; orig. pub. 1926), 56.

43. Wives: Gillies, *History*, iii. 366; R.K. Porter, *Travels in Georgia, Persia, Armenia, Ancient Babylonia, &c.&c., During the Years 1817, 1818, 1819, and 1820* (London, 1821-2), ii. 666; Górski, *Wierszem*, 40.

44. 'Three months': S. Marlowe, *The Shining* (New York, 1965; orig. pub. 1963), 347. Marlowe also alludes to Cleomenes' famous riposte in Herodotus: 'You say no easy thing for the Spartans, wanting to lead them three months' journey from the sea' (5.50.3).

45. Re-writing: Heine, *Complete Poems*, 145; Howard, 'Thalatta', 207; F.T. Csokor, *Als Zivilist im Balkankrieg* (Vienna, 1947), 149.

46. Loving the sea: S.E. Morison, *The Ancient Classics in a Modern Democracy* (Commencement Address Delivered at the College of Wooster, 12 June 1939; New York, 1939), 10.

5. The Sea is English

1. Pillar of smoke: A.R.E. Rhodes, *Sword of Bone: The Phoney War and Dunkirk, 1940* (London, 1942), 197. Other details from C. Seton-Watson, *Dunkirk – Alamein –*

Bologna: Letters and Diary of an Artilleryman, 1939-1945 (London, 1993), 36-7; J. Stedman, *Louisa's Boy* (Lincoln, 1990), 21; P. Wilson, *Dunkirk – 1940: From Disaster to Deliverance* (Barnsley, 1999), 127; D. Barlone, *A French Officer's Diary (23 August 1939-1 October 1940)*, trans. L.V. Cass (Cambridge, 1942), 58; Rhodes, *Sword of Bone* 192.

2. Dunkirk: *The Times*, June 4 1940, p. 7.

3. First glimpse, cellar: Rhodes, *Sword of Bone*, 199, 203.

4. 'England and her ships': J. Masefield, *The Nine Days Wonder (The Operation Dynamo)* (London and Toronto, 1941), p. xvi. Defeat into Victory (itself the title of Viscount Slim's 1956 book on the Burma campaign in the Second World War): Ruskin, *Works*, xxiii. 162 n. 5 (from a MS note on Xenophon), quoted by M.W. Mather and J.W. Hewitt (eds), *Xenophon's Anabasis: Books I-IV* (New York, 1910), 23; J. Thomson, *Liberty, The Castle of Indolence, and Other Poems* (Oxford, 1986; orig. pub. 1735-6), 62 (ii. 187-8). Thomson reverts to the image in the last book (v. 408-10) in speaking of Science, one of the virtues necessary to maintain Liberty: 'With XENOPHON, sometimes, in dire Extremes, / *She* breathes deliberate Soul, and makes Retreat / Unequal'd Glory' (p. 138). Cf. also Porter, *Travels*, ii. 466 on the retreat as 'more glorious than the most fortunate victory'.

5. Dunkirk again: I. Hay, *The Battle for Flanders 1940* (London, 1941), 4, 58-63.

6. Clearchus and Gort: M.C.A. Henniker, 'The Sea! The Sea!', *Army Quarterly* 59 (1949-50), 221-31, at 225, 222.

7. March to the Sea: W.S. Churchill, *The Second World War* (Harmondsworth, 1985; orig. pub. 1948-53), ii. 66-86. Run for the Coast: N. Harman, *Dunkirk: The Necessary Myth* (London, 1980), 103-23. Dunkirk itself, it should be remembered, was also a French affair: for a French allusion to the Ten Thousand, see a passage first included in the second edition of Aragon's novel on the fall of France, *Les Communistes* (Paris, 1966; orig. pub. 1949-51), iv. 248: 'we were like those soldiers of Xenophon seeing at last the Greek sea and calling it by its name: *Thalassa! Thalassa!*' (my trans.).

8. Dodds: J. Stallworthy, *Louis MacNeice* (London, 1995), 293.

9. *Sunday Dispatch*: quoted by P. Knightley, *The First Casualty: The War Correspondent as Hero and Myth-Maker from the Crimea to Kosovo* (2nd edn; London, 2000; orig. pub. 1975), 252.

10. 'Singular': T. De Quincey, 'Revolt of the Tartars: Or, Flight of the Kalmuck Khan and his People from the Russian Territories to the Frontiers of China', in *Works*, iv: *The English Mail Coach and Other Writings* (Edinburgh, 1862; orig. pub. 1837), 111-75, at 139.

11. Indomitable Londoner: B. Coulton, *Louis MacNeice in the BBC* (London, 1980), 52.

12. Thermopylae: Coulton, *Louis MacNeice*, 56.

13. Quoting Horace: P. Leigh Fermor, *A Time of Gifts* (Harmondsworth, 1979; orig. pub. 1977), 86-7. 'The last retreat': title of chapter 25 of Morris, *Farewell the Trumpets*, the final part of her *Pax Britannica* trilogy (two further chapters follow: 'On the Beach' and 'Home!'). Cretan mist: W.S. Moss, *Ill Met by Moonlight* (London, 2001; orig. pub. 1950), 125. Kristina Boden mentioned the film to me, and Steve Crook of the Powell and Pressburger Appreciation Society provided some more precise details.

14. 'The Sea at last ...' (ii. 200-5): Thomson, *Liberty*, 63.

15. Coolidge: in F.G. Kenyon (ed.), *The Testimony of the Nations to the Value of Classical Studies* (London, 1925), 17. Persian Wars spirit: H.G. Dakyns in C. Witt, *The Retreat of the Ten Thousand* (London, 1891), p. vi; Mather and Hewitt, *Xenophon's Anabasis*, 23; Hoffmeister, *Durch Armenien*, 252.

16. 'Need engenders virtue': J.W. Johnson, *The Formation of English Neo-Classical*

Thought (Princeton, 1967), 49, quoted in Thomson, *Liberty*, 38. Quotations from Thomson, *Liberty*, 62, 69, 70 (ii. 166-7, 428-30, 439, 444-5).

17. Quotations from Thomson, *Liberty*, 62-3, 64, 58, 71 (ii. 197-8, 222-5, 235-6, 60, 488).

18. Rollin: A.D. McKillop, *The Background of Thomson's Liberty* (Houston, 1951), 42. Preserving liberty: Rollin, *Ancient History*, iv. 79. Nautical imagery (ii. 150, 155, 157-8): Thomson, *Liberty*, 61; cf. ii. 263, 448-51 (pp. 64, 70) for similar imagery.

19. 'Earnest of Britain' (ii. 82): Thomson, *Liberty*, 59. Xenophon rewritten: Rollin, *Ancient History*, iv. 116.

20. Epigraph: Thucydides 2.42.4. Discipline dissolved, elections: Rennell, *Illustrations*, 250, 15. Cf. also Mitford, *History*, iii. 118 on Clearchus' summoning a meeting of his people 'as in civil assembly'; and C.G. Krüger (ed.), *Xenophon: Cyri Anabasis* (Halle, 1826), 154, on 3.2.9 ('civitatem peregrinantem'), a passage Robert Parker showed me. Athens in Asia: Taine, 'Xénophon', 50 ('république voyageuse qui délibère et qui agit, qui combate et qui vote, sorte d'Athènes errante au milieu de l'Asie'), cf. 76. 'Story of the Greeks': E. Hamilton, *The Greek Way to Western Civilization* (2nd edn; New York, 1948; orig. pub. 1930), 162.

21. Democracy, upbringing: Grote, *History*, vii. 307, 254, cf. 250-4, 328-30. Marathon: J.S. Mill, review of Grote, in *Essays on Philosophy and the Classics*, ed. J.M. Robson (*Collected Works of John Stuart Mill*, 11; London and Toronto, 1978), 273; orig. pub. *Edinburgh Review* 84 (1846), 343-77. On attitudes to Athenian democracy, see F.M. Turner, *The Greek Heritage in Victorian Britain* (New Haven and London, 1981), 187-263; J.T. Roberts, *Athens on Trial: The Antidemocratic Tradition in Western Thought* (Princeton, 1994).

22. English and Greeks: Anon., 'The Sea', 574; cf. e.g. K.B. Workman, *They Saw It Happen in Classical Times* (Oxford, 1964), 48.

23. Sea as home: G. Thorn-Drury (ed.), *The Poems of Edmund Waller* (London, 1893), 152 (from the poem 'Of A War With Spain, And A Fight At Sea'); J.L. Robertson (ed.), *The Complete Poetical Works of Thomas Campbell* (London, 1907), 188 (from 'Ye Mariners of England: A Naval Ode'). 'The sea is English': R.L. Stevenson, 'The English Admirals', in *Virginibus Puerisque*, in *The Works of R. L. Stevenson* (London and New York, 1922-3), 137-55, at 138-9 (orig. pub. *Cornhill Magazine* 38 (1878), 36-43); quoted by C.F. Behrman, *Victorian Myths of the Sea* (Athens, Ohio, 1977), 26.

24. Trip to Scilly Isles: G.H. Lewes, 'New Sea-side Studies (No. 1): The Scilly Isles', *Blackwood's Edinburgh Magazine* 81 (1857), 669-85, at 673, 677.

25. 'Amalgam', 'pet book': R. Ashton, *G. H. Lewes: A Life* (Oxford, 1991), 184, 187.

26. Marathon and Waterloo: E.S. Creasy, *The Fifteen Decisive Battles of the World, from Marathon to Waterloo* (London, 1851); Wordsworth, *Poetical Works*, iii. 147; see in general I. Jenkins, ' "Athens Rising Near the Pole": London, Athens, and the Idea of Freedom', in C. Fox (ed.) *London – World City: 1800-1840* (New Haven and London, 1992), 143-53; W. St Clair, *Lord Elgin and the Marbles* (3rd edn; Oxford, 1998; orig. pub. 1967), 261-80. 'New Athens': cited by St Clair, *Lord Elgin*, 163.

27. The Rhine: quoted in J. Murray (publ.), *A Hand-book for Travellers on the Continent* (London, 1836), 236; M. Shelley, *Rambles in Germany and Italy*, in *The Novels and Selected Works of Mary Shelley*, viii: *Travel Writing*, ed. J. Moskal (London, 1996; orig. pub. 1844), 61-386, at 89, with the editor's note.

28. *Hellas*: T. Hutchinson (ed.), *The Complete Poetical Works of Percy Bysshe Shelley* (London, 1952; orig. pub. 1904), 475.

29. 'All Greeks', 'chrystalline sea': Shelley, *Poetical Works*, 447, 468.

30. Bristol: Worden, 'Thalatta! Thalatta!'. Worden also translated Schiller's *Song of* *the Bell* and wrote other occasional pieces (e.g. a modern-sounding series of articles in 1894 entitled 'Touring in Europe on Next to Nothing').

31. I hope to discuss elsewhere the modern reception of the term 'anabasis'.

32. 'Descent to the Sea': V. Urošević, 'Descent to the Sea', in E. Osers (ed. and trans.) *Contemporary Macedonian Poetry* (London and Boston, 1991), 92. It is fascinating to read Urošević's poem alongside a passage near the start of H.D.F. Kitto's popular *The Greeks* (Harmondsworth, 1951), where Kitto re-tells the immortal story of the Ten Thousand's march to the sea, points out that 'thalassa' itself is not an Indo-European word, and then turns back ten or fifteen centuries to imagine a band of Greek-speaking people making its way south out of the Balkan mountains when it suddenly sees an immense amount of water – and learns from the natives that that is 'thalassa' (pp. 13-14).

33. Teaching Xenophon: quoted by N. Ascherson, *Black Sea* (London, 1995), 186. Villages: A.A.M. Bryer, *The Empire of Trebizond and the Pontos* (London, 1980), 187 (no source cited!).

34. 'Xenophonopolis': S. Bonsal, *Suitors And Suppliants: The Little Nations at Versailles* (New York, 1946), 181-3.

35. Smyrna: E. Hemingway, *The Collected Stories* (Everyman's Library 187; London, 1995), 37-8; cf. D. Roessel, *In Byron's Shadow: Modern Greece in the English and American Imagination* (Oxford and New York, 2002), 210-26. 'Present great *Anabasis*': A.A.M. Bryer, 'The Pontic Greeks before the Diaspora', *Journal of Refugee Studies* 4 (1991), 315-44, at 331.

36. Railways: Notz, *Deutsche Anabasis*, 56. Boer commando: Reitz, *Commando*, 296, 9 (Lucan 1.128: 'victrix causa deis placuit sed victa Catoni').

37. Naval action: Reitz, *Commando*, 297.

38. English Greeks: Taine, 'Xénophon', 93. Scillus: J.M. Merz, *Pietro da Cortona: der Aufstieg zum führenden Maler im barocken Rom* (Tübingen, 1991), plate 332 (painting lost during the Second World War). Kurdistan: S. Laveissière, *Adrien Guignet, peintre, 1816–1854* (Autun, 1978), 23-4 (painting now in the Louvre). I hope to discuss these paintings elsewhere. Note also that when Jean-Jacques-François Le Barbier designed engravings for an elaborate edition of Xenophon published in Paris during the French Revolution, the illustration for the fourth book of the *Anabasis* did not show the first sight of the sea, but the Spartan general Chirisophus sacrificing as some soldiers start to wade across the river Centrites, heroically naked (J.B. Gail (trans.), *Xénophon: Oeuvres complètes* (Paris, 1797-1819), iv. 95, depicting *Anab.* 4.3.17).

6. A Stray Genius

1. Letter about Haydon: *The Times*, 14 June 1940, p. 9 (Mr. L. Jassonides).

2. Haydon on the Ten Thousand: *Haydon's Pictures of Xenophon, Mock Election, &c. &c. &c; Now Exhibiting at the Egyptian Hall, Piccadilly* (London, 1832), 3, 5.

3. 'Immortal dinner': B.R. Haydon, *The Autobiography and Memoirs of Benjamin Robert Haydon (1786-1846)* (London, 1926), 269; references to Haydon's *Autobiography* will be to this edition (with introduction by Aldous Huxley) unless otherwise stated. Huxley: in Haydon, *Autobiography*, p. vi.

4. Ending of autobiography: R.J. Porter, ' "In *me* the solitary sublimity": Posturing and the Collapse of Romantic Will in Benjamin Robert Haydon', in R. Folkenflik (ed.) *The Culture of Autobiography: Constructions of Self-Representation* (Stanford, 1993), 168-87, at 183.

5. 'Tempestuous': R.D. Altick, *The Shows of London* (Cambridge, Mass., 1978), 413.

Haydon the writer: W.M. Thackeray, *Contributions to the* Morning Chronicle, ed. G.N. Ray (Urbana, Illinois, 1955), 154; M. Elwin, 'Introduction', in B.R. Haydon, *Autobiography and Journals* (London, 1950), p. xvii, quoting a review in *Blackwood's Magazine* in 1853; V. Woolf, 'Genius' in *The Moment and Other Essays* (London, 1947), 150-5, at 154.

6. Victoria's visit: B.R. Haydon, *Benjamin Robert Haydon: Correspondence and Table-talk* (London, 1876), ii. 45; cf. *Diary*, v. 9.

7. Age categories: 5.3.1, 6.5.4, 6.4.8. Carrying wounded: 3.4.32.

8. Catalogue description: Haydon, *Pictures of Xenophon*, 6.

9. 'Grouping': B.R. Haydon, *Lectures on Painting and Design* (London, 1844-6), i. 330. 'Overloaded': quoted by J. Barrell, *Painting and the Politics of Culture: New Essays on British Art, 1700-1850* (Oxford, 1992), 289 n. 101.

10. Novelty over: Haydon, *Diary*, iii. 597. 1820 exhibition: Haydon, *Diary*, iii. 598; *Autobiography*, i. 282-3. Egyptian Hall: Altick, *Shows*, 413.

11. *Childe Harold* (iii. 2. 1): Byron, *Complete Poetical Works*, ii. 77. Agincourt: *Henry V*, 3. 1. 1.

12. 'So so': W.M. Thackeray, *The Letters and Private Papers of William Makepeace Thackeray*, ed. G.N. Ray (London, 1945-6), i. 186. Reviews of the *Xenophon* exhibition: *Athenaeum* 231 (31 March), p. 211; *Gentleman's Magazine* 102 (May), pp. 440-1; *London Literary Gazette*, 24 March, p. 186; *Morning Post*, 29 March, p. 3; *Observer*, 25 March, p. 3, reprinted in *Morning Chronicle*, 27 March, p. 4; *Spectator* 196 (31 March), pp. 308-9.

13. Reform, Wilkie: Haydon, *Diary*, iii. 605, 635.

14. Sums: B.R. Haydon, *Description of Eucles, and Punch, with Other Pictures, Drawings, and Sketches, Painted by B. R. Haydon, Now Exhibiting At the Western Exchange, Old Bond Street* (London, 1830), 12; *Pictures of Xenophon* 8 (and in newspaper advertisements for the exhibition). 'Most English way': *Morning Post* 11 May, 1836 (quoted in W.T. Whitley, *Art in England, 1821-1837* (Cambridge, 1930), 315).

15. Victoria: Haydon, *Diary*, iv. 441, cf. *Correspondence*: ii. 202. Goethe's letter: Haydon, *Diary*, iii. 586-7.

16. Duke of Bedford as patron: B.R. Haydon, *Some Enquiry Into the Causes Which Have Obstructed the Advance of Historical Painting for the Last Seventy Years in England* (London, 1829), 9, 26. Raffle: details from *The Times*, 11 May 1836, p. 5; *Spectator* 411 (14 May), p. 469; Haydon, *Diary*, v. 346. Scores: Whitley, *Art*, 314, says that there was first a tie with Lord Mulgrave; the *Times* report has Mulgrave's throws as 10, 8, 11, with the Duke of Bedford as the clear winner, but the list of scores has 10, 9, 11 for Mulgrave – giving a tie. 'Perplexity': F. Haydon in Haydon, *Correspondence*, i. 164, adding that the Duke had sent Haydon fifty guineas and found himself entered for five shares; but *The Times* has the Duke's subscription as thirty guineas: he had subscribed fifty for the *Eucles*, according to the list in B.R. Haydon, *Description of the Picture of Pharaoh Dismissing Moses At the Dead of Night, After the Passover, and Other Pictures, Painted by B. R. Haydon, Now Exhibiting At the Western Exchange, Old Bond Street* (London, 1829), 12, and had lost on a re-throw (*Gentleman's Magazine* 100 (April 1830), p. 348).

17. Trebizond steamer: *The Times*, 10 May 1836, p. 5.

18. Russell Institution: Haydon, *Diary*, iv. 373. Letter: *Spectator* 429 (17 September), p. 892.

19. Location unknown: Pope at Haydon, *Diary*, v. 345 n. 7. Russell Hotel: *The Times*, 17 June 1940, p. 4 (Mr. W. Mannell from Guildford). Auction: Sotheby's, *British Paintings 1500-1900* (catalogue of a sale held in London on Wednesday 10 April, 1991), 52 (where the unpropitious claim that Haydon's painting 'was unsold' after its first exhibition is misleading).

20. Borrowing Rennell: Haydon, *Diary*, iii. 180.

21. Sketching: Haydon, *Diary*, iii. 188.

22. Planning: Haydon, *Diary*, iii. 433, 188, 378. Reviews of 1830 *Eucles* exhibition: *Morning Post*, 1 March, p. 3; *Spectator* 88 (6 March), p. 153; also *Athenaeum* 123 (6 March), p. 139, and 124 (13 March), p. 156; *Gentleman's Magazine* 100 (March), pp. 250-1; *Morning Chronicle*, 1 March, p. 3; *The Times*, 5 March, p. 3.

23. Painting: Haydon, *Diary*, iii. 427 (mistress), 431 (teeming mind), 537 (trumpet). 'Best read': Woolf, 'Genius', 154. Vandyke: Haydon, *Diary*, iii. 114.

24. Size: Haydon, *Diary*, iii. 431-2.

25. Portraits: Haydon, *Diary*, iii. 442 (feeble humanity); iii. 487-8 (peeping).

26. Futility: Haydon, *Diary*, iii. 432, 547.

27. 'Singular destiny': Haydon, *Diary*, iv. 406.

28. 'Go on': Haydon, *Diary*, iii. 432, and in W.B. Pope (ed.), *Invisible Friends: The Correspondence of Elizabeth Barrett Barrett and Benjamin Robert Haydon, 1842-1845* (Cambridge, Mass., 1972), 137. Lyppiatt: A. Huxley, *Antic Hay* (London, 1994; first pub. 1923), 42.

29. 'Let me recollect Xenophon': Haydon, *Diary*, iii. 433. Haydon could also have been thinking of the rousing rejection of the Persian demand that the Greeks hand over their weapons (2.1.12) – a rejection attributed to Xenophon in the translation he was using rather than to a young Athenian named Theopompus, as in most modern texts.

30. Reviews: see n. 12. Watts, Taylor: in B.R. Haydon, *The Life of Benjamin Robert Haydon, From His Autobiography and Journals* (London, 1853), iii. 364, 35. Illustrated histories: E. Taylor, *Historical Prints Representing Some of the Most Memorable Events in the History of Ancient and Modern Greece, with Illustrative Views* (London, 1844), 148; J.R. and C. Morell, *History of Greece* (London, 1873), 179 (the same illustration). Illustrated adaptations: H.L. Havell, *Stories from Xenophon Retold* (London, 1910), 192 ('Thalatta! Thalatta!' by Patten Wilson); Household, *The Exploits of Xenophon* 108-9 (featuring early work by Leonard Everett Fisher, a noted illustrator of children's books; the 1961 British edition has a more minimalist drawing by Bernard Blatch on p. 100).

31. Charlet: cf. M. Meisel, *Realizations: Narrative, Pictorial, and Theatrical Arts in Nineteenth-Century England* (Princeton, 1983), 210-11. David: A. Brookner, *Jacques-Louis David* (London, 1980), 139.

32. Exhibition catalogues: B.R. Haydon, *Explanation of the Picture of The Mock Election, Which Took Place At the King's Bench Prison, July, 1827; Now Exhibiting at the Egyptian Hall, Piccadilly* (London, 1828), 16; *Explanation of the Picture of Chairing the Members, a Scene in The Mock Election, Which Took Place At the King's Bench Prison, July, 1827; Now Exhibiting at the Bazaar, Old Bond Street* (London, 1829), 16; *Pictures of Xenophon*, 7.

33. 'Thalatta' scene: Haydon, *Pictures of Xenophon*, 6.

34. 'Stout Cortez': J. Keats, *Poetical Works*, ed. H.W. Garrod (Oxford, 1956), 38. First sights: Haydon, *Autobiography*, i. 14 (Reynolds), 67 (Marbles), 68 (Fuseli). Cf. I.R.J. Jack, *Keats and the Mirror of Art* (Oxford, 1967), 32 on the religious tone of the sight of the Elgin Marbles. (Jack's claim that Haydon lent Keats his copy of Chapman's Homer is incorrect.)

35. Flaxman's Britannia: J. Dobai, *Die Kunstliteratur des Klassizismus und der Romantik in England* (Bern, 1974-84), iii. 1005; M. Craske, *Art in Europe 1700-1830* (Oxford, 1997), 258-9. Haydon's Britannia: Haydon, *Diary*, i. 3-4.

36. Seaside trips: Haydon, *Autobiography*, i. 141; *Diary*, iii. 544.

37. Huxley: in Haydon, *Autobiography*, p. xvii.

38. Waterloo: Haydon, *Autobiography*, i. 212. 'Heir to Athens': D.B. Brown (ed.), *Benjamin Robert Haydon, 1786-1846: Painter and Writer, Friend of Wordsworth and Keats* (Grasmere, 1996), 19.

39. Phidias: Watts in Haydon, *Life*, iii. 364. Haydon and the Elgin Marbles: F. Cummings, 'Phidias in Bloomsbury: B.R. Haydon's Drawings of the Elgin Marbles', *Burlington Magazine* 106 (1964), 323-8; W. St Clair, *Lord Elgin*, index, s.v. Haydon. Artistic influence: Haydon, *Lectures*, ii. 210 n.; cf. T.S.R. Boase, *English Art 1800-1870* (Oxford, 1959), 161; Craske, *Art*, 271. Awareness of anachronism: shown by Haydon's remark in Pope, *Invisible Friends*, 182 (on the *Aristides*). 'Miracle no longer': Haydon, *Picture of The Mock Election*, 14.

40. National triumphs: Haydon, *Autobiography*, i. 212-13, 201, 283; *Diary*, iii. 374.

41. Géricault review: L. Eitner, *Géricault: His Life and Work* (London, 1982), 210. Fromentin: R. Benjamin, *Orientalism: Delacroix to Klee* (Sydney, 1997), 74. Father and son: L. Eitner, *Géricault's Raft of the Medusa* (London, 1972), 44-6, 155; Haydon, *Description of Eucles*, 12.

42. Letters: Haydon, *Diary*, iii. 582.

43. Excited: Haydon, *Diary*, iii. 559, 560. *Waiting for The Times*: illustration in C. Fox, ed. *London – World City: 1800-1840* (New Haven and London, 1992), 602.

44. 'Dowry of Englishmen': Haydon, *Diary*, iii. 557.

45. Reviews: n. 12. *Morning Chronicle* correspondence: 28, 30 March; 4, 9, 20, 24, 28 April (all p. 3); cf. the paper's *Eucles* review (n. 22), which again criticized the Royal Academy, with an extensive comparison between Haydon's career and James Barry's.

46. Eastlake: Haydon, *Diary*, iv. 146. Catalogue: Haydon, *Pictures of Xenophon*, 5, 6, 8.

47. Worries: Haydon, *Diary*, iii. 549.

48. Impossibility: Haydon, *Diary*, iii. 556-7, v. 430; W.W. Hazlitt, *Complete Works of William Hazlitt*, ed. P.P. Howe (London, 1930-4), xviii. 142-3.

49. Uphill: Haydon, *Autobiography*, i. 274. Sisyphus: G. Parry, 'The Grand Delusions of Benjamin Haydon', *Keats-Shelley Review* 31 (1980), 10-21, at 14; Haydon in Pope, *Invisible Friends*, 100. Dangers: Haydon, *Diary*, iii. 114, iv. 310; i. 279; iii. 89. Catalogue: Haydon, *Pictures of Xenophon*, 4-5.

50. Lazarus: C.R. Leslie, *Autobiographical Recollections*, ed. T. Taylor (Wakefield, 1978; orig. pub. 1860), 222-3. Eucles: Plutarch, *On the glory of the Athenians* 347c; Haydon, *Description of Eucles*, 3-5. First sketch for *Xenophon*: n. 22. Nero: Haydon, *Some Enquiry*, 33. Anchises: Virgil, *Aeneid* 2.708; for carrying the wounded as part of the modern iconography of retreat, see the cover of the 1974 paperback edition of T. Mains, *Retreat from Burma* (London; orig. pub. 1973). Mary: Haydon in Pope, *Invisible Friends*, 57, 144.

51. Precipice: in Pope, *Invisible Friends*, 146. 'Brink of ruin': Haydon, *Diary*, iii. 493.

52. Woman: Haydon, *Diary*, iii. 440. Naked: Haydon in Pope, *Invisible Friends*, 30. Masculine virtues: Barrell, *Painting*, 282. 'Marvel': Tarn, 'Persia', 11; for the sentiment, cf. M. Cary and E.H. Warmington, *The Ancient Explorers* (2nd edn; Harmondsworth, 1963; orig. pub. 1929), 169.

53. 'Happiness': Haydon, *Diary*, iii. 113.

54. Epigraph: Haydon, *Correspondence*, p. v, quoting *Childe Harold*, iv. 1209-12, 1225.

55. Hunt: quoted by A. Hayter, *A Sultry Month: Scenes of London Literary Life in 1846* (London, 1965), 105.

56. Need for a great work: Haydon, *Diary*, iii. 561; in Pope, *Invisible Friends* 76; in Haydon, *Autobiography*, p. xiv; Haydon, *Diary*, i. 406.

57. 'Kyber Pass': Haydon, *Diary*, v. 239.

58. 'Chattering Reformers': Haydon, *Diary*, iv. 556; cf. Barrell, *Painting*, 263.

59. Huxley: in Haydon, *Autobiography*, p. xiv. 'This calamity': Haydon, *Diary*, v. 373.

60. Death of art: Barrell, *Painting*, 262.

61. Badness: C. Dickens, *The Letters of Charles Dickens*, ed. K. Tillotson (Oxford, 1977), iv. 576. Haydon and Aristides: Boase, *English Art*, 211.

62. *Punch*: quoted by R. Fitzsimons, *Barnum in London* (London, 1969), 128.

63. 'Skilful retreat': Haydon, *Diary*, v. 544. On Haydon's suicide, see Hayter, *A Sultry Month*.

7. In the Tracks of the Ten Thousand

1. First view: H.F. Tozer, *A History of Ancient Geography* (2nd edn; Cambridge, 1935; orig. pub. 1897), 117-18, and cf. 317. Wooded valley: Haydon, *Diary*, iii. 188 (from Rennell, *Illustrations* 308, not verbatim); *Anab.* 4.8.2.

2. Swiss Alps: e.g. J. Pitton de Tournefort, *A Voyage into the Levant*, trans. J. Ozell (London, 1718; Fr. orig. 1717), ii. 185; P.-A.E.P. Jaubert, *Voyage en Arménie et en Perse* (Paris, 1821), 378; M.W. Wagner, *Travels in Persia, Georgia, and Koordistan: With Sketches of the Cossacks and the Caucasus* (London, 1856; Ger. orig. 1848-52), ii. 293-4; I. Bird, *Journeys in Persia and Kurdistan* (London, 1988-9; orig. pub. 1891), ii. 393; E.L. Weeks, *From the Black Sea through Persia and India* (London and New York, 1895), 9.

3. Oceanography: C.R. Markham, *Major James Rennell and the Rise of Modern English Geography* (London, 1895), 170.

4. 'The Ancients': R. Forster, 'Geographical Dissertation', in E. Spelman (trans.) *Xenophon: The Expedition of Cyrus* (London, 1740-2), ii, pp. iv-lxxix, at p. lviii. Rauwolff: in J. Ray (ed.), *A Collection of Curious Travels & Voyages*, i: *Dr Leonhart Rauwolff's Itinerary Into the Eastern Countries*, trans. N. Staphorst (London, 1693), 200-1. Honey: Pitton de Tournefort, *Voyage*, ii. 168-73.

5. Earlier travellers: Rennell, *Illustrations*, 307, 308, xxi.

6. Theches: Rennell, *Illustrations*, 250-1; cf. also 309-10.

7. 'Excellent': L. Robert, *A Travers l'Asie Mineure: poètes et prosateurs, monnaies grecques, voyageurs et géographie* (Athens and Paris, 1980), 198.

8. Following Xenophon: J.M. Kinneir, *Journey through Asia Minor, Armenia, and Koordistan, in the Years 1813 and 1814, with remarks on the Marches of Alexander and Retreat of the Ten Thousand* (London, 1818), 350n., 367, 476-97, vii.

9. Danger: Kinneir, *Journey*, p. vii, x, 396.

10. Great Game: Kinneir, *Journey* 482n., 367, 512-39, 520, viii; J. Williams, *Two Essays on the Geography of Ancient Asia, Intended Partly to Illustrate the Campaigns of Alexander and the Anabasis of Xenophon* (London, 1829), 1-2. Cf. P. Hopkirk, *The Great Game: On Secret Service in High Asia* (Oxford, 1991; orig. pub. 1990), 67-75, on Kinneir and routes to India.

11. Theches: Kinneir, *Journey*, 358, 495, 372 and n. Ginnis: Jaubert, *Voyage*, 372 n.

12. Seeing sea, Ulysses: Jaubert, *Voyage*, 371, 379.

13. 'Affecting', volume in hand: Porter, *Travels*, 666, 663. Russian Academy: S. Searight, *The British in the Middle East* (2nd edn; London, 1979; orig. pub. 1969), 251. Porter ended up as British Consul in Venezuela, where he painted Simon Bolivar.

14. Surveying the Euphrates: F.R. Chesney, *Narrative of the Euphrates Expedition:*

Carried on by Order of the British Government during the years 1835, 1836, and 1837 (London, 1868), 116, 124, 125, 127-8; *The Expedition for the Survey of the Rivers Euphrates and Tigris Carried on by Order of the British Government on the Years 1835, 1836 and 1837* (London, 1850), i. 287-9, ii. 232-3. Consul: J. Brant, 'Journey through a part of Armenia and Asia Minor', *Journal of the Royal Geographical Society* 6 (1836), 187-223 (with p. 188 on the pass used by Xenophon).

15. Elliot: W.F. Ainsworth, *A Personal Narrative of the Euphrates Expedition* (London, 1888), i. 87; J.S. Guest, *The Euphrates Expedition* (London and New York, 1992), 62-4, 154. Some of Elliot's notes are reproduced by J.B. Fraser, *Mesopotamia and Assyria, from the Earliest Ages to the Present Time; with Illustrations of their Natural History* (Edinburgh and London, 1842), 304-18, but there is nothing on his Xenophontic researches.

16. Coal: Ainsworth, *Personal Narrative*, ii. 287. Expenses: H.R. Mill, *The Record of the Royal Geographical Society, 1830-1930* (London, 1930), 47.

17. 'Cry of joy': H.K.B. von Moltke, *Briefe über Zustände und Begebenheiten in der Türkei aus den Jahren 1835 bis 1839* (8th edn; Berlin, 1917; orig. pub. 1841), 246, 424 (my trans.).

18. Tekeh: H. Southgate, *Narrative of a Tour through Armenia, Kurdistan, Persia, and Mesopotamia, with Observations on the Condition of Mohammedanism and Christianity in those Countries* (London and New York, 1840), i. 161. Steamer: W.J. Hamilton, *Researches in Asia Minor, Pontus and Armenia: With Some Account of Their Antiquities and Geology* (London, 1842), i. 158. Military advisers: R. Wilbraham, *Travels in the Trans-Caucasian Provinces of Russia, and Along the Southern Shore of the Lakes of Van and Urumiah, in the Autumn and Winter of 1837* (London, 1839); W. Strecker, *Ueber den Rückzug der Zehntausend* (Berlin, 1886); H. Kiepert, 'Gegenbemerkungen zur Erklärung des Rückzugs der Zehntausend', *Zeitschrift der Gesellschaft für Erdkunde* 4 (1869), 538-49 (answering an earlier piece by Strecker in the same issue). English predominance: K.H.E. Koch, *Der Zug der Zehntausend, nach Xenophons Anabasis, geographisch erläutert* (Leipzig, 1850), p. iii; C.F.M. Texier, *Description de l'Arménie, la Perse et la Mésopotamie* (Paris, 1842-52), i. p. vi. Cunaxa: K. Mason, *Notes on the Movements of the Greeks in Babylonia, before and after Cunaxa in BC 401, as described by Xenophon* (Basra, 1918).

19. 'Touristism': Anon., 'Life and Manners in Persia', *Fraser's Magazine* 54 (1856), 220-30, at 220. Childe Harold: V.H. Hobart, 'Thoughts on Modern English Literature', *Fraser's Magazine* 60 (1859), 97-110, at 105.

20. Passage to Nineveh: Layard, *Discoveries*, 59, 65.

21. Guide books: J. Murray (publ.), *Handbook for Travellers in Turkey: Describing Constantinople, European Turkey, Asia Minor, Armenia, and Mesopotamia* (London, 1854), 270; *Handbook for Travellers in Asia Minor, Transcaucasia, Persia etc.*, ed. C. Wilson (London, 1895), 202.

22. Hadrian's altars: Williams, *Two Essays*, 312-13 (contrast his more cautious assessment of Hadrian's antiquarians on p. 323).

23. Cairn: N. Hammond, 'Where the Greeks Cried "The Sea, the Sea" ', *The Times*, 30 November 1996, p. 16; T. Mitford, 'Thalatta, Thalatta: Xenophon's View of the Black Sea', *Anatolian Studies* 50 (2000), 127-31, at 129.

24. Arrian: Mitford, 'Thalatta, Thalatta', 129; V. Manfredi, 'The Identification of Mount Theches in the Itinerary of the Ten Thousand: A New Hypothesis', in C.J. Tuplin (ed.), *Xenophon and his World* (Stuttgart, 2004), 319-24. Cairns: Diodorus Siculus 14.29.4 (but a plural in this notoriously unreliable author cannot have much weight).

25. In an earlier article, by contrast, Mitford seems to have taken it for granted that both Hadrian's temples and his statue were in Trapezus ('Some Inscriptions from the Cappadocian *Limes*', *Journal of Roman Studies* 64 (1974), 160-75, at 160-2): he discusses a dedicatory inscription to Hadrian incorporated in the oldest church in Trapezus which could have come from one of these monuments.

26. More cairns: Ainsworth, *Travels*, 188; Hamilton, *Researches*, 166-7.

27. Photographing cairns: G. Gassner, 'Der Zug der Zehntausend nach Trapezunt', *Abhandlungen der Braunschweigischen Wissenschaftlichten Gesellschaft* 5 (1953), 1-35, at 18-20; V.M. Manfredi, *La Strada dei Diecimila: topografia e geografia dell'Oriente di Senofonte* (Milan, 1986), 225-6. I am grateful to Christopher Tuplin for discussion of this issue.

28. Libation: P. Briot, 'Identification of the Mount Théchés of Xenophon', *Journal of the Royal Geographical Society* 40 (1870), 463-73, at 463, 465-6, 473.

29. Honour: Briot, 'Identification', 468. Not on route: Bunbury, *History*, i. 378. Borit: H. Kiepert, 'Der Berg Theches in Xenophon's Erzählung des Rückzuges der Zehntausend, nach P. Borit', *Zeitschrift der Gesellschaft für Erdkunde* 5 (1870), 456-60; R. Cortambert (ed.), 'Extraits des procès-verbaux des Séances: Séance du 3 juin 1870', *Bulletin de la Société de Géographie*, 5th series, 20 (1870), 77-82, at 79-81. Briot: Kiepert in W. Strecker, 'Nachträgliches über Hocharmenien und den Rückzug der Griechen unter Xenophon', *Zeitschrift der Gesellschaft für Erdkunde* 18 (1883), 388-92, at 388 n. 1.

30. Flattery: P. Glazebrook, *Journey to Kars* (Harmondsworth, 1985; orig. pub. 1984), 147. Scholarly overview: Gassner, 'Der Zug', 12-20, with plan on p. 13. Two further mistakes: Grote did not specify the location of Mount Theches, and Kinneir thought Kolat Dag (but his text in fact has 'Koat Dagh') was the summit defended by the Colchians, and not Mount Theches. Gassner's mistakes are simply taken over by Manfredi, *Strada*, map 16. Insufficient honour: *Athenaeum* 123 (1829), 129-30, review of V. Fontanier, *Voyages en Orient entrepris par ordre du gouvernement français, de l'année 1821 à l'année 1829: Turquie d'Asie* (Paris, 1829); but see Fontanier, pp. 312 and 149.

31. Scotland: Glazebrook, *Journey*, 9.

32. Armenia: H.F.B. Lynch, *Armenia: Travels and Studies* (London and New York, 1901), i. pp. v-vi, 285; ii. 225.

33. To Persepolis: J. Ussher, *A Journey from London to Persepolis, including Wanderings in Daghestan, Georgia, Armenia, Kurdistan, Mesopotamia, and Persia* (London, 1865), p. v (utility), 495 (cricket), 644 (Russians); 342, 350, 388, 390, 395, 423 (Xenophon's route); 683-4 (sensations). Starting point: P. Fussell, *Abroad: British Literary Traveling Between the Wars* (New York, 1980), 208.

34. Back to the sea: C. Doughty, *Travels in Arabia Deserta* (London, 1936; orig. pub. 1888), ii. 573; Baker, *Albert N'yanza* 548-9. Steamboat: W.M. Thackeray, *Notes on a Tour from Cornhill to Grand Cairo* in *The Oxford Thackeray*, ix (Oxford, 1908; orig. pub. 1846), 136. Review of Ussher: *The Times*, 2 May 1865, p. 6.

35. Deprived of view: Bird, *Journeys*, ii. 395, 396.

36. Golden fleece: Hoffmeister, *Durch Armenien*, 140-2, 168 (my trans.). Hoffmeister devotes the second half of his work to an analysis of Xenophon's route, with seven pages on the site of Theches: here too he concludes that the Greeks went by the same route, and perhaps saw the sea from the same height – and probably even more unclearly thanks to the February clouds (pp. 242-9).

37. Internal ringing: F. Cumont and E. Cumont, *Voyage d'exploration archéologique dans le Pont et la petite Arménie* (*Studia Pontica* 2; Brussels, 1906), 363; cf. Dr Blau, 'Miscellen zur alten Geographie (I)', *Zeitschrift für allgemeine Erdkunde* 12 (1862), 296-

9, at 296. Hadrian: W. Weber, *Untersuchungen zur Geschichte des Kaisers Hadrianus* (Leipzig, 1907), 266 n. 976.

38. Review of Tozer: *The Times*, 23 September 1881, p. 4. Shouting 'Thalatta': H.F. Tozer, *Turkish Armenia and Eastern Asia Minor* (London, 1881), 431.

39. Animated guides: Grote, *History*, vii. 286.

40. Tozer: W.W. Jackson, 'Henry Fanshawe Tozer', *Proceedings of the British Academy* 7 (1915-16), 566-74, at 566 (quoting from *The Times*; and quoted in Horden and Purcell, *Corrupting Sea*, 539). Jackson adds that Tozer's 'account of Trebizond and the district around it is not to be surpassed' (p. 570). Home: Ascherson, *Black Sea*,176. One modern guidebook has the Greeks arrive at the sea even further west than Ordu, at Ünye (G. Horobin, *Turkey* (Odyssey Guides; Hong Kong, 1999; orig. pub. 1991), 260).

41. Not enthralling: Glazebrook, *Journey*, 148. Similar themes (without the self-consciousness) can be found in Hilton, *'Thalatta! Thalatta!'*, 225, 228 (bus journey with precipitous drops, difficulty of getting beer in Trabzon comparable with Xenophon's administrative problems there).

42. Staggering: G. Reitlinger, *A Tower of Skulls: A Journey through Persia and Turkish Armenia* (London, 1932), 309, 311. Grote: see the appendix at Grote, *History*, vii. 281-7, where special attention is indeed paid to the 'interesting scene' on Mount Theches.

43. Kara Deniz (Turkish for 'Black Sea'): Reitlinger, *Tower of Skulls*, 314.

44. Travellers and the past: R. Macaulay, *The Towers of Trebizond* (London, 1995; orig. pub. 1956), 31-6, 62 (Chantry-Pigg), 164-5 (Hamilton), 169 (*Argo*).

45. Travel liars: Macaulay, *Towers*, 15, 146.

46. 'Proper': Macaulay, *Towers*, 1, 28.

47. Vision of the church: R. Macaulay, *Last Letters to a Friend, 1952-1958*, ed. C. Babington Smith (London, 1961), 219 (cf. 159-60 for a letter after her own trip to Trebizond in 1954; she returned there in 1958, the year of her death); *Towers*, 64-6, 133, 200, 276, 73, 66.

48. Scholar and gypsy: J. Howard-Johnston and N. Ryan, *The Scholar and the Gypsy: Two Journeys to Turkey, Past and Present* (London, 1992), 5, 7, 135. It is perhaps disappointing that Howard-Johnston (Eton and Oxford) fails to evoke 'Thalatta! Thalatta!', in his sections of the narrative.

49. The sheep: D. Caroll and D. Davies, *Traveler's Turkey Companion* (Zollikofen, 2000), 241. But some modern guidebooks are content to offer a simpler pleasure by quoting Xenophon's account: see D. Darke, *Guide to Eastern Turkey and the Black Sea Coast* (London, 1987), 334, and esp. J. Freely, *The Black Sea Coast of Turkey* (Istanbul, 1996), 221-3, where the passage (accompanied by a picture of Xenophon's bust) provides a heroic finale for the modern traveller driving down to Trabzon at the end of his final route.

50. Dodds: Todd, 'E. R. Dodds', 97.

8. The Snotgreen Sea

1. 'La mer, la mer': P. Valéry, *Poésies* (Paris, 1942), 146. Mulligan: Joyce, *Ulysses*, 3, 5.

2. Marathon: Joyce, *Ulysses*, 119; Byron, *Complete Poetical Works*, v. 189 (*Don Juan*, iii. 701-4). Persian Wars: cf. D. Gifford and R.J. Seidman, *Ulysses Annotated: Notes for James Joyce's Ulysses* (2nd edn; Berkeley, Los Angeles, and London, 1988; orig. pub. 1974), 133. Xenophobia: V.J. Cheng, *Joyce, Race and Empire* (Cambridge, 1995), 186. Jingle: Schork, *Greek and Hellenic Culture*, 28, cf. also p. 22 on Dedalus' 'dismissal of the florid prose of the archbishop's letter that has been delivered to the newspaper office'. Camus: N.M. Leov, 'Thalassa, Thalassa: Camus's Use of Imagery in *La Chute'*, *New Zealand Journal of French Studies* 14 (1993), 5-29, at 24.

3. Parasangs: Joyce, *Ulysses*, 403.

4. Irishness: Joyce, *Ulysses*, 5, 7, 18.

5. Bile: Joyce, *Ulysses*, 6.

6. Xenophons Wake: Joyce, *Finnegans Wake*, 304, 308 (margins), 586 (parasangs), 547, 551, 93, 100, 324, 328 (galata et al.). 'Tha lassy': R. J. Schork, 'Tha Lassy! Tha Lassy!', *James Joyce Quarterly* 28 (1990), 293-6; Livy 1.9.10-12 and A. de Selincourt (trans.), *Livy: The Early History of Rome* (Harmondsworth,1971), 44.

7. Bosporus: L.O. Mink, *A Finnegans Wake Gazetteer* (Bloomington, 1978), 269.

8. 'Sea, sea': Joyce, *Finnegans Wake*, 626. 'Look, look': references at C. Hart, *Structure and Motif in Finnegans Wake* (London, 1962), 213. *Ulysses* reversed: M. Norris, '*Finnegans Wake*', in D. Attridge (ed.), *The Cambridge Companion to James Joyce* (Cambridge, 1990), 161-84, at 179.

9. California: Moore, *Fergus*, 3, 168-9.

10. Father Joyce: Moore, *Fergus*, 38; 'Old Father, Old Artificer', *Irish University Review* 12 (1982), 13-16, at 16.

11. Window-dresser: L. MacNeice, *The Strings are False: An Unfinished Autobiography* (London, 1965), 113.

12. Parasangs: MacNeice, *Collected Poems*, 116.

13. West of Ireland: MacNeice, *I Crossed the Minch* (London, 1938), 22.

14. Celtic spirit: MacNeice, *I Crossed the Minch*, 3, 19, 22-3.

15. Outsider: MacNeice, *I Crossed the Minch*, 3-4, 68.

16. Fathers and sons: MacNeice, *I Crossed the Minch*, 248. The poem was reprinted as 'The Hebrides' (*Collected Poems*, 64-6).

17. Sight of Atlantic: MacNeice, *Strings*, 111.

18. Lost Atlantis: E. Nicholson, 'Trees were Green', in T. Brown and A. Reid (eds), *Time Was Away: The World of Louis MacNeice* (Dublin, 1974), 11-20, at 14.

19. Waves and desert: MacNeice, *Collected Poems*, 193.

20. Round the Corner: MacNeice, *Collected Poems*, 518-9.

21. 'Round about here': G. Seferis, *Poems*, trans. R. Warner (London, 1960), 19; cf. T. Brown, *Louis MacNeice: Sceptical Vision* (Dublin and New York, 1975), 120-1. Redemption: A. Heuser (ed.), *Selected Literary Criticism of Louis MacNeice* (Oxford, 1987), 222-3. 'Good things': quoted in Brown, *Louis MacNeice*, 121.

22. 'Round a corner': MacNeice, *Strings*, 218, 220. 'Through that surrender': MacNeice, *Collected Poems*, 493.

23. Father: Stallworthy, *Louis MacNeice*, 454. 'Strand', 'Autobiography': MacNeice, *Collected Poems*, 226, 183. Biggest thing: MacNeice, *Strings*, 219.

24. 'Thalassa': MacNeice, *Collected Poems*, 546, with Dodds' comment on p. xv.

25. 'Fly, thalassa, fly': R. Pybus, *Flying Blues: Poems 1988-1993* (Manchester, 1994), 25, with n. on p. 141.

26. Amorous arrival: Pybus, *Flying Blues*, 83.

27. 'Railways! Railways!': S. O'Brien, *Downriver* (London, 2001), 74, 75. Desire: Lehmann, *The Weather in the Streets*, 229. Debussy: S. O'Brien, *HMS Glasshouse* (Oxford, 1991), p. viii.

28. Dust: J. Kaplinski, *Through the Forest*, trans. H. Hawkins (London, 1996), 57-8. I must thank Stephanie West for showing me this poem.

29. Homoeroticism: J. Biarujia, *Thalassa Thalassa* (Melbourne, 1983), 71, 24, 44, 45.

30. Love of the sea: Biarujia, *Thalassa Thalassa*, 47, 67, 27, 76. At the request of Javant Biarujia, I have (with some regret) changed the original version by restoring capital letters to proper nouns and adding italics to foreign words: the lack of these elements in the original was not an aesthetic choice but dictated by the word processor on which the book was set.

31. Deconstructed man: J. Laughlin, *Poems, New and Selected* (New York, 1998), 93.

32. 'dwang parasang': B. Zwaal, *dwang parasang* (Amsterdam, 1990), 19: 'strapatsen / snuiten hun neus / satraap / sluit zijn rijk / met een zakdoek / / de tienduizend / breken uit / door de nieszee / met moeiten / hatsjie thalassa / / de maan slaapt / nooit meer bij Endymion' (I am grateful to Gijsbert Loos for the translation). Sneeze: *Anab.* 3.2.9. Portia: *The Merchant of Venice* 5.1.108-9; Lorenzo had earlier exclaimed 'How sweet the moonlight sleeps upon this bank!' (5.1.54).

33. Chapter headings: Reynolds, *'Thalassa!'*, 308; Verne, *Journey* (trans. Malleson) 162; Keeling, *Adventures in Turkey*, 105; Lynch, *Armenia*, ii. 225; Fleming, *News from Tartary*, 231; Hay, *Battle for Flanders*, 58; cf. also the headings 'A Sail! A Sail' at Sue, *Romans*, 472 and 'Water! Water!' at Haggard, *King Solomon's Mines*, 82.

34. Exodus: E. Bille, *Thalassa* (La Chaux-de-Fonds, 1943), 8-9.

35. Hateful sea: W. Weyrauch, *Dialog mit dem Unsichtbaren: Sieben Hörspiele* (Olten and Freiburg im Breisgau, 1962), 182.

36. Earlier version: Glaeser's comments are quoted by Schmitthenner in Weyrauch, *Anabasis* (Hamburg, 1959), 40; cf. also H. Schwitzke, *Das Hörspiel: Geschichte und Dramaturgie* (Berlin, 1963), 377. Extracts from the first version were published in *Rufer und Hörer: Monatshefte für den Rundfunk und Fernsehen* 1 (1931-2), 504ff.: I have not been able to see this.

37. Gangland New York: Yurick, *Warriors*, 12, 109, 110, 112, 116-17.

38. Comic: Calvino, 'Xenophon's Anabasis', 20. Eat raw: *Anab.* 4.8.14.

39. 'The Ocean!': Yurick, *Warriors*, 177, 184.

40. Film guide: L. Maltin (ed.), *Movie and Video Guide* (Harmondsworth, 2001), 1529. Exoticism: J. Sunderland, *Bestsellers: Popular Fiction of the 1970s* (London, 1981), 161.

41. Library: W.C. Williams, *Paterson* (New York, 1963; orig. pub. 1946-58), 101, 100, 145.

42. Nostalgic sea: Williams, *Paterson*, 201-2. An earlier version is quoted by M.G. Lloyd, *William Carlos Williams's Paterson: A Critical Reappraisal* (Rutherford, NJ, 1980), 278-9: 'The sea of savage lusts, nostalgic / with its cry, Thallassa, Thallassa! [sic] / to draw us in, to draw the past / down on us. Until we drown in our / regrets and losses.'

43. Pound or Eliot: L.L. Martz, *The Poem of the Mind: Essays on Poetry, English and American* (New York, 1966), 153.

44. Poe: quoted Martz, *Poem of the Mind*, 154. Virtue: Williams, *Paterson*, 189. Savage lusts: quoted J.E. Breslin, *William Carlos Williams: An American Artist* (New York, 1970), 202.

45. 'Symbolic anguish': Calvino, 'Xenophon's Anabasis', 23.

46. Snow: E. Newby (ed.), *A Book of Travellers' Tales* (London, 1985), 251-2; B. Allen (ed.), *The Faber Book of Exploration* (London, 2002), 137-41; cf. also P. Gaskell, *Landmarks in Classical Literature* (Edinburgh, 1999), 97-8, who praises Xenophon's account as 'the real thing'. Eyvind Johnson: I rely here on G. Orton, *Eyvind Johnson* (New York, 1972), 64, 97-107; unfortunately *Molnen över Metaponten* has not been translated. Themistogenes of Syracuse has been revived in two other modern novels: Stephen Marlowe's *The Shining* (1965) and Michael Curtis Ford's *The Ten Thousand* (2001).

47. 'Grammar of the human foot': C. Middleton, *Selected Writings: A Reader* (Manchester, 1989), 190-1 (the poem was first published in book form in 1983, and written a few years earlier).

48. 'Feet': Liddell Hart, *T. E. Lawrence to his Biographer*, 176.

49. 'Aqueous reiterations': A. Powell, *The Valley of Bones* (London, 1997; orig. pub. 1964), 2. 'The women': W. Clark, *The Legal Status of Women in North Carolina: Past, Present, and Prospective* (New Bern, N.C., 1913), 24.

50. Eliot: quoted in J. Salzman and L. Zanderer (eds), *Social Poetry of the 1930s: A Selection* (New York, 1978), 323. Thunder: in Salzman and Zanderer, *Social Poetry*, 66. Exile: quoted in A.M. Wald, *Exiles from a Future Time: The Forging of the Mid-Twentieth-Century Literary Left* (Chapel Hill and London, 2002), p. vii (see further pp. 204-14 for a discussion of Funaroff and his milieu). 'What the Thunder Said' was first published in the magazine *New Masses* in 1932 and then included in Funaroff's 1938 collection *The Spider and the Clock*.

51. Greek freighters: J. Neugass, 'Thalassa, Thalassa', in G. Hicks, M. Gold, I. Schneider, J. North, P. Peters, and A. Calmer (eds), *Proletarian Literature in the United States: An Anthology* (London, 1936), 176-7.

52. Old Course: D. Young, *St Andrews: Town and Gown, Royal and Ancient* (London, 1969), 236. The story seems to suit another great St Andrews man, Andrew Lang, even better: Lang (whose grim childhood encounter with Xenophon was mentioned in Chapter 3) combined two of his interests, classics and golf, in skits like 'Herodotus in St Andrews' (J.B. Salmond (ed.), *Andrew Lang and St Andrews: A Centenary Anthology* (St Andrews, 1944), 124-7).

9. Thalatta! Thalatta!

1. 'Great moment': F. Stark, *The Valleys of the Assassins and Other Persian Travels* (London, 1982; orig. pub. 1936), 210.

2. Omissions: I. Murdoch, *The Sea, the Sea* (London, 1978); M. Crnjanski, *Lirika itake i komentari* (Belgrade, 1993), 329; H. de Campos, *Xadres de Estrelas: Percurso Textual, 1949-1974* (São Paulo, 1976), 41-5. Music: 'Thalatta! Thalatta!' was the title of a 1987 piano work by the Danish expressionist Axel Borup-Jørgensen and of a work for flutes by the avant-garde Dutch composer Rob du Bois.

3. Anatolian retreat: P. Karnezis, *The Maze* (London, 2004), 221, 203, 290, 361.

4. Epigraph: J. de Falbe, review of *The Maze*, *Spectator* 5198 (14 February, 2004), p. 35. I owe the thoughts of the last paragraph to John de Falbe (e-mail correspondence).

5. Mediterranean: Shelley, *Frankenstein*, 205; Bush, 'The Sea', 55. Bosporus: Mink, *Finnegans Wake Gazetteer*, 269; N. Reeves, *Heinrich Heine: Poetry and Politics* (London, 1974), 120. Persian Wars: P. Conradi, *Iris Murdoch: A Life* (London, 2001), 74; Leov, 'Thalassa, Thalassa', 24. Anabasis: *The Times*, 4 June 1940, p. 7; *Spectator*, 31 December 1864, p. 1491. Up to the sea: Schork, 'Tha Lassy!', 293.

6. 'Delightful passage': Gissing, *Private Papers*, 92. Even Gissing admits a jarring note in his translation. 'He took his leave' would have been more faithful to the Greek: the restrained Xenophon does not let in the personal 'of us'.

7. Carduchian guide (*Anab*. 4.1.24): Gissing, *Private Papers*, 92-3; Grote, *History*, vii. 263.

8. Lost in the desert: Reynolds, *'Thalassa!'*, p. vi.

9. 'Symbolic anguish': Calvino, 'Xenophon's Anabasis', 23.

10. Macronian peltast: *Anab*. 4.8.4-6.

11. 'All is safety there': J.H. Wiffen, *Julia Alpinula; with The Captive of Stamboul and Other Poems* (London, 1820), 143. (Wiffen – who also translated Tasso's *Jerusalem Delivered* – died suddenly a week before the Duke's victory in the Haydon raffle.) Ending at the sea: Thomson, *Liberty*, 63; Haydon, *Pictures of Xenophon*, 6; Marlowe,

Shining, 370; J.R. McElrath and A.P. Robb (eds), *The Complete Works of Anne Bradstreet* (Boston, 1981), 90; Shelley, *Frankenstein*, 205; S.S. Van Dine, *The Bishop Murder Case* (London, 1928), 10; cf. W. Young, *The History of Athens Politically and Philosophically Considered* (London, 1786; orig. pub. 1777), 207; G. Grundy, *A History of the Greek and Roman World* (London, 1926), 243. 'Glorious part': A. Boucher, *L'Anabase de Xénophon ou La retraite des Dix-Mille avec un commentaire historique et militaire* (Paris and Nancy, 1913), p. vi; cf. Tillyard, *English Epic*, 54 (Book 4 as end of the 'epic' part of the work).

12. Children's books: J. Barbary, *Ten Thousand Heroes* (New York, 1963); I have not seen A. Bonnard, *L'Invincible légion: adaptation pour la jeunesse de 'l'Anabase' de Xénophon* (Paris, 1957), but perhaps the title is enough. Argonauts: Witt, *Retreat*, 187-8; Hoffmeister, *Durch Armenien*, 168; Diodorus 14.30.5.

13. School editions of Books 1-4: W.W. Goodwin and J.W. White (eds), *The First Four Books of Xenophon's Anabasis* (London, 1880); Mather and Hewitt, *Xenophon's Anabasis*. A count of editions in the Bodleian and British Libraries reveals 34 single book editions for Books 1-4, 10 for 5-7; and 15 multi-book editions covering part or all of 1-4, 4 covering part or all of 5-7 (I exclude editions of the whole text).

14. Steamboats: Thackeray, *Notes on a Tour*, 136. Closure: D. Walcott, *Omeros* (London, 1990), 325; Arnold, *Matthew Arnold*, 150.

15. First edition: Bradstreet, *Complete Works*, 419-20. Since the second edition appeared only in 1678, after her death, it is not certain that Bradstreet herself made the alteration. But that between the first and the second editions 'So after all their travell ...' was changed to 'Thus finishing their travail ...', and so the repetition of 'after all' in successive lines avoided, suggests that the cutting of the six lines was not simply due to a publishing error.

16. Completed circuits: Stobart, *Glory*, 202; B. Johnson, *The Long March Home* (Folkestone, 1975), 116; Household, *Xenophon's Adventure*, 159, 8.

17. Concluding books interesting: Mahaffy, *History*, ii. 265. Book 4 best: G.M. Edwards (ed.), *The Anabasis of Xenophon: Book IV* (Cambridge, 1898), p. v; cf. E.D. Stone (ed.), *Xenophon's Anabasis: Book IV* (London, 1890), 5. Concluding books boring: Cousin, *Kyros*, p. xxx; cf. Bunbury, *History*, i. 355. Speeches: Horn, 'Last Three Books', 157; cf. Manfredi, *Strada*, 247. Pirates: Rennell, *Illustrations*, 286.

18. Lawrence: cited by Wilson, 'T. E. Lawrence', 37.

19. Burying alive: *Anab.* 5.8.11-12. An allusion to this passage was cut from the script of MacNeice's play on the Ten Thousand.

20. 'Two cries': Dupouy, *Poésie*, 13 (my trans.). Diario: O. Dunn and J.E. Kelley Jnr (eds), *The Diario of Christopher Columbus's First Voyage to America, 1492-1493, Abstracted by Fray Bartolemé de las Casas* (Norman, Oklahoma, and London, 1989), 59. Mistaken shouts: B. Keen (ed. and trans.), *The Life of the Admiral Christopher Columbus by his son Ferdinand* (London, 1960; orig. pub. 1959), 72, 75. Oviedo: quoted by D. Henige, *In Search of Columbus: The Sources for the First Voyage* (Tucson, 1991), 295. 'Tierra': S.E. Morison, *Admiral of the Ocean Sea: A Life of Christopher Columbus* (Boston, 1942), i. 311 n. 12; for the original, see A.B. Gould, *Nueva lista documentada de los tripulantes de Colón en 1492* (Madrid, 1984), 202. Cf. in general Henige, *In Search*, 165-75 on the source problems for the sighting of land (but he does not discuss the shout).

21. Adventurers and pirates: Defoe, *Captain Singleton*, 103; Gillies, *History*, iii. 374.

22. 'Land': Defoe, *Captain Singleton*, 45.

23. Desert and sea: Kinglake, *Eothen*, 185-6.

24. 'Useless purpose': E. Said, *Orientalism: Western Conceptions of the Orient* (2nd edn; Harmondsworth, 1995; orig. pub. 1978), 193.

25. Cycling holiday: Lawrence, *Home Letters*, 64.

26. Cartoon: *Mr Punch at the Seaside* (London, 1906), 55. Gin-twist: A. Maginn, 'A Twist-imony in Favour of Gin-Twist', *Blackwood's Magazine* 12 (1822), 635-8, at 638. Bloodthirsty: A. Bierce, *Shapes of Clay* (San Francisco, 1903), 98, 101. For slightly later pieces of *Punch* 'humour', see E.V. Knox (one of Ronald's brothers), 'Thalassa', *Punch* 157 (1919), 188 – the story of a boater hat that keeps blowing off until it is finally blown into the sea; and one of A.P. Herbert's Tommy series, 'What Tommy Saw at Brighton: Thalassa! Thalassa!', *Punch* 167 (1924), 10-11 – where Tommy is embarrassed at being caught eating cockles by a woman he knows from home.

27. To shout or not to shout: Watkins, 'At the Seaside', 416; Tozer, *Turkish Armenia* 431; Hoffmeister, *Durch Armenien*, 140-2, 168; C.F. Lehmann-Haupt, *Armenien Einst und Jetzt* (Berlin and Leipzig, 1910-31), ii. 687; Lawrence, *Home Letters*, 64; MacNeice, *Strings*, 111; Lewes, 'New Sea-side Studies', 678; Walker, 'A Trip', 436; Baker, *Albert N'yanza*, ii. 359.

28. Title: Skelton, *Thalatta!* p. vi; *Spectator* 1806 (7 February, 1863), p. 1611; W.A. Fraser, *Disraeli and his Day* (London, 1891), 241.

29. 'The American Xenophon': Coyle, *The Ten Thousand*, 195, 197, 248, 540.

30. Sherman: *The Times*, 20 December 1864, p. 6.

31. Ksenofon: Bryer, 'The Pontic Greeks', 332.

Select Bibliography

Ainsworth, W.F., *Travels in the Track of the Ten Thousand Greeks: Being A Geographical and Descriptive Account of the Expedition of Cyrus, and of the Retreat of the Ten Thousand Greeks, As Related by Xenophon* (London, 1844).
————— *A Personal Narrative of the Euphrates Expedition* (2 vols; London, 1888).
Altick, R.D., *The Shows of London* (Cambridge, Mass., 1978).
Anon., 'The Sea' (review of M.F. Maury, *The Physical Geography of the Sea*) *Dublin University Magazine* 4 (1855), 574-86.
Arnold, M., *Matthew Arnold*, ed. M. Allott and R.H. Super (The Oxford Authors; Oxford, 1986).
Ascherson, N., *Black Sea* (London, 1995).
Baker, S.W., *The Albert N'yanza: Great Basin of the Nile* (2 vols; London, 1962; orig. pub. 1866).
Barrell, J., *Painting and the Politics of Culture: New Essays on British Art, 1700-1850* (Oxford, 1992).
Benn, G., *Selected Poems*, ed. F.W. Wodtke (Oxford, 1970).
Betjeman, J., *Collected Poems* (4th edn; London, 1979; orig. pub. 1958).
Biarujia, J., *Thalassa Thalassa* (Melbourne, 1983).
Bierce, A., *Shapes of Clay* (San Francisco, 1903).
Bille, E., *Thalassa* (La Chaux-de-Fonds, 1943).
Bird, I., *Journeys in Persia and Kurdistan* (2 vols; London, 1988-9; orig. pub. 1891).
Bishop, H.C.W., 'From Kut to Kastamuni', *Blackwood's Magazine* 203 (1918), 241-61.
————— *A Kut Prisoner* (London, 1920).
Boase, T.S.R., *English Art 1800-1870* (Oxford, 1959).
Bonaparte-Wyse, W.-C., 'Θάλασσα, θάλασσα: Cridamen di Gré dins l'*Anabàsi* de Xenefoun', *Revue des langues romanes* 25 (1884), 153.
Bonsal, S., *Suitors And Suppliants: The Little Nations at Versailles* (New York, 1946).
Bradstreet, A., *The Complete Works of Anne Bradstreet*, ed. J.R. McElrath and A.P. Robb (Boston, 1981).
Briot, P., 'Identification of the Mount Théchés of Xenophon', trans. T.K. Lynch, *Journal of the Royal Geographical Society* 40 (1870), 463-73 (published under the name 'Rorit').
Brown, J.B., 'Thalatta! Thalatta!: Cry of the Ten Thousand', in E.C. Stedman (ed.), *An American Anthology, 1787-1900* (Boston and New York, 1900) 305-6.
Brown, T., *Louis MacNeice: Sceptical Vision* (Dublin and New York, 1975).
Bryer, A.A.M., 'The Pontic Greeks before the Diaspora', *Journal of Refugee Studies* 4 (1991), 315-44.
Bunbury, E.H., *A History of Ancient Geography* (2 vols; London, 1879).
Bush, D., 'The Sea, the Sea', *Poetry Wales* 21 (1985), 51-5.
Byron, G.G., *The Complete Poetical Works*, ed. J.J. McGann (7 vols; Oxford, 1980-93).
Calvino, I., 'Xenophon's Anabasis', in *Why Read the Classics?*, trans. M. McLaughlin (London, 1999; Ital. orig. 1991), 19-23.

Chambers, R.W., *The Gold Chase* (London, 1927).

Chesney, F.R., *Narrative of the Euphrates Expedition: Carried on by Order of the British Government during the years 1835, 1836, and 1837* (London, 1868).

Coleridge, S.T., *Collected Works*, xvi: *Poetical Works I*, ed. J.C.C. Mays (Princeton, 2001).

Corbin, A., *The Lure of the Sea: The Discovery of the Seaside, 1750-1840*, trans. J. Phelps (Harmondsworth, 1995; orig. pub. 1994, Fr. orig. 1990).

Coulton, B., *Louis MacNeice in the BBC* (London, 1980).

Cousin, G., *Kyros le jeune en Asie Mineure (Printemps 408-Juillet 401 avant Jésus-Christ)* (Paris and Nancy, 1905).

Coyle, H., *The Ten Thousand* (London, 1994; orig. pub. 1993).

Craske, M., *Art in Europe 1700-1830* (Oxford, 1997).

Defoe, D., *The Life, Adventures, and Pyracies of the Famous Captain Singleton*, ed. S.K. Kumar, introduction by P. Wilson (Oxford, 1990; orig. pub. 1720).

Douglas, F.S.N., *An Essay on Certain Points of Resemblance between the Ancient and Modern Greeks* (London, 1813).

Dupouy, A., *La Poésie de la mer dans la littérature française* (Paris, 1947).

Ellison, H., *Stones from the Quarry* (London, 1875; pub. under pseudonym H. Browne).

Ferenczi, S., *Thalassa: A Theory of Genitality*, trans. H.A. Bunker (London, 1989; orig. pub. 1938; Ger. orig. *Versuch einer Genitaltheorie*, Leipzig, Vienna, and Zurich, 1924).

Fleming, P., *News from Tartary* (Edinburgh, 2001; orig. pub. 1936).

Fortescue, J.W., 'A Day with Xenophon's Harriers', *Macmillan's Magazine* 71 (1895), 182-9.

Fraser, G.M., *Flashman at the Charge* (London, 1999; orig. pub.1973).

Funaroff, S., 'What the Thunder Said: A Fire Sermon', in J. Salzman and L. Zanderer (eds), *Social Poetry of the 1930s: A Selection* (New York, 1978) 63-6 (with biographical note on p. 323); orig. pub. in his *The Spider and the Clock* (New York, 1938), 25-32.

Gassner, G., 'Der Zug der Zehntausend nach Trapezunt', *Abhandlungen der Braunschweigischen Wissenschaftlichten Gesellschaft* 5 (1953), 1-35.

Gibbon, E., *The History of the Decline and Fall of the Roman Empire*, ed. D. Womersley (3 vols; Harmondsworth, 1994; orig. pub. 1776-88).

Gillies, J., *The History of Ancient Greece: Its Colonies and Conquests, From the Earliest Accounts till the Division of the Macedonian Empire in the East* (5 vols; Basel, 1790; orig. pub. 1786).

Gissing, G., *The Private Papers of Henry Ryecroft* (London, 1964; orig. pub. 1903).

Glazebrook, P., *Journey to Kars* (Harmondsworth, 1985; orig. pub. 1984).

———— *Captain Vinegar's Commission* (London, 1987).

Górski, K.M., *Wierszem 1883-1893* (Krakow, 1904).

Grant, A., *Xenophon* (Edinburgh and London, 1871).

Grote, G., *A History of Greece* (10 vols; London, 1904; orig. pub. 1846-56).

Haggard, H.R., *King Solomon's Mines* (Oxford, 1989; orig. pub. 1885).

Hamilton, W.J., *Researches in Asia Minor, Pontus and Armenia: With Some Account of Their Antiquities and Geology* (2 vols; London, 1842).

Havell, H.L., *Stories from Xenophon Retold* (London, 1910).

Hay, I., *The Battle for Flanders 1940* (London, 1941).

Haydon, B.R., *Explanation of the Picture of The Mock Election, Which Took Place At the King's Bench Prison, July, 1827; Now Exhibiting at the Egyptian Hall, Piccadilly* (London, 1828).

————*Some Enquiry Into the Causes Which Have Obstructed the Advance of Historical Painting for the Last Seventy Years in England* (London, 1829).

———— *Description of Eucles, and Punch, with Other Pictures, Drawings, and Sketches, Painted by B. R. Haydon, Now Exhibiting At the Western Exchange, Old Bond Street* (London, 1830).

———— *Haydon's Pictures of Xenophon, Mock Election, &c. &c. &c; Now Exhibiting at the Egyptian Hall, Piccadilly* (London, 1832).

———— *The Life of Benjamin Robert Haydon, From His Autobiography and Journals*, ed. T. Taylor (3 vols; London, 1853).

———— *Correspondence and Table-talk*, with a memoir by F.W. Haydon (2 vols; London, 1876).

———— *The Autobiography and Memoirs of Benjamin Robert Haydon (1786-1846)*, with an introduction by A. Huxley (London, 1926); Huxley's introduction is reprinted in his *The Olive Tree and Other Essays* (London, 1936), 239-61.

———— *The Diary of Benjamin Robert Haydon*, ed. W.B. Pope (5 vols; Cambridge, Mass., 1960-3).

Hayter, A., *A Sultry Month: Scenes of London Literary Life in 1846* (London, 1965).

Heine, H., *Historischkritische Gesamtausgabe der Werke*, ed. M. Windfuhr (16 vols; Hamburg, 1973-97).

———— *The Complete Poems of Heinrich Heine*, trans. H. Draper (Oxford, 1982).

Henniker, M.C.A., 'The Sea! The Sea!', *Army Quarterly* 59 (1949-50), 221-31.

Herbert, Z., 'Anabasis', in *Report from the Besieged City and Other Poems*, trans. J. and B. Carpenter (Oxford, 1987), 45.

Hilton, R., 'Thalatta! Thalatta!', *Blackwood's Magazine* 283 (1958), 224-30.

Hodgson, L.J., *Thalassa, Thalassa* (London, 1944).

Hoffmeister, E. von, *Durch Armenien: Eine Wanderung und der Zug Xenophons bis zum Schwarzen Meer* (Leipzig and Berlin, 1911).

Horden, P., and Purcell, N., *The Corrupting Sea: A Study of Mediterranean History* (Oxford, 2000).

Horn, R.C., 'The Last Three Books of Xenophon's Anabasis', *Classical World* 28 (1935), 156-9.

Household, G., *Xenophon's Adventure* (London, 1961; orig. pub. as *The Exploits of Xenophon*, New York, 1955).

Howard, B.W., 'Thalatta', *Scribner's Magazine* 22 (1897), 206-15.

Howard-Johnston, J., and Ryan, N., *The Scholar and the Gypsy: Two Journeys to Turkey, Past and Present* (London, 1992).

Huntford, R., *Nansen: The Explorer as Hero* (London, 1997).

Hutchinson, T. (ed.), *Xenophontis de Cyri expeditione libri septem* (4th edn; Cambridge, 1785; orig. pub. 1735).

Jaubert. P.-A.E.P., *Voyage en Arménie et en Perse* (Paris, 1821).

Johnston, M.A.B., and Yearsley, K.D., *Four-Fifty Miles to Freedom* (Edinburgh and London, 1919).

Joyce, J., *Ulysses* (Paris, 1922; reprinted Oxford, 1993).

———— *Finnegans Wake* (London, 1939; reprinted Harmondsworth, 1992).

Kaplinski, J., *Through the Forest*, trans. H. Hawkins (London, 1996).

Karnezis, P., *The Maze* (London, 2004).

Keeling, E.H., 'An Escape from Turkey in Asia', *Blackwood's Magazine* 203 (1918), 561-92.

———— *Adventures in Turkey and Russia* (London, 1924).

Kemper, S.H., 'O You Xenophon', *Atlantic Monthly* 126 (1920), 39-44.

Kinglake, A.W., *Eothen, or Traces of Travel Brought Home from the East* (Everyman's Library, 337; London, 1961; orig. pub. 1844).

Kinneir, J.M., *Journey through Asia Minor, Armenia, and Koordistan, in the Years 1813 and 1814, with remarks on the Marches of Alexander and Retreat of the Ten Thousand* (London, 1818).

Lang, A., 'Homer and the Study of Greek', in his *Essays in Little* (London, 1891), 77-92.

Laughlin, J., *Poems, New and Selected* (New York, 1998).

Lawrence, T. E., *Seven Pillars of Wisdom* (London, 1935).

———— *The Home Letters of T. E. Lawrence and his Brothers* (Oxford, 1954).

Layard, A.H., *Discoveries in the Ruins of Nineveh and Babylon: With Travels in Armenia, Kurdistan and the Desert* (London, 1853).

Lehmann, R., *The Weather in the Streets* (London, 1981; orig. pub. 1936).

Leov, N.M., 'Thalassa, Thalassa: Camus's Use of Imagery in *La Chute*', *New Zealand Journal of French Studies* 14 (1993), 5-29.

Lewes, G.H., 'New Sea-side Studies (No. 1): The Scilly Isles', *Blackwood's Edinburgh Magazine* 81 (1857), 669-85; reprinted in his *Sea-side Studies at Ilfracombe, Tenby, the Scilly Isles, and Jersey* (Edinburgh and London, 1858).

Liddell Hart, B.H., *'T. E. Lawrence': In Arabia and After* (London, 1934).

———— (ed.) *T. E. Lawrence to his Biographer, Liddell Hart: Information about Himself, in the Form of Letters, Notes, Answers to Questions and Conversations* (London, 1938).

Longfellow, H.D., *Poems and Other Writings* (Library of America, 118; New York, 2000).

Longfellow, S., and Higginson, T.W., *Thalatta: A Book for the Sea-Side* (Boston, 1853).

Lynch, H.F.B., *Armenia: Travels and Studies* (2 vols; London and New York, 1901).

Macaulay, R., *The Towers of Trebizond* (London, 1995; orig. pub. 1956).

McHugh, M.F., *Thalassa: A Story of Childhood by the Western Wave* (London, 1931).

MacNeice, L., *I Crossed the Minch* (London, 1938).

———— *The March of the Ten Thousand* (unpublished radio script, 1941; BBC Written Documents Centre).

———— *The Strings are False: An Unfinished Autobiography* (London, 1965).

———— *Collected Poems*, ed. E.R. Dodds (2nd edn; London, 1979; orig. pub. 1966).

Maginn, W., 'A Twist-imony in Favour of Gin-Twist', *Blackwood's Magazine* 12 (1822), 635-8.

Mahaffy, J.P., *A History of Classical Greek Literature* (2nd edn; London, 1883; orig. pub. 1880).

Mallowan, M., *Mallowan's Memoirs* (London, 1977).

Manfredi, V.M., *La Strada dei Diecimila: topografia e geografia dell'Oriente di Senofonte* (Milan, 1986).

Marlowe, S., *The Shining* (New York, 1965; orig. pub. 1963).

Martz, L.L., *The Poem of the Mind: Essays on Poetry, English and American* (New York, 1966).

Mather, M.W., and Hewitt, J.W. (eds), *Xenophon's Anabasis: Books I-IV* (New York, 1910).

Meyers, J., 'Xenophon and *Seven Pillars of Wisdom*', *Classical Journal* 72 (1977), 141-3; reprinted in his *The Wounded Spirit: T. E. Lawrence's* Seven Pillars of Wisdom (2nd edn; Basingstoke and London, 1989; orig. pub. 1973), 149-52.

Middleton, C., *Selected Writings: A Reader* (Manchester, 1989).

Mink, L.O., *A Finnegans Wake Gazetteer* (Bloomington, 1978).

Mitford, T., 'Thalatta, Thalatta: Xenophon's View of the Black Sea', *Anatolian Studies* 50 (2000), 127-31.

Mitford, W., *The History of Greece* (5 vols; London, 1808-18; orig. pub. 1784-1818).

Moltke, H.K.B. von, *Briefe über Zustände und Begebenheiten in der Türkei aus den Jahren 1835 bis 1839* (8th edn; Berlin, 1917; orig. pub. 1841).

Moore, B., *Fergus* (London, 1992; orig. pub. 1971).

Morison, S.E., *The Ancient Classics in a Modern Democracy* (Commencement Address Delivered at the College of Wooster; New York, 1939).

Morris, J., *Farewell the Trumpets: An Imperial Retreat* (London, 1998; orig. pub. 1978).

Neugass, J., 'Thalassa, Thalassa', in G. Hicks, M. Gold, I. Schneider, J. North, P. Peters, and A. Calmer (eds), *Proletarian Literature in the United States: An Anthology* (London, 1936), 176-7; also reprinted in J. Salzman and L. Zanderer (eds), *Social Poetry of the 1930s: A Selection* (New York, 1978), 177-8.

Notz, F. von, *Deutsche Anabasis 1918: Ein Rückzug aus dem bulgarischen Zusammenbruch in Mazedonien* (Berlin, 1921).

O'Brien, S., *Downriver* (London, 2001).

Pitton de Tournefort, J., *A Voyage into the Levant*, trans. J. Ozell (2 vols; London, 1718; Fr. orig. 1717).

Pope, W.B. (ed.), *Invisible Friends: The Correspondence of Elizabeth Barrett Barrett and Benjamin Robert Haydon, 1842-1845* (Cambridge, Mass., 1972).

Porter, R.K., *Travels in Georgia, Persia, Armenia, Ancient Babylonia, &c.&c., During the Years 1817, 1818, 1819, and 1820* (2 vols; London, 1821-2).

Procter, B.W., *English Songs and Other Small Poems* (London, 1832; pub. under pseudonym Barry Cornwall).

Pybus, R., *Flying Blues: Poems 1988-1993* (Manchester, 1994).

Reitlinger, G., *A Tower of Skulls: A Journey through Persia and Turkish Armenia* (London, 1932).

Reitz, D., *Commando: A Boer Journal of the Boer War* (London, 1929).

Rennell, J., *Illustrations, (Chiefly Geographical,) of the History of the Expedition of Cyrus, from Sardis to Babylonia, and the Retreat of the Ten Thousand Greeks, from thence to Trebisonde and Lydia* (London, 1816).

Reynolds, G.M., *'Thalassa!'* (London, 1906).

Rhodes, A.R.E., *Sword of Bone: The Phoney War and Dunkirk, 1940* (London, 1942).

Rollin, C., *The Ancient History of the Egyptians, Carthaginians, Assyrians, Babylonians, Medes and Persians, Macedonians, and Greeks* (13 vols; London, 1734-9; Fr. orig. 1730-8).

Ruskin, J., *The Works of John Ruskin*, ed. E.T. Cook and A. Wedderburn (39 vols; London, 1903-1912).

St Clair, W., *Lord Elgin and the Marbles* (3rd edn; Oxford, 1998; orig. pub. 1967).

Schork, R.J., 'Tha Lassy! Tha Lassy!', *James Joyce Quarterly* 28 (1990), 293-6.

—— *Greek and Hellenic Culture in Joyce* (Gainesville, Fa., 1998).

Shelley, M.W., *Frankenstein: The Modern Prometheus* (Oxford, 1980; orig. pub. 1818).

Shelley, P.B., *The Complete Poetical Works of Percy Bysshe Shelley*, ed. T. Hutchinson (London, 1952; orig. pub. 1904).

Skelton, J., *Thalatta! or The Great Commoner: A Political Romance* (London, 1862; signed 'S.'); serialized as 'Thalatta! Thalatta! A Study at Sea', *Fraser's Magazine* 65 (1862), 1-15, 151-68, 269-84, 415-31, 537-50, 671-97 (signed 'the author of "Catarina in Venice" ').

Stallworthy, J., *Louis MacNeice* (London, 1995).

Stobart, J. C., *The Glory That Was Greece: A Survey of Hellenic Culture and Civilisation* (London, 1911).

Sue, E., *Romans de mort et d'aventures* (Paris, 1993).

Taine, H., 'Xénophon: *L'Anabase*', in his *Essais de critique et d'histoire* (5th edn; Paris, 1887; orig. pub. 1858), 49-95.

Tarn, W.W., 'Persia, from Xerxes to Alexander', in J.B. Bury, S.A. Cook, and F.E. Adcock (eds), *The Cambridge Ancient History*, vi: *Macedon: 401-301 BC* (Cambridge, 1927), 1-24.

Tasso, T., *Jerusalem Delivered*, trans. E. Fairfax (London, 1962; orig. pub. 1600; Ital. orig. 1580).

Tennyson, A., *The Poems of Tennyson*, ed. C. Ricks (3 vols; London, 1987).

Thackeray, W.M., *Notes on a Tour from Cornhill to Grand Cairo*, in *The Oxford Thackeray*, ix (Oxford, 1908; orig. pub. 1846).

Thomson, J., *Liberty, The Castle of Indolence, and Other Poems*, ed. J. Sambrook (Oxford, 1986).

Tillyard, E.M.W., *The English Epic and its Background* (London, 1954).

Todd, R.B., 'E. R. Dodds: The Dublin Years (1916-1919)', *Classics Ireland* 6 (1999), 80-105 (reprints as Appendix A, pp. 92-8, E. R. Dodds, 'The Rediscovery of the Classics', *Irish Statesman* 2. 42 (10 April, 1920), 346-7).

Tozer, H.F., *Turkish Armenia and Eastern Asia Minor* (London, 1881).

—— *A History of Ancient Geography* (2nd edn; Cambridge, 1935; orig. pub. 1897).

Uroševik, V., 'Descent to the Sea', in E. Osers (ed. and trans.) *Contemporary Macedonian Poetry* (London and Boston, 1991), 92.

Ussher, J., *A Journey from London to Persepolis, including Wanderings in Daghestan, Georgia, Armenia, Kurdistan, Mesopotamia, and Persia* (London, 1865).

Verne, J., *A Journey into the Interior of the Earth*, trans. F.A. Malleson (London, 1876).

—— *Voyage au centre de la terre* (Paris, 1977; orig. pub. 1864).

Walker, E., 'A Trip to the Sea', *New Monthly Magazine* 29 (1830), 433-9.

Watkins, M.G., 'At the Seaside', *Cornhill Magazine* 32 (1875) 414-26; reprinted in his *In the Country: Essays* (London, 1883), 13-32.

Weyrauch, W., *Anabasis* (Hamburg, 1959).

Whitley, W.T., *Art in England, 1821-1837* (Cambridge, 1930).

Williams, J., *Two Essays on the Geography of Ancient Asia, Intended Partly to Illustrate the Campaigns of Alexander and the Anabasis of Xenophon* (London, 1829).

Williams, W.C., *Paterson* (New York, 1963; orig. pub. 1946-58).

Wilson, J., 'T. E. Lawrence and the Translating of the *Odyssey*', *Journal of the T. E. Lawrence Society* 3. 2 (1994), 35-66.

Wilson, W., 'Woodrow Wilson on the Teaching of Caesar', *Classical Journal* 21 (1925-6), 3-4.

Witt, C., *The Retreat of the Ten Thousand*, trans. F. Younghusband, preface by H.G. Dakyns (London, 1891).

Woolf, V., 'Genius', in her *The Moment and Other Essays* (London, 1947), 150-5.

Worden, J.P., 'Thalatta! Thalatta!' (Bristol, 1908).

Wordsworth, W., *The Poetical Works of William Wordsworth*, ed. E. de Selincourt (5 vols; Oxford, 1940-9).

Yurick, S., *The Warriors* (London, 1966; orig. pub. 1965).

Zwaal, B., *dwang parasang* (Amsterdam, 1990).

Index